The 123s of ABC in SAP

WILEY COST MANAGEMENT SERIES

The 123s of ABC in SAP

Using SAP R/3 to Support Activity-Based Costing

DAWN J. SEDGLEY

CHRISTOPHER F. JACKIW

John Wiley & Sons, Inc.

New York • Chichester • Weinheim • Brisbane • Singapore • Toronto

We dedicate this book to our mentor, Anton van der Merwe, without whom we would never have learned as much as we have, nor recognized the most important lesson in life.

Additionally, we dedicate this book to our families for their love, patience, support, and encouragement.

This book is printed on acid-free paper.

Copyright © 2001 by Dawn J. Sedgley and Christopher F. Jackiw. All rights reserved.
Published simultaneously in Canada.

No part of this publication may be reproduced, stored in a retrieval system or transmitted in any form or by any means, electronic, mechanical, photocopying, recording, scanning or otherwise, except as permitted under Sections 107 or 108 of the 1976 United States Copyright Act, without either the prior written permission of the Publisher, or authorization through payment of the appropriate per-copy fee to the Copyright Clearance Center, 222 Rosewood Drive, Danvers, MA 01923, (978) 750-8400, fax (978) 750-4744. Requests to the Publisher for permission should be addressed to the Permissions Department, John Wiley & Sons Inc., 605 Third Avenue, New York, NY 10158-0012, (212) 850-6011, fax (212) 850-6008, E-Mail: PERMREQ@Wiley.Com.

This publication is designed to provide accurate and authoritative information in regard to the subject matter covered. It is sold with the understanding that the publisher is not engaged in rendering legal, accounting, or other professional services. If legal advice or other expert assistance is required, the services of a competent professional person should be sought.

Library of Congress Cataloging-in-Publication Data
Sedgley, Dawn J.
   The 123s of ABC in SAP: using SAP R/3 to support activity-based costing / Dawn J. Sedgley, Christopher F. Jackiw.
      p. cm.
   Includes bibliographical references and index.
   ISBN 0-471-39700-8 (cloth : alk. paper)
      1. SAP R/3. 2. Cost accounting—Computer programs. I. Title: One-two-threes of ABC in SAP. II. Jackiw, Christopher F. III. Title.

HF5548.4.R2S43 2001
657'.42'028553769—dc21   2001017849

Printed in the United States of America.
10 9 8 7 6 5 4 3 2 1

CONTENTS

PREFACE

Given SAP's dominance in the enterprise resource planning (ERP) market, many companies and their managers encounter SAP AG applications in some form or another. Of those organizations, some utilize Activity-Based Costing/Management concepts to perform more accurate cost assignments or drive performance initiatives. Managers are then faced with trying to determine how Activity-Based Costing can be incorporated into the SAP environment. We have written this book to help business managers understand the capabilities of the SAP R/3 business application to support Activity-Based Costing, Management, and Budgeting. This book is not intended as a primer in Activity-Based Costing (ABC): many such conceptual introductions have already been written. In order to bring the focus on the application of ABC concepts to an SAP R/3 environment, it is assumed that the reader has knowledge of the ABC framework.

This book is divided into three parts: the conceptual foundation, the capabilities of SAP ABC, and integration with other tools. Part One consists of Chapters 1 through 4 and covers the basic conceptual fundamentals to lay the foundation for detailed discussions.

The conceptual foundation begins with Chapter 1, addressing the shortfalls of ABC and introduces the Resource Consumption Accounting philosophy (RCA). This philosophy is heavily incorporated into the design of the SAP Controlling (CO) module, which contains SAP's ABC functionality. The chapter also establishes the differences between ABC and RCA and provides support for the use of both approaches to support management costing needs. Chapter 2 expands the foundation to include analysis of the differences between the two main types of tools that support ABC concepts. Addressed are the core conceptual and technical differences between stand-alone ABC modeling tools utilized to support ABC and an "integrated" ABC tool.

Although it is assumed that the reader understands the basic concepts of ABC principles, we do not assume the reader has any familiarity with the SAP R/3 application. Therefore, Chapter 3 provides the reader with a basic understanding of SAP R/3, specifically the Controlling module, including the CO-ABC component.

Since there is relatively little information available on the subject of ABC within SAP, many misconceptions abound as to its capabilities and maturity. Chapter 4 chronicles the evolution of ABC within SAP R/3. This chapter is useful for managers to determine what overall capabilities are available within the given release of SAP R/3 their organization either currently utilizes or is considering implementing.

Part Two, the capabilities of SAP ABC, provides several chapters that detail the integrated ABC capabilities with each individual area within the SAP Controlling module. Chapters 5 through 9 are structured in a similar manner. Each chapter addresses the main functionality highlights of the individual area of focus, the information flows, sample key business decisions to be supported, implementation guidelines or considerations, and ends with a summary table to be utilized as a reference.

Part Three utilizes the same chapter structure to address the combined capabilities of SAP R/3 ABC with the Oros modeling tool (Chapter 10) and the SAP Strategic Enterprise Management (SEM) application (Chapter 11).

ACKNOWLEDGMENTS

The creation of a book is a combination of many people's thoughts and efforts. We recognize that many individuals helped with the completion of this project. We would like to thank the contributors listed individually here. Without their support of this project, taking time to painstakingly review chapters for quality and correctness of content, and providing their subject matter expertise, this endeavor would never have been possible. Their efforts are well received, greatly appreciated, and forever remembered.

We also thank all the clients and friends who repeatedly asked for this book to be written and inquired (nagged) as to its progress on a regular basis. We appreciate the significant support throughout the years made by: Kelly Kirwan, Gloria Marcinko, Elizabeth Martin, Sandra Otto, Tammy Schmeeckle, Samantha Walsh, and Kathleen Wilhide. Additionally, we thank Sheck Cho, Alexia Meyers, and John Wiley & Sons for all their hard work in bringing this book to completion.

CONTRIBUTORS

The following contributors were interviewed and regularly contacted to cover the subject matter contained within this book. These interviews and conversations were for the purpose of gathering information from the key SAP ABC representatives, or experience implementers, as to the importance and most beneficial functionality within their respective areas of expertise. We take this opportunity to thank them and make known their contributions to this book.

Anton van der Merwe

Mr. van der Merwe is a director in the Management Consulting Practice of PricewaterhouseCoopers. He provided conceptual content and reviewed and edited each chapter in this book. Mr. van der Merwe is well versed in advanced costing philosophies and the application of those concepts within organizations, especially through the use of SAP software. He has extensive experience in the implementation of the German cost management approach in both service and manufacturing industries. He has been a speaker at cost management forums on the subjects of Activity-Based Costing and the German approach to cost management. Mr. van der Merwe has additionally coauthored several works on Resource Consumption Accounting. His academic qualifications include a diploma in mechanical engineering, a Baccalarius Commerci (B. Comm) in Economics and Transportation Economics, and a Master's in Business Leadership (MBL/MBA), all from the University of South Africa. The latter included a thesis that entailed an international research project into 180 companies in seven countries that implemented the German cost management approach.

Peter von Zimmermann

Mr. von Zimmermann is currently a development product manager of a new accounting software application with SAP AG located in Walldorf, Germany. He has been with SAP AG for over 10 years and was responsible for the development of the SAP CO-ABC module. Mr. von Zimmermann edited several chapters, greatly lending his expertise to the content of this book, especially for Chapters 5 and 6. Mr. von Zimmermann received his diplomas in Computer Science and Business Administration from the University of Hamburg.

Roman Rapp

Mr. Rapp, Diplom-Wirtschaftsingenieur, is a development architect with SAP AG in Walldorf, Germany. He has been developing cost management concepts and solutions in SAP's ERP software for nearly five years. He is responsible for managing the joint venture development of the interface called the Bridge from ABC Technologies' Oros software to SAP R/3. He has also been conducting training and providing consulting expertise to international clients on implementing advanced cost management solutions, with a specialization on the banking industry. Since 1998 he has been a member of the Consortium for Advanced Manufacturing-International's (CAM-I) cost management symposiums, contributing to the Activity-Based Planning and Budgeting interest group. Mr. Rapp graduated from the University of Karlsruhe, Germany, in 1996 with a diploma in finance and industrial engineering. His remarks and thoughts are portrayed throughout this book and especially within Chapters 8 and 10.

David DuPont

Mr. DuPont also graciously provided his knowledge, experience, and expertise for Chapter 10. Mr. DuPont is cofounder of ABC Technologies Inc. and the manager of the European Development Center for ABC Technologies Inc. He has been a key developer and visionary for the Oros modeling software capabilities for 12 years. He received a B.Sc. degree in Electrical Engineering from the University of Ottawa, Canada, in 1984.

Joerg Funke

Mr. Funke has over 13 years of professional experience in cost management and accounting and has been employed by SAP AG, Walldorf, Germany for over 10 years. During his SAP career, Mr. Funke has held positions for consulting, product costing development, and various product manager roles. These product manager roles began with product costing, then to cost management, and to his current position as product manager of the Strategic Enterprise Management (SEM) and Cost Management (CO) applications. His knowledge and insight in the area of product costing were extremely useful for Chapter 7. Mr. Funke received his degree in Economics from the University of Bonn.

Gero Maeder

Gero Maeder, Ph.D., is an application developer at SAP AG, Walldorf, Germany. He started working for SAP in 1997, responsible for different components of SAP's R/3 software, such as Executive Information Systems and Business Planning. He has been involved with the SAP SEM application development since its inception. His core competency focuses on embedding ABC Technology's Oros software package within SEM-BPS as well as the dynamic simulations capabilities of Powersim. Mr. Maeder's thoughts and comments greatly increased the accuracy of Chapter 11. He graduated from the Technical University of Ilmenau, Germany, in 1992 in Electrical Engineering and received a Ph.D. in Engineering Sciences from Technical University of Ilmenau in 1996.

Todd Simon

Mr. Simon is a principal consultant for Alta via Consulting, specializing in the implementation of the SAP CO module involving financial and cost management processes. He has been consulting with clients in financial and cost management concepts for over five years, in industries ranging from automobile manufacturing to communications to airline maintenance and repair operations. The primary focus of his experience is in the implementation of advanced cost management concepts utilizing SAP. His work includes process reengineering, resource consumption analysis, Activity-Based Costing, and establishing performance metrics. Recently he has been involved with the creation of integrated planning tools using SAP's Sales and Operations Planning and ABC functionality for an uneven-demand environment. Mr. Simon edited several of the chapters in this book, providing keen observations on ways to make the subject matter more easily understood. He graduated from Northwestern University with a B.A. in Economics in 1985 and from the University of Michigan with an MBA in 1991.

Peter Bittner

Mr. Bittner, M.S., is a member of the mySAP.com workplace team at SAP AG, in Walldorf, Germany, where he is responsible for the coordination of SAP's user role development activities. Prior to this, he had more than six years of experience in the area of cost management as a project manager of an Activity-Based Costing implementation in the automotive industry and as the ABC product manager at SAP AG. Mr. Bittner's original background is physics, with practical experience in the design of integrated circuits. In addition to editing Chapter 4, he has coauthored several articles about the electrical characterization of semiconductors and is a key contributor to the book *The E-Business Workplace: Discovering the Power of the Enterprise Portals* (John Wiley & Sons).

PART ONE

LAYING THE FOUNDATION

1

COST MANAGEMENT: A BRIEF HISTORY AND THE CONVERGENCE OF PHILOSOPHIES

Since the mid-1980s, the business community in the United States has been challenging the value of management accounting data as a support tool to business decision making. The conclusion: Management accounting as it has existed since the industrial revolution is no longer sufficient in the new more complex business world. Early management accounting served the community well for a long time. As long as the primary costs in an organization could be accurately traced to products with labor hours, or perhaps machine time, management accounting had fine tools in place. As soon as this paradigm in the cost structure changed, so did the quality of cost information. In the current marketplace, the simplistic standard cost flow has become obsolete and has been replaced with the need for more comprehensive and meaningful information.

NEED FOR CHANGE

This story has been told in countless articles and books; customers want choice, in terms of services and product permutations. These choices drive complexity and complexity drives overhead, which, in turn, negatively impacts the ability of traditional managerial accounting to satisfy managerial information needs. Combine these issues with the rise of automation and the e-marketplace, and the dilemma of the accounting world is apparent. Certainly in the future complexity will only increase. The authors of the book *Blur: The Speed of Change in the Connected Economy* stated, "products and services are merging, buyers sell and sellers buy. Neat value chains are messy economic webs."[1] How can the accounting profession transform itself to address this relatively new and continuously changing complexity? The quest started around the early 1950s, and the struggle to convert accounting data into strategic decision support information still continues. No longer can the business community be complacent with old cost management methodologies. New and improved philosophies have come into play, or perhaps a convergence of philosophies. Two factors surfaced in the early 1980s that had a direct impact on management accounting. The first was the emergence of the personal computer and the accompanying decentralization of computing power. The second was the emergence of Activity-Based Costing (ABC).

Technology Evolves and Facilitates Change

With the change in the business environment pushing for transformation from one direction, rapid development in technology enabled change from yet another. The growth in personal computing power suddenly enabled an accounting workforce to go beyond the focus of basic transaction reporting. With the enabling technology, the accounting community suddenly had the ability to process data in ways previously never imaginable, and management starting seeing a glimmer of light. This decentralization of computing power, for better or for worse, provided accountants with a critical enabler to convert their traditional management accounting role into a truly analytical one. Management accountants and operations management could finally put their heads together with the power of the personal computer and begin to model the organization; thus the accountant's role shifted from being a glorified bookkeeper to a strategic decision support position.

Along with the benefits of increased computing power and decentralization came some less desirable results. First, the power to easily generate results on new dimensions often simply satisfied a whim merely to "spin" data. In order to get to the new dimensions and analytical views, tremendous effort was expended to merge financial and operational data into a usable format to work with and model these new views. This was particularly true of ABC models in the 1980s and 1990s. With information gathering and formatting taking such a significant effort, the quality and integrity of the data, let alone its timeliness, usually went unchallenged. Second, to accommodate the significant data-gathering effort, simplifications in modeling and gross organizational assumptions had to be made. These assumptions usually were frozen at a point in time, making the best analysis a stand-alone snapshot of the company at a selected point in time. Because these factors made the model almost instantly out of date, most organizations seriously doubted even the best analytical intentions.

Another effect on the technology lever of change is the impact of enterprise resource planning (ERP) software. ERP systems potentially span the entire corporate organization. An ERP vision incorporates the whole organization under one information technology roof. With ERP, the world of accounting can be integrated with operations and logistics. Full use of an ERP software eliminates most of the previous issues mentioned; simplification of the model, spinning data, merging data, and questions of quality. Rather than focusing on data collection and conversion, the data are available on a real-time basis. This one system can contain large amounts of organizational data, opening a window from accounting to other areas in the organization previously separated in silos. ERP software is utilized to integrate management statistics with financial data to finally get a fuller and timelier picture of the organization.

Even with advancements in technology in terms of raw computing power or the benefits of an integrated system solution, the underlying cost philosophy was, and still is, under attack. The following historical review provides details on the nature of the attack and the solutions proposed.

Evolution of Cost Management in the United States

Traditional Cost Management   The traditional world of management accounting was quite simple. The focus was on manufacturing as a whole and the ability to trace a cost to a finished good. Analysis of the results was clearly secondary to valuation. Cost could be analyzed and evaluated by converting the manufacturing costs of the company into three major pools:

1. Direct material
2. Direct labor
3. Factory overhead

Since the nature of early production consisted primarily of easily traceable direct costs, the allocation of the indirect costs (i.e., indirect labor, factory overhead, indirect materials) was a simple ratio of either the direct labor or the direct materials, whichever represented the best tracing tool. (See Exhibit 1.1.)

In this simplistic traditional cost environment, other nonmanufacturing costs were rarely considered in the equation. Once the "direct" cost no longer represented the majority of the cost in the assignment, the traditional methodology started to show cracks in assignment logic. High-volume products began being overcosted and low-volume products were undercosted. The direct cost relationship becomes further limited as the cost focus shifts from the cost of production to the cost of services packaged with the product. These service costs most likely were not even considered in the previous costing equation. Costs such as post-production support, sales services, and so on have quickly become a growing area in most companies. Companies that lead in today's marketplace differentiate

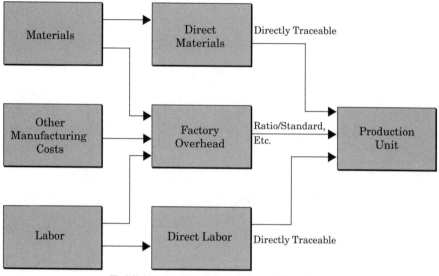

Exhibit 1.1 Traditional Cost Allocations

themselves from their competition not only in the products they produce but the customer services they provide. Therefore, the fastest-growing category of cost for many organizations has nothing to do with the direct costs of production but rather factory overhead and cost to serve the customers. The ABC philosophy was generated to address these ever-growing indirect overhead expenses.

Activity-Based View of Cost   The groundswell of ABC occurred in the mid-1980s. This approach was born to emphasize what is being done and what it costs to do it. Activity-Based Costing provided for a real understanding of the activities being performed by each department. While a direct cost method may assign costs to the correct objects, without the ABC view, it is still difficult to understand how to reduce costs or what the resources are actually doing.

The view of ABC originated in the resource center (albeit the resource view was most likely embedded within the general ledger [G/L] account coding), but the focus was to "convert" the G/L account view of the resources to a process perspective. Exhibit 1.2 illustrates a traditional ABC cost flow. In this example, the G/L account view within the *Distribution Support* resource/cost center is converted into the view of the processes supported by that center, for example, *Enter Documents* and *Schedule Laborers* processes. It is important to note that in this more traditional ABC view, the resource perspective was generally simpli-

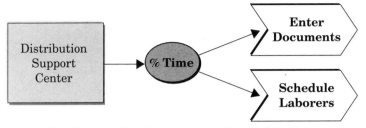

Exhibit 1.2   Traditional Activity-Based Cost Flow

fied. The normal conversion routine was to establish a "resource driver" via an interview process, thereby gaining a snapshot perspective of the effort expended on each activity. The most common process breakdown was formulated by interviewing the resources or the cost center manager to determine a percentage of time spent on each process. This weighting factor became the resource driver or apportionment tool for costs assigned to the process view.

Achieving the activity view in this manner did provide an activity perspective on costs. However, the perspective was achieved based on a primary assumption that, in order to reduce model maintenance workloads, the relationships would be frozen in a given point in time, for example, annually, semiannually, or quarterly at best. Also, in addition to the risks posed by using a stagnant model, the new activity view sacrificed and minimized the perspective of the resource view. The limited expression of resources along with the technical limitations of the computer hardware used to accommodate the models led to a number of weaknesses in the ABC models and in the information these models provided. Weaknesses in the ABC models were:

- Models were backward-looking, using only historical data. The models had no predictive perspective at all.
- Causal relationships, particularly those between resources and processes, were expressed only in value or in ratios/portions of value.
- Models were usually of a step-down nature, that is, costs flowed from resources, to activities, to final cost objects. Fully burdened resource costs were not provided.
- Models were very maintenance intensive.
- Models had limited ability to deal with complexity.
- Because they were stand-alone models, there was the need to "feed the beast" with all the information required to run the model.

Weaknesses in the information provided by ABC were:

- All costs for a period would be spread to products without regard for actual utilization levels. This full absorption approach spread costs to products indiscriminately. Companies that utilized ABC information potentially faced the fixed cost death spiral.
- Because the nature of cost was viewed inconsistently, the ability to provide accurate gross and contribution margin was limited.
- From a control perspective, the capabilities were limited in that plans were static, and the ability to generate authorized reports generally was not supported.
- Limited variance calculations was available.
- The weak resource expression led to ineffective capacity management capabilities.
- Activity-Based Budgeting (ABB) efforts have a tendency to overstate the budget because all costs are usually extrapolated, including fixed costs.

Traditional costing certainly no longer supports management accounting needs. ABC provides more analytical capabilities, yet, as can be seen from the weaknesses listed, it does not completely support the needs of management accounting. Therefore, there is an identified gap in the tools and abilities to fully support management accounting.

METHODS OF EXPRESSING CAUSAL RELATIONSHIPS

To understand the opportunity that went begging with ABC's mapping/tracing of resources to processes and the weaknesses identified, one must first understand the cost assignment options and the analytical differences in each of the methods available to express causal relationships. All examples within this section are between resources and activities; however, whether focusing on the resource or the activity, the underlying cost assignment principles are the same. These cost assignment principles may seem to have only subtle differences, yet analytically the differences are significant.

Assignment of cost can be divided into two major methods distinguished by their approach to cost valuation: (1) value-based assignments, and (2) quantity-based assignments. The first method, value-based assignment, pushes value/dollars (from the sender to the receiver) through the model. This method can be as simple as portioning out from the sender to the receivers money based on percentages. The second method, quantity-based assignment, pulls value/dollars (into the receiver from the sender) based on quantity flows. Hence value flow follows quantity flow.

Value-Based Assignment of Cost

The most common assignment method utilized with ABC is a value-based assignment. Value-based logic relies on a calculation to apportion costs from the source sender to the destination receivers. This calculation can be as simple as a ratio or a percentage agreed with the manager during an interview. The calculation can also be more representative of the relationships by utilizing statistics (e.g., head count), dollar values on the receiver (e.g., revenue dollars to allocate commissions), or even driver output quantities on the receiver (e.g., machine hours to allocate electricity expense). In the example from the illustration in Exhibit 1.2, costs are assigned from the *Distribution Support* cost center to the activities *Enter Documents* and *Schedule Labor* through a value-based assignment rule, percentage of time. This method can be utilized as a percentage of time and effort or even a quantity which gets converted to a percentage or ratio. To illustrate, in Exhibit 1.3, two value-based assignments are provided. Example 1 assumes the basis used to assign cost from cost center to process is an estimated percentage of time, with approximately 97% effort allocated to the *Enter Documents* activities. Example 2 assumes a statistical quantity, number of Full Time Equivalents (FTEs), is utilized to determine the value split between processes.

The value-based approach does not imply that quantities are not utilized, as supported by Example 2; it merely identifies the approach for the cost flows and the valuation of such as being based on dollar values. Characteristics of the value-based approach are:

- Only dollar values flow from the sender to the receiver, that is, it does not include a sender output quantity.
- The basis of the cost flow can utilize a dollar value or a quantity that is converted into a percentage or ratio in order to distribute the value.
- The basis utilized for sending the costs may or may not be highly correlated with the cause of the costs.
- Usually it is the main cost assignment method for supporting actual costing systems.
- Normally, 100% of the costs are flowed from sender to receivers, as in full-absorption costing.

Quantity-Based Assignment of Cost

In contrast to the value-based approach, the quantity-based approach, as its name indicates, utilizes quantities as the basis for cost assignment and valuation. A quantity-based assignment determines the amount to be charged based on a

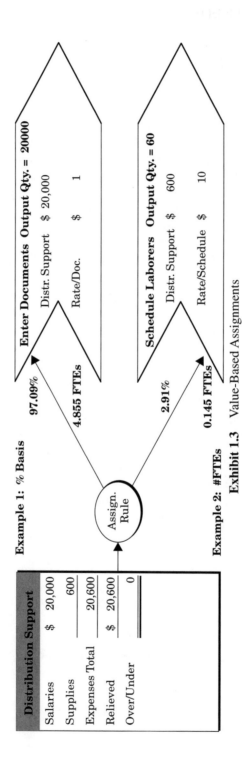

Exhibit 1.3   Value-Based Assignments

quantity, such as the cost center sending actual labor hours utilized to each process; in other words, a sender output quantity is the basis for the assignment. Rather than the posting being exclusively limited to a dollar amount, the sender quantity amount is the primary focus, posted on both the sender and receiver objects, and then dollar valuation occurs, based on a standard or an actual rate. In Exhibit 1.4, the same cost flow occurs as in Exhibit 1.3, only the additional consumption information for *LABHR* from the *Distribution Support* cost center is posted as consumed by the processes.

Some model limitations may still exist even with quantities included in the posting, based on the accuracy of the assignment basis, such as the percentage method. The primary improvement is that additional quantity information provides insight into the actual resource utilization on the receiver object. This improvement, however, highlights a primary issue, cost assignment accuracy, which is driven by the impact of utilizing assumptions versus known quantities. There are two components to this issue.

1. Many organizations do not track actual sender output quantities due to limitations in tracking capabilities or because the cost for capturing the information is more than the deemed value of the incremental accuracy.
2. Regardless of the approach utilized, value or quantity based, if utilizing a percentage, ratio, or statistical quantity with an actual costing system, the primary aim of the cost assignment is the posting of dollar amounts to the receiver object. Using this type of sender/receiver relationship basis, the total costs on the supplier are usually pushed entirely from the supplier to the consumer. Capacity analysis on the supplier is not the primary focus. For this logic to be credible, it must be assumed that capacity is readily changeable and fully utilized.

In order to address this issue, the quantity-based method supports taking the expression of the causal relationship one step further. The quantity-based method can be utilized to express a relationship between the sender output quantity correlated with the receiver output quantity. For example, instead of allocating electricity dollars based on machine hours, as mentioned earlier, the number of kilowatt-hours to be consumed for each machine would be determined per machine hour. Using this information, the total number of kilowatt-hours are linked to the total number of machine hours. Dollars, therefore, do not feature in the relationship definition; they merely serve to value quantities once the relationship has been defined. Exhibit 1.5 illustrates how this form of the quantity-based method would be used to express the relationship between the *Distribution Support* and its two activities, *Enter Documents* and *Schedule Labor.*

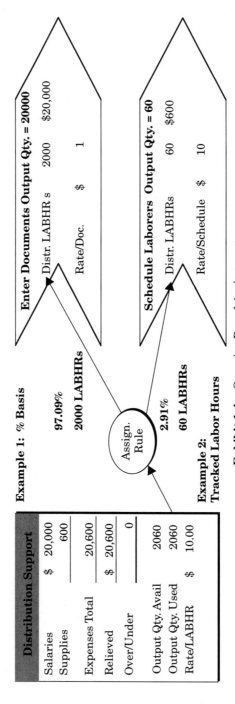

Exhibit 1.4 Quantity-Based Assignments

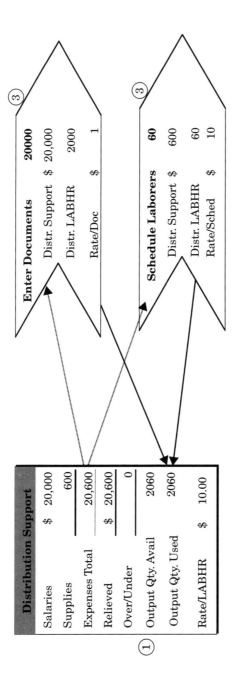

Distribution Support

Salaries	$	20,000
Supplies		600
Expenses Total		20,600
Relieved	$	20,600
Over/Under		0
Output Qty. Avail		2060
Output Qty. Used		2060
Rate/LABHR	$	10.00

Enter Documents   20000

Distr. Support	$	20,000
Distr. LABHR		2000
Rate/Doc	$	1

Schedule Laborers   60

Distr. Support	$	600
Distr. LABHR		60
Rate/Sched	$	10

② 10 Docs = 1 Labor hour
1 Schedule = 1 Labor Hour

Exhibit 1.5   Imputed Quantity-Based Assignment

In Exhibit 1.5 the relationship is defined in the following three steps:

1. The resource provider, *Distribution Support* cost center, establishes a quantity of its resource output available for consumption by the processes that it performs (the consumers). In this example *Distribution Support* has 2,060 resource hours available. Based on this output, the required expenses are planned. From this supply and its corresponding expenses, the *Distribution Support* cost center can determine the standard rate of providing the resource labor hours, *LABHR,* as $10 per hour.
2. The causal relationship is expressed in an output-quantity-to-be-consumed (distribution support labor hours) correlation to the output-quantity-to-be-produced (# of documents and # of schedules). In this example, the analysis reveals that for every 10 *Documents Entered,* 1 hour of *Distribution Support LABHR* is used, and for every 1 *Schedule Labor,* 1 hour of *Distribution Support LABHR* is needed.
3. The output of the receiver object or activity is forecasted. Then the amount of output required from the sender object or resource can be determined.

In Exhibit 1.5 the respective unit quantity standards translates as follows: for an output of 20,000 *Enter Documents* 2,000 hours of resource labor will be required, and for 60 *Schedule Labor* activities, 60 labor hours will be required. This results in total labor demand of 2,060. Note in this example no planned excess/idle capacity is assumed. Based on the established quantity relationships, dollars follow quantities and $20,000 ($10 × 2,000) goes to *Enter Documents* and $600 ($10 × 60) goes to the activity *Schedule Labor.*

Although applying this method is more complex, the first benefit realized is the limited need to capture resource sender driver information. In Exhibit 1.5, as far as actual data is concerned, the organization is required to capture only the quantities of the activities performed. It will be able to impute the resource driver outputs, that is, what is essentially a resource "backflushing" equation. Imputing based on standard results is a much more dynamic cost model than the static relationships that result when percentages, ratios, or fixed statistics (number of FTEs) are used. Further, compared to a snapshot in time, the correlated relationship of the resource to the activity is constantly being challenged by detailed variance information. This imputed quantity-based approach provides quantity information in terms of both demand and supply, allowing users the ability to perform a true capacity utilization analysis and providing insight into excess/idle capacity. Additionally, the sender's costs are assigned only when utilized and not necessarily in their entirety. An additional step is utilized to liquidate the variances captured, if required. Characteristics of the quantity-based approach are:

- Sender output quantity flows to the receiver utilizing different assignment methods. Then cost valuation occurs, relieving costs from sender to receivers.
- The basis of the sender output quantity assignment can utilize a dollar value or a quantity that is converted into a percentage or ratio in order to flow the quantity.
- The basis of the sender output quantity can also utilize a correlated relationship with the receiver output quantity to impute the sender output consumption by the receiver.
- The cost assignment method is utilized for supporting standard costing systems. Since output rates can be based on actual calculations, an actual costing system is also supported.
- When the quantity-based approach is utilized within an actual costing system, 100% of the costs are flowed from sender to receiver (e.g., full-absorption costing). When it is utilized for supporting a standard costing system, costs are flowed from sender to receivers based on quantities consumed. Potentially, not all costs or too many costs are relieved from sender resulting in an under/over absorption variance. This variance is liquated with various methods.

Quantity Structure   Both of the methods just described are used to express an individual relationship between a supplier and a consumer. A cost model that utilizes the quantity-based method to express the complete flow of the relationship, from resource input through the final output and product/service sale, is referred to as a quantity structure. A quantity structure facilitates the ability to accurately convert sales quantities into primary and support resource demand, for example. A distinguishing characteristic of the quantity structure is that sender output quantity consumed is correlated with the output quantity of the receiver. Therefore, the quantity structure is established by the linking of individual imputed quantity-based relationships defined between a resource and a receiver (a support resource or a process) and then from that sender to the cost object. The value-based method and the quantity-based method can both be deployed in the same cost model. A cost model that expresses only certain relationships using the quantity-based method (i.e., those between process and cost object) is considered a limited quantity structure.

Now we can turn to another cost management philosophy and offer a possible solution to current management accounting needs.

RESOURCE CONSUMPTION ACCOUNTING

Even in the best case, where costs are accurately traceable to products by the ratios of direct costs, the traditional cost management world provides very little analytical information. For example, it failed to explain which managers operate efficiently and effectively, or perhaps which machines are the most cost effective and require the least maintenance, or even more important, where is excess or strained capacity in the system? To review any of these questions, a more powerful managerial view of the resources must be provided that expresses resources in financial terms. The building blocks of Resource Consumption Accounting (RCA)[2] cover areas such as the resource view of costs, fully burdened resource costs, the inherent nature of costs, the changing nature of costs, a standard costing system, the allocation of fixed costs, and capacity management.

Resource View of Cost

The RCA view has its origins in Germany during the late 1940s. This view recognizes the need for more discrete cost pools and specific drivers. Additionally, it was the first approach to assign nonproductive costs to cost objects for the delivered products/services as opposed to just the manufactured products. The RCA concept developed into a very sophisticated costing methodology utilized by both production and service enterprises over the past half century, primarily in German-speaking Europe.

The tools of RCA bring a new level of focus to management accounting. RCA enables a detailed view of the resource and resulting management control capabilities. The goal is to provide, first and foremost, responsibility center reporting, to break down the organization into logical managerial subcomponents. These subcomponents or cost centers provide a framework for planning, control, corrective action, and analysis. The cost center view also provides insight to the organization's resources that have previously gone unnoticed. Rather than looking at the organization only in terms of the direct or indirect relationships of production costs, the entire organization is considered. Under the new view, production costs as well as those related to pre- and postproduction costs are considered in cost analysis.

But how does this resource view provide more information about the organization than the traditional method or ABC? It does so in two ways.

1. It provides the analysis tools at a lower level of control. The true custodians of the cost (departmental managers) get a direct look at their respective span of control. Simply increasing visibility is the first step.

2. Besides providing a more finite grouping of costs, the cost center view supports a more finite analysis of resource usage. Rather than looking at the cost as indirect and direct, RCA provides for more microanalysis by reviewing cost in terms of the cost center, such as *Facilities* or *Printing*. (See Exhibit 1.6.) Within each of these cost centers, the resources are dedicated to providing a particular resource output. In the case of *Facilities,* the output is the space provided by the building, that is, square footage (SQFT); when looking at the production work of the *Printing* area, the output is machine hours (MACHR). Obviously, similarities exist to the macrostructure of traditional cost management, but the resource view supplies the capability of "micro" analysis of generic resource pools.

Origin of the Quantity Structure and Fully Burdened Resource Costs

Resource Consumption Accounting is a view of cost, but it facilitates an approach to cost assignment as well. This approach primarily utilizes assignment of resource costs based on a quantity structure along direct causal relationships between support and direct resource pool; it does not consider the activity view. For example, in Exhibit 1.6, for every *LABHR* of output consumed

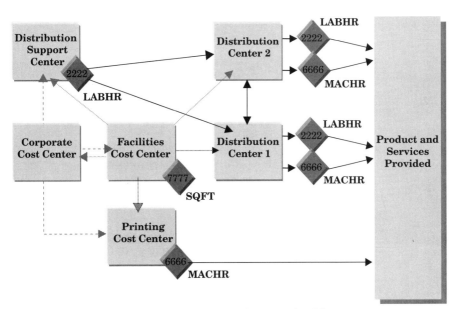

Exhibit 1.6   Resource Consumption View

from *Distribution Center 1, Distribution Center 1* consumes 0.1 *LABHR* of the *Distribution Support* cost center. This is a variable quantity relationship; as consumption of one output quantity increases, the consumption of the other output quantity increases. Additionally, there are fixed relationships defined by the quantity structure. For example, for every *LABHR* of *Distribution Center 1* consumed, a fixed consumption of 3,000 *SQFT* of the *Facilities* cost center is consumed per period, representing the work area for the labor crew. This approach results in fully burdened resource costs and a specific treatment of the nature of costs. The RCA approach starts with the sender output quantity. For each resource pool, this output is used to calculate a resource output rate. The resource output rate is an important parameter in determining the initial efficiency of converting inputs into outputs for each resource/resource pool. The resource output quantity and output rate together form the mechanism whereby costs are charged to the consumers of resources.

Initial Inherent Nature of Costs

At this resource view level, what else is provided? In addition to the "micro" view, two key components that the resource view provides are:

1. Insight as to the inherent nature of cost
2. An understanding of resource capacity

Resource Consumption Accounting recognizes that the resource pool is the primary determinant of the initial inherent nature of costs. Once a company has passed the budget cycle and has determined to invest in a specific mix of machine resources and a specified level of skill and technology, the nature of the costs required to achieve the resource strategy is defined. In the case presented in Exhibit 1.6, investment in a specific automated copy machine in the *Printing* department is closed when that machine is purchased. At that point, departmental capacity, human intervention, and support cost have all been defined for the time frame considered. The costs for this time period can easily be translated into its fixed and proportional components. Given this basic principle, the annual plan for the *Distribution Support* department from Exhibit 1.5 may be expanded. (See Exhibit 1.7.)

The expenses shown in this example are only those expense accounts for which the department is directly responsible, classified as primary expenses. Primary expenses are then further broken down and classified into their fixed and proportional components. The exhibit also shows the resource output rate for the expense inputs. It is important to recognize that this approach will result in the

Distribution Support	Resource Output: 2,060 Labor Hours		
Primary Expenses	*Fixed*	*Proportional*	*Total*
Supervisory Salary	$ 3,000	-	$ 3,000
Support Personnel Wages	-	$ 17,000	$ 17,000
Office Supplies	-	$ 600	$ 600
Total	**$ 3,000**	**$ 17,600**	**$ 20,600**
Resource Unit Output Rate	$1.46	$ 8.54	$ 10

Exhibit 1.7   Initial Inherent Nature of Costs and Resource Output

determination of very specific rates for each individual resource pool. Departments in different locations will not only have different rates but also different ratios of fixed and proportional costs within those rates. For example, because of relatively high social costs in Europe, not only will the distribution function in Europe be more expensive, its fixed cost component will be higher than, for example, the same type of the distribution function in Asia.

Changing Nature of Costs

An important factor to consider is that the inherent nature of cost can change at the time of consumption. The initial inherent nature of costs is determined by the characteristics of the invested resources that make up the supplying resource pool. But in cases where the service consumed is not related to the output of the consuming resource or activity, the quantity of service consumed, and thus the costs for that particular service, must be considered as fixed to the consumer, such as the *Facilities* example previously mentioned. Another example is that of the *Purchasing* department buying furniture for the *Distribution Support* cost center. Clearly, this expense does not relate to the output of the *Distribution Support* department, in terms of support man-hours, in the same way that the purchase of office supplies would, the latter being proportional to the *LABHR* output quantity generated by the *Distribution Support* department. The activity *Purchase Asset* has a rate of $10 per purchase that is all proportional costs. Exhibit 1.8 shows how the nature of cost changes at consumption in the case of furniture purchased for the *Distribution Support* cost center.

Distribution Support	Resource Output: 2,060 Labor Hours				
Primary Expenses	*Fixed Qty.*	*Prop. Qty.*	*Fixed*	*Proportional*	*Total*
Supervisory Salary	-	-	$ 3,000	-	$ 3,000
Support Personnel Wages	-	-	-	$ 17,000	$ 17,000
Office Supplies	-	-	-	$ 600	$ 600
Depreciation: Furniture	-	-	$ 1,060	-	$ 1,060
Secondary Expenses	*Fixed Qty.*	*Prop. Qty.*	*Fixed*	*Proportional*	*Total*
Activity: Purchase Asset	10	-	$ 1,000	-	$ 1,000
Total			$ 5,060	$ 17,600	$ 22,660
Resource Unit Output Rate: LABHR			$ 2.46	$ 8.54	$ 11

Exhibit 1.8   Changing Nature of Costs on Consumption

The impact to the fixed/proportional split of the *Distribution Support LABHR* is due to the secondary expenses. Secondary expenses are those that are internally allocated rather than primary expenses, which are representative of general ledger postings. The 10 purchase orders, planned for equipment to be provided to the *Distribution Support* cost center, are planned as a fixed quantity consumption, because the purchase orders will be raised regardless of the level of planned output of the *Distribution Support* department. Note that using the fixed-quantity consumption method results in all of the secondary costs posted via the *Purchase Asset* activity to change from proportional to fixed for the *Distribution Support* cost center. These costs are included as such in the *Distribution Support LABHR* output rate.

Standard Costing System

Resource Consumption Accounting usually utilizes a standard costing system approach. Standard unit rates per resource quantity output are calculated and utilized throughout the period to provide cost information based on actual quantities. Actual rates for resource output quantities are calculated, for informational purposes only. The actual rate is utilized to determine if standard rates should be updated. Cost valuation remains based on standard unit rate multiplied by actual quantity consumed. Therefore, both price and quantity variances are generated, providing more resource analytical information. This accounting method considers variances for input price, input quantity, output price, output quantity, and so on. With an actual costing system utilizing actual unit rates, these variances are liquidated through the actual rate and spread to the consumers of the actual quantities. With the standard costing system, these variances can be liquidated in various ways. The importance and greatest benefit of the standard costing approach is that variances are transparent and indicate potential areas for corrective action.

Allocation of Fixed Costs

A traditional full-absorption approach to cost accounting would allocate all fixed costs at the lowest product level. With RCA utilizing a standard cost approach, the liquidation of the excess/idle capacity variance is the primary fixed cost that must be considered for allocation. The variance for excess/idle capacity is allocated in the stepped recovery method, for example, to different levels of the Profit and Loss Statement (P/L). This is for the following reasons:

- In line with the principles of controllable and uncontrollable variance identification, the excess/idle capacity variance should not be spread out among the lowest-level products.
- For the sake of visibility and to clearly delineate responsibility for the variance, it is allocated to an appropriate, higher level in the stepped recovery report.
- Not spreading the variance to the individual product level enhances the relevance of the data for decision making.

Exhibit 1.9 is an example of how excess/idle capacity can be allocated. This example is for an airline focusing on flight profitability. In this example, Flight Crew excess/idle capacity is allocated at the flight business level and Human Resource excess/idle capacity at the enterprise result level.

Therefore, within the RCA philosophy, liquidation of excess/idle capacity is taken to the level of the organization responsible for that capacity. Doing this shows the resulting transparency of excess/idle capacity and helps to eliminate poor decision making caused by fully absorbed product and service costs.

Capacity Management Is Resource Focused

The allocation of fixed cost addresses how excess/idle capacity is liquidated to various levels of the organization within the RCA philosophy. Another important

Business-Class Passengers	Planned	Actual
Passenger Revenues	(50,000)	(45,000)
Passenger-Related Costs:		
Meals	500	480
Cabin Crew	2,000	2,000
Passenger Handling	2,500	2,400
Gross Margin 1: Business-Class Passengers	(45,000)	(40,120)
Flight ZZ999		
Σ Passenger Class Margins	(150,000)	(165,000)
Flight-Related Costs:		
Jet Fuel	15,000	16,000
Landing and Parking	8,000	8,000
Aircraft Maintenance	6,000	6,000
Gross Margin 2: Flight ZZ999	(121,000)	(135,000)
Route: Europe/Asia		
Σ Flight Margins	(2,250,000)	(1,975,000)
Route-Related Costs:		
Lounge Costs	55,000	50,000
Marketing Costs	800,000	910,000
Gross Margin 3: Route Euro Asia	(1,395,000)	(915,000)
Flight Business		
Σ Route Margins	(10,800,000)	(6,300,000)
Flight Business-Related Costs:		
Flight Business Overhead	1,700,000	1,500,000
Excess Capacity — Cabin Crew	-	**100,000**
Gross Margin 4: Flight Business	(9,100,000)	(4,700,000)
Enterprise Result:		
Σ Business Units Margins	(27,900,000)	(18,100,000)
Enterprise-Related Costs:		
Corporate Overhead	3,000,000	3,200,000
Excess Capacity — HR Dept.	-	**80,000**
Enterprise Operating Result	(24,900,000)	(14,820,000)

Exhibit 1.9   Product Stepped Gross Margin Report

aspect of RCA is the view of where capacity resides. Attempts have been made to incorporate capacity management into ABC. Resource Consumption Accounting takes the view that capacity resides in resources, based on the following considerations:

- The invested resource base is the output from the strategic planning process, during which initial capacity has been determined.

- The primary capacity measure in the model is the resource output quantity, which is established through the quantity structure approach.
- The domain of capacity management is wholly contained within the resource base.

Within this view, activities have no capacity in and of themselves; they are individually and collectively consumers of capacity output. The consumption quantities that activities consume reflect resource utilization, not capacity. Utilization and capacity can always be equal only in a closed and perfectly balanced system. To demonstrate that capacity is Resource, and not an activity, a one-resource to many-activities relationship can be used. Reduction in an activity output does not indicate an increase in excess/idle capacity. One activity may have been reduced while another activity consumed more of the labor-hour resource, potentially resulting in overtime and not the expected idle capacity. A highly recommended resource that completely addresses this concept is "Accounting for Excess/Idle Capacity in an Advanced Cost Management System: The Case for Resource Consumption Accounting" by Anton van der Merwe and David Keys.[3]

As with ABC, RCA has several weaknesses:

- With the more comprehensive view of resources, users encountered greater complexity.
- The iterative cost flows are more accurate but also less transparent and can become difficult to trace.
- The quantity-based relationships, and more so for the quantity structure, requires more up-front analysis work and therefore can be costly to implement. However, on-going maintenance is reduced.
- Most important, the causal relationships do not necessarily consider the activity view; they focus on the interrelationship between resource pools.

TANDEM SOLUTION: RESOURCE CONSUMPTION ACCOUNTING AND ACTIVITY-BASED COSTING

Although the RCA view and principles provide valuable insight, they only partially explain the view of work actually being performed and the complexity of resource utilization. The process or activity view is required to delineate the resource perspective into the activities performed in an organization. Key analyses are needed to focus on what processes the organization spends the most resources providing, which processes should be the focus of reengineering efforts, what outsourcing opportunities exist, and so forth. These questions can be answered only with the analytical tools of ABC.

The resources of the enterprise are the foundation of the proposed tandem solution of RCA and ABC. In this process, regardless of any analytical need, the mechanics of journalizing cost are established at the financial accounting level as a G/L journal entry. Costs are posted to accounts and grouped by responsibility centers. This process supports the purposes of departmental learning, optimization, and resource specialization. Resources are also paramount in planning and control. They are the basic units of input into the value chain, and therefore they are key elements in execution optimization as well as in changing and adapting the organization to meet its strategy. For these reasons, resources are at the foundation for any costing solution. This section illustrates the building blocks of the combined cost model to explain the mechanics of a combined cost solution and to highlight how these requirements are met.

Resource and Process View

By combining the view established through RCA with the view established in ABC, the loop can be completed and the best of both worlds obtained. Exhibit 1.10 adds the ABC view to the RCA view illustrated in Exhibit 1.6.

It is important to continue to recognize the value of the resource view and the analysis it supports. For the greatest accuracy and information, the ABC view is linked to the resource driver to create a causal relationship rather than the snapshot perspective previously adopted.

Fully Burdened Resource and Accurate Activity/Process Costs

A requirement for the ideal cost solution is that it should supply fully burdened resource costs, so that the enterprise can understand the true interrelationship of the senders and receivers of activities and resources. Normally, within ABC, this cost flow is simplified and is reflected in a unidirectional step-down method, as illustrated in Exhibit 1.11.

This step-down method of allocation generally does not recognize the fact that processes/activities should be allocated back to the resource pools, that is, the real consumers of support activities. Activity-Based Costing would establish a relationship between the support activities and the activities of the consuming cost center. This relationship may not be highly correlated, if at all, and therefore can be very inaccurate. This inaccuracy leads to erroneous activity rates. An appropriate example from the storyboard of how the RCA and ABC combined would address this relationship is the *Distribution Support* area, highlighted in

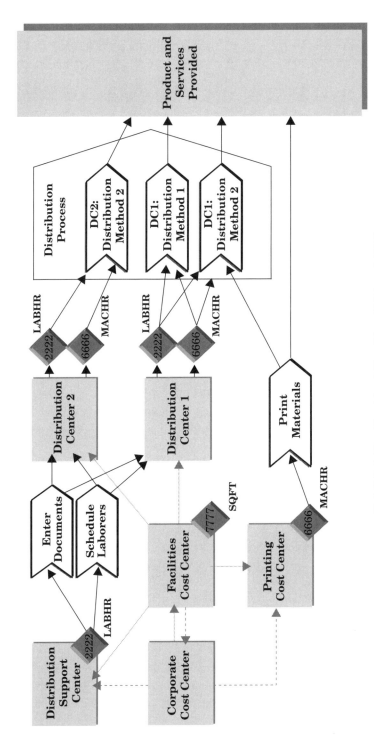

Exhibit 1.10 Combined Cost Flow RCA and ABC

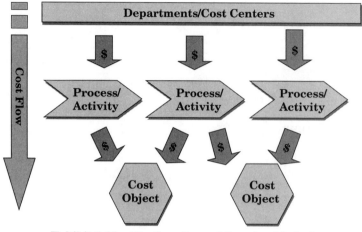

Exhibit 1.11   The Step-Down Allocation Method

Exhibit 1.12. By addressing this type of true cost flow, the mechanics of the costing system can support outsourcing decisions (for both resources and/or activities), capital replacement decisions, and the valuation of products and services with the fully burdened resource cost information.

Outsourcing Decision with Alternate Views of the Nature of Costs   For a detailed example, the outsourcing decision support capability of the tandem approach is considered. The information demands of different levels of management can result in conflicting information needs. This is well illustrated when information supplied by the management accounting system is compared with the information needs of managers who are making an outsourcing decision. For decisions of this kind, middle managers must consider fewer costs to be fixed than what they are typically presented with. The tandem model is based on what is considered to be a viable strategic plan. It is assumed that no organization plans for failure. Adjustments to the resource base—for example, outsourcing—can therefore only be incremental steps to the plan, triggered by change in the environment. The embodiment of the plan, optimizing execution, and enabling control is a primary objective of the solution.

Consider Exhibit 1.13, an example of the fully burdened resource costs for a *Catering* cost center of an airline. Often it is believed that all costs are variable at this level of decision making. However, this is not the case. The classification of costs into their primary (general ledger account) and secondary (allocated) cate-

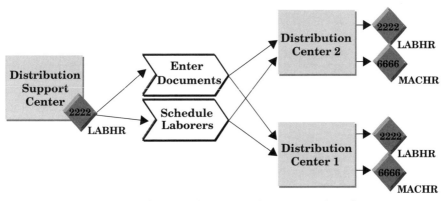

Exhibit 1.12   Combined Cost Flow RCA and ABC

gories is crucial. When considering outsourcing, the secondary costs, in particular, should be very carefully considered. The classification of primary fixed and proportional costs, although essential for making short-term operating decisions, is not relevant in the case of outsourcing decisions. If the catering function is to be outsourced, clearly all of the primary expenses will no longer be incurred, and therefore middle management will need to consider none of these costs to be fixed. However, this is not the case for the secondary expenses. If catering is outsourced, the fixed secondary expenses will result in excess/idle capacity for the providers of these services. For the *Human Resources, Water and Energy,* and *Facilities* departments, subsequent management actions are required to ensure that the resultant excess/idle capacity is addressed and the cost savings realized. It is more difficult to turn the secondary fixed costs, highlighted in Exhibit 1.13, into cost savings. Management, in making the outsourcing decision, cannot be oblivious to these costs, which will clearly not go away, but only shifted to another area in the organization, when the *Catering* department is outsourced. As this scenario illustrates, the tandem solution can supply information that is relevant to tactical management in cases where managers are required to take corrective actions as well as information that is relevant to operational decisions.

Finally, this scenario highlights another interesting point about the nature of costs—namely, that there is never really a business for which all costs would be variable, an approach generally applied when using ABC today. For any given strategy, considering the investment base and support services being provided, certain fixed costs will always be present. The only time all costs would be variable would be if it were the enterprise's strategy to go out of business.[4]

Catering Department	Planned Resource Output: 12,000 LABHRs		
Primary Expenses	Fixed	Proportional	Total
Supervisory Salary	$ 80,000	-	$ 80,000
Chefs' Salaries	-	$ 228,000	$ 228,000
Fringe Benefits	$ 60,000	-	$ 60,000
Depreciation—Equipment	$ 4,000	-	$ 4,000
Secondary Expenses	Fixed	Proportional	Total
Human Resources Activities: Set-up New Hires Process Payroll	$ 20,000 $ 20,000	$ 10,000 $ 5,000	$ 30,000 $ 25,000
Water and Energy: KWH	$ 8,000	$ 25,000	$ 33,000
Facilities: SQFT	$ 20,000	-	$20,000
Total	$ 212,000	$ 268,000	$ 480,000
Resource Unit Output	$ 17.67	$ 22.33	$ 40.00

Exhibit 1.13   Outsourcing the Catering Department Example

Need for a Standard Costing System

To achieve its strategy, the enterprise must be able to effectively plan and control its progress along the envisaged path. This is most effective when the costing model and system support frozen standards, including use with ABC. When the tandem approach of RCA and ABC is utilized, a standard costing approach should be utilized. Standards should be quantity standards, and values should follow quantities. The use of a standard costing approach is primarily the need for timeliness, among other things. RCA information is analyzed every period, if not within a period. ABC information is often analyzed more infrequently, such as quarterly or annually. If ABC is to be utilized in tandem with RCA, then ABC information must be as readily available as RCA data. Although real-time enterprise resource planning (ERP) systems strive to enhance the timely availability of information, it is not practically possible. Quantities are fairly well available to the cost system at the time that they are posted, but expenses cannot be gathered with such consistency. Even within an ERP system, the monthly payroll run is still a periodic processing event. Normal expenses are still received only after the service or product has been consumed. Timely monetary reflections of the organization's activities and outputs can be provided by a standard cost system that uses the real-time quantities available. On a real-time basis, managers can evaluate the impact of actual activity and output levels on planned profit and costs. They can take appropriate steps at an early stage to address any deviations. Yet they will be able to make a detailed variance analysis of actual expenses only after all relevant expenses have been collected. Additionally, once a standard costing system is in place, authorized reporting can be supported.

Organizational Control with Authorized Reporting   A primary objective of utilizing RCA with ABC is to enhance organizational control by providing valid yardsticks for performance measurement in spite of changes in the business environment. Exhibit 1.14 shows the original plan and actual expense for the period for the *Distribution Center 1* cost center. Note that this exhibit covers equipment and does not include labor costs; the latter is treated as a separate resource pool with its own output, *LABHR*. Also note that the actual output level for the period

Plan/Actual/VarianceReport Distribution Center 1				Output: Equipment Hours Planned Quantity: 10,000		Actual Quantity: 11,000	
Primary Costs				*Plan Fixed*	*Plan Proportional*	*Actual*	*Variance*
Oil and Lubricants				$ 100	$ 1,000	$ 1,270	$ 170
Diesel Fuel				-	$ 5,000	$ 6,000	$ 1,000
Consumables				$ 50	$ 200	$ 260	$ 10
Depreciation				$ 25,000	-	$ 25,000	-
Secondary Costs		Quantities					
	Plan Fixed	*Plan Proportional*	*Actual*				
Maintenance	$ 10	$ 1,000	$ 1,377	$ 10,250	$ 15,000	$ 34,425	$ 9,175
Plan & Schedule	-	$ 400	$ 433	$ 6,000	$ 8,000	$ 15,155	$ 1,155
Purchase Supplies	-	$ 100	$ 112	$ 500	$ 1,500	$ 2,240	$ 240
				$ 41,900	$ 30,700	$ 84,350	$ 11,750

Exhibit 1.14   Planned Output and Costs Used for Authorized Reporting

Service Description	Output	Fixed Rate	Proportional Rate
Equip. Maintenance: MAINTH	Hours	$ 10	$ 15
Equip. Scheduling: MGRH	Hours	$ 15	$ 20
Activity: Purchase Supplies	Purchase Orders	$ 5	$ 15

Exhibit 1.15   Service Outputs and Rates

was higher than planned. The rates charged by the secondary services in this example are shown in Exhibit 1.15. A fair amount of the input variances shown here should be attributed to the increase in volume from 10,000 hours to 11,000 hours. This distinction is provided by the authorized report shown in Exhibit 1.16.

The total input variance for *Distribution Center 1* equipment is now $4,780 in Exhibit 1.16, as opposed to $11,750 in Exhibit 1.14, and this variance is the responsibility of the *Distribution Center 1* supervisor. Cost variances can be broken down further into price, quantity, resource usage, and remaining variance (details not shown in the exhibit). Note that authorized secondary costs are based on authorized secondary quantities. The monetary secondary cost variances shown reflect the quantity variances only. For this example, since the system is a standard cost system, no price variances for secondary costs are provided.

Quantity Structure and Capacity Management

A primary responsibility of middle management is the monitoring and realignment of the deployed resource base. Excess/idle capacity information is an important input into this process. A quantity structure within a standard costing system will not only enable middle managers to monitor resource utilization during the process of executing the value chain; it will also help them to make capacity management decisions during the planning stage. In cases where resource skill or technology dictates the use of practical capacity during planning, the financial implications of this decision will be known up front. For example, when plant maintenance technicians will not be fully utilized for a planning period, the decision is made not to reduce the number of technicians. This decision is based on the fact that these highly skilled personnel require extensive training and cannot be readily hired off the street. A resource output rate based on practical capacity, such as the resource pool output quantity, and the planned product consumptions of this resource will result in the resource pool showing a dollar

Authorized Report Distribution Center 1		Output: Equipment Hours Planned Quantity: 10,000 Actual Quantity: 11,000			
Primary Costs			*Authorized*	*Actual*	*Variance*
Oil and Lubricants			$ 1,200	$ 1,270	$ 70
Diesel Fuel			$ 5,500	$ 6,000	$ 500
Consumables			$ 270	$ 260	$ (10)
Depreciation			$ 25,000	$ 25,000	-
Secondary Costs	**Quantities**				
	Authorized	*Actual*			
Maintenance	$ 1,200	$ 1,377	$ 30,000	$ 34,425	$ 4,425
Plan & Schedule	$ 440	$ 433	$ 15,400	$ 15,155	$ (245)
Purchase Supplies	$ 110	$ 112	$ 2,200	$ 2,240	$ 40
			$ 79,570	**$ 84,350**	**$ 4,780**

Exhibit 1.16   Authorized Report for Distribution Center 1

amount of costs that are to be underrecovered. This amount is a clear expression of the financial implication of the decision. In a similar vein, excess/idle capacity variances during execution will be an indication to middle management that changes have occurred in the business environment and must be addressed. The use of the quantity structure and standards in white-collar areas, such as human resources and purchasing, provides for an effective tool to apply capacity management principles in these historically elusive areas.

The presence of excess/idle capacity variances means that activities/processes are not fully burdened with all expenses for a given accounting period, as would be the case in most existing ABC systems. Although not allocating this variance bodes well for the accuracy of product costs and the relevance of information for making decisions, it does have an implication for alternative strategic cost rollups. The total costs of all activities/processes are now no longer a reflection of total enterprise expenses. The excess/idle capacity variance must therefore be added into the relevant level of the value chain to ensure that all costs are included in the strategic cost analysis. This by no means suggests support for the common practice of creating an activity called "Idle Capacity." The capacity variance should be applied directly to the responsible level of the P/L.

Quantity Structure and Planning/Budgeting   For the cascading organizational planning process, a reliable method for calculating both the resource quantities and the associated dollars is necessary to support a given strategy. This planning process of RCA is typically a reverse flow (backflush) of the standard cost model; a cost model based on a quantity structure is ideally suited to this process because it is geared to generating accurate planned dollar values. The combination of RCA with ABC means the inclusion of the activities/process in this backflush of the cost model. Therefore, this approach encompasses Activity-Based Budgeting. ABB is a limited quantity structure in that it normally defines a quantity-based assignment between processes and cost objects; however, traditional ABB is weak and often inaccurate when addressing the resource-to-process relationship. This is due to the fact that value-based relationships are often defined between the resources and activities in ABB models. To illustrate the benefit of combining RCA and ABB, an example of traditional ABB versus RCA and ABB is provided.

Taking another example from the airline industry, these examples will determine the planned costs of the cabin crew and their utilization on two aircraft types for the current period and the current flight timetable. These examples only address the resource-to-activity relationship, which is the relationship definition in contention. Exhibit 1.17 contains basic data that both examples will utilize. Note that the A7Y7 is a larger airplane that requires more cabin crew per flight. The total expense for the cabin crew is $4,000,000.

Example 1: Traditional ABB   Using traditional ABB principles, the budget is generated for 8,000 planned flight hours for both aircraft types for the period, as shown in Exhibit 1.18. In the top half of the exhibit, the planned full-time equivalents (FTEs) are used to split the planned $4,000,000 of cabin crew expense between the two aircraft types. This results in the values $1,600,000 and $2,400,000 as shown. These numbers are then used to calculate a budget, given the planned flight hours. Because it is common practice to consider all costs in ABC as variable, the calculated costs for A7X7 and A7Y7 will be $1,280,000 and $3,840,000, respectively. (See the bottom half of Exhibit 1.18.) The total newly calculated planned expense for cabin crew is thus $5,120,000.

Cabin Crew Utilization	*Aircraft Type:* A7 X7 (10,000 *Flight Hours*)	*Aircraft Type:* A7 Y7 (5,000 *Flight Hours*)
Cabin Crew Time	80,000 hours (40 FTEs)	120,000 hours (60 FTEs)

Exhibit 1.17   Actual Data Copied as Plan for Activity-Based Budgeting Example

Basis of the Calculation

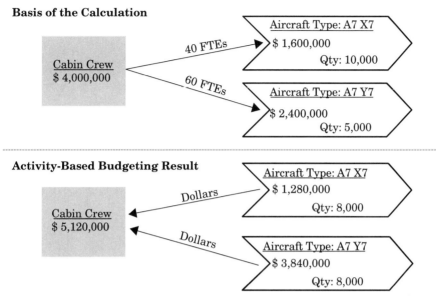

Activity-Based Budgeting Result

Exhibit 1.18   Traditional Activity-Based Budgeting

Example 2: ABB with RCA   However, using Resource Consumption Account-ing, one would first come up with the resource pool plan, which can be a copy of a previous time period or a fresh start. Cost would be classified as primary and secondary as well as fixed and proportional. The plan for the cabin crew is shown in Exhibit 1.19. Because of the complexity of the exhibit, the detailed secondary quantities are not shown here. These consumption quantities would be assigned to the cabin crew resource pool using quantity-based assignments.

Next, using the resource output quantity as the primary consumption link, we arrive at the dollar value for each aircraft type. (See the top half of Exhibit 1.20.) Planned excess/idle capacity is assumed to be zero; therefore, the amounts cal-culated are the same as when FTEs were used. Given the planned utilization for each aircraft type, new demand for cabin crew hours is calculated as 64,000 hours for the A7X7 and 192,000 for the A7Y7, which results in total planned cabin crew hours of 256,000 as shown in the bottom half of Exhibit 1.20.

The hours demanded are converted to the dollar amount that would be re-quired using the resource pool unit standards. Total hours (256,000) multiplied by the proportional cost rate ($15) gives the total planned proportional expense ($3,840,000). Add to this the $1,000,000 of fixed costs and we arrive at the total planned expense for cabin crew: $4,840,000. This number is $280,000 less than the amount calculated using traditional ABB.

Cabin Crew	Planned Resource Output: 200,000 Cabin Crew Hrs		
Primary Expenses	*Fixed Cost*	*Proportional Cost*	*Total Cost*
Supervisory Salaries	$ 190,000	-	$ 190,000
Crew Salaries	-	$ 2,900,000	$ 2,900,000
Uniforms & Clothing	$ 200,000	-	$ 200,000
Secondary Expenses	*Fixed Cost*	*Proportional Cost*	*Total Cost*
Human Resources Costs	$ 170,000	$ 60,000	$ 230,000
Aviation Medical Costs	$ 320,000	$ 40,000	$ 360,000
Facilities Costs	$ 120,000	-	$ 120,000
Total	**$ 1,000,000**	**$ 3,000,000**	**$ 4,000,000**
Resource Unit Output $	$ 5	$ 15	$ 20

Exhibit 1.19   Fully Burdened Resource Costs for the Cabin Crew

This example highlights only the error that traditional ABB will cause owing to the fact that fixed primary and secondary costs of the resources are usually ignored. For simplicity, both scenarios used the same total expense for cabin crew ($4,000,000). Since RCA includes secondary costs and an iterative method of allocation, it will give a more accurate reflection of total cabin crew costs. Also, utilizing RCA with ABC, the calculated support needs of the cabin crew's secondary quantities from the *human resources, aviation medical, and facilities* cost centers can then be utilized to derive their budgets in a similar fashion. The method for deriving these support budgets will also be iterative. Additionally, the presence of planned excess/idle capacity (not illustrated in this example) will result in a larger margin of error for the traditional ABB approach.

SUMMARY

A primary objective of this proposed cost management solution is that it supports proactive decision making better than what traditional prescriptive reporting does. Achieving this vision means converting from the traditional management accounting view into a hybrid world, combining the best characteristics of resource and activity-based analysis. The combination of Resource Consumption Accounting and

Basis of the Calculation

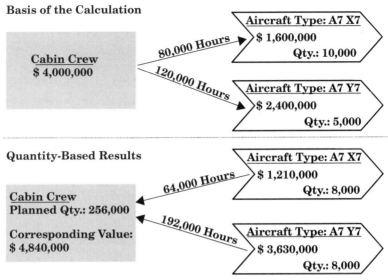

Exhibit 1.20   RCA and ABC Using Quantity-Based
Basis of the Calculation

Activity-Based Costing with the power of real-time integrated systems makes this vision attainable. The benefits obtained by utilizing RCA and ABC are:

- Analytical support for both resources and activities.
- The concept of processes consumed by resources ensures fully burdened resource rates and more accurately transfers costs to the activities that resource supplies. These fully burdened resource rates and more accurate activity rates provide better information for resource/cost center and/or activity outsourcing decisions.
- Inclusion of all costs in one costing model, direct and indirect.
- Applying the standard costing approach to both RCA and ABC for resource and activity consumption provides baseline information for analysis.
- The standard costing system supports variance analysis capabilities for both resources and processes.
- True capacity management is possible with the management of the capacity on the resource. The knowledge of how capacity is utilized is demonstrated through the activities.
- An accurate reflection of the nature of costs and how they change as consumed through the cost model supports gross and contribution margin reporting.
- The quantity structure supports accuracy and reduces maintenance for actual cost assignments and for planning, of which ABB is a limited quantity structure.

Resource Consumption Accounting	Activity-Based Costing
1. Focuses on resources.	1. Focuses on activities.
2. Understanding of resource costs and a fully burdened resource rate.	2. Understanding of activity/process costs.
3. Recursive flows between resource pools.	3. Step-down approach for resource to activity cost flows.
4. Direct expenses and indirect overhead expenses.	4. Indirect overhead expenses.
5. Actual cost flows are mainly quantity-based.	5. Actual cost flows are usually value-based.
6. Normally a standard costing system with frozen unit rates.	6. Normally an actual costing system.
7. Planned/budgeted cost flows are mainly quantity-based.	7. Planned cost flows usually value-based. Quantity-based ABB is a limited quantity structure.
8. Inherent nature of cost based on resource assets. Nature of costs can change on consumption.	8. Inherent nature of costs inconsistently viewed.

Exhibit 1.21   ABC and RCA Philosophies Summary

The key points highlighted within this chapter are summarized in Exhibit 1.21, focusing on the components of the ABC and RCA philosophies.

NOTES

1. Stan Davis and Christopher Meyer, *Blur: The Speed of Change in the Connected Economy* (Reading, MA: Perseus Books, 1998), p. 7.
2. Anton van der Merwe and David Keys, "Accounting for Excess/Idle Capacity in an Advanced Cost Management System: The Case for Resource Consumption Accounting," *Journal of Cost Management,* in press.
3. Anton van der Merwe and David Keys, "Resource Interrelationships to Obtain Fully Burdened Resource Costs: The Case for Resource Consumption Accounting 2," *Journal of Cost Management*, in press.
4. Anton van der Merwe and Christopher Jackiw,"Strategic Cost Management in the Airline Industry", in *Handbook of Airline Finance,* ed. (New York: McGraw-Hill, 1999), chap. 8.

2

SYSTEMS SUPPORT OF THE ACTIVITY-BASED COSTING PHILOSOPHY: STAND-ALONE ANALYTICAL ABC VERSUS INTEGRATED ABC

Chapter 1 addresses differing costing philosophies common throughout the business world today, ending with a detailed look into the Activity-Based Costing approach. When trying to support an ABC philosophy, three types of software applications can be used.

1. A custom-developed system may be designed to support a variety of functionality. However, this option is not addressed here, as the individual functionality can vary too widely.
2. A stand-alone analytical ABC tool, such as Metify ABM or Oros ® Analytics may be used.
3. An integrated enterprise resource planning system, also sometimes referred to as an enterprise-wide system, with embedded ABC functionality, such as SAP R/3, may be employed.

Many ERP vendors have directly developed or have formed partnerships to interface ABC functionality into their packages.[1] Additionally, some ABC companies have independently built interfaces to various ERP packages.[2] The maturation of ERP systems to include ABC functionality is an indication that the ABC costing philosophy is here to stay and is now considered a common or standard method for costing and supporting management analysis. Within SAP, ABC is no longer used as just an analytical tool but is integrated as part of the normal operational costing engine. The acceptance of the ABC costing philosophy into ERP systems raises several questions. For example, are ERP systems a replacement for stand-alone ABC applications? Are there benefits in utilizing both software products? Are there potential philosophical differences in how ABC is applied in each?

This chapter focuses on these very questions and on the differences between stand-alone and ERP ABC business application tools. Obviously, the ERP system addressed in this chapter is the SAP system, since SAP ABC functionality is the subject of the entire book. The following seven chapters will address the specific SAP ABC functionality. Chapter 10 focuses specifically on the Oros ABCPlus and SAP ABC integrated solution, tandem usage scenarios, and the benefits provided.

DEFINING DEFINITIONS

Before a comparison between these stand-alone and integrated ABC tools can be made, a definition for each application needs to be established. What exactly is a stand-alone analytic ABC or an integrated ABC system? It is very hard, actually impossible, to find a standard definition for either. To define them, the pieces need to be understood. A stand-alone analytical ABC system breaks down as follows:

> *Stand-alone:*   Of, relating to, or being a self-contained, usually independent operating, computer system or device: a stand-alone terminal.[3] Capable of operating without other programs, libraries, computers, hardware, networks, etc.[4] Operating, or capable of operating independently of a computer system.[5]

Although these statements do not provide a clear definition, a definite message is conveyed, that of being separate and independent. The "analytical" definitions at least are simplistic and straightforward: "pertaining or proceeding by analysis,"[6] or "concerning or involving analysis."[7] Basically, focusing on analysis. Therefore a stand-alone ABC system, such as Oros ABCPlus, is a separate system used to provide analysis information based on the Activity-Based Costing philosophy.

The integrated ABC system contrasts with the stand-alone ABC system. Unfortunately, today the word "integrated" is so overused by consultants that it has lost its impact. Mainly consultants use it to avoid having to say "interfaced," a word that elicits looks of panic and fear from the audience visualizing massive expenses from having to build and maintain these tables, links, and/or custom code. To truly understand the term "integrated," one must understand "interfaced." An "interface" is "a boundary across which two systems communicate"[8] or "the equipment or programs used to communicate between different systems or programs."[9] "Interfaced" is the act of using the "interface." Some other common words used to describe "interfaced" are links, point of interaction, common boundary, and to "interact or coordinate harmoniously."[10] The message gleaned from this definition is also one of distinct separation, with the addition of harmonious interaction. In summary, a stand-alone ABC system interfaces with other systems to receive necessary pieces of information to produce data to be analyzed, conveying information (ABM) for use in operational and strategic business decisions. To the contrary, "integrated" is defined as:

> *Integrated:*   To form, coordinate, or blend into a functioning or unified whole.[11] A popular computer buzzword that refers to two or more components merged together into a single system.[12]

Other key words used to describe "integrated" are to incorporate, combine, meld with, and enmesh. The message is clearly no longer about separation, but having become one with the other components. This oneness is the foundation of the following criteria:

- One source of information for management reporting eliminating potentially conflicting data.
- One system capturing actual information in real time for use in the ABC model. As transactions that impact the ABC model occur (e.g., process drivers being consumed or a G/L account posting), the ABC model is immediately updated with the data. Conversely, information calculated using the ABC model automatically updates throughout the system (e.g., inventory valuation with real-time updates to the financial ledger).
- One system for defining the organizational model used to support the ABM information produced. When new master data are added or the organizational environment shifts, the ABC model is simultaneously updated. For example, when a new customer is added, different pieces of information on that customer are entered into the master record. This new customer may be identified as part of customer group 2. The integrated ABC model has cost-to-serve processes assigned to all customers in customer group 2 based on a driver. The ABC assignment is updated immediately by the addition of the new customer. Therefore, there is real-time automatic update of the integrated ABC model whether due to changes in the master data or in the transactional data. Neither is stored in a different system.

Since ABC is a costing philosophy for the entire organization, to be an integrated ABC system, the ABC philosophy must be supported in one system that represents the entire organization. (This is not to imply that the ABC philosophy must be used for the entire organization.) Until the emergence of ERP systems, a single system potentially representing the entire organization did not exist. Since an ERP system encompasses the systems for most organizational functions, such as financials, purchasing, human resources, production, and costing, with real-time update of transactional data and model maintenance, only an ERP system can be called an integrated system. Therefore, only an ERP system with the capabilities to support the ABC costing philosophy throughout all components, not just the strategic components, is an integrated ABC system. And that is exactly what SAP provides. All other configurations of systems, such as a stand-alone ABC system interfaced with the financial and/or production systems, are "integrated solutions;" while these are no less or more valid, they definitely are different from integrated ABC.

DETAILED DIFFERENCES

Each type of ABC system—stand-alone or integrated—has advantages and disadvantages. This chapter is about understanding the inherent differences between the two types, before specific functionality is addressed in the later chapters. This chapter utilizes the following five categories to highlight the different natures of the two types of ABC applications.

1. Systems implementation
2. Costing conceptual design
3. Live processing environment
4. User friendliness
5. Organizational aspects

Systems Implementation

System implementations focuses on subjects associated with software implementation projects, such as scope definition, time lines, prototyping, promoting the system into production, and so on.

Implementation Scope   SAP is not usually purchased and implemented just to support ABC in an organization, even though it is possible. Many people ask if they can buy SAP and just implement the ABC module. Doing so is like buying an aircraft carrier to go water skiing. The beauty and strength of SAP lies in the high level of integration between modules, not necessarily focused execution for one area. The scope of an SAP implementation usually encompasses the replacement of several separate software packages used to support different functional organizations, such as financials, human resources, production, and warehouse management. Technical benefits drive the scope, such as reducing the number of interfaces, eliminating several different software packages and their licenses, maintenance, release upkeep, and merging onto one software with one platform.

Business benefits also drive the scope, such as single update of master date records, reduced reconciliation, greater functionality in a particular business application, and real-time capturing of the information.

Exhibit 2.1 illustrates the integration of ABC with some of the other major modules. The potential scope of the SAP implementation can be all of these areas, plus many others not depicted, or just some. Depending on the pieces selected for the scope of the implementation, the integrated ABC model design will be impacted. When integrated ABC is implemented depends on when each of the major pieces is installed. Chapter 3 provides a detailed overview of SAP modules and functionality.

As stated, the typical scope of an SAP implementation is not just for providing ABC functionality; in contrast, a stand-alone package is purchased specifically for that reason. Additionally, the SAP implementation may be a global implementation, with the first phase focusing on a pilot site, such as the United States, with add-on phases for the roll-out to other countries. Although stand-alone ABC systems are implemented in phases as well, these phases are compartmentally smaller. Normally there is a focus on certain types of costs, such as product costing or distribution costs, or some departments within an organization for the United States, not the entire U.S. organization. Huge differences exist regarding the driving factors behind the purchases of these two types of systems and therefore the scope of the projects.

Implementation Time Line   The defined phases of the SAP implementation scope encompass all functionality being implemented, not just the ABC component.

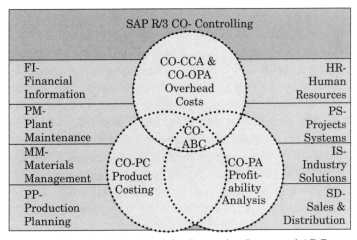

Exhibit 2.1   Major Modules Impacting Integrated ABC

This greatly impacts the implementation time line. Due to the integrated nature of an ERP implementation, the time line is typically measured in months to years for global roll-outs to several countries, as opposed to weeks to months for a stand-alone ABC system since consideration must be given to all integration dependencies (i.e., other functional areas such as production, materials management, sales, and human resources), their individual implementation time lines, system architecture, and organizational impacts. Also impacting the SAP implementation time line is the level of customization required over and beyond the SAP standard business model. Stand-alone ABC systems can be implemented much faster since other functional areas do not impact the ABC project as severely in a nonintegrated environment and their scope is smaller by nature. If implementing SAP ABC in a later release of the SAP total implementation cycle, the time line is much closer to a stand-alone ABC system. This timeline improvement is due to the focus being limited to only ABC functionality.

ABC Model Definition   Integrated SAP ABC should be built during the phase which the Controlling (CO) module is identified for implementation. Just prior to 2000, many companies implemented the CO module without implementing the ABC component, mainly due to time pressures to beat the Y2K deadline. Many organizations implemented CO with little functionality just to provide the basics for supporting financial reporting, with the intention to come back around in the second phase to build or expand costing and management capabilities. Since CO houses the organizational departments, their plans/budgets, the drivers and measures, the allocations, and the profitability reporting, it is often necessary to take a fresh look at these areas during the SAP ABC implementation. In order to not merely replicate the legacy costing and profitability system, an integrated solution analysis is required.

Due to limitations in system functionality, often legacy costing systems have master data that exists merely to support allocations. These systems are also usually built on an embedded G/L concept where the departmental codes, project codes, and other key piece of information have been embedded into the G/L account numbering scheme. During the beginning of the SAP implementation for the financial and controlling modules, the chart of accounts is usually restructured, impacting most allocations already defined, and the departmental definitions are revisited. This reevaluation is the first stage of the analysis, the final deliverable being the costing conceptual design for the CO module that must be systematically supported. This design may or may not contain the ABC philosophy, depending on the organization's costing requirements.

To define any ABC model, an activity analysis is performed regardless of the system supporting the ABC functionality. The activity analysis focuses on business processes, allocations, drivers, and reporting, and should be a part of the SAP integrated analysis used to design the CO module. However, the interviews and workshops of the integrated analysis are broad in nature and do not focus primarily on the activities of the organization. This analysis includes reviewing all inputs and outputs of all the departments, capturing information for investment projects and capitalization needs, depreciation review for financial versus cost depreciation, planning/budget policies and procedures, revenue determination and timing for recognition, and inventory tracking and valuations. Therefore, while the tasks performed to build the ABC/M model are similar, the CO module focus has to be more encompassing because of the integration impacts (organizational, scope) and the wider spectrum of costing philosophies supported. For those organizations that already have the Controlling module implemented, in order to just build integrated ABC, the activity analysis can be performed with additional tasks for reviewing the integration points to the other implemented SAP modules. Especially integration points with production and inventory valuation.

Master Data Creation   Once the ABC model has been defined, it can be built. First the master data needs to be established, and then the assignments and reporting can be implemented. Within the stand-alone ABC system, master data can be created very quickly since very few pieces of information are required. Additionally, the stand-alone model usually is not constructed for the entire organization and therefore less master data needs to be generated. This shortens the time it takes to build a model. In an integrated environment, master data records can have many information fields and several required fields that impact a large portion of the organization. Many areas of an integrated system use the same master data to track and control the transactions being generated by the organization's business processes. This control ensures a certain customer cannot be used with a particular pricing procedure, products can be purchased only from approved suppliers, salespeople cannot reduce the price to provide a contribution below a certain level, manager of Division 1 cannot run the allocations for Division 2, and so on. Also, the integrated environment potentially represents the entire organization and therefore it is more common to have hundreds to thousands of master data records, requiring more time for identification, clean-up, and conversion. Although the ABC assignment model within SAP probably will not encompass the entire organization, being a part of the SAP system means the ABC model does have access to the entire organizational model that has been implemented into SAP.

Prototyping   With a sample or all of the master data in place, prototyping of cost assignments and identification and creation of the reports can occur. In order to prototype in the SAP environment, all integration points have to be built and maintained. Since the CO module, and therefore ABC, is the receiver of most of the transactions, its prototype is greatly impacted by the design of the other components. Therefore, often the prototype cannot be finished until other teams get certain pieces of their respective prototype designs in place. Additionally, the time to complete the prototype is greatly impacted by getting the organizational representatives to agree on which processes should be supported in an ABC methodology and how. Decisions of one team, such as sales processing, can impact how the financials or controlling teams define their support of the processes.

Conversely, the lack of integration and dependencies throughout the organization allows for quick building of ABC models in using a stand-alone tool. This characteristic can be leveraged by developing ABC models to be utilized during the integrated SAP ABC system implementation blueprinting or design phase, potentially reducing the effort normally expended. Doing so will help to identify information that needs to be gathered, key areas for points of integration with other SAP modules, and reporting requirements for the integrated ABC implementation.

Promote to Production Path   Enterprise resource planning software in general, including SAP, is not just pulled out of the box, loaded onto a computer of choice, and turned on, as is the case with most stand-alone software. SAP requires configuration of options on how the business processes and their generated transactions should be supported, captured, and reported. Since changes are being made to the standard software, strong controls and change management procedures need to be established. These change control and documentation procedures are referred to as the promote to production. The promote to production path is the migration of program code, configuration, and master data through different technical environments to eventually reside in the final productive system. Whether implementing all the modules of SAP or merely a portion of functionality, such as integrated ABC, any configuration or program change must follow some sort of path to production, passing organizational authorization checks to determine impacts on other functional areas. Exhibit 2.2 illustrates a promote to production path.

In this example, there are four instances or environments of the SAP application, providing a very high level of safety, basically four separate software loads. These instances may be housed on separate hardware or the same hardware, like having a partitioned drive with Microsoft Office loaded on both drives. Within an instance, there can be multiple clients, which are reflections of the organizational model and the business processes to be supported with the resulting

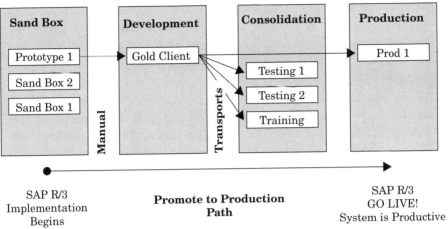

Exhibit 2.2   Promote to Production Path Example

data to be captured. For example, in Exhibit 2.2, the instance "Sand Box" has three clients, Sand Box 1, Sand Box 2, and Prototype 1. Some software changes may impact only a single client (client dependent), while other changes impact all clients in an instance (client independent.) An analogy is having Excel loaded on a computer four times (representing the four instances) using one of the four Excel programs. Three Excel files are created (representing the clients). If one of the files gets changed or deleted, the other files are not impacted (client dependent). However, if someone changes the coding of one of those four Excel programs, perhaps eliminating the Sum function, then all of the files in that Excel program (instance) will loose the Sum functionality.

The first instance, the "Sand Box" (names vary from location to location), is the initial trial-and-error area for determination of configuration and master data requirements. Sand Box 1 may be used for the entire project team to practice what they have learned in training and to try out ideas of how to configure the system to support the organizational business processes. Sand Box 2 may exist for particular areas within the system, for interfaces and conversion coding, for another phase that has started after the initial project, or for production support. There can be multiple Sand Box clients for different reasons. Regardless of the Sand Box schema, there is a prototyping client in which all configuration for the project is performed by each team (Financials, Human Resources, Production, Controlling, etc.). The initial focus is on providing the functionality requested from the area, while still trying to make sure the prototype works from an integrated standpoint. Different configuration scenarios are compared to determine the best final configuration.

The "Development" instance contains the preliminarily agreed-on configuration and programs that support the desired system and business design. The configuration and the programs can be automatically transported from the Sand Box instance to the Development instance. However, usually a manual rebuild of the configuration is performed to eliminate unnecessary or erroneous trial-and-error configuration from being moved. The main client in the Development instance is the pristine, proven environment normally without transactional data, often called the gold, core, or master client. This master client is highly controlled to ensure integrity and is used to transport, or copy, the configuration to the consolidation instance.

"Consolidation" is where integrated testing scenarios are performed, such as purchase requisitions to check, sales inquiry to cash, and period-end closing. Clients in the Consolidation environment are also used for volume/stress testing and training clients. Master Data conversions are usually performed here and a complete run through of the system is checked. If changes need to be made, the system configurator goes back to the prototyping client in the Sand Box to make sure the changes work there. Once approved, the changes move through the promote-to-production path until tested to satisfaction. Once everything passes testing, the Development core configuration client (Master, etc.) is often used to create the production client that is used to "go live" with the system.

Each organization has a different promote-to-production path driven by varying factors, such as hardware availability, sizing constraints, and risk tolerance. This is merely a sample promote to production path to stress the difference in the required steps necessary between implementing any integrated ABC system versus a stand-alone. A stand-alone ABC system needs to have the model defined and built. Testing must be performed for the functionality and for the interfaces to a stand-alone product. However, there is not as stringent a promote to production path as with the integrated SAP solution.

Overall, the differences from a system implementation standpoint between implementing SAP integrated ABC and a stand-alone ABC system are driven by size and time of the implementation. As with every project, scope drives time, and with an SAP implementation, the scope is usually much more encompassing.

Costing Conceptual Design

As a result of the integrated or nonintegrated nature of the solution, there are some potential philosophical differences between the two systems. The costing conceptual design category focuses on these differences. Some of the points are unique to the particular products being considered, that is, SAP. For example, areas highlighting the philosophical differences that exist between SAP and stand-alone ABC systems are primarily due to the integration of ABC into Resource Consumption Accounting, conceptually addressed in Chapter 1, which is the basis of the SAP ERP business application. Other points addressed exist regardless of the ERP solution chosen.

Quantity Structure   Chapter 1 addresses the traditional flow of ABC, which is usually a value-based approach sometimes using quantity drivers to determine a percentage split or ratio as the allocation basis. The traditional approach to value flow in the SAP system has been one of an entirely quantity-based consumption model where value follows quantity. This is apparent by the fact that most of the allocation methods supported by SAP are quantity-based. Using the quantity structure approach, percentages, ratios, and FTEs are not used to allocate costs between objects. Instead, for each object (cost center, activity/process) a quantified output is identified, associated with the dollars on the object, and a calculated standard unit rate is used to drive the cost assignment.

The quantity structure approach has implications for other philosophical areas, such as more accurate Activity-Based Budgeting. Some stand-alone ABC packages support a quantity structure in some manner, such as the Oros ABCPlus software using the Output Measurement Method (the Bill of Cost), which can be used for ABB. However, SAP also provides functionality supporting simultaneous consumption of the output quantity, both a fixed and a proportional output quantity, addressed in detailed in the "Fixed/Proportional Quantities" section of Chapter 5. This additional SAP capability provides the most accurate reflection of the organization and can impact accuracy of the information.

Excess/Idle Capacity   The quantity structure approach, combined with SAP's emphasis on resource consumption accounting, results in a specific accommodation and focus on the costs related to invested capacity and the excess/idle capacity variance. Resource pools within SAP are provided with more than one output field to allow for analysis and rate calculations based on, for example, planned output, practical capacity, or theoretical capacity. See the "Which Quantity Will Be Used to Determine the Driver Rate?" section of Chapter 5. Some stand-alone packages, such as Oros ABCPlus, can support any of these capacities as well. However, resource pools are considered the focal point for managing capacity-related costs in SAP, an approach not typically adopted when implementing stand-alone ABC packages.

True Reflection of Consumption Relationships   Most stand-alone ABC packages support a one-way flow of allocation (resource> activity> product) as the default allocation method. In the SAP system, an iterative allocation method has always been the preferred solution for the purposes of accurate valuation and fully burdening consumers with all relevant costs, particularly in the support cost center areas such as facilities, human resources, and information technology departmental costs. Within SAP's integrated ABC concept it is possible to allocate activities/processes back to cost centers/resources. For example, the *Purchasing* department performs the process of *Create Purchase Order* for items for the *Human Resources* department. Therefore, the process costs will not be allocated to products but will be charged directly to the consumer—the *Human Resources* department (resource> activity> resource). Chapter 5's "Activity-Based Costing Paradigm Shift" section contains a detailed example of the resource> process> resource cost flows and the benefits provided.

Assignment Rules Supported   Stand-alone ABC systems often support many different assignment methods, from simplistic tracing of costs via percentages or quantities converted to percentages, to some form of quantity-based approach, such as using bill of costs or resources, all usually using a process object. SAP's robust costing engine supports many different costing philosophies, not just ABC. Therefore, SAP supports these same allocation methods using processes as transfer objects as well as direct charge-out rules or traditional cost-plus methods. Additionally, SAP provides an allocation method called the Template. When used with the ABC functionality, the Template allocation method supports multidimensional rules, with IF-THEN statements, using any number of variables to determine which process to be used, how much of it to apply, and when to apply it. For example, in a paint shop, variables such as the surface area of a product, the part number of a base coat applied, the actual volume consumed, and the specific gravity of the base coat can be used to determine, in real time (since all the information is contained within SAP), which process and the process quantity to apply to product cost. Therefore the singular driver to consumer associations typically found in stand-alone ABC systems should not be directly applied to the integrated ABC model—it would forfeit both accuracy and flexibility.

Previously built ABC models may have limitations designed into the assignments due to the inability to capture the most accurate driver or to accurately impute a driver quantity. The SAP assignment capabilities support many ways to impute driver quantities. Also, the integrated nature of SAP provides for the capturing and use of thousands of drivers that may have been too cost prohibitive to capture previously, increasing the accuracy or validity of the assignments.

Scope of Conceptual Design   SAP systems by their very nature are all-inclusive when it comes to the accommodation of costs/expenses. SAP systems must not only consider product costs but also cost categories that often are ignored in stand-alone ABC systems. Examples of these are assets under construction, warranty repairs and insurance claim costs incurred (to be recovered from the vendor and underwriter, respectively), and major maintenance reserves to be capitalized. Additionally, the integrated nature of SAP supports cost transfers that are normally not considered or supported due to philosophical limitations by stand-alone ABC systems, such as direct G/L postings to a process activity, purchase orders assigned to an activity, or activities being integrated with sales orders for showing profitability impacts prior to a sale.

Costing Basis and Variances   Stand-alone ABC packages typically are full-absorption actual cost systems. SAP has an industrial-strength costing engine that allows for product costing on a moving average or frozen standard basis. SAP provides for automated inventory revaluation or variance liquidation depending on the product cost method used (moving average or frozen standard).

Additionally, using SAP, overhead costing can be performed using actual or frozen standard costing. This frozen standard, or unit driver rate, functionality extends beyond resource and overhead cost management (which provides excess idle capacity, price, usage, and quantity variances) to product costing (with price, quantity, usage, and lot size variances) and on into profitability analysis (providing sales price quantity and sales mix variances).

Inventoriable Costs   Stand-alone ABC systems generally are not integrated with the inventory control systems and therefore do not focus on the impacts or inclusions of activity costs for financial inventory valuation. However, inventoriable costs is a topic that must be closely evaluated with an SAP integrated ABC system since the activities can be automatically included for and directly impact the inventory valuation.

The differences from a costing conceptual design standpoint between implementing SAP integrated ABC and a stand-alone ABC system are addressed in detail throughout the rest of this book. Some highlights have been provided here.

System Live Processing

Quite possibly the largest gap between an interfaced and integrated solution is seen when reviewing the processing nature of the two options. System live processing focuses on the differences between the two systems' operational characteristics, such as timing, data types, data integrity, and processes for supporting intercompany accounting or period-end closing.

Real-time versus Periodic   The key difference between the integrated ABC system and the stand-alone is the timing, on-line real time versus batch. Integrated ABC is real-time recognition. Stand-alone is separate and therefore batch related. The integrated ABC model is required to accurately reflect the day-to-day fluctuations of an operational environment. Data updating and validation of the SAP cost model structure occur when the transactional data is posted in real time. Integrated ABC reporting of profit and cost occur in real time, if frozen standards are used. A full spectrum of variances is available once all actual expenses have been collected and assigned.

Contrary to the on-line view, stand-alone ABC systems are batch fed and updated monthly, more likely quarterly, with new information from the G/L and other sources for driver data. The stand-alone solution must also address cost model structure changes, for example, new cost centers and accounts. These "master data" structure changes usually are addressed less frequently, for example, quarterly or annually, to limit ongoing maintenance requirements.

The number one reason cited for moving from a stand-alone ABC system to SAP integrated ABC is to support increased speed for calculation, model updates, and dissemination of the ABC information. The main focus in the move is therefore to provide ABC information more rapidly and perhaps at irregular times to support the immediacy of current management queries and decisions, not to provide a historical view.

Driver Data Collection   All actual driver quantities must be manually loaded, uploaded, or interfaced into a stand-alone ABC system. Using the functionality within SAP, the ABC model can be designed to use drivers already captured within the SAP system, such as number of purchase orders, number of quality checks, number of goods issued, or number of production orders. Thus, integration reduces the number of interfaces/uploads required, thereby shortening or eliminating reconciliation and error correction procedures.

Data and Data Structure Integrity   One of the reasons companies purchase SAP is to obtain the structure and data integrity inherent to an integrated system. Master data resides and is maintained once in a single location and is accessible by all users in real time versus having to maintain master data in several legacy systems. Modules are also functionally integrated, such as the G/L and costing system, preventing misalignment from occurring. For example, when an account is created because of a need in financial accounting, that account is also created in the cost model. Further, significant control exists to limit access to make such changes. Stand-alone ABC systems, however, do not require all the validations and master data elements control points of the SAP system. Thus, within a stand-alone system, ad hoc data manipulation is much easier, allowing for simulation and "what-if" analysis to be conducted without compromising the integrity of the operational database.

Transaction-based System   At its root, SAP is a transaction-based system and provides audit trails throughout the system for all postings, including any ABC assignments. Also, if data is to be interfaced into SAP, it is rarely directly input into the database. Data is posted through transactions in order to pass the checks and balances within SAP. Transactions create a clear audit trail that lends credibility to reports by means of drill-down to posted documents and line items. For example, the drill-down of a revenue line in a profit report out of the Controlling module will drill back to a line item on a particular sales order in the Sales and Distribution module. A stand-alone system is normally uploaded with summarized data directly into the database. Also, due to the aggregation of the data, when an anomaly is detected, in stand-alone systems it is not possible to continually drill back to the originating transaction, which normally indicates the cause of the exception.

Currency   SAP supports a four-tiered currency tracking capability. The four tiers are for document level, object level, legal entity level, and consolidation level currencies. For example, assume a British-owned company with a U.S. subsidiary has a plant in Mexico that purchases materials from Brazil. The purchase document is captured using the Brazilian real currency a transactional/document posting. It is posted to the appropriate cost center (object tier) for the production plant in Mexico that uses Mexican pesos as currency. The production plant is for a legal entity that is based on U.S. dollars. The required currencies for consolidation are British pounds and the Euro. With integrated ABC, these four tiers are also relevant for the tracking of shared services or corporate allocations between legal entities.

Stand-alone ABC software packages do not accommodate the four tiers of currency. By their very nature they do not capture information at the document level. Usually the object level can be attempted, but often it requires all objects in the model to have the same base currency. The legal entity might be accommodated; however, some stand-alone packages require additional models to reflect the legal entity currencies. Consolidation is usually not a consideration of scope for stand-alone ABC projects because, as stated earlier, the focus on most modeling efforts usually does not include higher-level consolidations or legal needs.

Intercompany Accounting   The integrated nature of the SAP system supports intercompany accounting using activity costs. For example, a shared service company may be established that supports several other corporate legal entities. Within SAP, when a shared service activity is posted to a receiving cost center in a different company code, the corresponding posting is made to align the financial books of the legal entities, that is, the accounts receivable posting for the provider and vice versa. Therefore, the two companies share the same management accounting view yet have two separate financial accounting ledgers that are kept in sync. Stand-alone ABC systems may be used to determine the rates of a shared service process and even the assignment methods. However, they normally are not integrated to make the real-time corresponding postings that represent both the internal movement of costs and the external updates of the financial ledgers.

Product Costing   Stand-alone packages utilize a very flexible and uncluttered approach to product costing. Due to its tight integration with the logistics modules, however, SAP has a vast array of links and dependencies with statistics and production/conversion quantities. These include, for example, customized objects for the production strategies adopted, such as process manufacturing, make to stock, make to order, engineer to order, or even a services object. Planning dependencies exist for these objects for long-, medium-, or short-term planning. The accompanying material and external service purchase requests can be generated. In addition, information enables scheduling of work and the collection of actual material, time, and internal and external services consumed. There are statistics tied to the production object for the purposes of statistical quality sampling, for example, tolerances and the conversion of raw material units of measure (lbs, kgs, liters) to the output product unit of measure. Finally, financial requirements for inventory valuation at standard or moving average, the calculation of work-in-process, and variances are also provided for.

All of this is tied together by means of system configuration that makes the product costing area the least likely to be leveraged, if at all, in transitioning from a stand-alone system to SAP's integrated ABC. Also, all of the ERP systems that have incorporated the ABC philosophy have not necessarily integrated ABC with the operational logistics system. Most ERPs, other than SAP, have integrated ABC capabilities with their strategic components only.

Period-end Closing   The preceding points not only highlight the real-time and integrated nature of ABC transactions in an SAP integrated ABC system but also the potential difference in period-end closing for the two systems. A stand-alone ABC application that is not used for inventory valuation can be populated with the relevant data once the company's formal period closing has been completed. In an integrated ABC environment, the period-end close is now dependent on processing and closing out at least the product-related ABC information. However, due to the real-time aspect of SAP and the type of hardware used to support SAP, usually all of the ABC information can be processed within the normal period-end closing procedure, or shortly thereafter.

The integration and timing aspects of SAP versus a stand-alone system mainly drive these differences from a live processing environment standpoint.

User Friendliness

User friendliness of a software package has to do with the ease of learning, using, and manipulating it.

Ease of Use   As previously stated, the stand-alone ABC systems are not hampered with the interdependencies of an integrated system. Therefore, the ABC model is much easier and faster to create. To set up the integrated ABC model in SAP requires some configuration and an understanding and review of integration points. Also, the user interface is usually not as intuitive as a stand-alone ABC system.

Ease of Simulation   Given the speed with which a model can be developed in stand-alone ABC packages, creating different variations of the model to perform simulation is relatively easy. SAP facilitates model simulation by means of alternate plan versions. However, SAP validity checks force the simulations to adhere to existing master data and structures, a process that can be both cumbersome, unduly restrictive, and resource intensive. Additionally, simulations are usually performed to model the impacts of new potential structures, such as new markets, new customers, or new vendors. SAP usually represents the true current organizational structure, therefore these simulations would not be included in SAP.

Training Investment   Two types of training must occur: (1) ABC philosophy and (2) System training. The people responsible for the models and the receivers of the information must be trained in the ABC philosophy for them to understand the benefits or the impact on the type and accuracy of the information provided. This type of training is not impacted by the software application used. System training is broken into user training and modeler training. The SAP users are known as end users and must undergo training to become familiar with the SAP product itself and with the resulting organizational impact. This sort of training is usually delivered during the implementation phase of the project. Stand-alone ABC systems require less training due to a strategic focus and less complexity.

Modeler training is provided for the SAP integrated ABC superusers. Those users responsible for maintaining the CO conceptual design including the ABC view going forward, must have an understanding of all of the Controlling module functionality used in their organization and the interdependencies with the other modules. This is a great deal of formal classroom training and on the job training during the implementation. The modeling training for a stand-alone ABC system is measured in days to weeks, where the training for SAP functionality is measured in weeks to months.

Report Customization   Stand-alone packages usually have user-friendly and intuitive functionality, or a partnership with reporting packages, to aid in the creation of customized reports. SAP provides a vast array of standard reports and tools, such as report writer, report painter, and ABAP (program code), for complete report customization. However, the SAP tools require more training and a higher user skill level than the average stand-alone ABC reporting tools. Additionally, much of SAP reporting is being moved to the Business Warehouse (BW) application, which requires added training to understand what types of information are reported from which modules of the SAP core system.

Where the integrated nature of SAP provides huge benefits as far as added functionality and data consistency, when compared to a stand-alone ABC system, the same integration negatively impacts user friendliness.

Organizational Aspects

The organizational aspects category details the implications for an organization in moving from a stand-alone to an integrated ABC system. These aspects cover topics such as scope, organizational planning and control, and organizational buy-in.

Organizational Scope   As indicated earlier, SAP is all-inclusive by nature, particularly in the organizational realm. Enterprise resource planning systems are high-cost, large investments adopted by organizations as a whole. Although the stand-alone ABC system can be governed by a select few in the organization, the SAP ABC system cannot be champion owned; it must be *organization* owned. However, SAP implementations provide greater access to ABC functionality, which has far-reaching implications for how information is presented, viewed, and used. SAP also provides robust multilingual and multicurrency functionality for the seamless accommodation of global enterprises.

Organizational Planning and Control   Since most stand-alone ABC tools are after-the-fact actual cost systems only, in practice, often the management processes of planning and control are disjointed. Organizations that currently plan in their general ledgers and use stand-alone ABC systems for actual cost information can use SAP to integrate these management processes since SAP fully supports the integration of planning, control, and corrective action. In SAP, the default planning tool is the Controlling module, not the G/L. In integrated ABC, the organizational planning process can be directly linked to ABC-based performance measurement information. Terms like "responsibility accounting," "variance analysis in ABC," and "authorized (flexed) reports" can signal big and positive changes, but major change management effort is required to implement it throughout the organization.

Organizational Buy-in   Because SAP usually encounters a much broader organization than stand-alone ABC, gaining organizational buy-in often takes more time, with greater political maneuvering involved. Users can employ stand-alone ABC software to communicate ABC principles and benefits throughout the organization quickly, thus enhancing the success of the drive to implement integrated ABC at a truly operational level within the SAP system.

The size of each system drives the impacts to the organization. Stand-alone ABC systems can be champion owned and can exist only in certain areas of the organization, without ever being known by other areas. SAP integrated ABC provides ABC functionality and information potentially to the entire organization. Any SAP licensed users can access this functionality for their part of the organization, meaning ABC can be decentralized throughout the organization within SAP. This access greatly impacts the organization.

SUMMARY

In the past, stand-alone ABC systems were used within an interfaced solution to try to emulate an integrated ABC environment, which simply was not available yet. Now that integrated ABC is both available and achievable, many companies have asked the often-elusive key question: How should each of these systems be used? The answer to this question is determined by the quality and time aspects of the implementation. Quality is defined as the accuracy of the ABC model to reflect the actual organizational cost flows required for analysis. This accuracy may require an application that can support iterative flows between resources and processes, the ability to simultaneously consume fixed and proportional output quantities, real-time updates for inventory costing, and so on.

Time is defined by how long is needed to build a model, perform maintenance on the model, process the ABC information, and by how long the model exists (permanent or one-time specific analysis). The decoupling of the stand-alone ABC application from the core backbone processing systems provides speed and flexibility when building models. This speed better supports models built for temporary, specifically focused analysis, for example, process reengineering impacts and increasing capacity of a plant. However, the decoupling also increases the maintenance of the model and requires additional steps for synchronization and reevaluating the assignments. It also increases the time required for processing the data with batch interfaces needing error correction and reconciliation.

The integration aspect of the SAP ABC system increases the time required to build the model, from the standpoint of both analysis and actual construction. However, the processing maintenance is reduced when access to the information and organizational model changes is real time and on-line. Integration potentially eliminates some interfaces, depending on the scope of the SAP system, reducing the need for batch interfaces, reconciliations, and resource-intensive model updates.

In summary, if the organization needs immediate information, real-time analysis, and updates with actual results, then the solution lies with SAP's integrated ABC. If the requirements are to support situational analysis, such as "what-if" or simulation-type models, then the answer is a nonintegrated model, such as Oros ABCPlus. In the latter scenario, the requirements focus on rapid changes and adjustments to the model for hypothetical situations rather than actual results. Exhibit 2.3 provides a summary table of all of the categories and criteria as a reference.

NOTES

1. Many news releases describe mergers between SAP-ATI, Armstong-Laing and J.D. Edwards, and ACTIVA and Oracle.
2. Armstong-Laing independently developed an interface to the SAP R/3 CO application.
3. *Dictionary.com,* http://Dictionary.com.
4. *Free On-line Dictionary of Computing,* http://wombat.doc.ic.ac.uk.
5. *Merriam-Webster's Collegiate Dictionary,* www.m-w.com.
6. Ibid.
7. *All Words Dictionary,* www.allwords.com.
8. *Free On-line Dictionary of Computing.*
9. *Wordsmyth Dictionary,* www.wordsmyth.net.
10. *Merriam-Webster's Collegiate Dictionary.*
11. Ibid.
12. *Webopedia Dictionary,* www.pcwebopaedia.com.

Focus Points	Stand-alone ABC	SAP Integrated ABC
System Implementation Category		
Implementation Scope	Narrower focus on type of costs or piece of organization within a country	Much broader focus—pilots can be for one country, driven by IT and/or business needs
Implementation Time Line	Shorter—measured in weeks or months	Longer—measured in months or possibly more than one year (depending on scope)
ABC Model Definition	Requires activity analysis to define model	Best practice requires an integrated analysis, which encompasses an activity analysis to define all of CO and the touch points to other areas of the system
Master Data Creation	Swift with limited information required, smaller data set, limited required fields	Larger data set (whole organization) and its partners (customers, vendors, etc.), many more required and informational fields
Prototyping	Quick and easy due to nonintegration	Complex with system and organizational dependencies
Promote to Production	None to speak of	Stringent path to follow with authorization and control checks along the way. Many sign-offs and meetings over impacts of changes
Costing Conceptual Design Category		
Quantity Structure	Not fully supported since logistic modules do not exist to support product costing	Traditional backbone of controlling
Excess/Idle Capacity	Typically not consistently accommodated	Particular philosophical approach adopted
Consumption Simulation	Resource>activity>product	Iterative consumption model with the ability to flow from Resource>Process>Resource to the true consumer
Assignment Rules Supported	Single dimensional rules	Multi-dimensional "IF-THEN" rules
Scope of Conceptual Design	Typically limited to product costs	All organizational costs, including capitalized costs
Cost Basis and Variances	Frozen standard rates or fluctuating actual rates	Can support either rate method as well as extensive variance analysis across overhead, product and profitability analysis
Inventoriable Costs	Usually not a consideration	Process costs automatically included in inventory

Exhibit 2.3 Comparison by All Categories and Criteria Summary

Live Processing Environment Category		
Real-Time versus Periodic	Periodic	Real-time
Driver Data Collection	Cumbersome, batch oriented	Real-time or batch
Data and Data Structure Integrity	A classic stand-alone system	Fully integrated system
Transaction Based	Summarized batch feed — no transaction data	Transaction-based application
Currency	Some ability to handle multiple currencies	Four-tier currency tracking including process cost postings
Intercompany Accounting	Can model the assignments between companies but not make the accounting postings	Maintains internal/external accounting postings
Product Costing	Can model the cost assignments to product cost objects; however, lacks the logistics integration	Completely integrated with the logistics functionality, including the abilities of the logistics modules for capacity management, scheduling, unit of measure conversions, etc.
Period-end Closing	Typically not included	ABC determined product costs included, ability to completely include ABC costs for period-end closing
User-Friendliness Category		
Ease of Use	Very easy	Can be complex depending on design needs, not as intuitive, and requires more training
Ease of Simulation	Swift and flexible, but with fewer validations	Resource intensive due to all-inclusive nature and many validations required
Training Investment	Relatively low	Extensive training investment
Report Customization	Easy user-friendly functionality	Requires training (some extensive [e.g. ABAP]) and higher level of user skill
Organizational Buy-in Category		
Organizational Scope	Often not implemented organization wide, less robust in multi-lingual and multi-currency and therefore one model is limited in its ability to support a global view	An all-inclusive application with robust multi-lingual and multi-currency capabilities. Specifically designed to accommodate global implementations and considerations
Organizational Planning and Control	Management processes not usually fully supported	Full spectrum of management processes (planning and control) supported
Organizational Buy-in	Quick dissemination of concepts and benefits	Requires training, time, and commitment to yield full benefits

Exhibit 2.3   (Continued)

3

OVERVIEW OF SAP AND INTEGRATED ACTIVITY-BASED COSTING

Before proceeding with the details of integrated ABC in SAP R/3, a basic understanding of the SAP application must exist. Chapter 2 established the differences between stand-alone and integrated ABC systems in general. This chapter provides an overview of the SAP R/3 application as a whole and its components. For readers who are very familiar with the SAP R/3 modules and functionality, this chapter may not be relevant other than to establish a common understanding of acronyms.

The SAP R/3 business application is a tightly integrated, transaction-based, operational-level, enterprise resource planning system. This integrated nature of SAP generates the largest benefits of this software solution; however, this integration also causes the greatest difficulties in implementations. One area of SAP R/3 cannot be discussed, designed, trained, or scoped without understanding the next integrated piece of the system to be affected. SAP R/3 consists of application areas addressing financials, logistics, and human resources. Within each application area are one to many modules. These modules are logical groupings of system capabilities into areas of functionality, such as financials, production, sales and distribution, materials management, human resources, and so on. Exhibit 3.1 illustrates the core SAP R/3 modules. Each hexagon represents a module and the shading represents the application area.

HIGHLIGHTS OF THE CORE MODULES

Each module is a logical functional grouping of other components (or submodules) that focus on a specific area within an application. An example is the general ledger component versus the accounts payables component within the

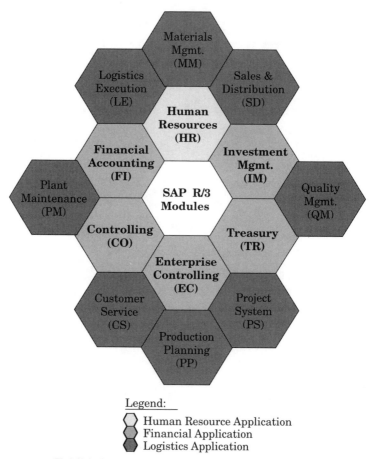

Legend:
Human Resource Application
Financial Application
Logistics Application

Exhibit 3.1   Overview of Core SAP R/3 Modules

Financial Accounting (FI) module. The following is a high-level description of each of the core modules that in no way completely defines all the capabilities of each module. For more detailed information on the functionality supported by these modules, see the SAP R/3 on-line documentation library.

Human Resources

The Human Resources (HR) module is the only module within the Human Resources Application and is designed to support the complete range of human capital areas. HR contains components for personnel management, time management, payroll, training and event management, organizational management, and travel management. Capabilities within personnel management specifically focus on support for administration, recruitment, benefits and compensation management, personnel cost planning, HR funds and position management, and retirement pension plans. The time management component contains work schedules, shift planning, time recording, time evaluations, and incentive wages. The payroll component is divided into a country view to deal with country-specific requirements for payroll processing. The training and event management abilities focus on event preparation, catalog, dates, costs, billing, prebooking, rebookings, cancellations, followups, and appraisals. Information generated from HR usually focuses on benefits, payroll, training, personnel development, planned costs, compensation, time and travel, and organization aspects such as vacant positions, job descriptions, and current organizational structures.

Materials Management

One of the main logistic application modules is Materials Management (MM). The MM module is designed to provide information, tracking, controlling, and management on the materials moved in, within, and out of the organization and the valuation of those materials. The MM module does not focus only on materials; it supports externally procured services as well. MM contains components for consumption-based planning, inventory management, purchasing, invoice verification, external service management, and information systems.

Consumption-based planning deals with stock replenishment utilizing material requirements planning (MRP), determining lot-sizing procedures, and performing forecasting, potentially with formulas. The inventory management component houses the material and service master records, and controls and tracks all the goods movements, receipts, issues, return receipts, stock transfers, reservations, physical inventory, stock determination, and batch handling. In addition, inventory management contains the actual costing material ledger that supports multiple currencies and valuations of a material as well as calculating an actual price from production. The purchasing area of MM provides the ability to determine possible sources to supply materials/services, the actual procurement of these materials/services, tracking the delivery from vendors, and monitoring the payments to those vendors. Within purchasing are the vendor master records, requisitions, requests for quotes, conditions and prices, purchase orders, and vendor confirmations among many other objects.

Invoice verification, as its name suggests, supports verification and material valuations such as Last In First Out (LIFO) and First In First Out (FIFO), revaluations for price changes, changes to the invoices for credits, taxes, cash discounts, checking the invoices, defining account impacts for invoices, canceling invoices, delivery costs, and determining invoice variances. The external services management component is provided to support the complete process of procuring external services from vendors, from bidding on invitations, to awarding the order, to acceptance of services. It is used to define the service specifications, enter the services performed, accept those services, and then verify the service invoice. The information systems within MM consist of vendor valuations, the purchasing information system, and inventory information.

Logistic Execution

The Logistic Execution (LE) module provides functionality to support the goods receipt of inbound deliveries, warehouse management, and shipping and transportation. Once the purchase order has been issued from MM, the process of goods receipts for those deliveries occur. This process consists of notifications for the deliveries, the actual inbound delivery, the stocking of the deliveries received, and posting of the goods receipt. Specific capabilities support transfer orders, goods receipts, monitoring, confirmations for inbound deliveries, batch splitting, determination of receiving points, parcel tracking, and incompletion logs.

Warehouse Management (WM) once was a stand-alone module and is now an integral component of the Logistics Execution module. Warehouse Management links together inbound and outbound logistics and manages inventory at a lower level of detail than the inventory management component of MM. It is utilized when organizations need to manage complex warehousing structures with bin locations; and process all goods movements, such as receipts, transfers, and issues quickly, to optimize the material flows through the warehouse. In addition to the normal inventory management capabilities, WM supports hazardous materials management, stocking and picking strategies, warehouse movements, storage unit management, and mobile data entry.

The outbound logistic execution activity deals with shipping. Shipping supports the picking, packing, posting goods issue, and printing of the shipments based on agreements with customers. Additionally, special requests or shipping conditions defined within the sales orders are considered. The final component of the LE module is for transportation, which focuses on both inbound and outbound transportation activities. These activities cover areas such as shipping types, documents, outputs, freight codes, processing reports, and leg determination (without optimization or geographical capabilities, which are supported by Advanced Planning and Optimization [APO]). Additionally, the transportation area has functionality to monitor shipments, the completions, the costs for those shipments, and billing of those costs.

Production Planning

The Production Planning (PP) module supports different production strategies, such as discrete, make-to-order/variant processing, repetitive manufacturing, process industry, and KANBAN. The PP module contains the basic data required to perform production, such as the bills of materials (BOMs), work centers, routings, line designs for repetitive manufacturing, and recipes for process manufacturing. Production Planning supports the production controlling and planning needs of the organization. Production controlling is essentially any aspect of the complete production process, from inputs to production, the flow through production, and the eventual completion of the production process. These controlling aspects of the PP module focus on order management, scheduling, trigger points, document management, production resources and tools, availability checks, preliminary costing, KANBAN controls, evaluations, goods movement, confirmations, backflushing, rework, statuses, and change management.

Production planning mainly deals with sales and operation planning (SOP), materials requirement planning (MRP), capacity planning, and product cost planning. The SOP capabilities support the integration of sales plans from the profitability analysis planning area used to determine the sales forecast that production must fulfill. Sales and operation planning supports different types of planning and populates demand management to feed important information for the master production schedule (MPS) and materials requirements planning by product. Once the lowest level of planning has been completed, MRP and distribution resource planning (DRP) determines material quantities, available inventory, and procurement/assembly dates required to supply the products for the demand. Simultaneously, capacity planning and product cost planning can occur throughout the planning process.

Project System

In addition to the production strategies listed for production planning, the Project System (PS) module is provided to plan and control the production execution of projects requiring capacity and scheduling capabilities similar to a production plant. The Project System module focuses on planning, tracking, controlling, and reporting on the materials, resources, and progress of large projects. The PS module is used to support production execution for industries focusing on construction, large-scale marketing campaigns, software or consulting services, and research and development. Project System is used to provide project information focusing on revenues and costs, resource needs and utilization, materials purchased and consumed, dates, milestones, and progress. Within the PS module, data elements include the projects, the networks (which are much like a production routing), the work breakdown structures focusing on areas of work or tasks, materials, resources, and accounts. The Project System module is tightly integrated with many other areas, such as purchasing, inventory management and materials planning for the control of materials, and the sales and distribution module for billing. Additionally, PS has capabilities for monitoring available funds, defining detailed planning, and supporting budgeting.

Plant Maintenance

Requirements to support the plant maintenance activities within an organization often are as sophisticated as those needed to perform production planning. The Plant Maintenance (PM) module supports varying requirements from scheduling resources, managing capacity, and tracking orders. Planning and execution within the plant maintenance areas is often at a very detailed level, and documentation is very important. Therefore, the PM module specifically addresses documentation needs. This module consists of three main areas focusing on:

1. Equipment and technical objects
2. Preventive maintenance
3. Maintenance order management

The equipment and technical objects area defines the maintenance objects, allowing for different classifications, and identifies the process for performing maintenance, such as the amount of time needed. It also contains the network (or tasks required to perform the maintenance), the maintenance bills of materials, measuring points and counters, permits, and warranties.

Preventative maintenance focuses specifically on maintenance activities that occur repeatedly in an organization. Plant Maintenance supports the planning of these events to ensure that breakdowns do not occur. The PM planning takes into account not only user-defined requirements but also external requirements, such as legal, environmental, or manufacture recommendations. The maintenance order management has the capability to capture notifications of a malfunction or exception situations, manage the maintenance orders for control and tracking, support capacity planning for technicians, collect completion confirmations, and maintain the maintenance history. The PM module usually relies on information from varying sources for computer-assisted design (CAD) schematics, data collection devices, measurement capturing, external benchmark or measurement standards, and dispatch/mobile devices. Therefore, SAP R/3 provides open access for integration with these types of external devices and systems. Additionally, like all the other modules, PM contains an information system to support reporting for the plant maintenance area. The information system focuses on information for location and planning, object class and manufacturer, damage analysis, object statistics, breakdown analysis, cost evaluations, sales notification analysis, and reliability information for failures and overhauls.

Quality Management

The Quality Management (QM) module supports the activities aimed at establishing quality standards, monitoring quality metrics, and documenting deviations. Therefore, QM focuses on planning, inspecting, sampling, testing, notifying, and documenting. The main basic data for QM consists of catalogs, sampling procedures, and inspection methods. Two forms of inspection planning can be utilized. One relies on material specifications to determine what materials should be inspected, what the inspection criteria are, and if test equipment is required. The other defines an inspection plan for one or more materials that lists what dimensions are to be inspected, what the specifications should be, and the inspection operations. To perform the inspection, an inspection lot is created, the results and defects are recorded, and the lot is completed. The inspection may utilize the sample management capabilities of QM.

Quality controlling is supported via statistical process control (SPC) capabilities, utilizing control charts to detect quality deviations. Based on the inspection results, quality certificates are awarded. These certificates can be user defined or based on general standards. When defects are determined, quality notification abilities support the labeling of the cause, such as poor quality of vendor material or an internal production issue. To ensure the results of an inspection that utilizes test equipment, QM facilitates test equipment management for testing and calibrating the test equipment. Additionally, QM can be used to capture actual costs of ensuring quality, such as appraisal and nonconformity costs.

Customer Service

The Customer Service module (CS) contains the previously stand-alone functionality of the Service Management (SM) module, with additional capabilities to service and support customers. The SM component of CS focuses on servicing items that have already been sold, that is, an installed base of products. For the actual execution of the servicing, CS-SM calls on the PM functionality for permits, measuring points, orders, confirmations, and notifications. CS-SM then provides the additional needs, such as service agreements, warranties, sales pricing and conditions, time sheet tracking, and billing functionality. In addition to the SM component, the CS module has capabilities designed to provide customer service, such as a customer interaction center, call management capabilities, and a solutions database. The customer interaction center (CIC) supports a call center that utilizes computer telephony integration (CTI). The agents perform their activities through the front office, a customizable desktop view. Multiple views can exist and can be personalized by agent or agent group. The CIC contains standard soft phone controls (telephony controls) and work modes such as login, ready to receive, answer, transfer, deflect, and drop calls. The CIC focuses on supporting extensive call logging, the ability to view call statuses, integration with interactive voice response (IVR), and customer information access. Unlike the CIC, the call management functionality focuses on managing service requests. Call management supports the call logging, call processing, call monitoring, call closure, and service order billing activities involved with responding to a service request. The final component, the solutions database, is a knowledge warehouse provided to preserve any type of expertise. Unlike the standard reporting tools with SAP R/3, the solutions database has been optimized for speed and search capabilities.

Sales and Distribution

The Sales and Distribution (SD) module is a very large module encompassing all areas of the sales and distribution processes. It is also a form of production supporting the make-to-sales orders (engineer-to-order) production strategy. The basic data structures of SD contain the definitions of the sales and distribution structures, such as customers, customer hierarchies, sales views for information on material masters, sales organizations, sales offices, sales groups, sales reps, divisions, distribution centers, delivering plant, and shipping point. Some of the main functionality SD supports deals with pricing, availability checking, credit and risk management, output determination, sales, foreign trade/customs, billing, payment card processing, and sales support. The pricing component is a very important area of the sales process. The SD module supports simple to very complex pricing schemes that usually rely on conditions for pricing and determining a myriad of discounts. Additionally, manual pricing or special functions can be used for determining pricing. When generating a sales order, pricing and availability are both determined. Availability checking concerns two areas: for the sales order and for delivery. Availability checking for the sales order determines if the appropriate items are available by the customer's requested date. This availability check can be performed against available to promise (ATP), a production allocation (amount available for a determined period), or against planning for production or procurement. Replenishment lead times can be included or excluded for the availability check. Availability for delivery determines if the items can be delivered within the required time frame. It is important to make sure the items are available; however, it is even more important to make sure the customer can pay for them. To ensure this, credit and risk management is integrated with the financial module's credit control functionality to manage the available credit of a customer. For every sale and billing, several different documents will be generated. Each organization and industry has different needs for how these documents should be formatted. To aid with this, output determination manages the messages and documents generated during the sales, shipping, and billing processes.

The SD sales process follows from the inquiry, to quote, to contract, to sales order. Customers calling with questions about a product, its costs, and its availability generate an inquiry. As requirements and dates get more formalized, the inquiry is converted to a quote. The quote is a commitment to the sale and can be generated from the inquiry or initiated from scratch. This quote can then be turned into a contract with a billing plan or directly utilized to create a sales order, formalizing commitments for resources and materials. The sales order can also be generated without an inquiry, quote, or contract. The sales order will have scheduled lines for when items will be completed and available to ship. In the unlikely event there is a return, SD supports returns of goods, potential subsequent deliveries free of charge, as well as back-order processing. If the sales order is for an international sale, the foreign trade/customs aspect of the SD module is utilized. The foreign trade/customs capabilities support declarations to the customs authorities, defining how invoices, packaging lists, or other documents should be printed or communicated, determining if a product qualifies as an originating product (potentially reducing custom duties), and the legal requirements for each country. Once any sale is finalized, or for periodic billing of make-to-sales orders, the billing component focuses on revenue recognition, resource-related billing for services and expenses incurred, invoicing, debit or credit memos, down payments, rebate agreements, installment plans, and intercompany sales processing. The billing invoice is used for the customer to make payment against. One form of payment is via the payment card process that is completely integrated in the sales, delivery, and billing process. Additionally, a sale support component of SD provides a means for tracking sales information and generating new business. It supports promotional campaigns, such as direct or Internet mailing, tracking direct calls and telemarketing activities, and comparing potential sales with actual sales. The completion of the physical sales process is the delivery of the product. The main distribution capabilities of the SD module are shipping and transportation, both of which are addressed in the Logistic Execution module section.

Financial Accounting

The Financial Accounting (FI) module is the core module within the financials application. Almost all functionality that resides in the other financial application modules relies on the implementation of at least parts of the FI module. Financial Accounting is designed to provide financial information from an external view. The main FI components offer functionality for the general ledger, accounts receivables and accounts payables, asset management, a special ledger used to meet user specific requirements, funds management, and legal consolidations. The general ledger (G/L) houses the chart of accounts as well as the account balances and line items. The G/L tracks all transactional postings, such as inventory updates, sales revenues, bank accounts, and expenses. Accounts Receivable (AR) and Accounts Payable (AP) are subledgers of the G/L that support the processes involved with the collection of revenues and payments of expenses. Combined AR and AP facilitate maintaining customer or vendor records, account balances and line items, payments, clearing, advice notices, dunning, interest calculations, check releases, and over/underpayment management. The AR/AP information systems support reporting for due date breakdown, payment history, days sales outstanding, overdue items, and currency risk. Asset management is another subledger to the G/L that focuses on the management of the fixed assets in an organization. Asset management maintains the master records for the assets, special valuations, country-specific requirements, and four types of depreciation calculations, one of which is for cost depreciation. The special ledger functionality supports the ability to create other ledgers or subledgers for specific user requirements. Special ledgers can pull information from other modules and can support simplistic allocations. In addition to the ledgers and subledgers, FI contains functionality supporting funds management and legal consolidations. Funds management provides the capabilities to define planned revenues and expenses for the management areas, monitor these transactions as compared to available funds, and prevent exceeding the budget. Once all transactions have been completed, consolidations can be performed. Legal consolidations functionality supports providing consolidated financial information for companies and business areas. Business areas are utilized primarily for external reporting of business segments across companies.

Treasury

The Treasury (TR) module supports all the business transactions and processes of the treasury department within an organization. The TR module requires that the FI module already be in place. The major treasury processes are cash management and cash budgeting, treasury management, market risk management, and loan management. The purpose of cash management is to manage the inflows/outflows of cash while maintaining enough liquidity to meet payment needs. Within cash management there is functionality to monitor and manage the inflows of cash received in various manners, such as electronic bank statements, manual bank statements, electronic deposits, manual deposits, lockbox, payments, bills of exchange, and payment advices. Other cash management capabilities support calculating interest, comparing value dates, analyzing cashed checks, determining current cash position, liquidity forecasting, and financial planning dealing with excessive cash balances. Cash budgeting focuses on a longer time frame than cash management and aims to monitor revenues and expenditure flows that might lead to over/undershooting the budget. Additionally, cash budgeting can be tightly linked with funds management.

Treasury management focuses on the financial transactions generated from investments purchased. These investments and transactions focus on money market, securities, derivatives, and foreign exchanges. The treasury management component also offers payment program capabilities. Once these investments have been purchased, the market risk management component aims to support valuating the financial instruments, performing risk calculations for those instruments, and determining actual market value of portfolios. When the treasury department is not busy managing investments, it is focusing on maintaining loans. Loans management supports the management of loans taken or given by the organization, such as mortgages, borrower's notes (mainly used for Germany and are similar to bonds), and policy and general loans. There are information systems for each of these main areas within the TR module, providing a myriad of information on loan assets, liabilities and deadlines, position or matrix evaluations, currency exposure calculations, and risk settings.

Investment Management

The Investment Management (IM) module focuses on the planning, budgeting, controlling, and reporting of large capital investment endeavors. The Investment Management module integrates with the order functionality of the Project System, Controlling, and Plant Maintenance modules to represent the measures (cost object) for the investment. Investment Management facilitates the defining and planning of the investment programs, requesting appropriations for the programs, capturing and measuring the costs, and reporting for the programs. The investment programs are defined, planned, and/or budgeted at a higher level than projects or orders. Therefore, investment programs usually represent a hierarchy group of investment measures (projects/orders). An appropriation request is used to request the planned capital required for the investment measure, usually because of the large capital amount involved. The approval process is user defined. Once approved, the investment measure is updated with a planned cost. Planning is accomplished in a bottom-up method. The budget usually consists of the bottom-up plan with corrections made and then distributed top down through the hierarchy back to the investment measures. These investment measures, which are either a project or an internal order (addressed in the next section), are used to capture actual costs, manage commitments, calculate overhead, and settle the costs to an asset or to an asset under construction (AUC) if needed. If settling to an AUC, different capitalization rules can be used, and capitalized versus not capitalized costs are automatically accounted for. This information is used to generate an origin list for the asset showing all internal and external resources and activities used to create the asset. Additionally, depreciation can be calculated and is integrated with the planned depreciation forecast functionality, ensuring that planned balance sheets are the most accurate reflection of the planned environment.

Controlling

The Controlling (CO) module is the symbiotic counter to the FI module and is designed to provide financial information from an internal managerial accounting view. To support this view of accounting, the CO module offers functionality for cost center accounting, activity-based costing, order and project accounting, product costing, and profitability analysis. Cost center accounting focuses on showing the expenses of the organization from a departmental view for the purpose of supporting responsibility accounting. Cost center accounting also supports the planning, budgeting, controlling, and allocation of departmental expenses. Additionally, many organizations desire to show the expenses of the organization within a process view. This process-oriented view is supported by the activity-based costing component.

Within organizations, costs might be incurred to support events and overhead-related projects. The order and project accounting capabilities of CO support planning, monitoring, capturing, and allocating the expenses related to these events. For production-related organizations, many of the cost centers capture expenses that later will be attributed to products to determine product costs. The product costing component of the CO module focuses on the creation of the standard product cost estimates, charging of overhead to production, capturing actual costs of production, calculating production variances, and settling production expenses to the appropriate profitability market segment. All of the expense objects—cost center, process, event or project, and products—allocate or settle costs to the profitability analysis component, which supports the generation of market profit and loss (P/L) statements at a gross and contribution margin level. The next section provides more details on the CO module components, especially for ABC.

Enterprise Controlling

The Enterprise Controlling (EC) module houses the components that have both an external financial view, such as FI, and an internal management view, such as CO. These components consist of consolidations, profit center accounting, and the executive information systems and business planning. This consolidation functionality encompasses the legal consolidation functions within FI and further supports consolidations for internal management via different consolidation types. The consolidation component facilitates the aggregation of business units, translation of currencies, and eliminations for interunit activity/transactions.

The Profit Center Accounting (PCA) component aims to support a management-oriented view of profits and losses. This management-oriented view is usually higher than a cost center or departmental view and needs to report balance sheet information as well as revenues and expenses, such as the divisional or regional view. Therefore, PCA supports within-company profit unit financial reporting. It facilitates both the period-accounting and cost-of-sales approaches for reporting. Capable of handling multiple valuation methods for transfer pricing to support external reporting versus internal management reporting, PCA also supports plans and has some allocation capabilities for the movement of expenses or revenues between profit centers.

The Executive Information System (EIS) supports flexible business reporting. It is capable of pulling from the information systems of the other modules, such as for human resources, financials, and logistics. The business planning component of the EC module focuses on supporting enterprise-wide planning at a higher level than operational planning.

HIGHLIGHTS OF THE CONTROLLING MODULE

The previous section provided a cursory overview of each of the core SAP R/3 modules. This section addresses the CO module and each of its components in greater detail. In order to better understand what the CO module is, one must understand what it is not.

- *CO is* not *just costs.* Many people mistakenly think that CO stands for cost management. While the controlling module does support cost management, it certainly is not limited to cost management. Much of the profitability reporting resides in the CO module.
- *CO is* not *focused on transaction or business process automation.* The other modules of the R/3 system primarily focus on the automation and execution of business processes and transactional postings for data capturing and tracking. The CO module is focused more on aggregate information with the added benefit of having drill-down capability to the actual transactional postings, providing a very robust audit trail.
- *CO is* not *configuration based.* Many CO implementations mistakenly design, manage, test, and implement the CO module like the other SAP R/3 modules, focusing on configuration as an indication of complexity. To estimate resource and time requirements, most projects use the number of configuration scripts. However, this heuristic in the CO module leads to understaffed CO engagements. The CO module is business decision oriented, not transaction focused. Its implementation parameters are more appropriately driven by the complexity of information and analysis rather than being configuration driven. Defining the conceptual design, the complete organizational costing model, drives the CO implementation. Time and expenses for a CO module implementation are driven by the master data, drivers, allocation methodologies and complexities, number of profit dimensions, cost objects, and events. It is not uncommon for the CO module implementation to require more analysis/design and less testing/construction time than other modules.

Basically, CO is very much *not* like the rest of the R/3 system in the nature of its focus or how it should be implemented. With that established, the question still remains; what exactly is CO?

- *CO is a conceptual design.* This initial conceptual design forms the backbone of the CO model. Therefore, it is very important that the CO module be designed with flexibility in mind so it can continue to support the changing organization. Many organizations "slam" the CO module in when they first implement SAP, not realizing the amount of work it takes to eventually redesign CO for analysis purposes rather than just expense capturing.

- *"CO is comparative analysis."*[1] Comparative analysis is taking many different objects and putting those objects into a common denominator for comparison purposes. The most obvious example is converting objects into the same currency. The CO module is used to make comparative analysis of many different objects such as materials, market segments, events, cost centers, and process views.

- *CO is contribution and Gross Margins.* The CO module contains the reporting tools used to provide contribution and gross margin reporting for multidimensional market segments fully burdened with downstream supply chain costs to provide cost-to-serve views.

- *CO is support for the controller.* The CO module was designed to support the decision-making needs of the controller. These include such decisions as which resources should be allocated to what organizations, what areas are candidates for outsourcing, which resources should support such process, what impacts will result from a strategic decision to spin-off/acquire a division, and so forth.

- *CO is comprehensive capacity management.* The CO module supports complete capacity management through the types of drivers it provides and the tight integration with the other SAP R/3 modules, especially the Production Planning modules. The ability to link processes with their resources completes the capacity management view. The support for capacity management is emphasized throughout this book.

- *CO is collaborative planning.* When building a quantity-based model, CO is collaborative in its very nature. Managers must work together to define the input/output relationships of resources to build the quantity structure. The quantity structure is about planning the supply and demand of resources throughout the organization.

- *CO is cost management.* The CO module supports an array of advanced cost management philosophies for the enterprise. Specifically addressed in Chapter 1 are the Resource Consumption Accounting philosophy, the basis of the Controlling module, and Activity-Based Costing, the topic of this book.

- *CO is controlling and performance monitoring.* Once the structures have been defined and planned, then controlling and performance monitoring can take place on the actuals and the variances calculated. These variances do not just focus on plan/actual, which only illuminates poor planning. Target/actual variances are the focus, highlighting what costs should have been given the actual volume.

- *CO is corrective action.* Once actuals are captured and charged, assigned, or allocated, corrective action can take place. Given that SAP R/3 captures transactions in real time, if the model has been designed with timing in mind, then corrective action can be applied almost in real time.

In summary, the CO module is a conceptual design built to provide comparative analysis, including contribution and gross margins, for the controller, based on comprehensive capacity management and collaborative planning, used to support cost management, controlling, and performance monitoring, in order to take corrective action to support a changing organization. That is a lot of functionality packed into one sentence.

In order for the Controlling module to provide this functionality, it is tightly integrated with the other core models. Exhibit 3.2 illustrates this integration.

A single picture cannot clearly depict all of the integration points between the CO module and the other modules. This is an extremely simplified example. The point, however, should be very clear, since the CO module is the sender and/or receiver of most expenses, revenues, and allocations; it has hundreds of

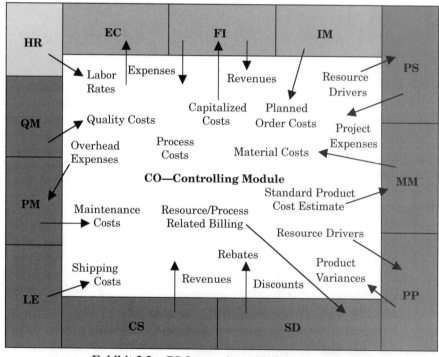

Exhibit 3.2   CO Integration with Other Modules

integration points with the other modules. In order to accommodate all of these integration points, the CO module components are divided into different types of analytical areas. These areas cover organization, event, process/activity, product, and market-related analysis. Each of the components of the CO module corresponds to an analysis area. Exhibit 3.3 illustrates the components that form the Controlling module.

As seen in the exhibit, the information from Exhibit 3.2 has been gathered into areas of analytical focus that are represented by the five components of the CO module[2]:

1. CCA: Cost Center Accounting
2. OPA: Orders and Project Accounting
3. ABC: Activity-Based Costing
4. PC: Product Costing
5. PA: Profitability Analysis

Each component is covered in detail in the following chapters, with stress on the integration with the Activity-Based Costing component. This section merely provides a preparatory overview.

HR	Financials			PS
	CCA—Cost Center Accounting			
	Labor Rates	Overhead Expenses	Resource Drivers	
QM	**OPA—Order & Project Accounting**	**ABC—Activity-Based Costing**	**PC—Product Costing**	
	Capitalized Costs	Process Costs	Material Costs	MM
	Revenues		Standard Product	
PM	Plan/Actual		Cost Estimate	
	Order Costs		Production	
	Resource/Process-Related Billing		Variances	
			Resource Drivers	
	PA—Profitability Analysis			
LE	Revenues	Discounts	Rebates	PP
	CS	SD		

Exhibit 3.3 Controlling Module Components

Cost Center Accounting

The core of the Controlling module is Cost Center Accounting (CCA), which is used to support an organizational view of expenses. The main focus is supporting responsibility accounting, with the cost center representing an area of accountability. The CCA functionality brings attention to the following questions, among others:

- What resources are being consumed where?
- What are the drivers of those resources?
- Where should these resources be deployed?
- What variances are generated by which resources?

To support this analysis, expenses are grouped within cost centers; output quantities are defined; planning is performed; actuals are captured; costs are charged, assigned, or allocated; target costs are calculated; and reports are generated. A cost center is an organizational unit generally having a physical location, existing for long periods of time (more than one year), and represents an area of responsibility where costs are incurred, such as the *Benefits, Training, Payroll* departments. Cost centers are grouped together and collected into a hierarchical tree, the standard cost center hierarchy, until the entire organization is represented. The standard cost center hierarchy contains cost centers for one or multiple companies representing the entire organization, regardless of legal boundaries. Each level above the cost center on the standard hierarchy represents a cost center group, also referred to as a node. Alternative views of the structure can be created by groups of cost centers outside of the "standard" view. This additional view allows tremendous flexibility to aid with allocation and reporting requirements, such as all HR-related cost centers across multiple companies in order to determine overall human resource expenses.

The cost center is usually the primary cost collector, where expenses are incurred and are traceable through the financial transactions. Expenses are representing by cost elements throughout the Controller Module. The cost elements are categorized as either primary or secondary. Primary costs are posted through the FI module and normally reflect cash flow, such as expenses for 430000 *Salaries,* 430162 *Water,* 400000 *Raw Materials,* and so on. These costs are contrasted with secondary cost elements, which are costs charged to a cost center through a charge-out or transfer pricing methodology. The consuming cost center has secondary control over these costs. Secondary cost elements do not reside on the chart of accounts since they are not used for external reporting and do not get direct postings from financial processes. Sample secondary cost elements are 900000 *Corporate Overhead* or 901000 *Facilities Allocation.* Since the CO module is also a debit/credit set of books much like the external G/L, drivers also utilize secondary cost elements when posting, such as 920000 *Labor Hours*. Similar to the cost center structure defined previously, these primary and secondary elements can be grouped for more specific analysis and to support allocation methodologies.

Once the primary expenses are posted to the cost centers, they are charged, assigned, or allocated to other cost centers or cost objects. Other cost objects within the CO module are processes, overhead orders, and market segments representing customers, products, and divisions. Additionally, there are cost objects for the other modules, such as production orders in PP, sales orders in SD, plant maintenance orders in PM, and projects in PS. In order to make some of these expense movements, a resource driver, called an activity type (actype), or a statistic, called a statistical key figure (SKF), are utilized. The actype and SKF are used as efficiency measures and as the basis for cost flows. The actype is used to represent a driver for a pool of costs within a cost center. Actypes usually represent capacity-related drivers such as square footage, machine hours, labor hours, or central processing unit (CPU) minutes. These drivers have capacity constraints and also have a direct causal relationship to the increase or decrease of expenses incurred in the cost center. This relationship between the expenses and the actype driver may establish a rate that supports both a fixed and a proportional component for the unit rate.

The following example illustrates the use of an activity type to assign cost. Assume *Prod Line 1* cost center provides machine hours for production. The actype *MACHR* is defined to represent this driver and the capacity is set for the year, such as 2400 hours. Cost center expenses are related to this driver for both plan and actual for fixed depreciation, fixed preventative maintenance hours from another cost center, variable electricity, and so forth. These expenses are divided by the 2400 hours, and a rate is calculated—for example, $10/MACHR—of which $7 is fixed and $3 is proportional. The statistical key figure is a statistic that does not have an associated rate and does not necessarily relate to the costs incurred within the cost center. Sample SKFs are for number of employees, full-time equivalents (FTEs), and number of purchase orders.

To support cost flows, CCA provides many methods for cost charging, assignment, and allocations. The actype can be directly charged to any cost object; for example, *Production Line 1* can charge 100 *MACHR* to a production order. Assignments can be made through determination of direct relationships, such as for every *MACHR* used for production, 1 *KWH* (kilowatt-hour) is required. As production consumes *MACHR*s, *KWH*s will be assigned accordingly. Actypes and SKFs can both be used for allocations, such as using the number of employees to allocate the payroll costs to the cost centers. Or the actype quantity for maintenance labor hours posted to each cost center can be used to allocate the *Maintenance Planning* cost center's expenses. Many other allocation/assignment methods exist, from simplistic percentage methods to more advanced utilization of "if-then" logic. Exhibit 3.4 illustrates the structures of the CCA module and is used to continue building a sample CO conceptual design.

Order and Project Accounting

Where CCA focuses on the area of responsibility, Order and Project Accounting (OPA) analyzes the events or overhead projects that occur in an organization. OPA is used to define, plan, budget, control, capture actuals, settle, and report on

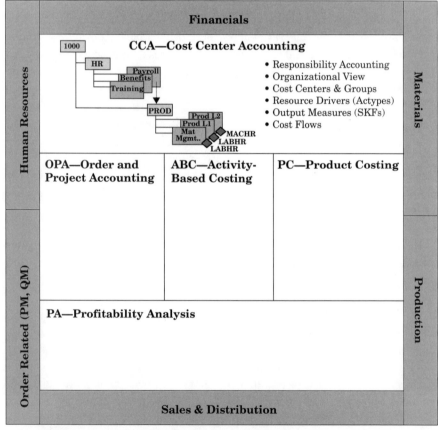

Exhibit 3.4   CCA Component of the CO Module Conceptual Design

overhead orders, called internal orders. An internal order is used to represent an event, such as a Christmas party, or a small project, such as an information technology (IT) initiative, that does not require full production scheduling, capacity management, and controlling functionality provided by the production or project modules. The internal order is used within organizations to represent a myriad of events/projects/jobs. It usually has a shorter life span than a cost center, does not consume permanent physical space, and may not have a single responsible party. The analysis supported by internal orders focuses on:

- What resources are needed to plan or budget this event/project?
- What commitments are outstanding?
- What costs have been incurred for the different stages of the internal order?
- What were the profits generated by this event?

To support this and other analyses, expenses and revenues are grouped within internal orders. Individual internal orders can be grouped together into internal order groups that are utilized as allocation receivers, for group allocations, and as reporting filters. Like the cost center, the internal order is a cost collector and can be posted to directly from other modules for financial postings or purchasing needs. The internal order can also post back to other modules to settle costs to sales orders for resource-related billing or to asset management for capitalizing an asset under construction. Internal orders provide a more detailed view of the events that are taking place within a cost center. For example, the *Maintenance* cost center might use internal order to represent each maintenance request, if the more advanced Plant Maintenance module functionality is not required. The *IT* cost center can use an internal order to represent each *IT* project, such as repair and maintenance of PC or software development requests. The costs incurred can be posted to the cost center and then moved to the internal order, or posted directly to the internal order by a G/L posting, or posted to both cost objects, in which case one receives an informational posting only. The cost center manager can see the overall costs for the area while the internal order provides the more detailed view for analysis.

Internal orders are also used for analysis not related to within cost center events. For example, the internal order can be used to represent the life cycle of a product or calculate accruals. Additionally, the internal order can be used for events or projects that generate revenues. Revenue recognition of an internal order differs from the cost center object, which generally does not contain revenues. The internal order has controlling capabilities more closely related to a production order than the cost center. It has status controls that determine when certain business transactions can take place, such as performing planning, issuing goods to the internal order, calculating revenue postings, or settling costs or revenues. In general, the internal order has more functionality than the cost center, except for its cost assignment capabilities. Internal orders allocate the costs to any other cost object based on percentages, fixed dollar amounts, or equivalency numbers only. For example, the training cost center creates and gives a training course to the production workers on how to use internal orders. An internal order, *T200,* is used to capture the costs for the creation and execution of the course. The internal order allocates (settles) to the production-related cost centers based on the number of attendees entered as equivalency numbers. Exhibit 3.5 illustrates this example for the OPA module added to the CO conceptual design.

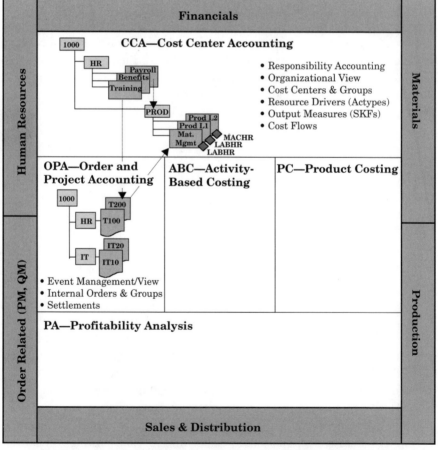

Exhibit 3.5 OPA Component of the CO Module Conceptual Design

Activity-Based Costing

Cost center accounting provides the organizational view of the expenses, high-lighting the resource perspective of cost. Further, cost center accounting gives the user the tools to critically assess the optimization of resources. However, it does not necessarily provide information on what activities those resources are performing for identifying opportunities for reengineering through process analysis. This process view is supported by the Activity-Based Costing (ABC) component of the CO module. There are two forms of ABC within SAP. The first is called Parallel and was the original ABC functionality within SAP. Parallel ABC functions like a stand-alone ABC system and supports modeling analysis rather than an integrated solution. Parallel ABC shares key data with the cost centers, receiving all expenses posted. Then within Parallel ABC, the ABC model is defined and executed. However, the directional flow of the data supports only the analysis of the results, not the application of those results throughout the rest of the CO module. Therefore, Parallel ABC is more of an "integrated snapshot" rather than a truly integrated solution. The second form of SAP ABC is operational ABC, which is completely integrated throughout the entire SAP R/3 application. Chapter 4 covers the evolution of ABC from parallel to operational ABC. Operational ABC is the topic of the rest of this chapter and the book. The ABC component aims to answer questions like:

- What are my process costs?
- What resources are required to provide a process?
- What cost objects such as products, customers, orders, and projects consume the processes?
- Why does a process for one organizational unit cost a different amount when performed by another unit?

To support this analysis, the process cost object is utilized. The term "process" within SAP ABC represents both the lowest-level activity and the aggregate activity level, defined as the process in traditional ABC. Therefore, within SAP ABC, the term "process" encompasses the activities of *Receipt Raw Materials, Inspect Raw Materials, Issue Raw Materials,* as well as the process of *Manage Materials.*

ABC is structured much like CCA. The process cost collector can be organized into a hierarchy (the standard process hierarchy) or into groups. Process groups can also be utilized to collect processes together to represent an aggregate level instead of creating an actual process, such as *Manage Materials.* The process cost is measured and assigned via a process driver or a statistic. Further analytical tools are available via additional fields on the process master record. These nonmandatory, informational fields support many different views of the process data. Sample fields are organizational units the process is performed for, such as company code, business area, sales division, or plant. There are attribute fields, such as external value added, internal value added, categories for whether the process is batch oriented or product related, and so on. Additionally, user-defined fields can be added to provide information for other analysis.

If the process will be utilized within a quantity-based approach rather than a value-based approach, other informational fields are entered. When the quantity-based approach is constructed, the process itself is the defined driver. This process/driver has the rate to be used for cost valuation. In this instance, the process will also have a secondary cost element that will be assigned for use with posting. Additionally, a process utilized within a quantity-based approach needs a unit of measure since it is the driver as well. For example, the process of *Perform Inspection* has the process driver number of inspections. The *Perform Inspection* process will be assigned the unit of measure "EA" for each inspection occurrence. If the process is utilized in the value-based approach, an SKF will be created representing the number of inspections, and an allocation will be made. Rates still can be calculated for the value-based approach; however, they are merely for informational purposes and are not used for cost valuation.

Given that the CO module is so tightly integrated with other SAP R/3 modules, the ABC model can impact or be impacted by any other R/3 module. SAP R/3 allows the posting of expenses from FI directly to a process, skipping the entire resource view for analysis. For product or service costing, the process can be incorporated into the structures used to update the material masters with the standard cost estimate. Actual production for any of the production-related modules can be updated with process costs in real time (with a standard rate) at any point within the production cycle, just like materials and other resources required for supporting production. Very simply put, the process can charge, assign, or allocate to any of the costs objects.

To illustrate this diverse and flexible tool, the process *Hire New Employee* can be allocated to the *Production* cost center based on the number of new hires brought in during that period. This cost flow from process to cost center is generally not supported by traditional ABC systems and is discussed in more detail in Chapter 5, in the "Paradigm Shift" section. Further, the process *Review* can be allocated to the training internal order *T100,* a training course on how to inspect the finished good products. The *T100* internal order can settle its costs to the process *Inspect,* which will later be consumed by another process, *Handle Returns,* and by production. This process assignment capability is clearly the most powerful functionality presented in ABC to date, allowing not only flexible but realistic assignment of cost. Exhibit 3.6 illustrates the addition of the ABC module to the CO diagram. Although the illustration

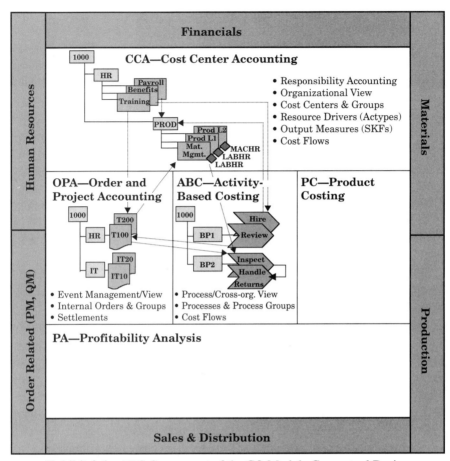

Exhibit 3.6   ABC Component of the CO Module Conceptual Design

may appear to be too complex for some organizations, the design possibilities are flexible enough to be simple as well.

Product Costing

The Product Costing (PC) component focuses on providing information for the analysis of planned and actual product and production costs. Its sole purpose is to support analysis focusing on:

- What service/products incurred costs?
- Given the volume produced, what should the costs have been?

- What product variances exist in production and why?
- How much costs are in work in progress?

The analysis for these questions relies on the planned costs for the products and service as well as the actual costs of production. The PC module is tightly integrated with the Materials Management module for updating the standard cost estimate and to the production modules for the calculation of actual production costs and variances. The standard cost estimate is calculated within PC for materials or services and updated to the costing view of the material masters. This standard cost estimate on the material master can be used for inventory valuations. The production cost collectors capture the plan and actual costs for production. Product costing uses these transactions to calculate work in process and to determine the variances and their causes. Once production is completed, PC is used to settle the production costs to the appropriate market segments representing that material or service.

Product costing often is a receiver of costs from the other CO components. Cost center accounting resource drivers (actypes) are assigned to the production method used to produce the product/service. Activity types such as labor hour, setup hour, machine hour, and kilowatt-hour are consumed by the production receivers. Even internal orders can settle to production receivers if necessary. Processes are integrated with both the standard cost estimates (planning) and to the production receivers for actual production costing. For example, every finished good *Material 1000* produced must have the process *Inspection* performed. During calculation of the standard cost estimate, one *Inspection* process will be included in the product cost. If the production order, *Order 1,* has an output of 100 finished goods, then a quantity of 100 *Inspection* processes will be posted to the production order during the actual assignment of costs. The production cost collectors have limited allocation capabilities and normally assume that 100% of the actual costs for the period are assigned to the appropriate market segment. Exhibit 3.7 illustrates the PC module integrated into the CO conceptual design.

Profitability Analysis

The Profitability Analysis (PA) component is the final cost object within the CO module and the main profitability reporting tool in R/3. Profitability analysis can be designed to utilize one or both of two basic analytical modes, account based or costing based. When account-based PA is used, the financial accounts are utilized for reporting and follow period accounting principles. The costing-based view provides a more market-focused view supporting user-defined value fields

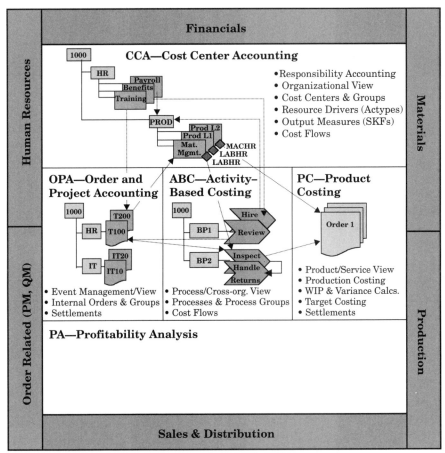

Exhibit 3.7   PC Component of the CO Module Conceptual Design

(rows on the report), which may consist of one or multiple accounts. Costing based utilizes the cost-of-sales approach. This book focuses attention on the costing-based view due to its flexibility and more common application. In either case, all overhead expenses are intended to finally reside in PA at the end of every period in order to provide a profit-and-loss report by market segment. Profitability analysis usually is structured to support analysis focusing on:

- Which customer, product, region is the most profitable?
- What processes are used to support specific segments?
- What is the marginal cost of product X for aggressive pricing?

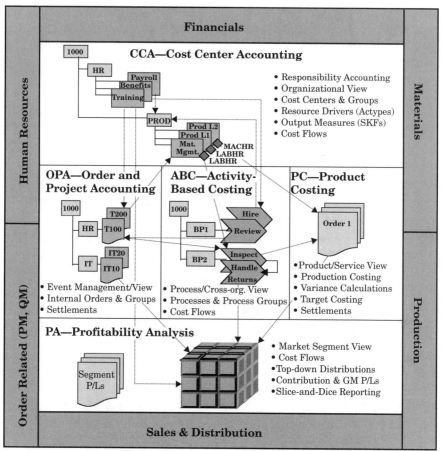

Exhibit 3.8   PA Component of the CO Module Conceptual Design

This and other analysis is performed on the market segments. These market segments are user defined and often include reporting dimensions (characteristics) for products/services, attributes of the products/services, customers, distribution channels, sales regions, and lines of business. Along with the defined reporting dimensions, rows for reporting need to be defined. These rows consist of value fields, which are the dollar and quantity values used for reporting and as the basis for allocations. Sample value fields are Revenues, Discounts, Corporate Expenses, Fixed Production Labor, Sales Quantity, Production Quantity, Number of Returns, and Number of Shipments. Profitability analyses can receive charges, assignments, and allocations from the other CO components as well as from other modules. Examples of external module postings are FI posting a one-time customer-related expense directly to the characteristic for that customer, or the SD module posting expenses and revenues related to sales activities, such as the revenues, discounts, and rebates. Cost centers can assign/allocate cost directly to any PA market segment, charging directly for labor of a cost center or allocating residual training expenses to all divisions based on revenues. For example, internal order *IT10*, utilized for the 4.6C SAP upgrade project, can settle its cost each period by percentage to each company. The process can be charged or allocated to a PA segment based on where the driver is collected. If the driver is the process, then the process charges directly to the segment. If the driver is collected in a value field, such as Number of Returns, then the *Handle Returns* process costs will be allocated to the segments. Product costing uses the production order transactions to calculate the variances. These variances are then settled to PA if a standard costing system is used. If an actual costing system is designed, the entire cost of production is settled to PA. Exhibit 3.8 illustrates the structure of the PA module integrated into the CO conceptual design.

SUMMARY

The SAP R/3 system is a tightly integrated enterprise resource planning (ERP) and controlling application. It focuses on the capturing, monitoring, controlling, and reporting of daily business transactions and the documents produced. SAP R/3 has expansive cross-functional capabilities that this chapter has mentioned only very briefly. The costing capabilities of the CO module cannot be addressed in one chapter, barely even one book. This chapter provides only a cursory, beginner's knowledge of the Controlling module's components and abilities. Exhibit 3.9 provides a summary table of the information contained within this chapter.

Highlights of the Core Modules	
Human Resources (HR)	The HR module focuses on personnel management, time and expense management, payroll, training and events, and organizational management.
Materials Management (MM)	Materials Management houses the master records for products and services. MM supports consumption-based planning, inventory management, purchasing, invoice verification, and externally procured services.
Logistic Execution (LE)	The main tasks associated with the LE module pertain to goods receipts of inbound deliveries, warehouse management, shipping, and transportation.
Production Planning (PP)	Production Planning supports differing production strategies from make-to-stock, to make-to-order, to repetitive, KANBAN, etc. PP contains all the bills of materials, routings, and recipes needed for production. All aspects of production execution and controlling are defined within the PP module. PP planning mainly focuses on SOP, MRP, capacity, and production cost planning.
Project System (PS)	Project System is another form of production geared toward large-scale project-focused industries such as construction, consulting, or aerospace and defense. PS has extensive resource management and scheduling capabilities and is completely integrated with the procurement and inventory management components of MM.
Plant Maintenance (PM)	Plant Maintenance focuses on scheduling resources, managing capacity, and controlling maintenance orders. PM functionality supports equipment and technical objects, preventative maintenance, and maintenance order management.
Quality Management (QM)	QM supports the activities for planning, inspecting, sampling, testing, notifying, and documenting. SPC utilizing control charts depicts deviations to be researched. Additional capabilities support sample management, test equipment management, and capturing costs of quality.
Customer Service (CS)	CS contains two focuses, service management and customer service. Service management deals with servicing the installed client base. Customer service revolves around the customer interaction center.
Sales & Distribution (SD)	SD encompasses many areas of functionality, such as engineer-to-order, master data structures for the sales organization and distribution methods, pricing, availability checks, credit issues, output requirements, customs, billing, and sales support.

Exhibit 3.9   Summary Definitions of Modules and CO Components

Financial Accounting (FI)	The FI module is the core module of the financials application. It contains components for general ledger, accounts receivables, accounts payables, special ledger, asset management, funds management, and legal consolidations.
Treasury (TR)	Once the FI module is in place, treasury capabilities can be used to support cash management and budgeting, treasury management, market risk management, and loan management.
Investment Management (IM)	Investment Management provides a hierarchical view of internal orders or projects representing a large capital expenditure requiring planning, budgeting, and funds management to ensure the budget is not exceeded.
Controlling (CO)	The Controlling module supports the internal management view of the organization. The CO abilities are structured around different types of analysis to support cost center accounting, event management, activity-based costing, product costing, and market-segment profitability reporting.
Enterprise Controlling (EC)	The EC module consists of three components focusing on consolidations, profit center accounting, and the executive information system.

Highlights of the Controlling Module

What CO is not	• CO is not just costs. • CO is not primarily focused on transaction or business process automation. • CO is not configuration based.
What CO is	CO is a conceptual design built to provide comparative analysis, including contribution and gross margins, for the controller, based on comprehensive capacity management and collaborative planning used to support cost management, controlling, and performance monitoring in order to take corrective action to support a changing organization.

Highlights of the Controlling Module Components

Cost Center Accounting (CCA)	CCA support the organizational view of expenses incurred. Cost center and cost center groups are used to represent the organization. Expenses are captured in primary and secondary cost elements. The actype is a capacity-based resource driver and the SKF is an output measure. Both are used for information and allocation purposes.
Order & Project Accounting (OPA)	OPA focuses on the expenses incurred for events and projects. The cost object used for this analysis is the internal order. The internal order is utilized to plan, budget, monitor, control, capture actuals, settle costs, and report.

Exhibit 3.9 *(continued)*

NOTES

1. Quote from the January 2000 interview with Sandra Otto conducted at SAP AG headquarters in Walldorf, Germany.
2. Cost elements are normally addressed when describing cost center capabilities and the flow of costs throughout the CO module since cost elements are definable within Cost Center Accounting (CCA). There is, however, a Cost Element Accounting (CEL) component of the CO module where cost elements are defined and maintained. Additionally, Profit Center Accounting (PCA) has not been listed as a component of the CO module since it belongs to the Enterprise Controlling module.

4

EVOLUTION OF SAP'S INTEGRATED ACTIVITY-BASED COSTING

The previous chapters focused on the costing philosophies supported by SAP and the conceptual differences that exist between an SAP ERP system and a stand-alone analytical system to support the ABC philosophy. This chapter is a historical perspective, focusing on how the SAP ABC system matured to its current state. Exhibit 4.1 depicts the time line of ABC functionality provided by each major release of SAP.

As illustrated in the time line, SAP has supported ABC since 1994, dedicating significant development efforts to expand and support the ABC philosophy. Therefore, the functionality provided within SAP has matured to provide an exceptionally advanced cost management solution. The next sections provide more information on each of the releases noted in Exhibit 4.1 and a projection of future SAP ABC capabilities to be supported. The following chapters describe in more detail the exact ABC functionality supported by the mySAP.com edition using the business applications in SAP R/3 Release 4.6C.

PRE–SAP R/3 2.2

Prior to Release 2.2, no true ABC functionality existed within the SAP system. Exhibit 4.2 depicts the standard flow for overhead costs to the product cost. The cost centers assign costs via an activity type, such as *Labor Hour for A1* or *Machine Hour* for A2. These activity types pull the direct costs to the production orders via the routings. Overhead allocations calculated via a costing sheet could also be attributed to the product/production order. Product costs and production variances are calculated and then transferred to a cost object for profitability analysis, such as Product 1.

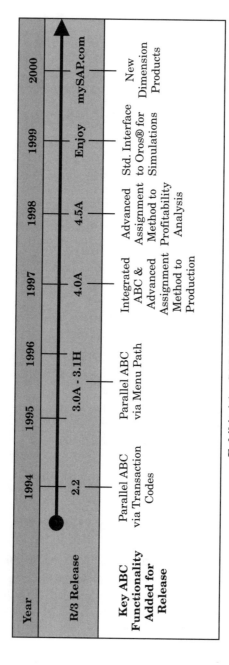

Exhibit 4.1 SAP ABC Functionality Timeline

92

Exhibit 4.2 Standard SAP Functionality Prior to ABC Being Supported

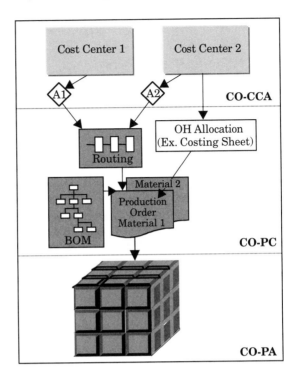

Although an activity/process object did not exist prior to Release 2.2, many users developed "workarounds" for this limitation in ABC functionality and still use these workarounds. The objects used to support ABC in the pre-2.2 Release would not be readily identified with ABC in the most traditional sense. Two examples of such possible workarounds are:

1. Activity type drivers to represent business processes
2. Internal orders to represent business processes

Example 1 An activity type (actype) is a single cost center pool of costs represented as a driver with an output measure. The actype can therefore be used to represent processes, which occur within a cost center. In Exhibit 4.2, this is depicted by *A2* representing a process named *Run Machine* instead of a resource driver named *Machine Hour.* Actual costs are split onto the actype based on equivalence numbers or a percentage. However, the limitation with the use of the activity type as a business process is that it cannot provide a view of activities across cost centers. Further, the activity type does not support attribute tags

Exhibit 4.3 Using Internal
Orders to Represent a Process
Example

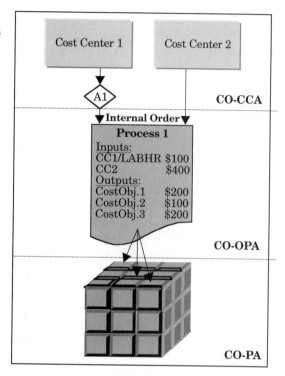

for more advanced reporting capabilities, such as a value-added measurement, or other analytical characteristics.

Example 2 To work around the lack of a true process view, internal orders could be used to provide an aggregation of a process view of costs as well as cost elements as seen in Exhibit 4.3.

In this example, the internal order is used to represent *Process 1*. The internal order captures the costs from each cost center either through a direct actype posting (A1) representing *LABHR* for *Cost Center 1* or through an allocation such as for *Cost Center 2*. The internal order allocates these costs to the cost objects via settlement rules. These settlement rules could be based on percentage, equivalence units (portions), or fixed dollar amount allocation methods. Additionally, the classification system, which supports functionality similar to tagging an internal order with additional information, can be used to provide the attribute functionality that the activity type lacks. A limitation of using the internal order to represent the process is that a rate cannot be determined for the internal order object, except through reporting.

These are just two examples of how clients desiring ABC functionality could support the philosophy prior to Release 2.2. A multitude of ways and cost objects exist within SAP; each has its own benefits and limitations. Even with these obvious limitations, it is important to note that ABC, even if only in its basic form, could be supported within SAP for decades. Future SAP releases supplied the demanded functionality and, more important, flexibility, evidenced in the progression of software releases reviewed below.

SAP R/3 2.2

Activity-Based Costing was first introduced in 1994 with SAP R/3 Release 2.2 via a transaction code, not through the standard menu path. Transaction code CP21 made available the ABC menu path from which the ABC transactions could be accessed. R/3 Release 2.2 provided a parallel view of ABC, much like having a stand-alone analytic system interfaced with the R/3 system. Parallel ABC was designed to provide users with process information to support strategic management decisions, harvesting the relevant data from the operational side of the system without actually impacting the operational flow of data.

Functionality Expansion

The overall functionality provided by the release of parallel ABC was akin to, but not as robust as, the functionality provided in a stand-alone analytical ABC system. The parallel system supported assignment of cost center (resource center) costs to a business process (activity/process) and then on to a cost object. Cost center/actype allocations to processes were also provided. Numerous allocation/assignment methodologies were used to assign costs from the cost center to the process and then to the cost object. The system supported cost assignment through percentage, ratio, fixed dollar amounts, or driver quantities as the basis.

As previously stated, one of the system weaknesses came from limited analytical tagging functionality. To address this limitation, the system was enhanced to allow attribute categories for user classifications on each of the processes. These categories were created for the common analytical tags of value added or non–value added, unit based versus batch based, or any user-defined attributes such as color, department, or value chain. Within each of the attribute categories, multiple attributes could be defined, such as high value added, value added, to non–value added. This provided more analytical capabilities than previously supported.

Parallel Analytical Activity-Based Costing   Parallel ABC is based on the concept of an alternative version for analysis, or a "delta version." The delta version is little more than an alternate view of costs being allocated. The postings made within the delta version are statistical, which means they are for information only and do not impact the true cost flows of the operational system. The delta version exists for both plan and actual data, and several delta versions can be created, allowing multiple "what-if" ABC scenarios to be examined. The actual version for the operative and delta version is always version 0. Although the parallel version has been compared to a stand-alone model, an interface from the general ledger or cost centers for expenses is not required. All cost information is housed within one system and is accessible by the parallel, delta version.

In Exhibit 4.4, the parallel version has its own view, the delta view, of the cost center costs, depicted with the version Δ added, such as *Cost Center 1Δ*. Any allocations executed on the parallel side do not impact the cost flows of the cost centers on the operational side, which represents the daily transactional system. Planned costs for the same cost center can vary between the versions used for the operational and parallel versions. When actual cost center postings are made, they are reflected within the parallel version simultaneously; that is, if new salaries are posted to *Cost Center 1,* they are also reflected in delta version *Cost Center 1Δ*, since there is only one version, 0, in which actuals are captured. This

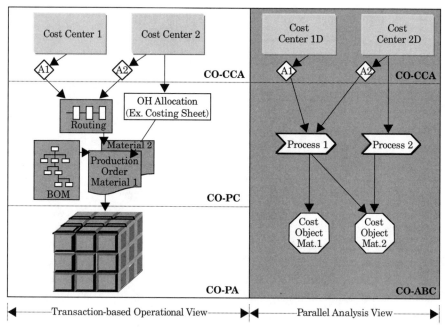

Exhibit 4.4   Parallel Activity-Based Costing

integration of the parallel view with the transactional posting side reduces the interface normally required to the G/L to gather the resource information.

The ABC functionality was not integrated with the operational system. The parallel ABC module is used to capture process information to support management decisions, and process improvement yet cannot be used to make actual cost assignments within and throughout the operational environment. Users who already demand the integration of the ABC results into the operational side of the system can create a simple workaround to use the information created on the analytic side as an allocation method for the operational side. This workaround is not necessary as of Release 4.0A.

Summary

With the introduction of the business process cost object in SAP Release 2.2, the support of ABC became more evident. A process view of the organization became available, enabling better management decision making. Cross cost center costs were captured and reported. The attribute tags supported further analysis capabilities. Exhibit 4.5 summarizes the key functionality provided with R/3 Release 2.2.

Functionality Provided with Release 2.2	Description
ABC analytical tools	• A process view of the organization with "what-if" scenario capabilities.
Eliminated interface	• Eliminated interface from general ledger or cost center system to a stand-alone analytic ABC tool, thereby eliminating the need for maintenance of that interface.
Integrated analytical and transaction-based operational tool	• Being within one system environment shortens the activities and time that are required for period-end/quarter-end closing activities. • Having one system eliminates the need for reconciliation of the two separate systems. • The transaction-based nature of SAP provides a transaction-level audit trail.
Wider access of ABC use and information throughout the organization	• More users typically are on the SAP system and therefore would have access to the analytical tool compared to those who have access to it only on their PCs.

Exhibit 4.5   ABC within R/3 Release 2.2 Summary

SAP R/3 3.0A THROUGH 3.1I

In 1995, SAP R/3 Release 3.0A provided the parallel version available in Release 2.2 through the standard menu path without the need to first access a transaction code. This change to a menu path made it obvious that SAP supported ABC functionality.

Functionality Enhancements

Where the previous 2.2 release actually introduced ABC functionality, the releases from 3.0A to 3.1I merely stabilized and expanded that parallel ABC functionality. In addition to visibility on the menu path, the link with Logistics Information System (LIS) was established and standard ABC reports were provided.

Logistics Information System   An additional benefit with Release 3.0 was the link between ABC and LIS within SAP. The LIS link can be used to provide the necessary actual driver data collection for the assignment of costs, such as number of purchase orders, of production orders, and of products sold. One common reason for failure of ABC systems is the increased data collection requirements. This linkage of ABC and LIS reduces the burden that often accompanies an ABC model of maintaining interfaces and actual data collection. Exhibit 4.6 shows an example of how this link can be used.

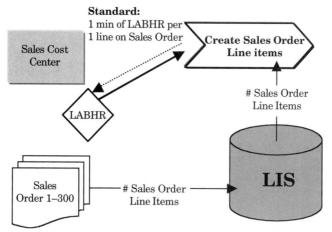

Exhibit 4.6   Logistic Information System (LIS) Link

The sales orders are created and tracked in the SD module. The LIS keeps track of the number of line items created on the sales orders. During the period-end close, the process driver is automatically updated with the actual number of sales order line items. No interface is required. The LIS captures hundreds of standard drivers that can be used for process allocations. Additionally, user-defined LIS key figures, drivers, can also be generated.

Summary

With Release 3.0A though 3.1I, the SAP's support of ABC capabilities became more transparent. Additionally, functionality was enhanced and new functionality was added. Exhibit 4.7 summarizes this functionality.

SAP R/3 4.0A

Release 4.0 in 1997 provided a quantum leap in support of advanced cost management using ABC. The ABC functionality was integrated with the operational aspects of the SAP CO system, most important in the area of product costing and

Functionality Provided with Release 3.0A to 3.1I	Description
ABC more visible	• Menu paths for ABC functionality were provided.
Link with LIS	• Reduced/eliminated some driver interfaces by pulling the driver quantities from other SAP modules. • Allowed for expansion of the ABC model since the model may have been designed with limitations on drivers where no actual system existed to capture the required drivers.
Standard ABC reports	• During these releases the standard SAP ABC-provided reports were added and enhanced.

Exhibit 4.7   ABC Functionality Changes with R/3 Release 3.0A
                to 3.1I Summary

also with the production modules. This true integration created the first and, to this day only, transaction-based, operationally integrated ABC ERP software package. The first target for this ABC functionality was the management of inbound logistic and production costs as well as better assignment of overhead costs.

Functionality Enhancements

Release 4.0A provided many new ABC functionality enhancements. These can be grouped into two key areas:

1. *Advanced cost assignment logic.* Rather than limiting users to static assignment parameters, a tool known as the process template allowed users the power of dynamic "if-then" Boolean logic.
2. *ABC Integration.* This integration was between CO-ABC and the other CO components; Cost Center Accounting, Order and Project Accounting, product costing (CO-PC) and the production modules, and also with the market segments in the profitability analysis module (CO-PA). Each is described in more detail in the next five chapters.

Advanced Cost Assignment Logic   A main reason why ABC failed in many organizations is that the design of the ABC model was such that existing systems could not readily accommodate the performance parameters of the model. The main design issues when building an ABC model are master data maintenance and dynamic determination of the appropriate driver and quantities for a cost object. Due to the integrated nature of an ERP package, SAP had the additional design challenge of needing the ability to create a quantity structure between the logistics modules and the business process. Release 4.0 introduced the process template assignment methodology to solve these issues. This tool provides a method that incorporates some of the cost objects with "if-then" formula logic.

The cost objects for Release 4.0 were processes, cost centers, activity types, and the production cost objects: production order, material, project, run schedule header, maintenance order, service order, and so on. "If-then" logic is the basic Boolean logic used for code that includes operands such as: If process 1 AND material 1 Then multiply by two. Pieces of information from the bill of material or routing can be automatically accessed, such as material unit of measure or work center number. Perhaps a mathematical formula is appropriate to calculate the quantity of a process consumed. The resulting benefit of the process template was the ability to:

- Create a quantity structure between the production objects and the process.
- Make very complex cost assignments.
- Potentially reduce master data maintenance.
- Address the need for a dynamic determination of the appropriate driver for the cost object.

The process template allocation method is addressed in detail in Chapters 5 through 8.

Activity-Based Costing Integration   The process template supports the integration of ABC throughout the operational system. Exhibit 4.8 illustrates the previous separation between the transaction-based system with the parallel analytical tool removed.

With the barrier down, the process can now be used as a sender and receiver throughout the controlling and production modules of the SAP ERP package. No longer is process information restricted to the analytical (Parallel ABC) module. Note that even though the process information has been truly integrated, the remnant parallel ABC version still exists, allowing for "what-if"

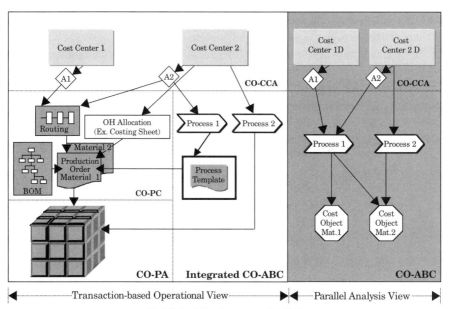

Exhibit 4.8   Integrated ABC

scenario analysis without impacting the operational design. This ABC operational integration was supported via three key areas:

1. Integration with CO-OM
2. Integration with CO-PC and production modules
3. Integration with CO-PA

Regarding the Integration with CO-OM, the Overhead Management (OM) components of CO are CCA (cost center accounting), OPA (order and project accounting) (not depicted in Exhibit 3.8), and ABC. Chapters 5 and 6 provide many detailed examples of the CO-OM and ABC integration. The two pieces of functionality created to support the ABC integration with overhead management are:

1. The ability to use the process as a cost object and the process quantity as a driver throughout the operational environment and not just for analytical analysis. Specifically for this area, the process can be used to transfer process costs to cost centers, other processes, and internal orders.
2. The ability to create complex resource costs to process assignments, which is supported by the template allocation capabilities.

Release 4.0 also offered integration with CO-PC and the production modules. Integration with product costing and production was provided via the process template. The process template is used to assign overhead process costs to production cost objects, such as production orders, service orders, projects, run schedule headers, and materials. As discussed in Chapter 1, traditional costing uses direct materials and labor with a percentage for allocating overhead to calculate production costs. Now, with the complete integration of ABC with the production module, the process can be used as a driver for making assignments of overhead costs to products. The process template assigns process costs to be used for the:

- Calculation of any of the standard cost estimates of a material/service
- Actual allocation of overhead expenses to production cost objects
- Determination of the target production costs
- Calculation of process variances

Chapter 7 provides detailed examples of the integration of ABC with product costing.

As depicted in Exhibit 4.8, this release also provided integration with CO-PA, through standard allocation methods such as percentage based or direct charging. The process template's advanced assignment functionality was not available for use with assigning to market segments until a later release. Exhibit 4.9 illustrates the ABC to PA integration for Release 4.0A. Chapter 8 provides detailed examples of the ABC integration with CO-PA.

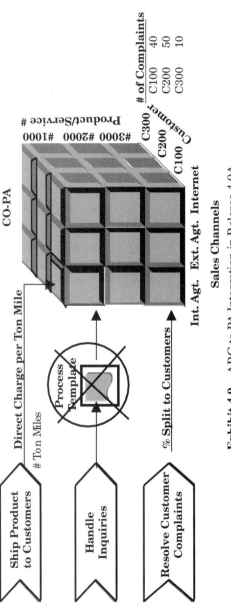

Exhibit 4.9 ABC to PA Integration in Release 4.0A

Functionality Provided with Release 4.0A	Description
Integrated ABC	• Provides more accurate product costing.
Process Quantity as a Driver in Integrated Environment	• Provides more accurate allocation of overhead costs via a process driver.
Structured business process template	• Allows the creation of a process routing. • Reduces maintenance. • Automates resource consumption and capacity planning.
Business process template	• Supports advanced assignments of business processes using formulas to the production modules.
Process view included for cost estimates	• Using the process template, provides a more accurate method of assigning production support costs to product cost. The product costing information is more accurate, which can lead to different decisions on make/buy, outsourcing, product mix, etc.
Process to market segments	• Functionality similar to other stand-alone tools, but not as advanced as with the process template capabilities, in this release.

Exhibit 4.10   ABC within R/3 Release 4.0A Summary

Summary

The key benefit for Release 4.0 was the integration of the ABC philosophy throughout major portions of the R/3 operational environment. This integration allowed micro-ABC standards to be used for execution within one system. Exhibit 4.10 summarizes the key functionality for this release.

SAP R/3 4.5A

SAP R/3 4.5A was released in 1998, fairly soon after 4.0B, and contained the rest of the ABC integration of the process template throughout the operational environment.

Functionality Enhancements

Release 4.5A provided the complete integration of the advanced process template allocation methodology by integration with the sales and distribution module and integration with the CO-PA module. Additionally, the process is integrated with the Routing.

Integration with Sales and Distribution Module   With this release the process template could be used to assign process costs to the sales order. This provided that the same functionality previously available for the other production methods could be used for make-to-sales-order production.

Integration with CO-PA Module   The integration of the process template with CO-PA provided the capabilities to have the advance assignment capabilities for process costs to support cost-to-serve and downstream analysis. Exhibit 4.11 illustrates the process template being used for the assignment of overhead costs to the market segments.

The process template can readily accommodate the complexity usually associated with the assignment of cost-to-serve costs. These types of cost often have "IF-THEN" as the basis for charging.

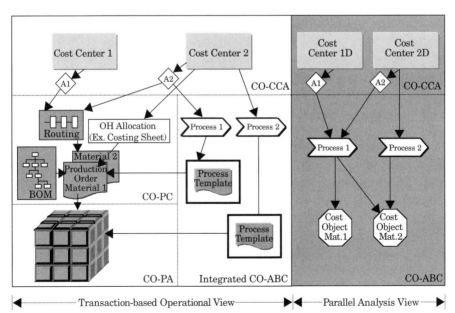

Exhibit 4.11   Process Template Integration with CO-PA

Example 1   IF the sale is via the Internet, THEN allocate .6 of *Create Sales Order* process costs.

Example 2   IF *Resolve Customer Complaint* is for Customer 1 and Product 2, THEN assign 1.1 of the process.

By accommodating complexity within the formulas, there is no need to create additional master data to represent the complexity. Thus, no *Resolve Customer Complaint—Easy* or *Resolve Customer Complaint—Difficult* processes have to be created, as is often done in ABC models to accommodate such complexity.

Complete Integration with Production Module   Another piece of new functionality Release 4.5 provided was the ability to assign a process to the production routing work center. This provided the benefit of having the process cost allocated at the standard process rate immediately instead of having to run the process template during period end. See Chapter 7 for a more detailed example.

Summary

Release 4.5A completed the integration of the process template and its advance assignment capabilities throughout the operational environment. Exhibit 4.12 lists the functionality provided with this release.

Functionality Provided with Release 4.5A	Description
Process template to SD module	• The process template integration with SD allowed for more accurate costing for make-to-order manufacturers.
Process template to CO-PA	• The process template integration with CO-PA supported the complexity issues with cost-to-serve and provided a more accurate assignment methodology.
Complete integration with production	• Integration of the process with the production routing allows process cost to be allocated real time at a standard rate. Previously, the assignment of process costs took place at period-end closing, at which time the impacts could be analyzed.

Exhibit 4.12   ABC within R/3 4.5A Summary

SAP R/3 ENJOY (4.6A/B)

Almost all of the pieces for the operational integrated ABC system were put in place prior to Release 4.6A in 1999. With 4.6A, called Enjoy, the focus became more on where to go next with integrated ABC. Since the operational integrated ABC system was in place, the next step was to accommodate functionality for strategic ABC capabilities and complete integration of the process.

Functionality Enhancements

The Enjoy release offered two additional pieces of integration:

1. Integration with the ABC Technologies, Inc. (ATI) Oros software
2. Direct posting to the process in plan and actual

Additionally, nomenclature for the process template changed to be just the template, since the "IF-THEN" Boolean logic had been expanded to work between any object within CO, not just with the ABC processes.

SAP ABC and Oros   Oros is the leading stand-alone analytical ABC software package. In September 1998 SAP AG announced that it had bought an interest in ATI. This relationship provided the following:

- A bridge tool to easily perform simulations of "what-if" ABC scenarios. Simulations are not generally performed in the operational environment of the SAP ERP package due to the strict master data validations set in place for the transactional system. Simulating strategic decisions and their impacts on the ABC model within the operational environment requires the creation of master data that may have to be discarded.
- Changed the perception in the United States that SAP does not provide ABC functionality. Due to this new relationship, users would assume that SAP would soon provide or already did provide ABC functionality. The advanced ABC capabilities of SAP were unknown to most outside of Europe.
- Modeling and prototyping of the ABC model via the Oros tool prior to the model being incorporated into the daily operational SAP system.

This partnership generated the ABC Technologies product called the Bridge. The Bridge product is a standardized supported interface between the SAP and the Oros software packages. See Chapter 10 for details on the Bridge Capabilities and benefits of using SAP ABC with Oros modeling.

Direct Financial/Procurement Posting to a Process   Prior to the Enjoy release, resource costs had to be collected on the cost center or internal order and then posted to the process. With the Enjoy release, SAP provided the ability to make account postings directly onto the process. For example, an organization uses a process *Perform Inspection* and purchases an outside service provider to do the inspections due to the lack of internal resources. A direct G/L posting of the expense to whichever account desired, such as *Subcontracting,* depending on the organization's chart of accounts, can be made to the process *Perform Inspection* when the invoice is processed. Purchase orders can also be directly assigned to a process. For example, the process representing the service of *Process Mortgage Loan* can order mortgage forms on a purchase order, and upon receipt the purchase order can be charged directly against the process.

Although posting directly to a process is systematically supported, in certain cases when used inappropriately, it is conceptually dangerous. Posting an account directly to the process results in the responsibility accounting view being bypassed. Also, capacity management may be lost since the relationship between the resource center cost driver and the process driver is not used. The ability to perform Activity-Based Budgeting can also be curtailed since the link between the cost center and the process has been circumvented.

Summary

With the Enjoy release, three key pieces of functionality were provided. These are addressed in Exhibit 4.13.

mySAP.com (USING R/3 RELEASE 4.6C)

The 1999 SAPPHIRE Conference, held in Philadelphia, was all abuzz with the new edition of SAP, mySAP.com. Every presentation and demonstration pod was geared toward addressing this new edition of the SAP products. So what exactly does it have to do with core functionality like ABC? The core R/3 modules became business applications used with the mySAP.com release. So even though there was a new focus with all the special functionality of mySAP.com, the core business applications of SAP are still enhancing their own functionality. The latest release used with mySAP.com is Release 4.6C.

Functionality Enhancements

With mySAP.com using Release 4.6C, three new pieces of functionality were added:

Functionality Provided with Release 4.6A	Description
Standardized interface with Oros tool	• Using the Bridge, the Oros product can be used to perform simulations to determine impacts on the operational ABC design. Simulations are not usually performed in SAP due to the stringent master data validations that must be in place.
Direct posting to the Process	• Integration with the FI allows a direct account posting to the process as the cost receiver. • Integration with the MM allows a process as the receiver of a purchase order.
Nomenclature change	• The change from the process template to simply be known as the template seems somewhat of an unperceivable difference. The Boolean logic was now available for nonprocess-related drivers as well. This change does denote that ABC is no longer a special function in SAP. It has completely matured to be one of many methods that can be used for costing, allocating, analyzing, and reporting within SAP.

Exhibit 4.13   ABC within R/3 Release Enjoy (4.6A/B) Summary

1. Easy Planning and Execution
2. Internal Service Request
3. mySAP.com Workplace

Easy Cost Planning and Execution   Easy Cost Planning and Execution (EP&E) is the combination of planning with a user-friendly Web graphical user interface (GUI). For example, an Easy Cost Planning and Execution model can be set up to determine the cost of an external training event. The end user can enter the event and then will be prompted to fill in the Web GUI fields for cost of the course, number of attendees, dates, mode of travel such as flight, cost of flight, number of nights in hotel, hotel cost ranges, and so on. All these questions are based on the ECP&E model configured. Once the end user finishes answering the questions, the model calculates the planned costs and informs the end user. Once the end user accepts it, the plan data for that cost center manager's budget is automatically updated. The process cost object has been completely integrated with this functionality, thereby allowing any process to be added as a determinate for planned costs. For this example, if the flight and hotel options are selected, the model can include the *Make Reservations and Issue Ticket* process costs for the estimate. This concept is akin to the concept of feature costing, where users fill in the desired features and the costing engine in the background calculates the estimated costs.

Internet Service Request   The Internet Service Request (ISR) functionality provides direct billing or charging of shared services. An example of the ISR is an office move. A request can be generated to move several employees' offices and provide a speaker phone for a new conference room. In the ISR model, several activities are predefined to occur for this event. The move requires labor hours from the *Facilities* department to move furniture and boxes. *Set Up PCs* and *Set Up Phone Line* processes are required from the IT department. A purchase of a phone is needed for the new conference room. The ISR model makes the requests. In the background the costs are calculated and posted to the responsible cost center, making the hidden factory completely transparent. The person making the request has a user-friendly Web GUI front end collecting all of the relevant information. This functionality eliminates the need for allocations and provides a method for standardizing internal business events that happen regularly. The dynamic nature of the ISR model captures the specific nuances of the individual events, which supports the most accurate assignment of the provided internal services.

mySAP.com Workplace   Two main pieces of functionality within the mySAP.com Workplace facilitate the continual integration of ABC throughout the organization: (1) roles and (2) miniapplications.

The role capability allows organizations to group tasks, specific SAP transactions, reports, and other non-SAP information, together as one role. For instance, a role for a process analyst can be created that includes: ABC transaction codes within the SAP component system, the SAP New Dimension product Strategic Enterprise Management (SEM) for Business Planning Simulation, Oros and PowerSim for ABC model simulations, several Web pages that provide benchmarking information, process management reports from R/3 and the Business Warehouse (BW), information gathered from the Knowledge Warehouse content, and access to other non-SAP systems or external organizations in the supply chain. The Workplace provides anything and everything that users in that defined role would need to perform duties efficiently.

Additionally, the integration of the miniapplication (miniapp) functionality supports the role. A miniapp functions to deliver up-to-date information to the role user. Miniapps provide access to applications, information, and services. Common applications used are e-mail, calendars, and access to legacy systems or any component of mySAP.com, such as the ABC submodule. Information can be of any type, but the most beneficial are miniapps that deliver alerts for exception reporting. For instance, a miniapp can be created to provide an alert on all processes that have reached 90% of their planned budget for the month or to provide a trend of process quantities to date. Additionally, miniapps can push information to the user's desk, in contrast to traditional reporting which needs to be specifically executed. Up-to-date information on key performance indicators

(KPIs) relevant for the user's work can be provided at a predetermined refresh rate, avoiding time-consuming searches for key pieces of information. The main complaint in today's world of business and even personal life is that there is access to too much data and not necessarily any information. The miniapps help to focus the role-based user on the area of greatest need by generating instant information from reports full of data.

Role functionality using miniapps provides a powerful tool to aid employees to be the most efficient in their tasks. This functionality is strengthened by the ability to have the miniapp information linked to mobile devices, ensuring that the relevant information is always available to users.

Summary

Until mySAP.com, the added functionality supported ABC. This release integrated existing ABC functionality with new functionality being added elsewhere in the system. The ABC functionality within SAP has matured and probably will not be expanded on, just incorporated into new functionality being added to mySAP.com intracomponents or New Dimension products. Exhibit 4.14 summarizes the functionality added with mySAP.com using Release 4.6C.

FUTURE FUNCTIONALITY

The mySAP.com edition using Release 4.6C incorporates the current ABC functionality but does not enhance it in any way. This is due to the ABC philosophy in SAP having completely matured. So what does that leave for future ABC functionality to be added in SAP? From a cost calculation and integration standpoint, absolutely nothing. The next new costing philosophy will have to be generated by the academics, and SAP will build functionality to support it.

Functionality Enhancements

Functionality that can be provided or is being considered for the future deals more with:

- Specialization to support the IBUs (industry-specific business units)
- Greater flexibility with reporting tools
- More integration with the New Dimension products, such as Strategic Enterprise Management (addressed in greater detail in Chapter 11)

Functionality Provided With mySAP.com	Description
Easy cost planning and execution	• An ECP&E model provides feature-costing module of an internal project or event to determine the planned cost, which can include process costs.
Internet service request	• An ISR model provides direct charging for shared services. The cost calculation is performed in the background and can include process costs of processes used to perform or support the service.
mySAP.com workplace	• Roles can include all ABC functionality through ABC transaction codes, access to ABC model simulation tools such as Oros or PowerSim, process reports generated from any source, and any information from the Internet. • Miniapps provide access to applications, information, and services. The alert capabilities direct employees to focus on the issues at hand. Process information can be accessed for any miniapps designed.

Exhibit 4.14   ABC within the mySAP.com using Release (4.6C) Summary

Industry-specific Business Unit Specializations   Industry-specific use of ABC may generate the need for certain formulas to be created as standards for the IBUs. For example, the banking industry has led the drive for many formulas to be provided—between processes and market segments—as the industry's focus is very cost-to-serve oriented. The public sector IBU may drive certain formulas to become standard between the processes and internal orders— to help with the complexity of allocating costs to classes or academic programs that are handled as events. So although no new ABC functionality is being added, new formulas may be added to make commonly used functions/formulas available to increase user friendliness and shorten project implementations.

Reporting Flexibility   Standard, Report Painter, Report Writer, and ABAP/4 written reports support the reporting capability of the intracomponents of mySAP.com. The next focus for completely integrating ABC is with the BW tool,

Potential Functionality Provided in Future Releases	Description
IBU specializations	• Support of standardizing formulae to make implementation faster and more user friendly.
Reporting flexibility	• Integration with BW and enhancement or standard reporting capabilities.
New Dimension products	• Complete ABC integration and support of those applications.

Exhibit 4.15   Potential Future Functionality Summary

and involves creation of standard data extractions built into the BW tool. It also involves bringing some of the flexible reporting capabilities of the BW tool back into the CO module for ABC reporting.

New Dimension Products Integration   As the New Dimension products continue to be refined and added to, the ABC developers are focusing on ways to integrate current ABC functionality to support these applications.

Summary

The current focus for SAP ABC developers and product managers is the complete integration of the ABC philosophy throughout any SAP application or tool. Exhibit 4.15 summarizes functionality slated to be added in the future releases of the business applications with mySAP.com.

The following chapters address in greater detail the functionality mentioned only briefly in this chapter. The functionality is based on the mySAP.com using Release 4.6C.

EVOLUTION OF ACTIVITY-BASED COSTING SUMMARY

This chapter provided a historical look at the evolution of the ABC philosophy as supported by the SAP E/3 software. A projection of future ABC functionality to be added is also provided. Exhibit 4.16 provides overall key highlights for each of the releases.

Release	Key Highlights
Pre R/3 2.2	• ABC philosophy had not been built into SAP. • ABC philosophy supported using other SAP functionality with limitations.
R/3 2.2	• ABC philosophy supported via parallel ABC. • Eliminates interfaces from general ledger or cost centers, reducing maintenance. • An integrated analytical and transaction-based operational tool, reducing the need for reconciliation between two separate systems. • Wider access of ABC use and information throughout the organization. • One integrated environment shortens the activities and time required for period-end/quarter-end closing activities. • The transaction-based nature of SAP provides a transaction-level audit trail.
R/3 3.0A–3.1I	• ABC more visible since it has been incorporated into the standard menu path. • Indirect activity allocation provides quantity structure capabilities and reduces actual data collection where a strong correlation between process and resource driver exists. • Link with LIS reduces/eliminates the driver interfaces required by pulling the driver quantities from other SAP modules and allows for the expansion of the ABC model since the model may have been designed with limitations on drivers since no actual system existed to capture that information. • Standard SAP ABC reports were added and enhanced.
R/3 4.0A	• ABC philosophy integrated into the operational transaction-based environment. • Driver/quantity measure comparison demonstrates when to use an actype, process, or SKF. • Resource to process to resource assignment supported, providing more accurate charging of internal services and better information for outsourcing decisions. • Process quantity as a driver in the integrated environment, providing more accurate assignment of overhead costs. • Structured Business Process template that provides a bill of process and reduces maintenance. • Process template supports advanced assignments of business processes using formulas to the production modules. The product costing information is more accurate, which can lead to different decisions on make/buy, outsourcing, product mix, etc. • Process view included for cost estimates, including the standard cost estimate.

Exhibit 4.16   Summary of the Evolution of ABC in SAP

	• Process to market segments allocation methods supported with functionality similar to other stand-alone tools, but not as advanced as with the process template capabilities.
R/3 4.5A	• The Process template integration with SD allows for more accurate costing for make-to-order manufacturers. • The Process template integration with CO-PA handles the complexity issues with cost-to-serve and provides a more accurate assignment methodology.
R/3 4.6A	• Oros Bridge developed to provide a standardized and supported interface between SAP CO module and the Oros Modeling tool. • Integration of the process with the work centers in the routings within the Production module. • Integration with the FI (Financial Accounting module) to support direct G/L account to process postings. • Integration with the MM (Materials Management Module) to support purchase orders being assigned directly to a process.
mySAP.com Using 4.6C Release	• Easy Planning & Execution integrates the process into a feature costing model to support internal projects and planning functions. • Internet Service Request integrates the process into a direct charging and billing approach for shared services and internal support departments. • Workplace miniapps and roles integrate the process to aid in making the worker more efficient via exception reporting and role definitions.
Future	• IBU specializations providing support of standardizing formulas to make implementation faster and more user friendly. • Integration with BW and enhancement of standard reporting capabilities. • Complete ABC integration and support of New Dimension products.

Exhibit 4.16   (*continued*)

____PART TWO____

SAP R/3 INTEGRATED
ACTIVITY-BASED
COSTING

5

INTEGRATED ACTIVITY-BASED COSTING WITH RESPONSIBILITY ACCOUNTING

Prior to the year 2000, there was a huge rush to partially install or completely implement enterprise resource planning (ERP) tools. This push was driven primarily by the need to replace non-Y2K-compliant software packages or outdated technology platforms. After the turn of the millennium, organizations were drawn to customer-related and Internet supporting software applications and implementations, thus pulling the focus away from backroom automation and transactional execution, at least temporarily. While the rush for Internet marketplaces, business to business (B2B), portals, and e-commerce is well founded and can provide huge benefits, to get the most from these tools, the backroom costing engine needs to be fully in force to support them.

These new software applications provide greater access for the internal user to more information and other users, such as suppliers and customers. Easier and quicker access to information can mean more business and opportunities, but it does not guarantee that the new business will be profitable or the relationship cost justified. To be profitable, a company must be very focused on determining whom to do business with and in what manner. This boom in software and hardware technology is akin to immediately laying thousands of new highways and different transportation modes, thus gaining access to an unlimited numbers of people and places. But several questions still beg to be answered. Where should we as a business go? Do we have the resources to get there? Whom should we go with? How much will it cost us? The companies that will benefit the most from all the technology advances will be the ones that can quickly and accurately identify, from all of the new information and opportunities, which business should be pursued and what unprofitable ventures should be left for competitors to chase after.

The SAP Controlling module houses both the costing engine capabilities and the profitability information needed to provide effective decision support for questions like these. The costing engine is designed to plan, collect, and attribute the appropriate costs throughout the organization. The accuracy and timeliness of the cost information greatly impacts the preparation of the profit information. The underlying costing philosophy of the CO module is based on Resource Consumption Accounting (RCA), described in detail in Chapter 1. This costing philosophy is built on the principle that all indirect and direct costs within the organization start with a responsible person or entity. Responsibility accounting is therefore the first place to begin. Profitability or market segment analysis will be the end result (discussed in Chapter 8). Within SAP CO, responsibility accounting is synonymous with cost center accounting.

COST CENTER ACCOUNTING CAPABILITIES

Cost center accounting is the cornerstone of the CO module and is normally the first submodule of CO to be implemented. Cost center accounting supports capturing cost center expenses for both planned and actual; calculation of driver rates, allocations, assignments, or direct charges of expenses; variances; and comprehensive reporting. From the responsibility accounting view of CCA, a further delineation of costs into a process view is the goal of Activity-Based Costing (ABC). Since this further analysis of cost is an expansion of the more traditional view, the ABC functionality is completely integrated with the CCA functionality.

All of the functionality supported by CCA along with the ABC integration cannot be addressed in one chapter, let alone one section. Therefore, this section focuses only on the integrated ABC and CCA functionality that helps to set SAP apart from other systems supporting ABC. This functionality concerns planning capabilities, driver rate calculations, and variance analysis. The cost assignment methods in CCA and ABC will be addressed in the "Information Flows" section later in this chapter.

Plan Reconciliation

SAP supports a fully integrated planning cycle from sales, production, investment, cost centers, and processes, through product costing, eventually focusing on profitability planning. The focus of this section is on the planning/budgeting of cost centers and processes, in particular, cost centers and processes that are quantity dependent, that is, have a directly correlated output driver for the resource or process. With this type of relationship, the resources and/or processes are more than simply pools of costs with value allocations.

In quantity planning, there are two components of output planning:

1. Output expressed in terms of a measure or driver—the planned output
2. Output in terms of users of resource drivers or processes—demand

The first component is an output—the planned output—that the cost center or process manager intends to provide expressed in terms of a measure or driver, such as supply. When determining the output quantity, the manager asks: How much of my service do I think they will need from me? or How much do I think my cost center or my process can provide? The second measure of output is in terms of the users of the resource driver (actype) or process, that is, demand. The consumers forecast the need or demand of the process or actype. This demand is referred to as scheduled quantity. The scheduled quantity is the amount the consumers plan to consume of the drivers and answers the manager's question: How much do they plan to consume from me?

This approach is akin to the one taken for zero-based budgeting. In zero-based budgeting, each cost center manager plans the year based on supply and demand of resources and processes rather than using last year's data as a starting point with a set percentage increase/decrease. Exhibit 5.1 illustrates the use of plan and schedule output fields.

For this example, the manager of the *IT* cost center plans to provide 190 *LABHR* (labor hours) as output. For simplicity, all of the *IT* cost center/*LABHR*

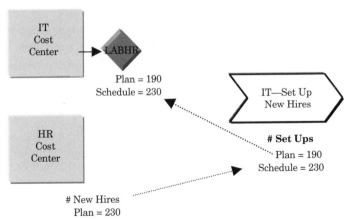

Exhibit 5.1   Planned versus Scheduled Output Quantity

is consumed by one process *IT—Set Up New Hires,* setting a one-to-one relationship between the drivers. The *IT—Set Up New Hires* process consists of activities such as providing a PC, establishing network security, and arranging licenses for software. The manager of the process plans to provide 190 *Set Ups* to the *HR* cost center. The *HR* cost center measure # *of New Hires* has a one-to-one relationship established with the *IT—Set Up New Hires* process. Therefore, once the HR cost center plans 230 # New Hires, a scheduled demand for 230 *Set Ups* is placed on the process that then places a scheduled demand of 230 *IT LabHrs.*

Obviously, with both a plan supply and a planned demand (scheduled output), a business decision must be made. Will efforts be made to adjust the supply to more closely align with demand? If demand cannot be expanded, how will this constraint be managed? The plan reconciliation functionality allows the responsible cost center or process manager to determine whether to accept the planned output or to convert the scheduled output to the new planned output. Having the two fields also allows, for example, the *Maintenance* cost center manager to see what additional maintenance labor hours are required for next year. The manager can then determine the appropriate course of action to take: Is the discrepancy enough to warrant hiring an additional labor resource, will overtime suffice, can outside services be procured? Because a relationship must be established between the drivers, the plan reconciliation functionality is supported only by a quantity-based model. This approach supports a focus on capacity management during the budgetary cycle by providing relevant and actionable information prior to the start of the fiscal year.

Driver Rate Calculations

The driver rate calculation functionality within CCA is completely integrated with ABC. Therefore, both resource driver (actype) and activity/process (process) driver rates can be calculated simultaneously. Several decisions must be made when determining how actype and process rates should be calculated for the organization. These are categorized as conceptual design issues and driver rate options.

Conceptual Design   The following conceptual design issues significantly impact the calculation of actype and process rates:

1. Methodology for internal resource allocation: step-down versus recursive
2. Methodology for process allocation: An ABC paradigm shift
3. Establishing the fixed/variable nature of cost and quantities

Step-down versus Recursive   The allocation of indirect internal services has long been an issue in the cost management community. Everyone agrees that these costs need to be allocated; however, in the past software was limited in its capabilities for support. The methodology decision between step-down or recursive allocation, hinges on weighing the importance of two variables: (1) complexity level of the costing model designed and (2) level of accuracy. The following text addresses the step-down approach, the recursive approach, and how the SAP recursive approach has altered the ABC paradigm.

The *step-down allocation methodology* is a simplified method for allocation of internal services. In a step approach, costs are assigned from the internal department with the widest customer base first. Once this department has all costs allocated out, the next department in the chain is allocated. Once costs are fully allocated in the sequence, the cost center can *never* receive service costs from another allocating cost center.

The step-down approach is significantly better than the direct method, in which internal service departments are assigned only to production cost centers, in that the department-to-department relationship is accepted. However, the step-down approach does not take into account self-consumption, for example the *Facilities* cost center consuming its own square footage, or the reciprocal relationships of most internal service centers. For example, if *Information Technology* department serves *Human Resources* when providing data services, and HR manages the employee services for IT, what is the proper sequencing? Further, if an outsourcing decision is made, how does management know the fully burdened cost of either the HR or IT departments?

Exhibit 5.2 illustrates an example of the step-down cost flow method. The *Utilities* cost center is allocated first based on the kilowatt-hours (KWHs) consumed by the receiving cost centers. Next, the *Facilities* and *Maintenance* cost centers are allocated, respectively.

The benefit of the step-down approach is simplicity. The cost flows are easily traced. However, the disadvantage of this approach is that it does not necessarily reflect causal relationships. The true cost flows within an organization are not represented, and therefore inaccuracy in cost rates still prevails.

The *recursive (iterative) approach* differs in that true organizational cost flows are reflected, or at least a much closer approximation is made. In order to support this portrayal of organizational expense flows, the system must provide the ability to flow costs back to cost centers and/or processes that have already been allocated. Exhibit 5.3 illustrates this difference using the same cost and quantity information used in Exhibit 5.2.

In reality, the *Utilities, Maintenance,* and *Facilities* cost centers can consume each other as well as themselves; for example, *Facilities* needs office

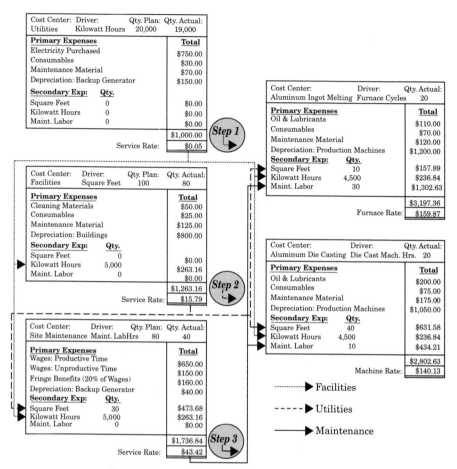

Exhibit 5.2   Step-down Allocation Approach

space for its own personnel. This causes a recursive cost flow that must be considered during the driver rate calculation. In SAP, when selected as iterative, the price calculation transaction will iterate the cost flows repeatedly until the change in the rate becomes negligible. With the step-down approach, the price calculation simply iterates once, needing to go no further to finalize the calculation of the driver rates. Exhibit 5.4 summarizes the differences between the rates.

The product/service profitability will be impacted by the more accurate assignment of the support costs using the recursive approach. The recursive method provides greater accuracy and more information for analysis. However, as the costing model more accurately reflects the cost movements within

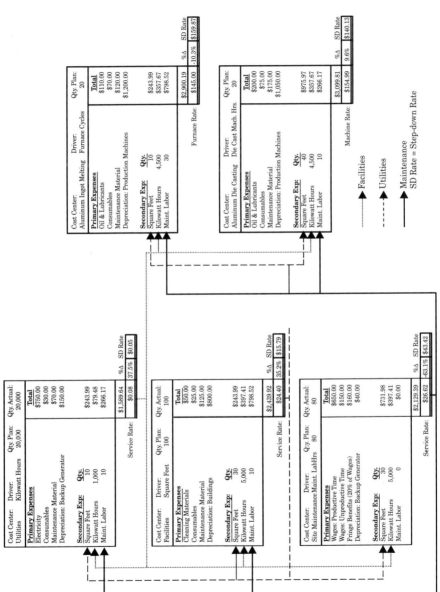

Exhibit 5.3 Recursive Cost Flows Approach

125

Driver Name	Step-down Method	Iterative Method	% Change
Furnace Cycles	$159.87	$145.00	-10.3%
Die Cast Hours	$140.13	$154.99	9.6%

Exhibit 5.4   Result Comparison of Step-down vs Recursive Allocation Approach

the organization, it also becomes increasingly intricate. This disadvantage is apparent in the reduced visibility and difficulty in tracing allocation flows at first sight as the model becomes more complex.

The SAP system supports both methods of assignment designs as well as a combination. The recursive design is suggested for support cost centers that are over a determined materiality limit, contain large fixed costs, have a quantifiable cost driver, and are consumed in different quantities by the receivers, such as *Utilities, Facilities,* and *Maintenance,* not necessarily the *Corporate Planning* department.

ABC Paradigm Shift   Most ABC systems are built on the principle that expenses flow from the cost centers to activities/processes and on to cost objects. If recursive cost flows are supported systematically, it is within an area only, for example, cost center-to-cost center iterations or process-to-process. Rarely does an ABC system allow circular cost assignments from cost center-to-process-to-cost center. The example in Exhibit 5.3 focuses only on a recursive cost flow between cost centers to:

- Narrow the illustration to the fact that SAP supports this method.
- Demonstrate the impacts on accuracy.
- Prevent distraction often caused by the statement: "SAP supports recursive cost flows between processes and cost centers."

This last statement has started many heated conversations between ABC proponents and SAP developers and consultants, mainly because it is a shift from the traditional ABC philosophy. This functionality supports the use of ABC beyond that of product/customer costing to include service costing for internal services. Exhibit 5.5 illustrates how internal support process costs can be assigned in SAP versus how they are usually allocated in a traditional ABC approach.

For this example, Step A has the *Human Resource* department tracing 100% of its expenses to the *Process Performance Review* activity.

A possible SAP approach includes assigning, in Step 1a, the *Process Performance Review* activity to the true consumers, the cost centers, based on the # *Employees,* each requiring one review. This is a directly correlated assignment of costs. Note that the *Human Resources* cost center would receive some of the process back since it also has employees that are reviewed. Each of the cost centers allocates expenses to its processes in Step 1b.

Since traditional ABC supports process being assigned only to other processes or cost objects, the cost for the *Process Performance Review* process will be assigned to the other processes (Step 2) or perhaps directly on to a cost object. The problem with this approach is that the *Process Performance Review* process is not directly correlated to *Create Sales Order Line Items, Remove Pallets* processes or to any cost object. The real consumer of this process service is the cost center and the employees being reviewed. If forced to move in the traditional direction, an allocation is used to spread the *Process Performance Review* costs to these other processes.

This process-to-process allocation has the following limitations:

- A weakly correlated allocation is used instead of the direct causal relationship that exists between the process and consuming resource center.
- The impacts of the process allocations are not visible within the receiver cost centers, thus they are not included in the resource driver rates. This

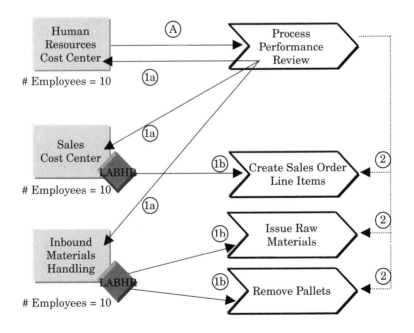

Possible SAP Approach

(1a) Process → Cost Center

(1b) Cost Center → Process

Traditional ABC Approach

(2) Process → Process

Exhibit 5.5   Cost Center-to-Process-to-Cost Center Allocation

omission makes product/service costing less accurate and the information used for outsourcing decisions incomplete. Also, cutting processes without reducing resources results in zero cost savings. Therefore, all costs impacting the function need to be considered in the outsourcing decision.

- When volumes change in a process-to-process model, the impact is not transparent throughout the environment, and impacts on the cost center resources are lost (i.e., Activity-Based Budgeting cannot be fully supported).
- The process-to-process approach uses the relationship to reflect interaction levels within the value chain at the time that they are defined. If these relationships change, the mapping has to be redone—that is, the model has to be updated. Using resources and quantities, the relationships, once established, will be updated dynamically based on defined unit standards.

In summary, the ability to systematically support a recursive cost flow from cost center, to process, to cost center for driver rate calculation increases the accuracy and information available. The dynamics of the cost model can also be further enhanced when relationships are expressed in quantities as opposed to values.

Fixed and Proportional Values and Quantities   Adding a level of complexity, another impact on the driver rate calculation is the view of fixed and proportional costs and quantity consumption. Many ABC systems contain a view of fixed and proportional values either through tags/attributes or through the creation of two separate accounts to represent this split, for example, *Electricity-Fixed* and *Electricity-Variable*. However, within SAP, the technical aspects of the cost element, representative of a G/L account and/or internal account for cost assignments, allows for both the fixed and proportional nature of the costs to be accommodated in a single entity. Additionally, SAP supports functionality to accommodate the simultaneous consumption of fixed and variable quantities. Usually, ABC systems require the quantity consumption to be identified as one or the other; they cannot easily support instances where both are required. As an example, in the automotive industry, melting the aluminum ingots requires a furnace. Since it takes too long to heat to the required degrees to support production, the furnace is kept at a constant temperature regardless of production output and therefore has a fixed consumption of kilowatt-hours. The furnace also has a variable quantity consumption of kilowatt-hours based on production output when more aluminum has to be heated to above melting point. Within SAP the KWH has a fixed and a variable quantity consumption. Other systems often require the same measure to be broken out so it can be identified as fixed or variable (i.e., KWH-Fixed and KWH-VAR). The following text provides examples of the impacts of fixed and proportional values and fixed and proportional quantity consumptions on the calculated driver rates and analysis.

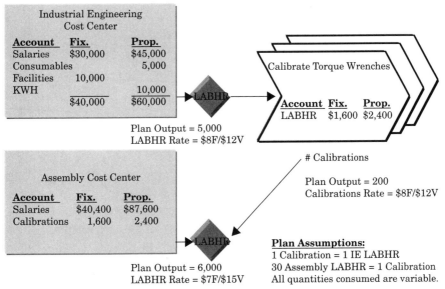

Exhibit 5.6 Fixed/Proportional Value Impacts on Driver Rates

The first example focuses on the *fixed/proportional values* impacts. The managers of cost centers can plan one account for *Salaries* with a fixed value covering the salaried employees and with a proportional value that represents the hourly staff. Planning the fixed and proportional amount supports the calculation of a dual-component driver rate, containing a component for fixed and another for proportional. Exhibit 5.6 illustrates the impact of fixed/proportional costs on the driver rate.

The *Industrial Engineering* (IE) cost center supports several processes, one of which is the *Calibrate Torque Wrenches* process. The calibrations are performed to support the *Assembly* cost center. During the price calculation, these separate fields are taken into account and used to determine a dual-component rate representing the fixed and proportional components of the driver rates. The *IE LABHR* is calculated and when consumed by the process, it consumes the fixed and proportional costs. These costs are then reflected in the process driver rate, and so on throughout the model. Planning values without the fixed/proportional view provides the *IE LABHR* rate of $20/hr, limiting the information provided and therefore analysis capabilities.

Many organizations take the view that all process costs are variable, which this principle contradicts. The variability of cost always depends on the definition of time frames and the relevant range being considered. However, in reality, since processes consume resources that may have fixed and proportional components of costs, there can be a fixed and a proportional nature to process costs that

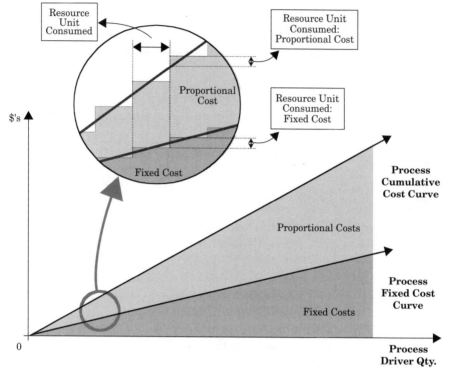

Exhibit 5.7   Relationship of Process Quantity to Process Costs

cannot be ignored or implied to be purely variable. Exhibit 5.7 illustrates the impact of the nature of resource costs on process costs.[1]

This exhibit represents the impacts on the nature of the process cost as the process quantity increases. For each process quantity consumed, there is an equivalent consumption of a resource driver quantity. The resource driver quantity has a fixed and proportional component to its rate. Therefore, the process inherits the nature of the resource costs, and when the process rate is calculated, it has a fixed and proportional component as well. Note that in Exhibit 5.6, the process driver rate has the same fixed/proportional component structure as the resource driver rate. This is because the process inherits its nature of cost from the resource driver. Since one resource driver feeds this process, the fixed/proportional ratios are exactly the same. If the process consumes multiple resource drivers, then the nature of the process costs will be a blend of the various resource drivers' fixed and proportional ratios. When the process is consumed by the receiver object (the *Assembly* cost center in this example), its fixed and proportional driver rate then impacts the *Assembly LABHR* driver rate components and eventually resides on the product, service, customer, and so forth.

The next example focuses on the impact to driver rates from *Fixed/Proportional quantities.* The example in Exhibit 5.6 illustrates the importance of having fixed and proportional information. The resources and process driver rates are calculated with a fixed and proportional component to the rate. This view on the rate is necessary in order to make accurate outsourcing decisions. Therefore, the split of the value flows is very important for organizations that consider outsourcing or benchmarking against external metrics. Yet, to be most accurate, the nature of the quantities being consumed should also be planned in a fixed and proportional amount. As mentioned previously, the ability to plan fixed and proportional quantities simultaneously is another aspect of the SAP functionality that sets it apart from most ABC systems. Exhibit 5.8 illustrates the impact of having fixed and variable consuming quantities for the calculated driver rates and cost flows.

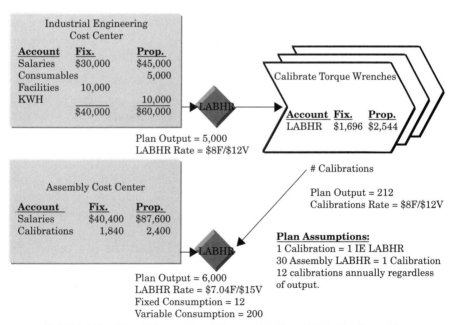

Exhibit 5.8   Fixed/Proportional Costs with Fixed/Variable Quantities

Take the previous example and add in the concept of fixed and variable quantities. Assume that regardless of *Assembly* operations output, 12 *Calibrations* are needed due to a routine schedule performed every month. The following equation is applied to determine the fixed and proportional *Calibrate Torque Wrenches* process costs to be attributed to the *Assembly* cost center:

$$(FixQty*FixRate) + (FixQty*PropRate) + (VarQty*FixRate) + (VarQty*PropRate)$$

(12*$8)Fixed	+	(12*$12)Fixed	+	(200*$8)Fixed	+	(200*$12)Prop
$96 Fixed	+	$144 Fixed	+	$1,600 Fixed	+	$2,400 Prop

The result is the $1,840 in fixed and $2,400 in proportional *Calibrate Torque Wrenches* process costs on the *Assembly* cost center.

As costs flow through the model, they become more fixed in nature, not proportional. The driver rate results in an increase of only $0.04 for the fixed tier of the rate. In this illustration, the amount may be negligible. However, it can change a product or service from being profitable to being unprofitable. The break-even point is also affected by this change, as are any outsourcing decisions being made. The impact of using fixed and proportional quantities increases based on depreciation and the level of technology invested, the latter being a primary determinant of the fixed and proportional ratios of an enterprises costs.

Driver Rate Options   In addition to the two conceptual decisions just addressed, step-down versus recursive and fixed/proportion reflections of costs, there are several other decisions that impact the driver rate calculation in SAP. These decisions answer the following four questions:

1. What type of costing system should be used?
2. Which quantity will be used to determine the driver rate?
3. For what time period will the rate be applicable?
4. How should the component costs of the driver rate be viewed?

One of the first decisions to be made when implementing the SAP CO module is whether the costing engine will be set up as a standard costing or an actual costing system. In a standard costing system, the standard driver rate is determined by the price calculation transaction. The price calculation gathers the planned values determined by all the planned relationships between the cost centers and processes. The price calculation then divides these amounts by the planned output quantities. The standard rate is used to provide detailed analysis information and to calculate variances. Using standard rates provides the ability to determine efficiencies and utilizations. When used with the target functionality, the standard rate determines what the costs should be, given the actual output levels. Moreover, it also provides information on areas for improvement and variance details to help determine whether the variance is due to spending and/or productivity fluctuations. For the purpose of valuating transactions, each posting of a quantity, for actypes (resource drivers) or the processes, automatically utilizes the standard rate.

Although a standard costing system is usually preferred, many companies and certain countries require an actual costing system. In the actual costing system, the driver rates are determined by running the actual price calculation transaction at period end. The actual costs incurred on cost centers and processes are then divided by the actual output quantities posted during the period. The actual driver rate does not provide insight into the variances causing the rate fluctuations. These causes can be due to spending, volume, efficiency, and price variances. Therefore, the actual driver rate can be a misleading indicator for operational improvement.

There are two methods for valuating with actual rates within SAP. The first is to use the standard driver rate during the period to valuate the transactional postings. At period end, an actual rate is calculated and adjustment postings are made. This method of valuation provides some information for analytical purposes since it uses the standard rate in the interim. The other valuation method is to have only the actual quantities posted during the period with no value and then at period end, once the actual price calculation is run, the actual values are posted instead of an adjustment from standard. Exhibit 5.9 provides a summary comparison.

The second question to ask is: Which quantity will be used to determine the driver rate? In any output plan, when expressed in terms of quantities, there are always two components of output in SAP: (1) planned output field and (2) capacity field. The planned output is the quantity of the driver the manager of the cost center or process intends to provide, normally practical capacity. The capacity is the total output quantity the driver can provide, potentially theoretical capacity. For example, cost center *Utilities* has a resource driver of megawatt-hours (MWHs). The *Utilities* cost center represents a subelectrical plant on the factory

Type	Formula	Use	Valuation
Standard	Planned value divided by planned quantity	Detailed analysis, used for target costing, helps to identify causes of variance	Immediate
Actual	Actual value divided by actual quantity	Legal requirements, or for industries where standards are volatile, e.g., high-tech industry	Period end

Exhibit 5.9   Type of Costing System Comparison

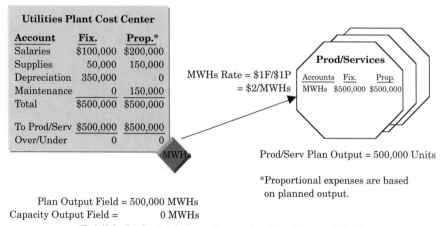

Exhibit 5.10   Unit Rate Determined by Planned Field

site. It has the capacity to produce 1 million MWHs; however, given the planned production output, only 500,000 MWHs are planned to be provided.

With all quantity permutations considered, the driver rate may be established in a number of ways. The first is to use the planned field, assuming organizationally that plan and capacity are viewed as one in the same. The second option is to use the capacity field, recognizing that capacity and supply are not conceptually the same. The final option ignores both quantity amounts and allows the driver rate to be established manually. This calculation determinant is defined in the driver's master data record.

The planned field does not necessarily need to reflect just the planned output for the year. The capacity output of the driver can be entered here as well or any quantity, regardless of logic. The purpose of the planned field selection is to indicate to the driver calculation that the fixed and proportional components of the driver rate should be determined by the output quantity entered into this field. Exhibit 5.10 illustrates an example of the planned field and the impact on the driver rate.

This example is only for planned costs. The fixed *Salaries, Supplies,* and *Depreciation* costs are based on the utility plant size that is driven by the capacity output, that is, 1 million MWHs. Since the planned field uses the same output quantity for calculating both the fixed and proportional portions of the driver rate, the driver rate is burdened with all capacity costs. This results in the products/services being burdened with all of the *Utilities* costs as they consume the resource driver, including the planned excess/idle capacity. Therefore, the product/service costs is overburdened with costs, potentially leading to erroneous product/service costing information or product/service mix decisions. Additionally, the excess/idle

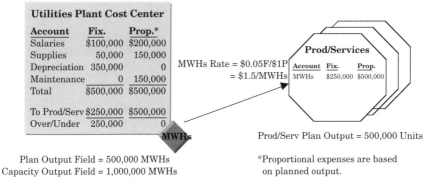

Exhibit 5.11   Unit Rate Determined by Capacity Field

capacity is not transparent on the sender cost center. Using the planned output as the denominator for determining the rates is a business decision usually chosen by organizations performing full-absorption costing.

If the driver is selected to be calculated based on the capacity field, then both the capacity and planned fields need to be entered. The planned output is entered in the planned field and the capacity in the capacity field. The capacity field selection indicates to the price calculation transaction to calculate the fixed component of the driver rate based on the capacity field quantity and the proportion component from the planned field. Exhibit 5.11 illustrates the difference in the driver rate and information provided.

Using both the planned and capacity output quantity fields results in the fixed portion of the resource driver rate being reduced by half. The impacts of this change are:

- The products/services consume the appropriate amount of *Utilities* costs that they drive, which supports a more realistic reflection of product/service costs and avoids poor product/service mix decisions.
- The resulting $250,000 of unused capacity temporarily remains on the cost center and is therefore visible.
- The excess/idle capacity is moved to the appropriate level on the P/L for responsibility accounting and capacity management.

The third potential option selected on the driver master record is manual and indicates to the price calculation to ignore this driver for calculation as its rate has been manually defined, that is, it is a political rate. Exhibit 5.12 illustrates a summary comparison of the field selections.

Planned field versus capacity field is also systematically available for use when determining process driver rates. However, the concept of capacity on a process is

Field Selection	Description	Costing Impacts
Planned Quantity	Fixed and proportional driver rates are determined from the planned field.	Overburdened rates (full absorption)
Capacity Quantity	Fixed component of driver rate is determined from the capacity field. Proportional component of driver rate is determined from planned field.	Excess/idle capacity visible by resource center
Manually Entered	Political rate is determined off-line and manually entered.	Usually not the most accurate; leads to over-underabsorption of the cost centers without rational insight to the cause

Exhibit 5.12   Field Selections for the Driver Quantity Comparison

philosophically flawed, whether supported by the system or not, as discussed in Chapter 1. The functionality is available simply because the capability was traditionally available for resource driver calculations and the system programs were merely extended to include process drivers. Therefore, for companies desiring to model capacity on a process, SAP does have the capabilities to support that model.

The third question to ask is: For what time period will the rate be applicable? When planning for cost center and processes, dollars and quantities can be planned by period or in total for the annual period. When planning in total, a distribution method is selected to spread the dollars and quantities across the periods. Therefore, in the end, there are values and quantities planned by period. These amounts can be exactly the same or vary period to period. Based on the organizational needs, the driver rate is selected as calculated by period, average, or cumulative.

If the driver rate is to be calculated by period, the price calculation derives the plan rate for each period by dividing period cost by the period output quantity. Doing this may result in a different driver rate for each period. The actual price calculation transaction is used to determine an actual driver rate by period. Exhibit 5.13 illustrates an example of planned driver rates by period, assuming 100% of the planned output quantities are consumed by some receiver.

With the period-based driver rate, certain countries that have holidays, say, for all of the month of August, would have a very high rate that month due to the fixed salary expenses being divided into lower levels of output. Therefore, a period-based driver rate might be misleading. To smooth out the effects on the driver rate

Row Name	Period 1	Period 2	Period 3	Period 4	Annual Total
Proportional Cost	$1,000	$2,000	$5,000	$2,000	$10,000
Fixed Costs	$10,000	$4,000	$6,000	$10,000	$30,000
Total Costs	$11,000	$6,000	$11,000	$12,000	$40,000
Quantities	1,000	2,000	5,000	2,000	10,000
Period Rate	$11.00 $1P/$10F	$3.00 $1P/$2F	$2.20 $1P/$1.20F	$6.00 $1P/$5F	
Net Cost Center over-/under-absorption	$0.00	$0.00	$0.00	$0.00	$0.00

Exhibit 5.13 Period-based Driver Rates (Plan) Example

Row Name	Period 1	Period 2	Period 3	Period 4	Annual Total
Proportional Cost	$1,000	$2,000	$5,000	$2,000	$10,000
Fixed Costs	$10,000	$4,000	$6,000	$10,000	$30,000
Total Costs	$11,000	$6,000	$11,000	$12,000	$40,000
Quantities	1,000	2,000	5,000	2,000	10,000
Average Rate	$4.00 $1P/$3F	$4.00 $1P/$3F	$4.00 $1P/$3F	$4.00 $1P/$3F	
Net Cost Center over-/under-absorption	$7,000	($2,000)	($9,000)	$4,000	$0.00

Exhibit 5.14 Average-based Driver Rates (Plan) Example

of fluctuating fixed expenses or volumes, the average driver rate can be used. The average driver rate is calculated by dividing the total costs for all periods by the total quantity for all periods. Doing this results in the same driver rate for each of the periods. The average driver rate can be used only for the calculation of planned driver rates. Exhibit 5.14 illustrates the impact of the average rate being used compared to the period driver rate. The results show that using an average rate may cause planned over-underabsorption as more of the fixed costs are pulled in the months with higher activity than lower activity. Usually this is not an issue, since fixed costs often are evenly spread across the periods, eliminating the net cost center over-underabsorption.

In order to remove cost fluctuations in the periods, the actual price calculation for cumulated rates accumulates the year-to-date actual total costs and the year-to-date actual total activities of the previous periods. So for March there is an average price for periods 1 to 3; in April there is an average from 1 to 4; finally, in December there is the average over the whole year that is the same average price. All relationships in all the periods are then reevaluated with this new driver rate. The result requires entries in the current period to be made to clear out previous months. When using the cumulative driver rate, it may appear that some receivers had postings in the current period when in reality they did not. These postings are merely clearing postings, adjusting the cumulative effect for activity in previous periods. This method is very useful especially for actual price calculation as it can be calculated during the year whereas the average price can be calculated only at the end of the year. To determine actual average prices, it is recommended that cumulative price be used. This makes sense for planning only if it is necessary to compare planned prices with actual ones and if great fluctuations are reflected in the different prices per period. Exhibit 5.15 illustrates an example of the cumulative driver rate calculation.

All the decisions to this point deal with how the driver rate will be calculated. In addition to decisions on rate calculation methods, an analytical breakdown of the rate calculation can also be provided, to answer the question: How should the

Row Name	Period 1	Period 2	Period 3	Period 4	Annual Total
Proportional Cost	$1,000	$2,000	$5,000	$2,000	$10,000
Fixed Costs	$10,000	$4,000	$6,000	$10,000	$30,000
Total Costs	$11,000	$6,000	$11,000	$12,000	$40,000
Quantities	1,000	2,000	5,000	2,000	10,000
Cumulative Rate	$11.00	$5.66	$3.50	$4.00	
Actual Posting	$11,000	$11,320	$17,500	$8,000	$47,820
Clearing Posting		($5,340)P1	($6,480)P2	$4,000P3	($7,820)
Total Posting	$11,000	$5,980	$11,020	$12,000	$40,000

Exhibit 5.15   Cumulative-based Driver Rates (Actual) Example

component costs of the driver rate be viewed? This breakdown of the rate into defined components of cost is referred to as the primary cost component split. The driver rate may be analyzed in any number of user-defined components or groupings of accounts, such as *Salaries, Depreciation,* and *Facilities.* The detail available through cost component splitting is based on the primary cost structure; therefore, primary costs must be planned in the same detail to support this analytical tool.

The primary cost component split supports transparency of the costs that impact the driver rates. This transparency to the components of the underlying resources may shed light on the formerly buried information delivered in most ABC solutions. Exhibit 5.16 illustrates the primary cost component split.

The breakdown of the *Maintenance* cost center *LABHR* is simply the total for each account grouping (this example does not have account groupings but accounts for simplicity) within the *Maintenance* cost center divided by the total costs for the cost center. To determine the primary cost component split for the *Perform Preventive Maintenance* process driver, number of events, the *Maintenance LABHR* split is combined with the additional process costs for consumable materials (oil, grease, rags, gloves, etc.) and supplies (order forms and tracking sheets, etc.) for $1,000 each. The additional process costs impact the percentage split for the originating accounts. As the *Perform Preventive Maintenance* process is combined with the cost center expenses, the primary cost component split for the *MACHR* is impacted.

There are two benefits of the primary cost component split. First, it maintains the integrity of the originating resource costs and allows for a transparent and visible impact of originating costs on the driver. This reference point allows management to investigate the whole picture in improvement efforts. The second benefit is the ability to use the primary cost component split in conjunction with other product cost component splits to see the originating accounts impacts on product/service costs, thereby providing the user with another perspective, the resource view. The product cost component splits are addressed in Chapter 7, in the section entitled "Different Cost Estimates Supported."

Variances

Variance calculations capabilities within SAP are very robust. There are three levels for which variances are calculated:

1. Overhead variance,
2. Product variance,
3. Profitability variance.

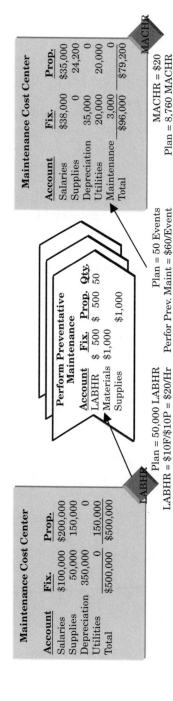

Maintenance Cost Center

Account	Fix.	Prop.
Salaries	$100,000	$200,000
Supplies	50,000	150,000
Depreciation	350,000	0
Utilities	0	150,000
Total	$500,000	$500,000

Maintenance LABHR

Account	$(000s)	%
Salaries	300	30%
Supplies	200	20%
Depreciation	350	35%
Utilities	150	15%
Services	0	0%
Total	$1,000	100%

Plan = 50,000 LABHR
LABHR = $10F/$10P = $20/Hr

Perform Preventative Maintenance

Account	Fix.	Prop.	Qty.
LABHR	$ 500	$ 500	50
Materials	$1,000		
Supplies		$1,000	

Plan = 50 Events
Perfor Prev. Maint = $60/Event

Perform Preventative Maintenance Event

Account	$	%
Salaries	300	10.00%
Supplies	1,200	40.00%
Depreciation	350	11.67%
Utilities	150	5.00%
Materials	1,000	33.33%
Total	$3,000	100.00%

Maintenance Cost Center

Account	Fix.	Prop.
Salaries	$38,000	$35,000
Supplies	0	24,200
Depreciation	35,000	0
Utilities	20,000	20,000
Maintenance	3,000	0
Total	$96,000	$79,200

MACHR = $20
Plan = 8,760 MACHR

Aluminum Ingot Melting MACHR

Account	$	%
Salaries	73,300	41.84%
Supplies	25,200	14.49%
Depreciation	35,350	20.18%
Utilities	40,150	22.92%
Materials	1,000	0.05%
Total	$175,200	100.00%

Exhibit 5.16 Primary Cost Component Split

The overhead variances are addressed in this chapter. The product variances are addressed in Chapter 7. The profitability variances are not addressed since they are not impacted by the integration of ABC throughout the SAP system.

Variance analysis can focus on three different causes:

1. Plan versus actual
2. Target versus actual
3. Over-underabsorption

Variance analysis focusing on plan is merely a comparison between a static plan and actual data results. Although this analysis of variances is perhaps the most common in application, it is also the most meaningless. Plan amounts compared to actual results offer little insight to the effectiveness or efficiencies the organization experienced during the period. The target versus actual basis is a comparison of actual costs with calculated target costs. Target cost is derived based on actual quantities produced against the anticipated standard rate, thus segregating the component of variance due to volume. Over-underabsorption is the difference between debits and credits on the cost centers or processes.

Further, variance can be categorized in two groupings, where variances are defined as:

1. Input-based variances
2. Output variances

This variance analysis can be expanded again with multiple variance categories that can be calculated. Exhibit 5.17 lists the groupings, the categories, and additional information.

The plan reconciliation, driver rate calculations, and variance functionality between the cost center accounting and activity-based costing submodules set the ability of SAP business applications to support Activity-Based Costing/Management ABC/M apart from other software. Comparing planned supply with planned demand helps to manage capacity for the upcoming year. All the driver rate options accommodate a spectrum from a simple rate (i.e., political rate) to a very advanced and extremely accurate unit driver rate to be calculated, depending on the organization's level of cost management complexity. Additionally, all the potential categorizations of variances provide detailed information in a real-time environment to make proactive changes.

INFORMATION FLOWS

Within SAP, there are many information flows between cost center accounting and Activity-Based Costing. These flows are expanded by SAP's ability to support the

Variance Group	Variance Category	Description	Example
Input	Input Price (IPV)	Caused by a difference between plan and actual prices of the materials, actypes, or processes. IPV = (Act. Price – Plan Price) × Act. Input Qty.	Process 1 plans to consume 100 Actype 1 @ $15, in actual 100 Actype 1 @ $20 Input Price Var. = $500
Input	Resource Usage (RUV)	Caused by using a different material, actype, or process than planned. RUV = Act. Cost – Target Costs – Input Price Var.	Process 2 consumes Actype B with rate of $20 versus planned Actype A with rate of $15 Resource Usage Var. = $5
Input	Input Quantity (IQV)	Caused by a different quantity of material, actype, or processes that were planned for. IQV = (Act. Input Qty. – Plan Input Qty.) × Plan Price	Process B plans to consume 1 Process A, actual used 2 Process A with a std. rate of @ $15/Process A instead of just 1 Process A. Input Qty. Var. = $15
Input	Remaining Input	Caused by choosing not to calculate any of the above variances or not recording the consumption quantities.	Any, or all, of the above examples can be included here. Remaining variance is more of a tree where it is the high level and the previous are lower-detail branches.
Output	Output Price (OPV)	Caused by standard price changing between planned and actually posted, e.g., manual update of a process rate. OPV = Act. Acty × (Plan Price – Actual Price)	Planned output of Process 3 is 100 Qty. @ $20. Rate changed to $10, 100 Process 3 are demanded. Output Price Var. = $1,000.
Output	Volume (VV)	Fixed costs are calculated within a rate based on planned output. Actual output varies and draws more or less fixed costs. VV = Fixed Plan Costs × (1 – Operating Rate)	Actype 1 plans to have a fixed consumption of 100 qty. of Process 1 @ $20F/$0P Rate. Planned Fixed Costs are $2,000 Actual Qty. = 120 $2,000*(1 – 120/100) = ($400) is volume variance
Output	Secondary Fixed Cost (SFCV)	Some secondary fixed costs are dependent on operating rate. SFCV = planned fixed costs – target fixed costs.	Process 1 has a planned variable consumption of Actype 2 of 100 qty. for its planned output of 100. Actual was 120, target qty. of Actype 2 consumption is therefore 120. Actype 2 has a rate of $10F/$10P. $1,000 – $1,200 = ($200) is secondary fixed cost variance.
Output	Quantity	Caused by a difference between the actual quantity consumed from the process and a manually entered quantity.	There is an assignment in place to determine the process consumption by cost object; however, the actual total

Exhibit 5.17 Multiple Variance Categories

| Output (cont'd) | Quantity (cont'd) | OQV = (Act. Qty. – Manually entered Qty.) × Actual Price | process output quantity (not by cost object) is captured as well. The Assignment determined 100 is quantity of the process allocated out, but the actual posting shows a quantity of 110 is consumed at $10/process = Output Qty. Var. of $100. |
| Output | Remaining | Output variance has been deactivated for calculation. | Any, or all, of the above output variance will then be located in remaining variance. |

Exhibit 5.17   *(continued)*

process flow back to the cost centers. There are five main methods for assigning resource costs to processes and vice versa:

1. Assessment and distribution cycles
2. Direct activity allocation
3. Indirect activity allocation cycle
4. Target = actual
5. Template allocation

These methods for cost transfers are described in detail with an example for each. At the end of this section, a summary chart compares the methods to one another. All examples are provided using a standard costing system. Refer back to the actual costing system description to see how to reevaluate the standard to an actual costing system.

Assessment and Distribution Cycles

Assessment and distribution cycles are the only method of allocation that supports the value-based approach. Since they are both value based and cover the same spectrum for an allocation basis, these two types of cycles are addressed together. Exhibit 5.18 illustrates the different allocation basis within the assessment and distribution cycles.

Many different rule combinations can be created within allocation cycles based on sender and receiver information. The few shown give an indication of the most common types of receiver rules in allocations supported by cycles. All of the costs on the sender do not need to be allocated. There are additional options allowing for partial allocation of the senders based on the sender rules.

Allocation Basis	Example: Sender	Example: Receiver Results
Fixed Portion	Corporate Financial Planning department contains $600,000 in expenses. The actual Strategic Business Unit (SBU) split is based on the fixed portion allocation basis. The portions are converted to a percentage.	SBU1 Portion = 0.2 $120,000 SBU2 Portion = 0.2 $120,000 SBU3 Portion = 0.6 $360,000
Fixed Dollar Amount	$600,000 of expenses for the Corporate Financial Planning department is allocated to the SBU planning cost centers based on a set dollar amount.	SBU1 Fixed $200,000 SBU2 Fixed $200,000 SBU3 Fixed $200,000
Fixed Percentage	$600,000 of the Corporate Financial Planning department is selected for allocation to the SBU planning cost centers based on a fixed percentage.	SBU1 % = 20 $120,000 SBU2 % = 20 $120,000 SBU3 % = 60 $360,000
Variable Dollar Amount	$600,000 in expenses for the Corporate Financial Planning department is selected for allocation based on the planned salaries for each SBU.	SBU1 Plan Salaries = $1M $125,000 SBU2 Plan Salaries = $1M $125,000 SBU3 Plan Salaries = $2M $300,000
Variable Quantity	$600,000 in expenses for the Corporate Financial Planning department is selected for allocation based on the number of employees for each SBU.	SBU1 #Employees = 1,000 $125,000 SBU2 #Employees = 1,000 $125,000 SBU3 #Employees = 2,000 $250,000

Exhibit 5.18   Sample Allocation Basis for Cycles

Assessment Cycles   An assessment is an allocation method that uses an aggregate account to move both primary (G/L accounts) and secondary cost elements (internal allocation accounts) between senders and receivers. In an assessment, the sender will have a credit for the assessment cost element and the receiver will have a debit for the same cost element. The receiver will not see the detailed accounts of what was allocated using the assessment cost element, such as *Salaries, Supplies,* and *Depreciation.*

Exhibit 5.19 depicts the *Market Research & Development* cost center making a 50% allocation to each of the *Research Market Patterns* and *Develop Service/Product Attribute* processes. The cost center contains both primary and secondary costs, and the allocation methodology can be applied to both planned and actual dollar values. The assessment cycle will split the costs to the two processes and post using a single assessment account, for example, *Allocated 99999.*

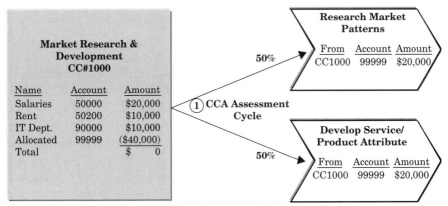

Exhibit 5.19   Assessment Cycle Results

The cost center has been relieved of all the costs and the processes have received their corresponding 50% allocation. The assessment account is a secondary cost element that is defined to provide detailed information about the sender, for example, Corporate Overhead, without providing details of the costs allocated. One assessment account can be used to reflect all allocations, which limits the visibility of an audit trail. Multiple assessment accounts are usually created to provide better visibility, for example, account 99999 for *Market Research* costs, 99998 for *Corporate Overhead* costs, and so on.

Distribution Cycles   A distribution is an allocation method that allocates cost in the original detailed account structure. It can be used only to allocate primary costs using the original account. Therefore, any secondary costs that the cost center contains cannot be allocated using the distribution cycle. Exhibit 5.20 illustrates the results of the distribution cycle for the same allocation portrayed in Exhibit 5.19.

Only the primary expenses have been allocated. The secondary expenses, account *90000 IT Department,* remain on the cost center. In terms of impact on processing, the distribution cycle requires more system effort due to the posting of several line items compared to a singular item in the assessment cycle. For instance, if the *Market Research & Development* cost center contained 300 cost elements, 600 total postings would be made after the distribution cycle is executed versus two postings for the assessment cycle. The larger number of postings generated by the distribution cycle impacts the time and resources required to run the cycle as well as the database size over time.

An assessment uses the aggregate account, and a distribution uses the detailed accounts in order to move expenses from a sender to a receiver based on

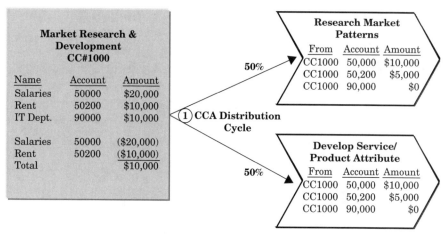

Exhibit 5.20   Distribution Cycle Results

a fixed portion, fixed dollar amount, percentage, and so on. The assessment and distribution cycles can use the cost center or a process as either the sender or the receiver. For example, the process *Perform Employee Review* can be allocated via either cycle type to all cost centers based on the number of employees reviewed. In addition, cycles can be created with more than one segment within them, allowing for multiple allocations to be created within one cycle, where each individual allocation is defined as a segment. Further, when the cycle segments generate a recursive loop, the system allows for the design of iterative relationships. For example, segment 1 allocates the *Facilities* department to all the cost centers including the *IT* department. Segment 2 allocates the *IT* department costs to all the cost centers including the *Facilities* cost center, generating a recursive allocation. Both the assessment and distribution cycles will iterate between the segments, calculating the recursive loop until a minimal decimal change has been achieved; in other words, a value-based recursive allocation is possible using SAP.

Within the assessment cycle the allocation structure functionality supports multiple secondary cost elements in one segment. Doing this provides an interesting combination of an assessment and distribution cycle supporting less data but more information than an assessment cycle using one assessment account and can potentially eliminate the need for distribution cycles. When using an assessment with the allocation structure, 300 detail accounts can be allocated with 15 secondary accounts, instead of one summary element.

Direct Activity Allocations

A direct activity allocation is the direct recording and posting of either an activity type (resource driver) or a process driver quantity. This method is a direct charging of the driver quantity to the receiver. When the posting is made, the sending cost center or process name, its driver name, quantity consumed by the receiver, and the receiver information are entered. Once the posting is saved, the value is immediately relieved from the cost center or process based on the quantity times the standard or political rate. Exhibit 5.21 illustrates an example of a direct activity allocation using a process as the sender.

In this example, the *Human Resources* cost center actually tracks the number of applications reviewed for positions logged by a cost center. Therefore, a direct *Review Employment Application* process can be posted. Additionally, the dockworkers in the *Shipping* cost center track their labor hours for preparing and delivering the shipments; however, they do not track *LABHRS* by customer. The *Shipping LABHRS* is directly posted to the *Deliver Shipment* process.

The direct activity allocation is very useful and integrated throughout SAP. It is used when backflushing the production orders during order confirmation to automatically relieve the cost centers of the resource-related production costs of the order, for example, labor hours, setup hours, machine hours, and so forth. The Cross Application Time Sheets (CATS) capability uses direct activity allocations to automatically post labor hours from time sheets. Additionally, the Business Application Program Interfaces (BAPIs) are set up to facilitate the automatic transfer of any data from external systems.

The direct activity allocation requires that the quantity be known and is real time. If the quantity is known and the posting is periodic in nature, not real time, or the quantity is not known but can be imputed, then an indirect activity allocation cycle can be used.

Indirect Activity Allocation Cycle

Structurally all SAP cycles have a similar design. The difference lies in what is allocated by the cycle. The assessment and distribution cycles allocate (post) dollar values, not quantities. In order to allocate quantities using the cycle-supported allocation basis, an indirect activity allocation (IAA) cycle is required. The IAA cycle supports several allocation methods. These include the cycle allocation basis described previously, such as fixed portion, fixed percentage, and so on. These methods are the ways the quantities can be traced out to the receivers (receiver

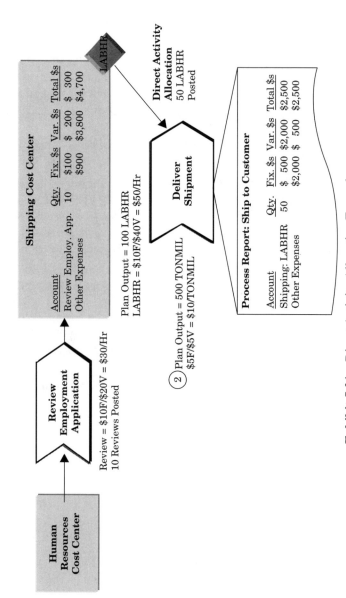

Exhibit 5.21 Direct Activity Allocation Example

148

rates). In addition, three methods exist for defining how much of the sending quantities will be allocated out:

1. Fixed quantity
2. Posted quantity
3. Inversely calculated

The fixed quantity method defines a fixed amount of a sender quantity to be allocated out to the receivers; for example, Cost Center 1 always posts out a quantity of 30 labor hours only due to an agreed internal service contract, regardless of the fact that 40 labor hours were actually worked. These 30 labor hours may be traced out using a percentage split of 50% to Process 1 and Process 2, or a fixed quantity can be assigned to each receiving process; however, only 30 Labor Hours will be allocated.

The posted quantity takes the quantities posted for the period; for example, instead of the fixed quantity used previously, the allocation takes the whole 40 labor hours posted and then allocates them to the receivers based on a percentage, such as splitting it 50% to Process 1 and Process 2, each receiving 20 labor hours.

The greatest benefit of the IAA cycle is its ability to inversely determine a sender quantity based on receiver information. Exhibit 5.22 illustrates this IAA functionality.

As shown on the Exhibit, there are 3 main steps.

Step 1: Using surveys or interviews of employees to determine the percentage of time an employee spends performing an activity, a standard relationship between an employee labor hour and the process can be defined. This is accomplished during the planning phase of the indirect activity allocation. During actuals, this same relationship is used to determine how much of the resource driver is allocated to the processes. Doing this eliminates the need to have employees continually maintain information sheets on the processes they perform and how much time they spend on each. This standard relationship creates a fairly accurate approximation and eliminates the need for capturing the information at the resource level. Only the number of times the processes are performed needs to be tracked.

Step 2: The indirect activity allocation cycle is run for plan. The cycle determines the planned output quantity for the resource drivers, *LABHR* and *MGHR*, using the planned output driver quantities of the process and the relationships defined.

Step 3: The price calculation is run to determine the driver rates. The resource driver rates are calculated and the dollar values are posted to the process. Then the process driver rate is determined. The rate also can be set manually instead of calculated.

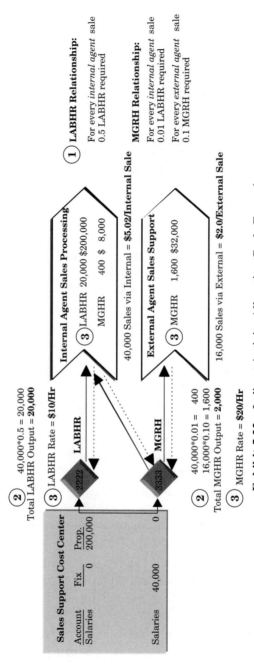

Exhibit 5.22   Indirect Activity Allocation Cycle Example

① **LABHR Relationship:**

For every *internal agent* sale 0.5 LABHR required

MGRH Relationship:

For every *internal agent* sale 0.01 LABHR required

For every *external agent* sale 0.1 MGRH required

Internal Agent Sales Processing

③ LABHR   20,000 $200,000
   MGHR   400 $ 8,000

40,000 Sales via Internal = **$5.02/Internal Sale**

External Agent Sales Support

③ MGHR   1,600 $32,000

16,000 Sales via External = **$2.0/External Sale**

② 40,000*0.5 = 20,000
Total LABHR Output = **20,000**

③ LABHR Rate = **$10/Hr**

LABHR

2222

MGRH

3333

② 40,000*0.01 = 400
   16,000*0.10 = 1,600
Total MGHR Output = **2,000**

③ MGHR Rate = **$20/Hr**

Sales Support Cost Center

Account	Fix	Prop.
Salaries	0	200,000
Salaries	40,000	0

150

When the IAA cycle is run for actuals, the standard rate for the drivers already exists and the price calculation does not need to be run, unless actual rates are being used. It is important to remember that although the example only depicts the process quantity determining the resource driver quantity, the resource driver and/or other process drivers can be used to impute a process driver output. For example, the resource driver *Number of Machine Hours* (*MACHRs*) for a production cost center can be used to impute the process driver quantity for the *Perform Emergency Maintenance* process. The illustrated example is not all-encompassing of the functionality of the IAA cycle, and the quantities do not need to be imputed if they are known. However, the greatest benefit of the indirect activity allocation cycle is the ability to impute the resource or process driver quantity for allocation use when capturing the actual quantity is not possible or cost justifiable.

Target = Actual

The target = actual functionality is similar to the indirect activity allocation cycle. This transaction also imputes the output quantity of one driver based on another and posts quantities with their corresponding values. However, unlike the IAA cycle, where the relationship is defined in the cycle, the target = actual relationship is established during planning. Therefore, the planned output is known; however, the actual quantities are imputed instead of captured. The planned relationship serves as the basis for calculating actuals when the target = actual transaction is executed. Exhibit 5.23 illustrates the target = actual functionality for an example in Period 3.

The *Customer Support* cost center provides *LABHR* resources for the *Handle Inquiries* and *Resolve Customer Complaints* processes. Exhibit 5.23 contains 4 steps.

Step 1: As before with the IAA cycle, a relationship needs to be established. This relationship is automatically created when planning is performed instead of being explicitly written as in the IAA cycle. Therefore, for target = actual, Step 1 is created based on the planned consumption performed by the managers in Step 2.

Step 2: Managers plan how much output of other cost centers or processes is needed in order for them to supply their output. For example, the process managers for the two processes will plan the amount of *Customer Support LABHR* needed for the next year, evenly distributed across the months, for the planned process driver output.

Step 3: The price calculation is run and the planned resource costs are posted to the processes by period. The price calculation takes into account all planned recursive allocations.

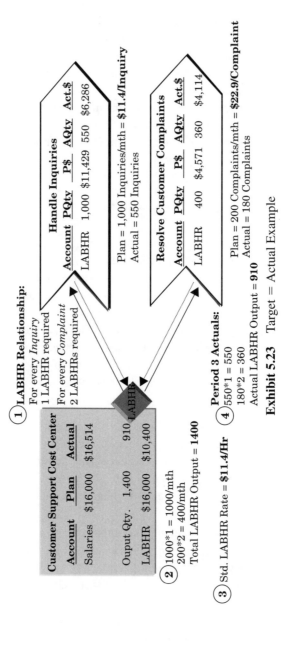

152

① LABHR Relationship:

For every *Inquiry*
1 LABHR required
For every *Complaint*
2 LABHRs required

Handle Inquiries

Account	PQty	P$	AQty	Act.$
LABHR	1,000	$11,429	550	$6,286

Plan = 1,000 Inquiries/mth = **$11.4/Inquiry**
Actual = 550 Inquiries

Resolve Customer Complaints

Account	PQty	P$	AQty	Act.$
LABHR	400	$4,571	360	$4,114

Plan = 200 Complaints/mth = **$22.9/Complaint**
Actual = 180 Complaints

LABHR

Customer Support Cost Center

Account	Plan	Actual
Salaries	$16,000	$16,514
Ouput Qty.	1,400	910
LABHR	$16,000	$10,400

② 1000*1 = 1000/mth
200*2 = 400/mth
Total LABHR Output = **1400**

③ Std. LABHR Rate = **$11.4/Hr**

④ Period 3 Actuals:
550*1 = 550
180*2 = 360
Actual LABHR Output = **910**

Exhibit 5.23 Target = Actual Example

Step 4: The actual process driver quantities for Period 3 are captured; 550 *Inquiries* and 180 *Complaints*. These process driver quantities are then used when the target = actual transaction is run to impute the actual *Customer Support LABHR* consumed, 910 *LABHRs*.

The target = actual functionality calculates the target input quantities based on the receiver's output quantities. This relationship is not explicitly written, as in the indirect activity allocation, but is determined based on the planned requirements. There are two benefits of using the target = actual instead of indirect activity allocation.

1. Cost centers or process managers planning how much input quantities they need of other cost center or processes is easier than defining a cycle.
2. The target = actual functionality supports recursive quantity consumption flows. These recursive flows are not taken into consideration if designed in separate indirect activity allocation cycles.

Companies use target = actual even though they still track the actual quantity of the resource driver. The resource driver actual quantity is tracked in aggregate, but not by process; for example, number of *Customer Service LABHRS* is tracked but not necessarily the hours by process/activity. This information indicates the causes of variances; the imputed capabilities are used merely to spread the actual resource driver quantity among the processes.

Template Allocation

The template method of cost assignment was first introduced in Chapter 4. To briefly reiterate, the template is a tool that facilitates simple to complex assignments of costs between cost objects, for example, cost centers, processes, market segments, production orders, and so forth, using Boolean ("IF-THEN") logic. The template is used to establish a quantity-based relationship between these types of cost objects for allocations to be made based on operational metrics in a timely manner. The greatest benefit of the template is its ability to dynamically determine which resources or processes are to be consumed by each receiver.

Two aspects are important in the structure of the template:

1. Designing templates
2. The assignment of the template to the receiving object

The assignment of the templates differs depending on the receiving object. Templates used for cost centers and processes are defined on the master record;

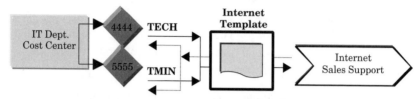

Exhibit 5.24   Cost Center to Process Template Example

for example, the template used to assign resource costs to the *Internet Sales Support* process is assigned to the process master record. In the following chapters, each template example explains how it is assigned to the receiver. For this example, the template named *Internet* (Exhibit 5.24) is used to assign *IT* department costs to the *Internet Sales Support* process using technician labor hours, *TECH,* and telephone minutes, *TMIN,* as the drivers.

The template structure is generally similar regardless of the sender and receiver objects. Two key pieces of information define the template:

1. Its name
2. The environment

The environment determines what information is available from SAP and/or external systems for use in template calculations. The environment acts as a filter in order to make the amount of information to search through manageable. For example, if a company uses templates to assign resource costs to the process, there is no need to search through the hundreds of pieces of information provided for assigning processes to production cost objects. Environments exist to support each of the major integration points of a process with other receivers, such as environments for assignments between cost centers to processes, processes to internal orders, processes to different production objects, processes to market segments, and so on. The following chapters provide examples of templates focusing on these specific integration points with ABC.

Two standard environments are used to assign resource cost to processes:

1. Business process planning (BPP)
2. Structured business process (SBP)

The business process planning template supports the assignment of cost elements to the process, such as *Salaries, Supplies,* and *Consulting fees.* The structured business process environment is used to assign resource drivers and/or other processes to a receiver process. For the example in Exhibit 5.24, the *Internet* template uses the structured business process environment to assign the *TECH* and *TMIN* drivers to the *Internet Sales Support* process. The structured

Environment   **SBP**   Structure Business Process

Template   **Internet**   Example CCA-ABC Template

Type	Name	Object	Activation	Plan Var. Qty.	Plan Fix Qty.	Actual Var. Qty.	Actual Fix Qty.	Un.
Cost Center/ AcType	IT Dept./ Tech Hour	IT/TECH	ACTIVE	FORMULA		FORMULA		EA
Cost Center/ AcType	IT Dept./ Tech Hour	IT/TECH	METHOD		10		10	EA
Cost Center/ AcType	IT Dept./ TMIN	IT/TMIN	ACTIVE	FORMULA		FORMULA		EA

Exhibit 5.25   Detailed CCA-ABC Template Example

business process template is similar to a routing for a process. It defines the quantities consumed in order to execute the process.

Once the template name and environment are entered, the structure of the template is defined. (See Exhibit 5.25.) The structure of the template includes: type, name (different from the template name), object, quantity columns, and activation indicators. The "Type" field determines the definition of the row within the template. Selection choices are:

- Business process
- Cost center/activity type
- Subtemplate (including another template)
- Calculation row (business processes)
- Calculation row (cost centers/activity types)
- Comment

The type defines what is to be consumed by the receiver, the *Internet Sales Support* process.

Depending on the type selected, the "Object" will display the appropriate match-code. For this example, the Cost Center/Actype is selected. Therefore, when selecting the object to be used, the list of Cost Center/Actype combinations is made available. The "Un." field is for the Unit of Measure and is automatically defaulted from the object master data record, as is the "Name" field.

The "Activation" field can be active, inactive, or have a defined method. In this example, the plan and actual variable quantities for *IT Tech* and *TMIN* have been chosen as active, indicating they will always be posted, as opposed to inactive, which prevents postings. The third option, a method, uses Boolean logic to determine the appropriate time for posting the process. For example, the *IT Tech* "Plan" "Actual Fixed Quantity" fields use a method to indicate "IF *#Internet Sales Support* processes are > 1000, THEN fixed quantity posted = 10." This formula is used to accommodate the additional *IT TECH* hours required for maintenance that takes place once a certain volume has been achieved in a period.

A number is directly entered into the quantity fields or a formula is defined using a function. Functions are the individual pieces of information that the environment contains. They are predefined systematic places where information can be gathered as a parameter for the formula. The function hierarchy and sample functions provided in the structure business process environment are:

- Process—ProcessPlanQuantity
- General Data—LastFiscalYear or ActivityTypeActualQty
- Mathematical—Trunc (Truncate)

There are hundreds of standard functions available, making the creation of the template fast and easy. For this example, a function is used in the formulas to calculate the required resources. In order to determine the *IT/TECH* variable quantity consumed for plan, the function PlanProcessQty is used in the formula PlanProcessQty*0.1. For the Actual Var. Qty. field, the formula uses the function ActualProcessQty multiplied by 0.1. The system will determine the planned process driver quantity and then determine the number of *IT Tech* hours required, such as 1000 planned *Support Internet Sales* process output requires 100 *IT Tech* hours. The quantities and activations defined in the template build the entire quantity relationship used by the template.

When creating the template, users need only select the functions they desire and select operands as they apply. The template builds all the necessary requirements and formulas in the background. Users need only to become familiar with the transaction; they do not need to understand ABAP code in order to have access to a quick definition of complex and very advanced assignments of processes. The template is by far the most advanced form of assignment methodologies available today.

Exhibit 5.26 illustrates a pictorial recap of the allocation methods addressed in this section.

Exhibit 5.27 summarizes the information flows that can be used with a process as either a sender or a receiver.

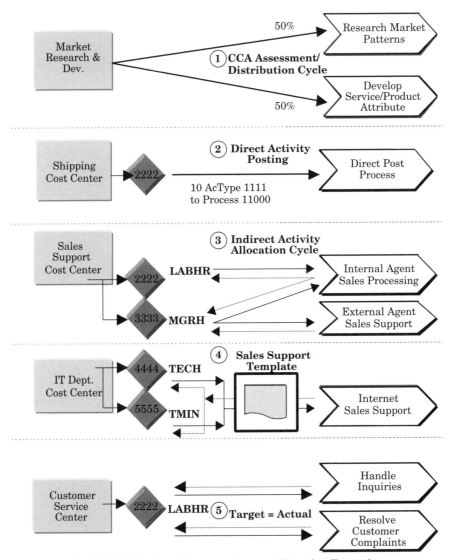

Exhibit 5.26 Cost Center to Process Allocation Examples

SAMPLE KEY BUSINESS DECISIONS

The combination of responsibility accounting and ABC information can support hundreds of key business decisions. A select few have been grouped together and are listed in Exhibit 5.28 to show key advantages of this integration.

Information Flow	Comments	Assignment Basis	Type of Posting	Timing	Usability	Handle Complexity
Assessment Cycle	Allocations from a cost center to a process, or from a process to a cost center using an assessment cost element.	Fixed %, fixed portions, fixed amount, variable tracing based on value field dollars or quantities.	Value based	Period end	Moderate	Limited
Distribution Cycle	Allocations from a cost center to a process, or from a process to a cost center using the detailed accounts, but no secondary cost elements.	Fixed %, fixed portions, fixed amount, variable tracing based on value field dollars or quantities.	Value based	Period end	Moderate	Limited
Direct Activity Allocation	Direct process charge to the cost centers or of a cost center/actype to a process.	Actual quantity.	Quantity with value	Real time	Easy	None
Indirect Activity Allocation	Inverse calculated supports imputing quantities and reduces the need to capture actuals for a driver quantity. Also supports quantity splitting.	Fixed %, fixed portion, fixed quantities, variable tracing based on value field dollars or quantities.	Quantity with value	Period end	Moderate	Limited
Target = Actual	Actual driver quantity imputed from planned relationship.	Imputed quantity.	Quantity with value	Period end	Easy	Limited
Templates	Dynamic determination of the process driver consumed by a cost center process. Provides a process routing.	Simple to complex formulas and "IF-THEN" rules (methods).	Quantity with value	Within period*	Advanced	High level easily supported

*Can be daily, weekly, periodically, quarterly, annually, etc.

Exhibit 5.27   Information Flows between CCA-ABC and Vice Versa

Sample Key Business Decisions	Value based	Quantity based
What are the true resource and process driver rates? What root costs comprise the rate?	√	√
Which departments or processes should be outsourced?	--	√
What are the process costs and how do they impact the cost center?	√	√
What is the bill of resources for the process?	--	√
Which resources should be used and where should they be deployed?	--	√
Given the product mix and volumes produced, what should the overhead expenses be? How can volume variance be isolated?	--	√

-- Indicates the inability to use this method or it is not suggested for use.
√ Indicates that the method supports the analysis required to address the business decision.

Exhibit 5.28   Responsibility Accounting & ABC Sample Business Decisions

Accurate Driver Rate Calculations/Primary Cost Component Splits

The driver rate calculations for both the resource drivers and the process drivers can be very accurate. Virtually any conceptual design desired is supported, from simplistic—for example, pure spreading of overhead costs—to very complex and advanced. Therefore, the driver rates can be very inaccurate or approach precision depending on the business need and the design modeled. On the simplistic side, there is the pure value-based approach, that is, cost distribution method, focusing on moving dollars in a sometimes noncausal manner to support basic analysis of overhead costs. An advanced approach, the quantity-based approach, relies on the defined quantity relationships to determine fully burdened unit driver rates. This approach increases the accuracy of cost transfers within the organization and those overheads are transferred further, eventually residing on the appropriate final cost object. This accuracy eventually impacts final reporting information, such as the product, regional, customer, SBU, and corporate P/Ls.

The unit driver rates are the microstandards for an actype or process used to make these more accurate costs transfers. The rates then support authorized expenses and reporting and the calculation of variances. Additionally, the driver rate can provide information on the component breakdown of its own costs by the fixed and proportional structure of the rate and via the primary cost component split, which provides indications for where to begin reducing costs.

Outsourcing Decisions

Once the more accurate driver rates are available, including the fixed/proportional components, cost centers and processes can be benchmarked to outside providers to drive efficiencies in those areas. Only after fully burdened rates are developed is there a tool to compare to the external competition.

Companies create their own internal support organization based on the assumption that there is enough volume to produce a cost savings by providing the service internally rather than externally. The aim is to provide the service cheaper than can be acquired externally without a decline in the quality of service or negatively impacting the core competencies of the organization. In order to determine how well these internal support units are performing and/or whether they are no longer cost justifiable, the fixed cost impacts need to be evaluated. There are two fixed cost impacts: (1) direct and (2) indirect. The direct fixed costs are easily recognizable. Most of these costs are usually depreciation related and already identified. The secondary fixed cost impacts are visible only if the quantity-based approach is used with calculated unit driver rates for the support cost centers and processes. If this information is not available, impacts on upstream excess/idle capacity generated by the outsourcing cannot be gathered. When a process or cost center is outsourced, many upstream fixed costs still remain, such as a manager, even though there may be fewer people to manage.

Business Process Analysis

Many different types of process analysis can be performed. Evaluating the process costs and their impacts on the cost centers consuming those processes is usually the first point of focus. For process costs analysis, the focus is on the breakdown of the inputs and the outputs of processes and how the processes roll up to provide the overall view of the macro-value chain. Inputs are defined as the allocations of resources to processes. The allocations can be established via the value-based or the quantity-based approach. The accuracy of input assignments is driven by the allocation method used. These input cost assignments also drive the accuracy with which the nature of the process costs is determined, that is, fixed/proportional. The mix of the fixed/proportional components of the resource costs determines the nature of the process costs. As with the input assignments, the output assignment accuracy is dependent on the allocation method. Focusing on the inputs and outputs provides answers to questions such as: What drives the process costs? Which resources does a process require? Which resources are most expensive? What are the impacts of fixed costs? Which cost objects drive the process costs?

In order to reengineer, first there must be established an understanding of process costs, what drives these costs, what consumes the processes, and so forth. Yet to completely support process reengineering, whether it is little *r* or big *R*, the quantity-based approach must be used, focusing on the bill of resources or routing for a process (i.e., the structured business process template) and all the quantity relationship dynamics. Otherwise, process-reengineering changes may optimize for the subcomponent while negatively impacting the entire organizational design. Other miscellaneous types of process analysis can be supported via user-defined fields on the process as well as tags, for attribute information such as value added and batch oriented. Additionally, the process information can be used for external benchmarking. Similarly, if some processes are designed across organizational structures, such as distribution center 01 and 02, then benchmarking of processes can be supported internally as well, leading to indications of potential areas for standardization of process execution for optimization.

Capacity Management

To determine which resources should be deployed where, resource consumption must be focused on. Many objects within an organization are directly consuming these resources (i.e., products, customers, or other internal units) and processes. Capacity resides at the resource level, not the process level. If a process remains idle in a period, does the organization have 100% underutilization for the resources that feed that process, for example, labor hours? Not likely; the resources supporting the process are most likely consumed by multiple other processes and potentially some process-oriented events (which stand-alone ABC systems usually do not address). As the actual consumption of processes changes, the resource demands are continually shifting. Cost center accounting focuses on the identification of resources, the collection of resources into cost centers, and the management of the capacity for each resource within a cost center. Activity-Based Costing focuses on taking some of those resource capacities and applying them to perform activities. The marriage of the two philosophies of Resource Consumption Accounting and ABC provides the best-practice solution for analysis and control.

Variance Capabilities

Target costing information, which is provided only by a standard costing system, answers the questions of what overhead expenses should be given the actual quantities or how can volume variance be isolated. By now most organizations have caught on to the fact that the actual driver rate provides misleading or incomplete information for the purpose of analysis. A real-time informational system merely provides those actual rates more often; they are no more accurate or informative than before. A standard-costing system provides better information for analysis and is the only type of system that can answer these questions.

Most current literature derides standard cost, mainly because of terminology problems or, more accurately, a bad perception of standard costs than anything else. The old standard costing systems that used unrelated percentage overhead allocations or noncausal drivers should be avoided. Yet standard costing systems have always been, and still are, built on the approach of having a microstandard for production-related areas. The overhead area was the one that was grossly lacking. Applying the theory of microstandards using quantity relationships to the overhead areas as well as to the production areas is what generates the accuracy of the quantity structure method. The standard costing system of SAP can be extremely accurate depending on the level of detail the microstandards are built to accommodate. When microstandards are applied to ABC, they provide an Activity-Based Costing/Management system that can give real-time information for day-to-day decision making.

Obviously that standard costing system of the past has made a giant leap, at least if using SAP. With any standard costing system, variances are used to determine the actual costs and to provide information for proactive corrective measures. All types of variances are provided from SAP, enough to drown the average analyst in detail. However, each organization can choose which variance to focus on. As the users of the information become more knowledgeable, eventually they can master all the analytical tools provided by this type of solution.

IMPLEMENTATION GUIDELINES

Implementing the SAP ABC solution is less of a technology-based issue and more focused on the change management component. The quotes provided in Exhibit 5.29 revolve around the impacts to the organization in terms of change.

Calculated Rates versus Politically Set Rates

The focus of the integration between the cost center accounting and activity-based costing components is to drive efficiencies and thereby reduce costs. As long as an organization uses the value-based approach for allocations, it will not be able to determine efficiencies accurately. It is usually easy enough to prove that the

Type	Implementation Guidelines
Organization	Which rates should be politically set versus system calculated?
Organization	What are the impacts to the organizational planning/budgeting cycle due to changes introduced by the quantity-based approach?
Organization	What is required for the integration of the organization processes of perform planning with capture actuals?
Organization	When should SAP ABC be implemented?

Exhibit 5.29   CCA-ABC Implementation Guidelines

SAP system using the quantity-based approach can precisely calculate the driver rates and provide useful information on the rate components—for example, fixed/proportional and the primary cost component capabilities. Therefore, the logical conclusion is to allow the system to calculate the driver rates. However, in reality, since the political rate is the easiest place to hide inefficiencies, second only to sandbagging the budget, getting an organization to stop using negotiated rates usually is very difficult.

At first, most organizations agree that political rates should be abandoned and as they gain more of an understanding, two groups of people form. The first group, generally consisting of poor managers, realize they will be caught out; the second group, generally good managers, realize they can finally quantify why they need their budgets. This political change must be pushed down from the top in order for it to succeed. Calculated driver rates using the quantity-based approach provide more accurate cost flows in the organization, leading to better decision making, while simultaneously eliminating the time required for internal rate negotiations. With the obvious informational quality improvement and the managerial conflict that may result, upper management must evaluate this approach in light of the organizational culture, politics, and readiness for change.

There are several valid reasons why political rates are being used in an organization. One supports the concept of transfer pricing, setting the requirement of paying only a certain amount for a service. Then the provider must supply the service for less. Political rates also can indicate areas that should be outsourced if the rate is intentionally set for this analysis purpose. Another reason political rates are used may be that management dictates that a certain investment be made; in order to not hold people responsible for that decision, a political rate is set (i.e., high-dollar technical purchases that will not be optimal for several years). Or perhaps a political rate is set to establish stretch goals. The different types of analysis desired, the requirements for cost assignment information and accuracy, and the performance metrics to be supported all have to be taken into consideration when determining which driver rates should be calculated instead of manually defined.

Planning/Budget Cycle Impacted

For the driver rate calculations to be most accurate and for efficiencies to be tracked in the organization, the planning/budget cycle needs to shift from a value-based approach to a quantity-based approach. Currently most organizations take a snapshot in time as a starting point and reevaluate the dollars based on a percentage increase or decrease. Some companies use several key metrics to impact the plan/budget, such as sales quantities, production quantities, and so on. However, in order to truly manage the organization's resources, a quantity-based approach needs to be accepted.

This is usually not a shift for the production/direct service–related cost centers or processes, as they generally tend to be quantity based. However, quantity relationships need to be applied to the next level of cost centers, the support cost centers, which directly feed those front-line cost centers, and then introduced into the administrative cost centers as the costing conceptual model matures. There is currently a flurry of activity around throwing away the budget since it is not accurate. People now spend all their time coming up with the next budget and justifying the old one. The focus is shifting to analyzing only actuals. This approach is similar to the one used with the quantity-based approach. Once all the quantity relationships are established, target (authorized) versus actual becomes the analysis basis, not static plan to actual comparisons. The only fact about the plan, given the new economy ever-changing environment, is it is usually wrong and almost certainly outdated by the next month.

As stated, quantity relationships are determined during the planning cycle. However, this is not the same planning cycle that academics are saying to discard. This planning cycle becomes more of an industrial engineering activity of determining the quantity relationships and microstandards for the cost center and process drivers. Once these are established, actual quantities and dollars can be measured against target. Doing so requires variances to be analyzed to determine if the difference is due to a market shift or if a standard needs to be updated. Because the focus is on target costs for actual quantity consumption, the second easiest way to pad the budget is identified when the actual quantities being consumed are nowhere near what the cost centers or processes said they would need. With this inefficiency highlighted, changes can be made to reflect a more realistic representation of true requirements and the microstandard for the driver rate can be adjusted. Therefore, the budget cycle in SAP can be shortened by focusing only on the quantity relationships that have been impacted by organizational shifts, instead of continually replanning all costs regardless of whether the relationships have changed.

Integration of Organizational Processes

The portion of the planning/budget cycle focusing on cost center and process costs is used to define the quantity relationships between all the cost center resources and processes. Once these relationships are established, the same relationships support actuals—that is, the relationships are planned based on defined causal relationships in an organization. Therefore, actual and plan now become attached; traditionally, these organizational processes have tended to be separate. This attachment eliminates time wasted trying to explain variances due to different structures for plan compared to the actual environment, based on separate systems in some cases, with separate designs, and so forth.

Fear of Activity-Based Costing

Many organizations began an ABC/M initiative at one time, only to have it fail miserably. Therefore, there is a residual perception that ABC projects are great pet projects for someone and provide no real benefits to the organization. In one example, an organization allowed four people, with vice-presidential roles, to spend two years process-mapping the HR department. Many of the failures were due to the inability of systems to support the ABC model desired. However, an integrated system can handle many of the traditional reasons for previous ABC failures, such as large data volumes and the need for multiple interfaces. Moreover, many failures are attributable to poor model designs.

These issues combined with the horrible tales from the ERP front add to the fear of performing ABC in an SAP implementation. SAP implementations have been bogged down with complaints about the length of implementations, cost of the projects, and impacts on the organization. Usually these complaints also are driven by a poor system design (and by not accepting the SAP business process philosophy). Implementing ABC within SAP is a scalable endeavor. Small portions of the organization can be targeted and shifted to an ABC focus. Changing to the more accurate quantity-based approach while using SAP also can be implemented in manageable pieces. The entire organization will not necessarily have all its costs using the ABC philosophy or resource quantity approach. At times a process view is not necessary or does not warrant the cost for the benefits returned. Therefore, the SAP system does not require everything to flow through ABC. The quantity-based solution, whether ABC or resource based, is scalable and manageable.

SUMMARY

Integration of ABC/M with the responsibility accounting capabilities within SAP provides several benefits. These include but are not limited to:

- The costing model can be designed to support varying degrees of complexity, from a step-down, value-based model using simplistic allocation methods to an advanced iterative, quantity-based consumption model incorporating fixed/proportional values and quantities.
- Microstandard unit rates can be created for cost center/actypes and processes based on plan or capacity output, to be used for cost assignments, performance measurement, benchmarking, and so on.
- There are capabilities for calculation of unit rates for different costing methods (standard versus actual) and periods (seasonality).
- The varying allocation methods address assignment issues relating to timing for postings, ease of use, and ability to handle complexity.

Exhibit 5.30 provides a summary table for the contents of this chapter.

NOTE

1. Anton van der Merwe and David Keys, "The Initial Inherent Nature of Cost and Accounting for Excess Capacity: The Case for Resource Consumption Accounting," *Journal of Cost Management,* in press.

Summary Area	Summary Description
Area-Specific Focus	
Plan Reconciliation	Example: *HR Dept.* scheduling the *Set Up New Hires* process that then schedules the *IT Dept. LABHR* resource. Benefit: Comparison of scheduled demand against planned supply to highlight areas for capacity management.
Driver Rate Calculation: *Step-down versus Recursive*	Example: Support Cost Center Benefit: Recursive calculation provides more accurate rates that support more accurate product, customer, etc., reporting.
ABC Paradigm Shift	Example: Cost center to process to cost center for consumption of support processes. Benefit: Fully burdened unit driver rates for the resource drivers increases accuracy and better supports outsourcing decisions.
Fixed/Proportional Values and Quantities	Example: Ingot furnace consumes both fixed/proportional quantities of electricity. Benefit: Accurate portrayal of fixed/ proportional costs required to support adequate information for decision making.
Nature of Process Costs	Example: 100 of Actype 1 @ \$2F/\$4V Rate and 50 of Actype 2 @ \$4V Rate are consumed by Process 1 with output of 100, then process rate = \$2F/\$6V (assumes the nature of the resource costs). Benefit: Accurate portrayal of fixed/proportional costs and consumption relationships required to support adequate information for decision making.
Standard Versus Actual Costing System	Example: Using a frozen unit driver rate or fluctuating monthly driver rates based on actuals. Benefit: Both methods supported, actuals can be valuated on standard during the period to get useful information and then revaluated at period end.
Plan or Capacity Denominator	Example: Driver rate determined on plan output or theoretical capacity. Benefit: Impacts whether product/services are fully absorbed or not.
Time Periods for Driver Rates	Example: Period, average, cumulative. Benefit: Supports multiple rate time determinations mainly used to smooth fixed expenses.
Primary Cost Component Layout	Example: Salaries, depreciation, supplies. Benefit: Provides visibility to the costs that comprise a process driver rate for indication of where to begin cost reduction initiatives.
Variance Calculations	Example: Input price, resource usage, output quantity. Benefit: Provides valuable information for process analysis and proactive corrective actions.

Exhibit 5.30 Summary Table for Process Integration with Responsibility Accounting

Information Flows	
Assessment and Distribution Cycles: The ability to allocate values for process costs based on a percentage, portion, or fixed dollar amount.	Example: *Market Research & Development* cost center to *Research Market Patterns* process. Assessment uses an aggregate account for allocation and distribution uses the original detail accounts. Benefit: Ability to simply allocate costs potentially with less need for accuracy.
Direct Activity Posting: The ability to directly charge a process to any cost object, e.g., cost center or other processes. Actual posting only.	Example: *Shipping LABHR* to *Deliver Shipment* process. Benefit: Real-time recognition of the process driver and resulting cost charge at standard unit process rate.
Indirect Activity Allocation: The ability to have the system automatically calculate the required processes needed to support the costs for plan or actual. No need to capture planned or actual resource or process driver quantities as they can be imputed via a relationship with another driver.	Example: *Sales Support LABHR* planned output determined by 1:0.5 ratio with *Internet Agent Sales* process driver quantity. Benefit: Reduced driver collection for areas where a strong correlation between drivers can be established. Sender quantity is not required because it can be imputed.
Target = Actual: The ability to have the system automatically calculate the required resource or processes driver quantity needed to support the process for actuals only, based on plan unit standards. No need to capture actual resource or process driver quantities as they are imputed via a relationship with another driver.	Example: *Customer Service LABHR* quantity is planned onto the *Handle Inquiries* process for a given process driver output, thus establishing the relationship. Actual process quantities are captured and impute the number of actual LABHRs that should have been worked. Benefit: Reduced driver collection for areas where a strong relationship can be established during planning. Supports recursive quantity consumptions.
Template: The ability to have the system calculate processes needed to support other processes or cost centers for plan or actual, possibly using advanced formulas and methods using Boolean logic.	Example: *Internet* template example to assign the *IT Dept. TECH* and *TMIN* drivers. Benefit: Dynamic determination of the process driver consumed by another process or a cost center. Provides a bill of resources for a process.

Exhibit 5.30 *(continued)*

Sample Business Decisions	
What are my true resource and process driver rates? What costs are comprised in that rate?	Supported via the accuracy that can be designed into the unit driver rate calculation for both the cost center/actype and the process drivers. The unit driver rate can be broken down by fixed/proportional and using the primary cost component to see types of costs. Benefit: Accuracy, more information for process improvement initiatives.
Which departments or processes should be outsourced?	Because the driver rates can be calculated fixed/proportional and with the accuracy of the quantity-based approach, outsourcing decisions can be supported. Benefit: True understanding of the upstream impacts to excess/idle capacity when a process is outsourced, i.e., what costs remain once the process is outsourced.
What are the process costs and how do they impact the cost center? What does the bill of resources routing contain to provide the process?	Multiple types of process analysis supported, including a higher-level understanding of the relationships that can be impacted by process reengineering. Benefit: Better information for decision making. Better understanding of components of process and process cost behavior.
Which resources should be used and where should they be deployed?	The use of the quantity-based approach with ABC defines the relationships with the resource drivers, where capacity resides. Impacts to the processes can then be used to see the impacts on the resource driver capacity. Benefit: Optimizes resource/process needs throughout the organization. Helps to define capacities correctly.
Given the product mix and volumes produced, what should the overhead be? How can volume variance be isolated?	The ability to calculate target costs along with the multiple variances fosters an environment where proactive changes to the environment can be administered. This is based on the microstandard for the process using a standard costing philosophy. Benefit: Provides more information for the determination of what is impacting the environment and what corrections are needed.
Implementation Guides	
Calculated versus Politically Set Rates	Which rates should be politically set versus system calculated?
Planning/Budget Cycle Impacted	What are the impacts to the organizational planning budgeting cycle due to changes introduced by the quantity-based approach?
Integration of Organizational Processes	What is required for the integration of the organization's processes of perform planning and capture actuals?
Fear of ABC	When should SAP ABC be implemented?

Exhibit 5.30   *(continued)*

6

INTEGRATED ACTIVITY-BASED COSTING WITH OVERHEAD ORDER ACCOUNTING

Chapter 5 stressed the responsibility accounting concept, focusing in detail on the optimization of individual cost centers and their combined usage with ABC. Cost centers are defined organizational units that are usually stable over an extended period of time. Therefore, cost centers can be an amalgamation of multiple events or occurrences for which detailed costs are required in order to perform analysis. For example, the *Vehicle Fleet* cost center may contain the costs for owning, running, and maintaining several hundred vehicles. Information on which vehicles are increasing costs may be desired. This analysis is not necessarily process related and is better defined as a view of the events that drive costs potentially captured within a cost center or across many cost centers. Analysis on each individual vehicle requires a cost object to represent this smaller pool or view of costs. To provide this more detailed information, overhead orders are utilized.

OVERHEAD ORDER CAPABILITIES

The SAP R/3 application contains many different types of orders. These orders are designed and utilized to support events in production, sales, plant maintenance, and overhead-related efforts. When focusing purely on overhead-related expenses, the internal order cost object is utilized. Internal orders capture expenses or revenues related to either overhead or investments. The investment focuses on internal assets and the allocation of related expenses to either the asset under construction account or, when completed, to a fixed asset. Therefore, internal orders monitor costs for either controlling overhead expenses or for capitalizing in-house construction. The internal order is the most discrete object within the CO module capturing the expenses and activities for a single event.

The capabilities of the internal order are supported by the production cost objects as well, such as production orders, sales orders, and projects. Specifically of interest are a comparison of the internal order with a project and the determination of when to utilize each. Both internal orders and projects are utilized to track overhead or investment-related events. The key difference between these two cost objects lies within the production-related capabilities of scheduling and capacity management. The internal order lacks these types of abilities while the project does not. If the overhead-related event requires the support of detailed scheduling and capacity management, such as for labor resources, then the project should be utilized. This chapter addresses only the internal order functionality and integration with ABC. However, the information flows between the internal orders and the processes hold true for projects and processes.

Multiple Applications

The greatest benefit of the internal order is definitely its flexibility in application. Internal orders are designed to support planning, capturing, and allocating costs for internal jobs or events. Since the object focus is at a more finite level—the event or job instead of the entire area of responsibility as with the cost center— internal orders provide the ability to monitor and control business transactions that occur during the entire life cycle of the event. How the internal order is applied within an organization is primarily driven by time frames. Internal orders can be applied short term or long term. The short-term application focuses on event management or job costing. The long-term application focuses on the life cycle of an object, a product, or a project.

Event Management/Job Costing   Event management concentrates on capturing the costs of a particular event, such as hosting the annual corporate party or creating a marketing campaign. These types of events do not necessarily require the structured controlling capabilities of the internal order and are mainly utilized to capture the costs and/or revenues for informational or allocation purposes. When used for informational purposes only, the internal orders might utilize statistical capabilities. This capability allows an internal order to be defined as statistical, capturing transactional postings for informational purposes only, without the added ability of then allocating those expenses/revenues. Statistical postings support two cost objects receiving the same posting simultaneously. For example, when the internal order is selected to be statistical, for an actual expense posted to the cost center and internal order simultaneously, the cost center holds the actual expense and the internal order has the same posting for information.

When the cost center line item is selected for further detail, it will display which internal order received the statistical posting. Since statistical orders do not actually contain the transactional posting, only the information, they cannot send expenses or revenues to another receiver. In this case, the internal order is used to match expenses and revenues to see if the event was profitable or to provide a lower level of information detail.

Job costing is another form of short-term or time-restricted usage of the internal order. The job costing application of the internal order is for services or production-related events for which the more robust stand-alone production modules are not utilized. Warranty contracts, maintenance services for the customers, minor construction for an asset, internally manufactured tools, and production orders within the Controlling module (often used if a production module is not implemented) are several examples of job costing. These types of jobs often require the order functionality of the production-related models without the scheduling and capacity management capabilities. The internal order's structure, status management, and settlement capabilities are utilized for job costing.

Every internal order is generated within an order type. Order types are created for the different types of events within an organization, such as for marketing, service requests, and assets. The order type defines the structure and capabilities of the internal orders through the definition of different parameters. These parameters control how the internal order will look, whether revenues can be captured, when data can be deleted, which informational fields are seen and if they are required or optional, number ranges for determining the number of the internal order, how it can be planned/budgeted, and so on. The order type also identifies the status management and allowed allocation receivers. There are two types of internal order status management: (1) system standard delivered and (2) user defined. Status management helps to track what stage the internal order is within its life cycle. The system standard statuses are consistent for every order type and cover statuses such as created, released, technically completed, or closed. The system status identifies the business transactions performed for the order and additionally restricts the transactions allowed during various statuses. For example, the business transaction for planning cannot take place if the order has been closed. Any user-defined statuses work in conjunction with the system statuses. Therefore, each organization can define the stages for the different types of internal orders to support the kind of job costing it performs.

Beyond how the internal order looks, how it is processed, and what the defined statuses are, the order type identifies what cost objects may receive costs/revenues of a completed order. Several potential receivers are available to internal orders, such as a fixed asset for in-house construction, G/L accounts for updating work in process or material warranty reserves, any cost center, processes, other orders, and market segments. Once the event/job is completed, the costs and revenues are as-signed to the appropriate receiver. This cost assignment rule is defined utilizing the settlement rule(s). For example, an order type utilized for in-house construc-tion of an asset might have as a selection parameter that a fixed asset is the only type of receiver allowed. Which particular fixed asset the internal order settles the costs to is defined directly in the internal order settlement rule. Additionally, when the settlement rule is defined, it is chosen as either a periodic or a full set-tlement rule. Full settlement indicates that all of the costs and revenues of the in-ternal order should be settled and allocated to a receiving object. Period settle-ment indicates that the internal order will continually receive costs/revenues on a periodic basis that should be settled in a stated periodic increment, that is, each month. For instance, the in-house asset internal order is settled periodically to an asset under construction account. When the job is completed, the costs of the built asset are fully settled to the fixed asset number in the Asset Management mod-ule. Another example is for resource-related billing, where each month a set amount of expenses incurred for servicing a customer are transferred to a sales order for billing. At the end of the service contract, all remaining expenses are fully transferred for billing.

Life-Cycle Costing   Long-term (i.e., over more than one fiscal year) utilization of an internal order usually revolves around life-cycle costing of an object. The time frame is normally longer than a year; more likely it is multiple years. Ex-amples are tracking repairs over the life of a specific asset, such as a vehicle fleet, or for tracking the total cost of providing a product from research and develop-ment to patent. The multiple-year focus for the minor repairs on any type of as-set provides useful information on which assets are driving up costs and when they should be replaced. The application of internal orders for long-term pur-poses can also support the capturing of expenses that must be recognized in the period incurred for FI reporting yet are recognized in a different period or year for internal management reporting purposes.

These are just a few ways in which internal orders are applied within an or-ganization. Additionally, internal orders are used for distributing accruals and to provide a focus on revenue management. Since internal orders are very flex-ible and have more authorization capabilities than the cost center, internal or-ders usually are widely implemented. The ability to use internal orders in flex-ible ways to represent standard and nonstandard occurrences in an organization provides the ability to utilize processes in many ways as well. Most important, since internal orders flow outside of the CO module, process costs are included in other modules for different purposes. For example, internal orders utilized for asset creation capture process costs that are then capitalized. Also, internal orders utilized for resource-related billing for providing a service transfer process costs to sales orders for the determination of billed revenues.

Planning Possibilities

Since internal orders can be used for almost any application, planning and budgeting capabilities must be robust in order to accommodate every need. Planning capabilities support both overall (high-level) to very detailed planning. Unit cost planning, which is similar to a bill of materials and resources, is also supported when utilizing internal orders. In this instance, internal orders function more like production/service orders. Internal order planning is completely integrated with other organizational plans, such as cost center and profit center planning, as well as with financial special ledger planning.

Overall Planning   In the event that the internal orders are utilized for multiple fiscal years, overall planning supports a high-level plan. This overall planning is for the entire internal order covering all years estimated or for each individual fiscal year. Overall planning is used to plan cost and revenues for an internal order when the time frame is too far in the future to accurately determine a more detailed plan. The overall planning capabilities support a planned estimate for the order without any supporting account detail.

Detailed Planning   Where overall planning supports an internal order with planned expenses of $100,000 for each year from 2002 through 2005, as the fiscal planning begins for year 2002, detailed planning for the internal orders is performed. This detailed planning supports planning primary cost elements, activity types, processes, and statistical key figures on the internal orders. When activity types and process quantities are planned on the internal orders, standard rates are utilized to calculate the planned dollar values in the internal order. If utilized, statistical key figures are usually planned on internal orders to support reporting needs, such as cost per statistical key figure.

Resource Planning   In addition to high-level and detailed planning, resource planning is also available. Resource planning is performed below the primary cost element level. A resource represents a procured good or service that rolls up into one primary cost element. For example, planning is often performed for a primary cost element, such as *Consulting Fees*. However, this primary cost element reflects the expense for all externally procured consultants. Resource planning provides the ability to further define resources that are included within this account, at a prescribed price per period of time. For example, *Consultant-1* is $10/hr and *Consultant-2* is $100/hr but both are planned on cost element 450000 *Consulting Fees*. Internal resources are captured within secondary cost elements via the process and activity types and are supported via detailed planning, not resource planning.

Integrated Planning   The detailed planning performed on the internal order is contained within order accounting only. However, many organizations desire to have this plan information combined with cost center and process cost planning to determine the overall planning impacts to the organization as a whole. To accommodate this requirement, integrated planning is supported among internal orders, cost centers, and processes. This support provides the ability to have activity types and process quantities planned on the internal orders, resulting in a scheduled demand against the supplying process and cost center/activity type. For example, if 100 *LABHR*s of the *Maintenance* cost center are planned onto an internal order, the cost center will automatically see a scheduled demand for that quantity if integrated planning is being used. Throughout the planning process, the quantities of activity types and processes planned to be consumed might change. When the price rates are recalculated for the internal orders selected utilizing integrated planning, any price changes for the activity type and process rates will then be automatically updated on the internal order as well. Additionally, with integrated planning, planned internal order settlements (allocations) are also supported, such as planned settlements to the market segment planned P/L. Further, linkages are provided through integrated planning to objects in profit center accounting and special ledger planning, thereby updating the corporate and internal management P/Ls in the event these internal orders cross organizational boundaries.

Unit Costing   Unit cost planning is utilized to determine the cost of providing a job/event. This type of planning is at the detailed planning level. Unit costing is facilitated via the base object costing functionality located within the product costing area. Base object costing functions like an Excel sheet that supports the inclusion of materials, activity types, and processes required to perform a job or event. Once the base object representing the job/event is created, it is pulled into the internal order to produce the plan. Base object costing is normally performed to estimate the cost of new products or services or changes to current products and services. Additionally it can be used to cost nonstandard materials, services, or events such as a conference. For example, a base object can be unit costed for a conference, pulling in materials for general supplies required, products for promotional giveaways, or internally supplied actypes for labor hours or processes used to support the conference.

Internal orders support very high level planning for a lump sum representing multiple years or for each individual year. Further, detailed planning can be performed by primary cost element, actype, process, etc. on each individual order, potentially utilizing the unit cost functionality to perform the detailed planning. The absolute lowest level of planning supported by the internal order is resource planning of individual resources contained within a primary cost element. In addition, multiple plan versions are supported and the unit costing is completely tied in with the easy cost planning and execution capabilities addressed in Chapter 4 in the section on mySAP.com. For example, ECP&E is used within an organization for requesting meeting rooms. The user enters the number of people; number of days; travel to be incurred; whether breakfast, lunch, or dinner needs to be provided; and other information in whatever manner the ECP&E has been defined. In the background, an internal order is generated and automatically planned with the appropriate cost. The requesting cost center can see the planned costs for the meeting event. If accepted, the plan is established on the internal order. Actual expenses are charged against the internal order and then settled to the appropriate receivers.

The type of planning utilized usually is driven by the time frame of the internal order. For internal orders that exist across multiple years, overall planning is performed for those future years. As the time frame draws nearer, detailed, resource, or unit cost planning can be performed. If this lower-level planning is possible during the normal planning/budgeting cycle, then integrated planning should be selected to provide an overall integrated plan. For low-level planning that occurs on the fly within the plan/budgeted year for common events, such as meeting scheduling or maintenance events, Easy Cost Planning and Execution can be utilized.[1]

Budgets, Funds Management, and Commitments

The "plan" is commonly accepted as the determined course of action and the requirement to ensure achievement of the objectives. The fiscal year plan is usually the bottom-up approach of planning the resource needs of individual areas in order to achieve certain objectives, aggregating into the corporate financial plan. The planning capabilities of the internal order have already been addressed. The "budget" is the authorization of the plan, at which point funds have been allocated to ensure that the needs of the plan are met. Budgeting is usually a top-down approach determining the revenues and expenses for the organization and pushing them down through the organization to then reside at the lowest individual level. Budgets are often generated from a plan that has been altered by upper management, setting new targets for the objectives and finalizing the plan number as the budget.

Within SAP R/3, the budgets (allocations of funds) for internal orders can be performed utilizing a bottom-up or top-down approach. When budgeting is completed, the budget becomes the final approved costs for the internal orders or groups. Then funds are reserved for these budgets. The management of these funds focuses on whether outstanding commitments exist and if the budget has the funds to pay these commitments. For example, an internal order is created to support an IT project for implementing a new software package. This internal order is planned based on the determination that $250,000 is required. Once approved, making no adjustments for this example, the budget is set at $250,000 and these funds are reserved for the internal order. This job requires the purchase of several external materials and services, which need to be reflected as commitments of funds for the internal order. Commitments are generated through purchase requisitions for internal orders or manually created. When a purchase requisition/order is made for these materials or services, a commitment is made against those funds on the internal order to prevent overspending. These commitments are reduced automatically when the goods receipt transaction is performed. The goods receipt changes the commitment to be an actual expense on the internal order. Manual funds commitments are entered for expenses that probably will occur; yet it is unknown which business transaction method will generate the expense. Additionally, internal allocations, such as from processes or cost centers, will reduce the funds for the internal order as well. Setting the budget, the funds reservations and different planning levels, and tracking actual costs and commitments as well as revenues, provides stringent monitoring and controlling capabilities that can be applied for any of the potential applications of the internal order.

INFORMATION FLOWS

The integration of ABC with order accounting supports a bidirectional flow of information. Processes can post to internal orders, and internal orders can post to processes. All of the information flows possible between the cost center and processes are also valid for internal orders and processes. In addition to these standard methods, the overhead calculation and internal order settlement methods are added as other forms of cost assignment. Therefore, the cost flows supported between the processes and internal orders are:

- Assessment/distribution cycles
- Direct activity allocation

- Indirect activity allocation
- Target = actual allocation
- Template allocation
- Overhead calculation
- Internal order settlement

Process Assessment/Distribution Cycles to Internal Orders

Assessment and distribution cycles are the allocation methods used to support a value-based model, where the costs are pushed down throughout the organization. Within an allocation cycle, the process or group and the cost elements or group are selected as the senders, and the internal order or group is then chosen as the receiver. Recall from Chapter 5 that the basis for these cycles are fixed percentages, fixed dollars, fixed ratios, or variable portions based on an actype, process, cost element, or statistical key figure value or quantity. For the examples illustrating the assessment cycle, Exhibit 6.1, and distribution cycle, Exhibit 6.2, from a process to an internal order, costs must already reside on the process. A cost center to process assessment has already occurred using secondary cost element 999888 to allocate $500 of the *Facilities* cost center (CC1100) to the *Print Materials* process. A cost center to process distribution has also allocated $1,000 in *Salaries* (430000) from the *Printing* cost center (CC1200) to the *Print Materials* process. Additionally, $200 of copy expenses from an outside printing service and $800 of external temporary help are directly posted from FI to the *Print*

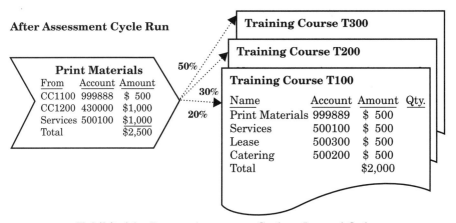

Exhibit 6.1 Process Assessment Cycle to Internal Order

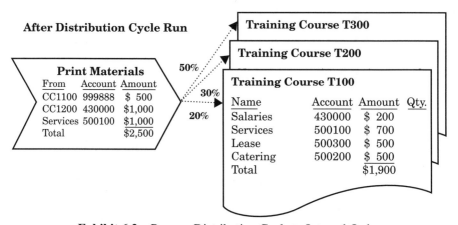

Exhibit 6.2   Process Distribution Cycle to Internal Order

Materials process using the *Service* account 500100. Therefore, the *Print Materials* process has both allocated and direct expenses for these examples. Exhibit 6.1 illustrates the results of an assessment cycle utilized to allocate the *Print Materials* process costs to the receiving internal orders representing training courses.

For the assessment cycle, all of the costs are allocated using one secondary cost element (999889) to the receivers based on a percentage split. The assessment results in $500 ($2500*20%) in *Print Materials* process costs being allocated to training course T100. Since distribution cycles recognize only primary cost elements, the $500 of allocated *Facilities* expenses will be ignored, causing a different result from the assessment cycle. Exhibit 6.2 illustrates the results of the same example using a distribution cycle instead of an assessment cycle.

The costs for the 999888 secondary cost element are left unallocated on the *Print Materials Process* using the distribution cycle, resulting in a $100 ($500*20%) difference for *Training Course T100* between the two examples. Two hundred dollars of the *Salaries* (430000) costs originally allocated from the *Printing* cost center is posted from the process to the *Training Course T100* internal order. Additionally, the distribution cycle locates the primary *Services* account (500100) and allocates 20% ($200) to the *Training Course T100* internal order as well. Since the T100 internal order already had $500 in *Service* costs directly charged to it, the total *Service* costs is $700.

The most common value-based allocation is the assessment cycle utilizing the allocation structure that reduces the amount of line items posted by the distribution cycle while providing more detail than the assessment cycle posting with only one secondary cost element (eliminating the need to have several cycle segments to support this detail). In general, internal orders are not common

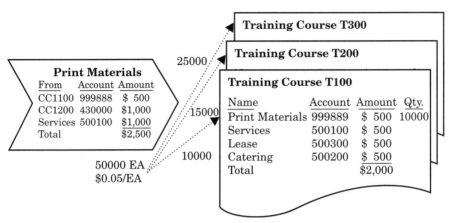

Exhibit 6.3 Direct Activity Allocation from a Process to the Internal Orders

receivers of an assessment or distribution cycle. This is due to cycles being sender based periodic to receivers, which should be stable over the long term. Internal orders are usually short term in nature, except for the life cycle example.

Direct Activity Allocation to the Internal Orders

The first quantity-based assignment method is the direct activity allocation (DAA). For the DAA, the sender, sender quantity, and receiver are known. In order for the process to be utilized in a quantity-based method, it must have a secondary cost element and a unit of measure assigned in the master record, such as 999889 and each (EA), respectively. A process rate (price) also must exist. This rate is a planned standard to be utilized during the period when the DAA is posted. If utilizing an actual costing system, the rate can be later revaluated by the actual process rate. Using the same *Print Materials* example, Exhibit 6.3 illustrates the DAA from a process to the internal orders.

The results of the DAA are intentionally the same as the assessment cycle to stress the different information received. The key differences between the assessment cycle and the DAA is the additional quantity information provided by the DAA and timing. The assessment cycle is allocated at the end of the period whereas the direct activity allocation can be posted daily or at the completion of the actual copy run, providing immediate information on costs and quantities. In addition, unlike the assessment cycle, the direct activity allocation exists only for actual postings. The plan equivalent of a DAA is performed using detailed planning on the internal order.

Indirect Activity Allocation Cycle to Internal Orders

The indirect activity allocation (IAA) cycle allocates the process output quantities along with the value amount. Recall from Chapter 5 that the IAA can have a sender rule for a fixed quantity, the posted quantity, or inversely calculated. The IAA provides the most benefit when one quantity inversely determines the process output quantity, since it reduces the need to track a measure and to support quantity splitting. The IAA is a hybrid of the assessment and direct activity allocation methods of allocation. The IAA allocates similar to the assessment cycle, providing the same basis for allocations and posted at period end. However, the allocation is quantity based, like the direct activity allocation, and therefore the process has a secondary cost element, unit of measure, and a rate associated with it. Exhibit 6.4 illustrates the same assessment example utilizing the IAA cycle.

In this example, since the quantities by receiver are not known, the percentages are used to split the quantities between receivers. If the quantities by receiver are known, the DAA is utilized. Since this example uses the same percentage allocation method as used in the assessment example, the only difference here in the results is that the IAA posts a quantity as well. A quantity provides useful information if internal service agreements are based on transaction volumes. Also, since the IAA cycle is intended for stable receivers, like the assessment and distribution cycles, an internal order is generally not a receiver.

Target = Actual Allocation

The target = actual allocation is utilized to impute actual consumption based on a planned relationship. For example, 10000 KWH of electricity are planned for 1000 production MACHR. The planned relationship is 10:1. Therefore, for every actual MACHR consumed, 10 KWH will also be consumed. Therefore, if actual production utilizes 2000 MACHRs, 20,000 KWHs will be consumed. With an internal order, this allocation method functions more as a plan = actual because the lot size of the internal order effectively is one. Exhibit 6.5 illustrates a target = actual allocation of a process to the internal orders.

Since quantities of the internal order will not increase or decrease because it does not have an output quantity, the target = actual will not flex the required processes to be consumed. The amount planned simply is posted for actual. If a standard costing system is utilized, any variance in costs on the process will therefore be price related since the volume has not changed. This variance will be liquidated with another allocation or if an actual costing system is utilized the actual process rate liquidates the variance based on actual quantities consumed.

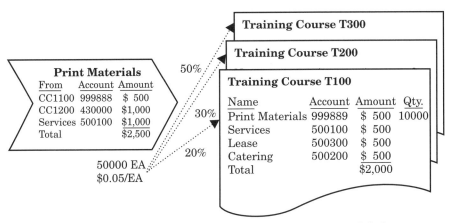

Exhibit 6.4 Indirect Activity Allocation Cycle to Internal Order

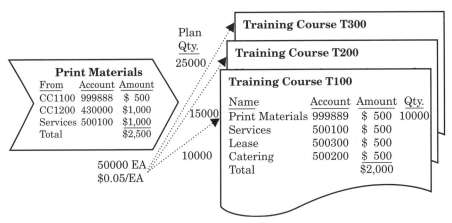

Exhibit 6.5 Target = Actual Allocation from a Process to the Internal Orders

The target = actual allocation between processes and internal orders requires the use of plan integration. This allocation method may not be widely applied; however, there are some instances where it proves useful. For example, a shared service organization has contracts with specifically agreed-on quantities that can be charged, such as one *Prepare Period-end Reports* process per period. The process can represent the service provided and the planned quantity represents the agreed-on volume charge. The internal order is utilized to represent the receiving organization. When executed, the target = actual allocation automatically makes the actual quantity posting each period to the receiving internal orders, reducing manual efforts. The internal order can be utilized to generate an invoice instead of having the process charged directly to the receiving organizational unit's cost center. Using the internal order for this type of resource-related billing for a shared service is a common occurrence, especially in organizations where all units do not utilize the SAP R/3 system or where the shared service group is a completely separate legal entity, and invoices must be issued.

Template Posting Process Costs to Internal Orders

The examples provided for the previous allocation methods are very simplistic and unrealistic for most organizations. The assessment, distribution, and indirect activity allocation cycles example is completely subjective, relying on assumptions regarding the percentage of volume split. Those assumptions are created at a single point in time and do not reflect the dynamics of the organization. The direct activity allocation, using the number of copies, is appropriate only if the actual number of copies is tracked and all copying requires the same amount of effort. Once a performance variance in the quantity measure is identified, such as one-sided versus two-sided, or black-and-white versus color, the accuracy of DAA is in question. Based on the potential types of copies, it can be seen that assumptions and conditions might be required to accurately relate the *Print Materials* process costs to the corresponding training course internal order when actuals are not tracked. To accommodate these assumptions or conditions, the template allocation is required.

In order to define the template from the process to the internal orders, the template name and environment are defined. For this example, the template name is *Printing*. The template also requires an environment—007 is provided for internal orders—which filters the list of potential logical and mathematical functions, providing only those pieces of information valid for use with an internal order. For the 007 environment, the function areas (hierarchies) and one sample function of each are:

- Process: ScheduledProcPlannedQty
- Unit costing: UnitCostingLotSize
- General data: StatisticalKeyFigure
- Internal order: OrderCharValue (a characteristic of the internal order)
- Mathematical: CEIL (round up to the highest whole number)

Once the template name and environment are entered, the structure of the template is defined. (See Exhibit 6.6.) The structure of the template includes: Type,

| Template | 007 | | | Internal Order | | | | |

| Template | **Printing** | | | Printing Process Assignment | | | | |

Type	Name	Object	Un	Plan Quantity	Plan Activation	Actual Quantity	Actual Activation	Actual Alloc. Event
Process	Print Materials	RP100	EA	FORMULA	METHOD	FORMULA	METHOD	

Exhibit 6.6   Template Allocation to Internal Order

Name (different than the Template Name), Object, Unit, Quantity Columns, Activation indictors, and Actual Allocation Event. Since this template is to assign the *Print Materials* process to the internal orders, the "Type" field is selected as Business Process instead of Cost Center/Activity Type, Subtemplate (including another template), Calculation Row (Business Processes), Calculation Row (Cost Centers/Activity Types), or Comment. The Object represents the code for the process. Once filled in, the "Name" and "Unit" (Un) fields are automatically populated.

The plan and actual qty fields contain the formula used to distinguish between the training courses. Since the *Print Materials* process unit of measure is EA to represent the number of copies, the quantity fields are used to calculate the number of copies. For this example, a template is utilized since the number of copies is not directly tracked and there are some differences in the level of effort to print materials that are one-sided compared to two-sided. Here the "IF-THEN" for the different internal orders can be entered, such as "IF *TR100* THEN 200*1*#*Attendees*" and "IF *TR200* THEN 75*2*#*Attendees.*" The 200 and 75 represent the number of pages in a training course book and the 1 and 2 represent the effort multiplier if the copies are one-sided or two-sided. The number of attendees (#*Attendees*) is an SKF captured on the internal order. Therefore, if there are 50 attendees for class *TR100* and 100 for class *TR200,* the number of copies, weighted for complexity, utilized to consume the *Print Materials* process will be 10,000 and 15,000, respectively. By using the template, the actual quantity of copies made does not need to be tracked or entered in the system. Additionally, the template allocation can be run daily if desired.

Once the formula is defined, the plan and actual "Activation" field is set. The activation is defined as Active, indicating the *Print Material* process is always applied. Alternatively, a method can be defined to identify a logical condition of when the process should be applied. For example, perhaps there is an internal service agreement that a business area (BA100) does not pay for the *Print Materials* process. A method is defined that states "IF Business Area is not *BA100* THEN Active." When the template is executed to assign the process costs to the internal orders, those for *BA100* will not be charged *Print Materials* processes. The actual "IF-THEN" wording does not appear as written in this text. The statements must follow the correct syntax and the functions are used to fulfill the requirements for making the "IF-THEN" statements. The user needs only to select the desired function (OrderBusinessArea), the operand ($\neq$), and the value (*BA100*); then the statement code is built.

The "Actual Allocation Event" field determines when in the life cycle of the internal order a process should be assigned. For example, a function representing the internal order statuses can be created. Then support processes can be assigned to the internal order only during a certain status, such as the *Plan Training Schedule* process allocated during the Plan status, or *Print Materials* during the Released status, and so on. The flexibility and ease for creating complex calculations and determining which process should be applied when, and to which cost objects, are the most advanced assignment capabilities available.

Internal Order Overhead Calculations

The overhead calculation method supports percentage or quantity surcharges for allocating overhead costs. Overhead calculation is a value-based allocation. It is similar to the template allocation in that it is a generally defined rule on the receiver object. However, while the template uses the more appropriate drivers, the overhead calculation does not. Overhead calculations can consider dependencies, such as for a specific company compared to another. Overhead calculations utilize a costing sheet, which defines the cost elements to be considered on the sender, the overhead rate to be charged, and which cost element to utilize when posting. The overhead rate can be a percentage, such as 10%, or a quantity rule stating that, for example, for each quantity an additional $100 is charged to the receiver. Costing sheet *ABC1* has been created to make a surcharge from the *Print Materials* process to the training internal orders. Within the costing sheet, a "base" is defined, indicating which cost elements on the internal orders are to be considered in the calculation. For this example the "base" includes all cost elements; therefore it captures all the actual costs on the internal orders. The overhead rate is determined to be percentage and/or quantity and the amount is set. Costing sheet *ABC1* has an overhead rate that is percentage based with the value of 30%. Also defined on the costing sheet is the account and sender to be credited. Cost element 660000 for *Overhead Surcharges* has been assigned to the *Print Materials* process. Exhibit 6.7 illustrates the overhead calculation between the process and the internal orders.

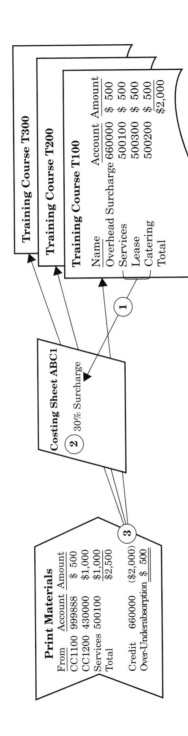

Exhibit 6.7 Overhead Calculation of Process to Internal Order

Contained within the master data for each of the internal orders is a field identifying which costing sheet should be applied for overhead calculations. Each of the training internal orders has the assignment for costing sheet *ABC1*. Three steps are taken when the overhead calculation is executed:

1. All the cost elements on the internal order are totaled.
2. The overhead rate is applied, determining the surcharge based on the 30% percentage overhead.
3. The resulting surcharge posting is made. Since all three training internal orders contain costing sheet *ABC1* in the master data, each receives the 30% surcharge posting. Internal order *T100* had $1,500 in expenses prior to the overhead calculation, resulting in a $500 surcharge posting to the *Overhead Surcharges* account. *T200* and *T300* have $2,000 and $3,000 in expenses, respectively, resulting in surcharges of $600 to *T200* and $900 to *T300*. Total credit to the *Print Materials* process is $2,000 ($500 + $600 + $900).

This cost-plus method of overhead charging is a common allocation method, especially in the production area. As depicted in Exhibit 6.7, one potential drawback of overhead calculations is that the utilization of a surcharge can generate over/under absorption on the sending process.

Internal Order Settlements to a Process

A settlement is the allocation method utilized to relieve the costs for any type of order, for example, internal orders, production orders, and maintenance orders. The allocation abilities of the settlement are limited compared to the other methods already addressed. Supported allocation methods are percentage based, fixed amount, or equivalents (ratios). The settlement consists of the rule and the structure. The settlement rule is defined in the master data of the internal order and identifies the receiver object and the allocation basis. The settlement structure defines which settlement cost elements, if any, are used to move the expenses from the internal orders to the cost objects. Exhibit 6.8 illustrates different ways of defining the settlement structure.

This exhibit illustrates three sample settlement structures. One method not depicted supports all cost elements being combined into one settlement account if desired, perhaps named *Internal Order Settlements*. In this case, the receiver would display $3,500 in that one settlement account. With this design, little detail is provided other than indicating the sending internal order. In order to understand what the $3,500 consists of, the internal order would need to be investigated. Beyond the single settlement account approach, other structures can be designed. Structure 10

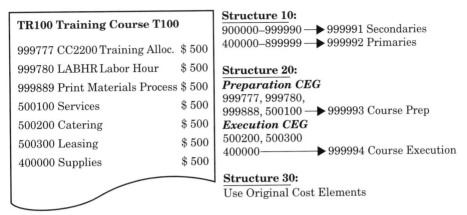

TR100 Training Course T100	
999777 CC2200 Training Alloc.	$ 500
999780 LABHR Labor Hour	$ 500
999889 Print Materials Process	$ 500
500100 Services	$ 500
500200 Catering	$ 500
500300 Leasing	$ 500
400000 Supplies	$ 500

Structure 10:
900000–999990 ⟶ 999991 Secondaries
400000–899999 ⟶ 999992 Primaries

Structure 20:
Preparation CEG
999777, 999780,
999888, 500100 ⟶ 999993 Course Prep
Execution CEG
500200, 500300
400000 ⟶ 999994 Course Execution

Structure 30:
Use Original Cost Elements

Exhibit 6.8   Sample Settlement Structures

shows slightly more detail, indicating to the receiver at least that $1,500 is from internal costs and $2,000 is from external costs. Again, for more detail about the individual accounts, the internal order has to be investigated. Structure 20 breaks the costs out into the reasons for the costs. The receiver can see that $2,000 of training expenses is due to the course preparation and $1,500 was for actual course attendance. Structure 30 provides the most account detail, having all the cost elements settle with the original account number. Therefore, the receiver has the complete breakout of costs; however, this structure has two drawbacks.

1. It can result in large data volumes.
2. The receiver costs will be mingled with all other postings for the same accounts, supporting a detailed account view yet making it difficult to easily identify original costs postings from settled costs from the internal order.

Each organization defines the level of transparency as supported by the settlement structure to suit its needs.

Most internal orders will settle to a cost center or market segment, perhaps even another internal order. However, an internal order can also settle to a process. This is a viable business case only in the relatively few instances where the event occurs specifically for a process. Exhibit 6.9 illustrates at a high level the internal order and process interrelationship.

In this example, the *TR100* training course internal order is provided specifically for learning the policies, procedures, and methods for resolving customer complaints. The internal order could settle back to the *Customer Service* cost center and then be allocated to the *Resolve Customer Complaint* process based on the time customer service representatives spend resolving complaints. However,

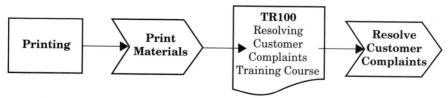

Exhibit 6.9   Process to Internal Order to Process Information Flow Example

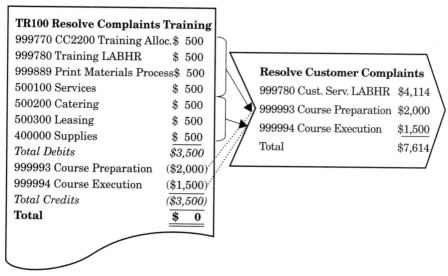

Exhibit 6.10   Internal Order Settlements to Process Receiver

some of these training costs may be spread across all of the processes performed by the *Customer Service* representatives. Directly settling the *TR100* internal order to the *Resolve Customer Complaint* process is more accurate. Exhibit 6.10 illustrates the *TR100* internal order settling to a *Resolve Customer Complaint* process using the settlement structure, Structure 20.

The intermingling of events and activities provides the ability to accommodate cost flows for processes supporting events and attributing the cost of events that occur for a specific process. This combination of discrete events with ongoing activities, along with the cost center accounting integration, provides the ability to support overhead management accurately and effectively. Exhibit 6.11 provides a summary of the internal order and process information flows.

Information Flow	Comments	Assignment Basis	Type of Posting	Timing	Ease Of Use	Handle Complexity
Assessment Cycle	Allocations from processes to internal orders utilizing an assessment cost element or an allocation structure. Not usually utilized with short-term internal orders.	Fixed %, fixed portions, fixed amount, variable tracing based on cost elements, SKFs, processes, or actypes.	Value based	Period end	Moderate	Limited
Distribution	Allocations from processes to internal orders utilizing the detailed accounts. Not usually utilized with short-term internal orders.	Fixed %, fixed portions, fixed amount, variable tracing based on cost elements, SKFs, processes, or actypes.	Value based	Period end	Moderate	Limited
Direct Activity Allocation	Direct process charge to the internal order.	Actual quantity	Quantity-based with value	Real time	Easy	None
Indirect Activity Allocation	Inverse calculated supports imputing quantities and reduces the need to capture actuals for a driver qty. Also supports quantity splitting. Not usually utilized with short-term internal orders.	Fixed %, fixed portion, fixed quantities, variable tracing based on cost elements, SKFs, processes, or actypes.	Quantity-based with value	Period end	Moderate	Limited
Target = Actual	Requires integrated planning to be utilized for the internal orders.	Takes quantities from the detailed plan and posts them for actuals.	Quantity-based with value	Period end	Moderate	None
Templates	Dynamic determination of the process driver consumed by an internal order.	Simple to complex formulas and "IF-THEN" rules (methods).	Quantity-based with value	Within period	Advanced	High level easily supported

Exhibit 6.11   Summary of Process and Internal Order Informational Flows

Information Flow	Comments	Assignment Basis	Type of Posting	Timing	Ease Of Use	Handle Complexity
Overhead Calculations	Utilizing a costing sheet to determine an overhead surcharge. Some ability for defining conditions (dependencies).	Percentage and/or quantity-based surcharge.	Value based	Period end	Moderate	Moderate
Settlements	Internal orders settle to processes.	Percentage, fixed dollar amount, equivalents	Value based	Period end	Moderate	Limited

Exhibit 6.11   (*continued*)

SAMPLE KEY BUSINESS DECISIONS

With the flexibility in application of the internal order and the complete integration with the process capabilities, many business decisions can be supported by using both these cost objects. Exhibit 6.12 lists only a few that highlight the key integration between internal orders and processes.

Process Support of Events/Jobs

The different allocation methods from a process to the internal order support both value-based allocations, such as assessments, to more advanced quantity-based assignments that potentially address complexity and timing issues for job costing, such as the template allocation. The process allocation capabilities combined with an internal order, representing events or jobs, provides an additional level of information granularity. For example, internal orders for trade shows, marketing campaigns, or conference hosting provide another cost bucket to pool costs, including processes, prior to associating those costs directly to the receiver cost objects. In this manner, the internal order acts like a production order representing internal events. The processes utilized to support these events are more accurately assigned to the consuming cost object. When internal cost management decisions are considered, the complete cost of these events can be weighed to determine if the benefit is justifiable. Given that revenues can also be captured on the internal order, profits by events can be identified. These profits are overstated

Sample Key Business Decisions	Value Based[a]	Quantity Based[a]
What are the impacts of internal services for event management of job costing?	√	√
What events occur to support processes?	√	--
Should the event be procured or internally provided?	√	√

√ means approach supports decision
- -means approach does not support

Exhibit 6.12   ABC and Order Accounting Sample Business Decisions

if processes, representing internal services, are not attributed to the internal order. Additionally, with the statistical internal orders, it is possible for decision support to assign process costs to the internal order for informational purposes only, while actually allocating the process costs in a different manner directly to the cost object.

Beyond the transparency of event costs, revenues matching, and information benefits just addressed, integrated ABC with order accounting supports a broader cost focus as well, such as with capitalization, depreciation, and accruals. Process costs attributed to internal orders for events such as IT projects or constructing an asset in-house can be included in the portion of costs capitalized. When using internal orders for investment endeavors, process costs are included in depreciation calculations. Additionally, organizations might defer certain process expenses to a different period or year for internal management reporting, although they are recognized as a period expense for external reporting. In these cases, the internal order holds these expenses and then settles them at a later time. The application of the internal order throughout the organization is designed specifically to support enhanced analysis.

Events Supporting Processes

It is easy enough to imagine several instances where events consume different activities. However, it is less likely that events occur to support processes, although there are always the exceptions. If an event occurs specifically to support an ongoing process, the internal order can be used to attribute these costs directly to the process. The example utilized in the Information Flows section is the *TR100* training course designed and executed for the sole purpose of educating attendees on the policy, procedures, and skills required to resolve customer complaints. Settling these costs back to the *Customer Support* cost center and then allocating them to the *Resolve Customer Complaint* process is inefficient and potentially inaccurate. The settlement allocation of the internal order is always a value-based allocation. A quantity-based allocation from the internal order to the process is not supported, since a single event has a lot size of one. The costs settled from the internal order to the process are fixed expenses. These costs are not variable, since they are not driven by the output quantity of the receiving process. By settling the costs of the internal order to the process, two pieces of information are gained: (1) the complete cost of the event itself, to be used for make-buy decisions, and (2) a more detailed view of the costs required to provide the process. The complete view of all costs related to the process helps identify potential impacts when evaluating outsourcing decisions. If the event is outsourced, such as *TR100*, the impacts to the *Print Material* process and one level farther back to the cost center, where the capacity resides, can then be determined.

Make, Buy, and Divestment Decision Support

Before the event is even initiated a decision needs to be made as to whether the event or asset should be supplied in-house or procured externally. This type of decision is supported by the planning capabilities of the internal order. The make-buy decision has two different focuses: The first focus is whether the noncore event should be performed or outsourced completely, such as providing a conference, building tools and dies, or creating and executing a training course. The decision to produce a training course internally, for example, versus externally procuring it requires planning the cost elements, processes, and potential allocations the course would consume. The unit costing of a base unit object can also be used for the job-costing events. If the event/job is to be produced in-house, the second make-buy decision focuses on whether to utilize internal resources only or to purchase third-party services/products. In the training example, the decision to create and execute the training course is decided; the decision to externally procure the space and catering is determined as well. Both space and catering are available from internal resources; however, the space is not suited for a training course, and the catering cost differential, or the quality compared to the cost differential for utilizing the corporate cafeteria, drove the decision to procure.

In addition to support make-buy decisions, the process cost integration with the internal orders provides complete costing information supporting divestment decisions during life-cycle costing. For example, research and development projects or job costing, such as for automobile refurbishments, often have costing requirements by stages. If the costing requirement is exceeded, the event is canceled due to an inability to recuperate the expenses or a reduced probability of obtaining the estimated profitability margin.

Type	Implementation Guidelines
Conceptual Design	How does internal order process costs impact financial reporting?
System Design	Is there a need for statistical internal orders?
Organizational Impact	Which internal orders should be integrated in planning?

Exhibit 6.13   OPA-ABC Implementation Guidelines

IMPLEMENTATION GUIDELINES

The integration of ABC into order accounting supports endless possibilities for including process costs throughout the organization. However, there are several areas to focus on when trying to integrate processes into order accounting. Exhibit 6.13 lists a few points to be addressed during the implementation.

Thinking Outside the Normal ABC Box

Traditional ABC does not usually take into consideration impacts of process costs back onto the financials. The financial information tends to feed from the general ledger to the ABC system without a reciprocal feed. However, given that the internal order is capable of updating the financial G/L, process information can now be used for integrated updates for the purpose of capitalization and depreciation calculations and for accruals. Therefore, when designing integrated ABC within SAP, these types of costs must be considered within the scope of the ABC model.

Statistical versus Real Internal Orders

Statistical postings within SAP are a very powerful tool with an equally powerful potential to cause reconciliation nightmares. With internal orders, statistical posting can be generated in two ways.

1. Have a real internal order receiving the actual posting and simultaneously posting to another cost object, such as a cost center that receives an informational posting
2. Flag the internal order as statistical, in which case it receives the informational posting and another cost object, such as the cost center, receives the real posting

With either method, for reporting purposes, the same expense appears to reside on both objects. An additional field on the posting line items indicates the value type as either real or statistical. However, this identifying field may need to be added to the standard format of the report; often in user-defined reports it is mistakenly or intentionally left out.

The decision as to whether to flag the internal order as statistical or not is based on the allocation methodology selected to relieve the internal order of its expenses. For example, the *Vehicle Fleet* cost center uses internal orders to represent each vehicle. If the vehicles themselves are directly assignable to cost centers that utilize the vehicle, then the internal orders should be real. All vehicle costs are captured on the internal order, and informational postings are made to the *Vehicle Fleet* cost center for overall responsibility reporting. In this example the internal order provides two functions: (1) it captures the cost of the vehicle to be tracked over time to determine when the vehicle needs to be replaced, and (2) it supports the direct assignment of the vehicle expenses to the consuming cost center. The internal order for each vehicle is settled to the cost center that utilizes the vehicle. If, for instance, the receiving cost center is for sales and the vehicles used for making sales calls have more maintenance activities and a higher probability for wrecks, given the percentage of usage, these costs are directly attributed to the cost center. Alternatively, if the vehicles are not assigned to specific individual cost centers and are allocated out based on days used, the internal order can be flagged as statistical to track the cost per vehicle to determine the time for replacement. The cost center then holds the actual expense postings for the asset and charges based on the days utilized by the consuming cost center.

Integrated Planning Impacts

When internal orders are used to represent random or small events, planning often is not done in advance. Internal orders considered during the normal fiscal year planning cycle are those that tend to represent larger-scale projects or repeatedly performed jobs that require detailed or resource planning. In these cases, a decision is made as to whether integrated planning is required. By utilizing the integrated planning capabilities, the impacts of the planned consumptions of a process onto an internal order are recognized for calculating the scheduled process quantity and for the process price calculation. Internal orders utilizing integrated planning must settle their planned costs that return to a cost center or process in order to be included in the price calculation. These planned settlements of internal orders also assure that internal order costing and the processes utilized for those orders are included through all cost flows, which eventually reside in the planned P/L by market segment. This integration supports a much more accurate reflection of potential profitability by segment. However, as each view of costing is added—cost center accounting, process costing, and order accounting—the complexity of the model has a potential to increase. By choosing not to have integrated planning, the interrelationship of the loop is broken. The magnitude of the impact varies depending on the dollar amount that flows through order accounting.

SUMMARY

The integration of the order accounting and activity-based costing components supports accurate process costs for noncore events and jobs performed within an organization. The information flows between the two cost objects support simplistic to very advanced assignment capabilities. The added process costs view provides needed information for understanding the impacts for make-buy, outsourcing, and divestment decisions as well as any other decisions focusing on the costing impacts of events within an organization. Exhibit 6.14 is a summary table representing the key points of this chapter.

NOTES

1. Chapter 5 did not address planning capabilities of the cost center. Most of the planning capabilities listed for the internal order are also available for the cost center, such as overall and detailed planning and budgeting, commitments, and fund management capabilities.

Summary Area	Summary Description
Area-Specific Focus	
Multiple Applications	The internal order can be utilized to represent the most discrete cost pools. Internal orders generally are used to track and control events and jobs or long-term endeavors such as life-cycle costing.
Planning Capabilities: *Overall Planning*	Planning lump sum for multiple years or per year.
Detailed Planning	Planning internal order groups or individual internal orders with cost element/groups, activity types, processes, and statistical key figures.
Resource Planning	Planning at a resource level that combines to represent the costs of a primary cost elements, i.e., specific materials within the *Materials* account or individual consultants within the *External Services* account.
Integrated Planning	Integrated planning supports the update of scheduled drivers quantities for activity types and process planned onto the internal order during detailed planning. Integrated planning also allows for planed settlement to occur.
Unit Cost Planning	Utilizing base object planning capabilities to generate a bill of costs including materials, processes, and activity types in order to plan an event or job.
Budgets , Funds, and Commitments	Budgets can be defined for internal orders, setting aside an allotment of funds to cover commitments created manually or from purchase requisition and orders.
Information Flows	
Assessment and Distribution Cycles:	Utilized to allocate values for process costs to internal orders based on a percentage, portion, or fixed dollar amount. Benefit: Ability to allocate costs simply, potentially with less need for accuracy.
Direct Activity Allocation:	Directly charging a process to internal order. Actual posting only. Benefit: Real-time recognition of the process driver and resulting cost charge at standard unit process rate.
Indirect Activity Allocation Cycle:	An allocation method like an assessment or distribution that utilizes quantities and has the ability to automatically calculate the required processes needed to support the internal order. The process driver quantities can be imputed via a relationship with other drivers already posted to the internal order. Benefit: Reduced driver collection for areas where a strong correlation between drivers can be established. Planned sender quantity is not required because it can be inputed.

Exhibit 6.14   Summary for Process Integration with Overhead Order Accounting

Target = Actual Allocation:	The target = actual allocation requires that integrated planning is utilized. Instead of flexing the actual quantity of one driver to determine the target consumption of another, the process quantities planned in detailed planning are posted as actual quantities to the internal orders. Benefit: Automatic posting of an actual quantity reducing manual efforts.
Template:	Supports conditional requirements for determining the process and quantity to be posted as well as when the process should be posted and during which stage of the internal order life cycle, if necessary. Benefit: Dynamic determination of the process driver consumed by the internal order.
Overhead Calculations:	Overhead calculations utilize costing sheets to determine a surcharge based on a percentage and/or a quantity. Benefit: A value-based allocation that can support some form of dependencies and calculation capabilities that the assessment cycle cannot support.
Settlements:	Settlement is the allocation method supported to relieve the internal orders of costs and revenues based on percentages, fixed dollars, or equivalents (ratios).
Sample Business Decisions	
What are the impacts of internal services for event management or job costing?	The inclusion of process costs onto the internal orders supports a fully burdened event/job costing. Additionally, process costs can be assigned to other modules for capitalization of an asset and expense recovering for sales orders. Benefit: Integration with other modules, accuracy for event/job costing.
What events occur to support processes?	Settling internal orders to processes supports a more direct assignment of costs if the event/job can be specifically attributed to providing the service. Benefit: Ability to completely understand impacts or resources and events supporting processes that are outsourced.
Should the event be procured or internally produced?	The planning capabilities of the internal order in addition to including process costs support a more accurate estimate of the costs for performing an event/job. Benefit: With a fully burdened cost for an event or job, decisions for make-buy or termination can be more accurately evaluated.
Implementation Guides	
Capitalization costs and depreciation simulations	How do internal order process costs impact financial reporting?
Driven by allocation needs	Is there a need for statistical internal orders?
Included in yearly planning/budgeting cycle	Which internal orders should be integrated in planning?

Exhibit 6.14   *(continued)*

7

INTEGRATED ACTIVITY-BASED COSTING WITH PRODUCT COSTING AND PRODUCTION CONTROL

Since the inception of Activity-Based Costing, it has been the goal of Corporate America to integrate, not interface, process information into the world of product costing, production monitoring, and control. The assignment of overhead costs via a process, a two-step method, raises the level of accuracy compared to the traditional method of attaching a percentage overhead surcharge to the direct material or labor costs. As stated in an SAP white paper, "along with greater transparency in overhead cost areas, cost origin-appropriate allocations of overhead in Product Costing is the central goal [for integrating] Activity-based Costing."[1]

The power of the SAP product costing (PC) submodule functionality is in its complete integration with the production modules. This functionality provides the ability to support different types of production methods, valuation across multiple periods beginning with plan on to simultaneous and then final costing, and a high level of accuracy for determining the product costs. The integration of Activity-Based Costing further enhances this functionality, removing ABC from the modeling role and integrating it into the operational day-to-day solution.

This chapter focuses on the integration of ABC to the product costing module; it does not provide a detailed explanation of all of the SAP product costing abilities. As mentioned in Chapter 4, the product costing functionality supports product cost planning, cost object controlling (capturing of actual costs, work in process, and variance calculations), material valuation, and multilevel actual price calculation. Product cost planning is performed via different types of cost estimate tools, where cost estimates define the determination of cost of goods sold, cost of goods manufactured, different material prices, and inventory valuation. Actual costs are captured by period, order, and sales order for intangible goods or services. Once actual production costs and quantities have been collected, the variance analysis can be performed. Additionally, the product cost business application supports the actual costing/material ledger capabilities that are used if actual costing for materials, period valuation of material stock, multiple valuations (such as legal or profit center), or material stock in multiple currencies is necessary.

PRODUCT COSTING ANALYSIS CAPABILITIES

With a high-level definition established, the question still remains: What specifically does the product costing module do and how is ABC integrated? The following sections address each of the major areas of the product costing submodule.

Types of Production Strategies Supported

The traditional flow of ABC for product costing starts in resources flowing through to the processes and on to the cost object. A cost object can represent any receiver of cost, such as the customer, a product, or an advertising campaign. The SAP system contains several cost objects. Each cost object is used for different analysis and reporting purposes. The product costing cost objects are designed to support different types of production and are the focus of this chapter. Exhibit 7.1 lists the different types of production strategies along with additional information. Regardless of the type of production environment or the product costing cost objects used, the ABC submodule is completely integrated with the product costing submodule. This integration supports process cost assignments to the appropriate cost object or material.

Every type of production environment is supported, including the service sector. The differences between these production environments are great when considered from a production/logistics standpoint. However, from an ABC standpoint, there is little difference between the production types, other than the cost objects used and the timing of costing. Therefore, for the sake of simplicity, all examples within this section are based on a make-to-stock production environment. This chapter does not ignore service costing since the Service Management module is considered a production module; therefore, the functionality listed is applicable for services. Furthermore, services are addressed again in Chapter 8.

Different Methods of Product Cost Planning Supported

All forms of production generally use a planned product cost as a method for planning, tracking, and inventory valuation. Within product costing, planned

Type of Production	Description	Cost Objects	Products Costing By
Make-to-Order	Make-to-Order manufacturing supports products that are configurable to meet the specific customer's needs, e.g., a direct-ordered laptop computer.	Sales orders and production orders	Sales order (focus is a particular quantity)
Make-to-Stock	Make-to-Stock related manufacturing supports production that has lot size constraints, e.g., batches of chocolate chip cookies.	Production orders, product cost collectors	Order (focus is a particular quantity)
Engineer-to-Order	Engineer-to-Order products are large-scale, customer-specific projects, e.g., construction of a building.	Projects (WBS-elements), networks, and orders	Order (focus is a particular quantity)
Repetitive	Repetitive manufacturing is used for products that have a stable design and are mass produced, such as a disposable razor or 3/4-inch bolt.	Product cost collectors, run schedule headers, and cost object hierarchies	Period (focus is a particular time frame)
KANBAN	KANBAN is used to support JIT production for environments that choose to not hold intermediary stocks.	Product cost collectors	Period (focus is a particular time frame)
Process	Process manufacturing is used for nondiscrete, continuous process industries such as chemical companies.	Process orders, product cost collectors, and cost object hierarchies	Order if batch related or period based
Service	The Service Management module is used to determine and track the cost of providing a service.	Sales orders, internal orders, general cost objects, service orders	Intangible goods and services

Exhibit 7.1 Types of Production Strategies

product costs are determined in one of two methods: (1) quantity-structure and (2) non–quantity-structure.

Quantity-structure planning requires structured objects such as a bill of material (BOM) or a master recipe to capture material costs, a routing to capture the costs of operations, and so on. Similarly, a template is used to determine the quantity requirements and point of valuation of process drivers. The combination of the information contained in these structures is used to determine the product costs for a given time frame. This method for determining the estimated product costs is useful when the product consists of standardized structures and is consistent in nature.

The non–quantity-structure approach allows the end user to create a product cost without structures by directly entering the materials, internal activities (ac-types), and/or processes required to calculate the planned product costs. This form of product cost planning is very useful when determining the planned cost of a new product or enhancements to current products. Both of these methods can be used to determine the cost estimate of a product or service.

Different Cost Estimates Supported

Product cost planning supports the generation of a cost estimate using either the quantity-structure or the non–quantity-structure approach. A cost estimate is a list of costs (materials, internal activities, processes) for a cost object (part, component, product, service). The cost estimate is used as the basis for production controlling, profitability analysis, price determination, and inventory valuation. SAP supports several different cost estimates for varying needs. Exhibit 7.2 lists the cost estimates and additional information.

Each cost estimate is supported by multiple cost component splits, cost components, potentially two cost component layouts, and an itemization.

Cost Component Splits   Product cost functionality provides alternative aggregation and views of the resulting cost information. These views and aggregations are referred to as cost component splits. There are several cost component splits standard to product costing: cost of goods manufactured (COGM), cost of goods sold (COGS), sales and administration, inventory (commercial and tax-based). The cost component split merely filters costs based on the type of information desired. All examples contained within this chapter use the current cost estimate with the cost of goods manufactured cost component split.

Cost Components   Cost components are groupings of cost elements (e.g., materials, direct labor, process costs, etc.). Users define the cost components to match their organizational information needs. These cost components are also selected as containing fixed and/or proportional (variable) costs and as relevant for the different cost component splits (e.g., COGM or COGS and if used for inventory valuation.)

Type of Cost Estimate	Description	Calculation	Updates	Used For
Standard	A frozen standard for a material usually set at the beginning of the fiscal year or new cyclical season and not intended to be changed.	The quantity structure multiplied by the standard material prices, actype, and process rates	The Standard Cost field on the Material Master/Cost view	Calculation of target costs and total variances
Modified	A revised standard used during the year or season to recalculate the product cost to reflect permanent engineering changes, e.g., material change to the BOM.	The current quantity structure multiplied by the standard material prices, actype, and process rates	The Planned Price fields 1, 2, or 3 on the Material Master Cost view	Calculation of target costs
Current/ Production Version Specific	A current standard to provide the most recent information.	The current quantity structure multiplied by the current material prices, actype, and process rates	The Planned Price fields 1, 2, or 3 in the Material and Master Cost view	Calculation of WIP, scrap, with target costs and variances.
Inventory	A cost estimate to provide an inventory valuation.	The current quantity structure multiplied by the tax-based and commercial prices	The Tax and Commercial Balance Sheets	Valuation of materials in stock

Exhibit 7.2   Comparison of Cost Estimate Types

Cost Component Layouts   The cost component layout is a breakdown of the calculated product costs. Two different types of layouts are possible for each cost estimate.

1. One layout focuses on the split of the product cost, for example, grouping cost components together, such as materials, direct labor, indirect labor, machine costs, and so on, all user defined.

2. Another layout focuses on the primary source of costs, such as materials, energy, depreciation, and wages. (This layout is the primary cost component layout described in Chapter 5.)

Itemization   A further analytical view is provided through the itemization of the cost estimate. The itemization functionality provides detailed information about the origin of the costs grouped into the cost components. Exhibit 7.3 illustrates a sample cost estimate with the cost component splits, cost components, and itemization. This example uses the standard cost component layout; therefore, it does not depict the primary source of the costs (e.g., wages, depreciation, electricity, etc.).

The itemization shows the detailed information of the costs that are rolled up into the cost components. The materials (category M) roll up into cost component 10 for Direct Materials. The actypes (category E) roll up into 20 Direct Labor and 30 Direct Machine, respectively. The costing sheet (category G) used in this example to calculate indirect material costs based on a percentage of direct materials is contained within 40 Indirect Material. A template (category X) is used for posting the *Final Inspection* and *Receipt FG* processes that roll up into cost component 50 Process Costs.

This cost estimate example can be generated with or without the quantity-structure and is provided to show the information cost estimates contain. This example is used throughout the chapter to illustrate the impacts of integrating process information with product costing.

Different Methods for Transfer Pricing Supported

SAP product costing supports multiple values for inventory based on different currencies and on different methods of valuation for transfer pricing. Valuation methods supported are legal, group, and profit center valuation. Legal valuation uses transfer prices for intercompany transfers, whereas group valuation does not use transfer prices at all and therefore does not contain any internal profits. Profit center valuation uses transfer prices every time a profit center change occurs in a value chain. All of the methods for transfer pricing include the process costs.

Different Variance Calculations Supported

At the core of control and accountability is variance analysis. Variance can be calculated based on three different bases:

Material: Prod/Serv #1000	Cost of Goods Mfg'd. Cost Component Split:				
	Cost Components	*Overall*	*Fixed*	*Var.*	*Cur*
Cost Component Splits:	10 Direct Materials	$1,000		$1,000	USD
Cost of Goods Manufactured **$3,000**	20 Direct Labor	$ 500	$250	$ 250	USD
Cost of Goods Sold $3,500	30 Direct Machine	$ 500	$400	$ 100	USD
Sales & Administration $ 0	40 Indirect Material	$ 300		$ 300	USD
Inventory (Commercial) $3,000	50 Process Costs	$ 700	$ 70	$ 630	USD
Inventory (Tax based) $3,000	Cost of Goods Mfg'd.	$3,000	$720	$2,280	USD

Itemization of Cost of Goods Manufactured:									
ItmNo.	*Catg.*	*Resource*	*Cost Element*	*Total*	*Fixed*	*Var.*	*Cur*	*Qty.*	*Unit*
1	M	Raw Material	400000	$ 500		$ 500	USD	1	EA
2	M	Semi-finished	400010	$ 500		$ 500	USD	2	EA
3	E	CC100 WC1 LABHR	950010	$ 500	$ 250	$ 250	USD	10	HR
4	E	CC200 WC2 MACHR	950020	$ 500	$ 400	$ 100	USD	10	HR
5	G	PPC1	400000	$ 300		$ 300	USD		
6	X	Final Inspection	950100	$ 200	$ 20	$ 180	USD	1	EA
7	X	Receipt FG	950200	$ 500	$ 50	$ 450	USD	1	EA
Cost of Goods Manufactured				$3,000	$ 720	$2,280	USD		

Exhibit 7.3   Cost Estimate for Prod/Serv #1000 Example

1. Total
2. Production
3. Planning

Variance can be further categorized as input-based variance or output variance. This variance analysis can be expanded again with multiple variance categories that can be calculated. Exhibit 7.4 lists the categories, the groupings, and additional information.

The ability to include a process view in any type of production, for differing cost estimates, or transfer pricing, and to calculate a multitude of variance categories provides a completely integrated operational ABC system for the support of product costing, production control, and monitoring. The following section addresses the ways in which process costs are integrated with product costing.

INFORMATION FLOWS

Three main methods integrate the ABC information with product costing:

1. Direct activity allocation to charge out process costs
2. Templates used for calculating and posting process costs
3. Direct process assignment via the routing

Variance Group	Variance Category	Description	Example
Input	Input Price	Caused by a difference between plan and actual prices of the materials, actypes, or processes.	Process 1 in Std. Cost estimate is 1 @ $15 for the plan, in actual 2 @ moving average of $20. Input Price Var. = $10
Input	Resource Usage	Caused by using a different material, actype, or process than planned.	Process B with rate of $20 is used versus Process A with rate of $15. Resource Usage Var. = $5
Input	Input Quantity	Caused by a different quantity of material, actype, or processes.	Plan used 1 Process A, actual used 2 Process A with an std. rate of $15/Process A. Input Qty Var. = $15
Input	Remaining Input	Caused by any input difference not assigned to one of the other input variances.	A Costing Sheet adds 100% of Raw 1 as indirect material cost. Raw 1 increased from $15 to $20, allocation increased $5 as well and is calculated as Remaining Input Var. Not ABC related.
Output	Mixed price	Caused by different production alternatives for the same materials.	Mixed price is $15, consisting of $10 for alternative A and $20 for alternative B. A production for alternative A will show a mixed price variance of ($5), assuming no other variances. If the ratio between alternatives A and B is the same as planned, the total mixed price variances will be 0. (Not ABC related.)
Output	Output price	Caused by standard price changing between cost estimate and delivery to stock.	Normally a standard price change should be created only via a new standard cost estimate, which would prevent output price variances to occur. Not ABC related.
Output	Lot size	Caused by planned quantity different than confirmed quantity.	Lot size variances occur when some actypes/processes to be consumed are not based on a planned lot size. If the lot size changes, some of the drivers may not change, such as the # *Setup Hrs* or *Perform Inspection*. The cost impact is shown as a lot size variance.
Output	Remaining	Caused by any output difference not assigned to one of the other output variances and rounding errors.	This is the catch-all bucket for unknown discrepancies that the system cannot classify. This should not be ABC related.

[a]Variance examples provided within this exhibit are using a lot size of 1 except for the Output variance and Lot size variance.

Exhibit 7.4 Multiple Variance Categories

Exhibit 7.5 Direct
Activity Allocation to
Production Cost Object

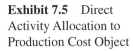

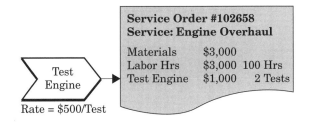

Direct Activity Allocation to Production Cost Object

The DAA transaction can be used to charge the process directly to the production cost object (e.g., production order, service order, project, etc.). Exhibit 7.5 illustrates a direct activity allocation to a service order. A service order for the overhaul of an engine has been placed at an airline maintenance shop. In order to ensure that the engine works properly, the process of *Test Engine* is performed. Depending on the condition of the engine, the *Test Engine* activity may be required more than once and can vary between service orders for different engines, impacting the cost of providing the service.

   A DAA is available only for making an actual posting of process costs based on a quantity. Therefore, this method of assigning process costs to product cost objects is not supported for planning. In order to build the process cost relationship to the product cost objects for plan, the process can be added to the unit cost, integrated through a template, or assigned directly to the routing.

Template to Production Cost Objects

The template can be used to calculate and post planned and actual process costs to the material or production cost objects. (See Exhibit 7.6.) A template is indirectly assigned to the material master for planned/actual product cost assignments. In planning, the template is used when calculating the cost estimate. This cost estimate can be used later to determine target production costs. The same template is used to assign actual process costs to the production cost objects once the appropriate defined event has been encountered, for example, final confirmation of the production order or at a project's milestone confirmation. The following sections provide detailed examples of a template for product costing, integration with the cost estimate, and assignment of actual process costs.

Detailed Example of a Template This template example, *ProdExample,* assigns the *Final Inspection* and the *Receipt FG* process costs to the product cost estimates

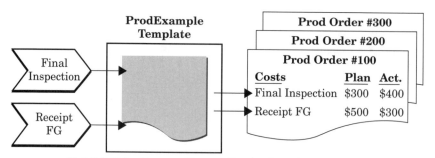

Exhibit 7.6   Process Costs to Production via a Template

Type	Name	Object	Un	Plan Quantity	Plan Activation	Actual Quantity	Actual Activation	Actual Alloc. Event
Business Proc	Receipt FG	Receipt FG	Ea	Total_ Order_Qty.	Active	Total_ Order_Qty.	Active	Order End
Business Proc	Final Inspection	Inspection	EA	1	Method	1	Method	Order End

Environment: 001 — Cost Estimate/Production Order
Template: ProdExample — Example Prod. Cost Template

Exhibit 7.7   A Detailed ABC-PC/PP Template Example

and to the production order for plan and actual production costs. The template is created using the standard environment 001, filtering the information (Functions) related to Projects, Services, and so on. Several standard production-related template environments are:

- 001 Cost estimate for Material/Production orders
- 004 Network (Project Related)
- 008 Sales order
- 009 Process Order
- 011 Service Order

Exhibit 7.7 illustrates the template definition structure. Recall that the "Type" field defines the sender cost object. In this example, the Business Process type is used. Therefore, when selecting the actual object to be used, the standard process hierarchy is made available for the process to be selected. For this example, the plan or actual quantity fields use a function instead of directly entering a quantity. For the 001 Environment, the function areas (hierarchies) and one sample function of each are:

- Process—Scheduled_Process_Planned_Qty
- Order Data—Total_Order_Quantity
- Materials—Material_Characteristic_Value
- BOM—Number_of_BOM_Items
- Routing—NumberOfWorkCenters
- General Data—Actual_Cost_On_Object
- Mathematical Equations—Frac (Fractions in an equation)

In Exhibit 7.7, the function Total_Order_Quantity is used to determine how many *Receipt FG* processes should be posted to the production order. The template also has defined that one *Final Inspection* process will be posted for both the plan and actual. The *Receipt FG* process is selected as Active, indicating that the process will always be posted. The *Final Inspection* process uses a method defined as Total_Order_Quantity > 100. When the template is run, it will check the total order quantity; if it is greater than 100, then it will post the one planned/actual process quantity.

The final definition of the template is the actual allocation event. To accurately reflect process costs when they occur and not necessarily just periodically, the actual allocation event is used. Exhibit 7.8 illustrates how process costs are recognized over time using the "Event Activation" field.

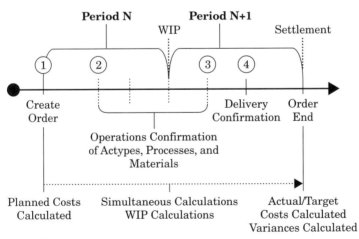

① Post *Create Production Order* process

② Post *Issue Raw Materials* process

③ Post *Final Inspection* process

④ Post *Receipt to FG* process

Exhibit 7.8 Process Costs Recognition over Time Example

The processes can be allocated to the production order or to any production cost object at any point throughout the life cycle. Certain processes' cost may be attributed when the order is created, or during an operation confirmation or an order end. By using the Event Activation field, the process costs are recognized at the appropriate time in the correct period. As seen in Exhibit 7.7, for the template example, the Activation Field is defined as Order End.

Using this example, when a production order with quantity of 300 is confirmed, completed, and closed (Order End), the resulting process charge to the production order will be 300 *Receipt FG* and 1 *Final Inspection.*

Template Integrating the Process with the Cost Estimate   Now that the template functionality has been fully described for the product cost controlling area and its capabilities explained, how is it used to integrate the process with the materials? Exhibit 7.9 illustrates how the processes *Final Inspection* and *Issue Raw Material* impact the Cost Estimate with Quantity Structure of Prod/Serv #1000.

The example illustrates the original cost estimate, Exhibit 7.3, being generated with a quantity structure. The BOM is used for the materials and the routing is used to determine direct labor and machine costs. The drivers, A1 for LABHR and A2 for MACHR, are defined on the work centers (WC) of the routing. Each driver has a standard rate that has already been calculated or manually entered. The costing sheet (PPC1) allows formulas for the calculation of values, not quantities, to be created in order to attribute overhead expenses. A common example is allocating a percentage of the direct material costs as indirect costs to cover nontracked costs, such as receiving, batch acceptance testing, storing, and issuing of raw materials.

The template is assigned to each material via the material master and several connective configuration steps for product costing. Once these steps have been completed, process costs via the template are included in the product cost estimate.

Template Integrating the Process with the Production Cost Object   Process costs are available on the production costs object for planned, actual, and target costing. When a production cost object, such as a production order, is created, the planned cost of the production order can be calculated. The planned production costs pull the structures, including the template, in a manner similar to the cost estimates being generated with a quantity structure. Companies desiring to review the production order cost prior to the actual production can calculate planned production costs in order to determine if the production order is cost justifiable.

Given that many companies do not rationalize whether to take an order, the system allows users to not create the planned production costs, if desired. In this instance, the companies choose to focus on capturing of actuals and a comparison

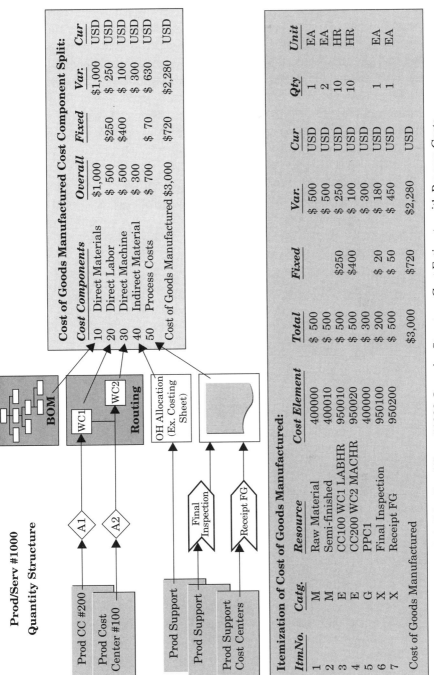

Exhibit 7.9 Prod/Serv #1000 Quantity Structure Cost Estimate with Process Costs

with target costs. The defined template is used to assign actual process costs to the production object. The template can be run within a period or during period-end closing. Once the template has been used to post the actual process production costs, the target costs can be generated. They are generated either using the standard or the current cost estimate with the actual quantities of the production cost object to forecast what the actual production costs should have been. Since the process costs are included in the cost estimates, target process costing also takes place. Exhibit 7.10 illustrates the actual and target production costs comparison. This example has actual production output quantity of one. Therefore, the target information is equal to the cost estimate provided in Exhibit 7.9.

This example demonstrates how the template is created, included in the cost estimate, and integrated with the production cost object for planned, actual, and target costing. The template functions and methods support the ability to generate very complex calculations for determining when and how much of a process should be assigned.

Process Integrated with the Routing

The integration of the process with production was first accomplished via the template. Later, in Release 4.5, the process could be directly assigned to a work center on a routing. Exhibit 7.11 demonstrates the impact on the cost estimate with quantity-structure illustrated in Exhibit 7.10. The process assignment for *Receipt FG* has moved to be included in the routing instead of being calculated using the template. Note that for the *ItmNo.* 7 within the *Itemization* section of the exhibit, the *Category* for the *Receipt FG* process has changed from an X to a P. The P represents that the process is directly assigned to the object, in this instance via the routing.

The impact to planning is merely which structure, the routing or the template, the process quantity is pulled from. For actuals, the impact is on the timing of when the process quantity and costs are recognized. If the process is directly assigned to the work center and confirmation is done by operation, then process costs will be recognized when the work center is confirmed rather than at order end, as the template in Exhibit 7.7 was defined. The timing for both methods can be designed to be the same. Having the process on the routing provides two benefits.

1. Users can backflush at standard quantity with an adjustment posting for any usage difference, if desired. Doing this can reduce the requirements on the system. If the process quantities do not vary greatly or the cost impact is minimal, this method can be used to automatically assign process costs to a production cost object.

Resource	Cost Element	Act. Total	A. Fixed	A. Var.	A. Qty.	Tgt. Total	T. Fixed	T. Var.	T. Qty.	Variance
Raw Material	400000	$ 550		$ 550	1	$ 500		$ 500	1	$50
Semi-finished	400010	$ 500		$ 500	2	$ 500		$ 500	2	$ 0
CC100 WC1 LABHR	950010	$ 550	$275	$ 275	11	$ 500	$250	$ 250	10	$50
CC200 WC2 MACHR	950020	$ 450	$360	$ 90	9	$ 500	$400	$ 100	10	($50)
PPC1	400000	$ 315		$ 315		$ 300		$ 300		$15
Final Inspection	950100	$ 200	$ 20	$ 180	1	$ 200	$ 20	$ 180	1	$ 0
Receipt FG	950200	$ 500	$ 50	$ 450	1	$ 500	$ 50	$ 450	1	$ 0
Total		$3,065	$705	$2,360		$3,000	$720	$2,280		$65

Cost Report for Production Order #10000 for Prod/Serv #1000:

Exhibit 7.10 Production Cost Comparisons

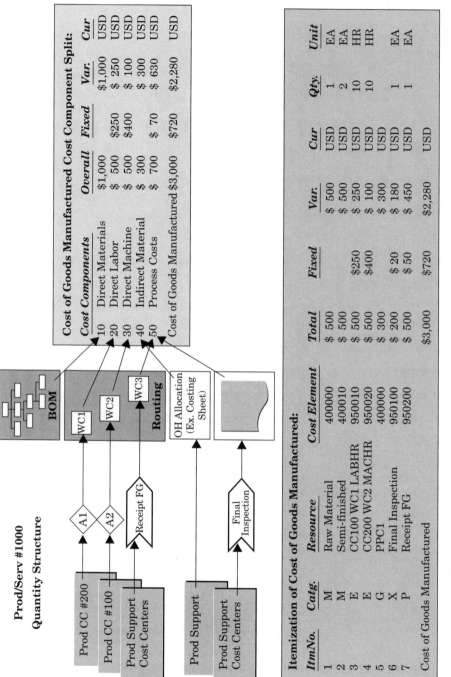

Exhibit 7.11 Process Integration with the Production Routing

Information Flow	Comments	Assignment Basis	Type of Posting	Timing	Usability	Handle Complexity
Direct Activity Allocation	Only used for actual process postings to production cost objects, e.g., production order, service order.	Actual quantity	Quantity with value	Real time	Easy	None
Templates	Integrates process cost to the cost estimates and production cost objects. Uses formulas, "IF-THEN", and event activations to accurately attribute product costs.	Simple to complex formulas and "IF-THEN" rules	Quantity with value	Within period	Advanced	High level easily supported
Process on Routing	Backflush at standard during confirmation. Impacts routing and work center design.	Standard quantity or actual quantity	Quantity with value	Real time	Moderate	None

Exhibit 7.12 Comparison of Information Flows between ABC and Product Costing

2. If the process is influenced only by formulas that already exist on the routing, it is unnecessary to create a template to mimic the same capabilities of the routing.

Exhibit 7.12 compares these methods (the DAA, the template, and the process on the routing). These methods of process integration are not the only ones that can be used to assign process costs to the materials and production cost objects. Product-related process costs can be merely allocated out to the products based on percentages or noncausal drivers using the ABC assessments or distributions cycles to production orders.

SAMPLE KEY BUSINESS DECISIONS

Multitudes of key business decisions can be supported by the integration of the ABC and product costing submodules. However, a select few listed in Exhibit 7.13 have been chosen to highlight the advantages of this integration.

Key Business Decision	Value Based[a]	Quantity Based[a]
Which processes impact production or service orders and when?	--	√
What are the impacts of process cost on inventory, planned product costs, and production costs?	--	√
What process variances exist and what drives those variances?	--	√
What are the impacts of Sales and Operational planning on planned process outputs?	--	√
Where is excess/idle capacity generated if a product/service is eliminated?	--	√
What are the process cost impacts on future products or enhancements?	--	√

[a]— represents not supported. √ represents supported.

Exhibit 7.13   Key Business Decisions Supported by the ABC-PC Integration Sample

Process Integration with Products and Production Objects

The ability to post process costs via the three methods defined in the "Information Flows" section directly addresses the question: Which processes impact production or service orders and when? The key aspect of the question is the impact on the timing of the process cost recognition for the sake of accuracy. The direct activity allocation transaction recognizes process costs immediately on the cost object and works only for actual process cost postings. The timing of the template posting is determined by the activation field and allows process costs to be attributed to the correct periods based on the events driving the processes. The process assignment to a work center supports process cost recognition when the operation or the whole product cost object is confirmed.

Processes Incorporated into the Cost Estimates

The process integrated with the cost estimates provides valuable information for determining the impact of process costs on product/service costs, inventory values, and production costs. The ability to include the process costs within the cost estimates allows process information to be integrated with:

- *Product prices.* Product pricing can be determined more accurately to ensure that all relevant costs are included.
- *Inventory valuations.* With the process included in the cost estimate, during inventory valuation, the inventory cost estimate is combined with the quantity in stock to determine the value. Therefore, the allowable process costs can be incorporated automatically into the inventory valuation.
- *Target production costs.* Target production costs use a cost estimate to determine what the costs of the product should be, given the actual quantity outputs. With the inclusion of process costs in the cost estimate, process impacts can be determined when the production costs are captured and analyzed.
- *Variance calculations.* Variance calculations use the planned production costs to compare to actual or target. Therefore, since the process costs have been included in the planned production costs, variances for processes can be calculated as well.

Process Variance Calculations

Many different variance categories address input and output variances. Of these, process variances can be generated for:

- Input price
- Input usage
- Input quantity
- Input remaining
- Lot size
- Output remaining

Two key points for the calculation of variances are:

1. If the cost component is not marked as inventoriable, then a variance is not calculated for those items. Therefore, if cost component 50 Process Costs is not marked as inventoriable, variances (other than plan versus actual) for process costs will not be calculated.
2. These variances are calculated on the production cost objects of which the service order and project network or work breakdown structure (WBS) may represent a service. Calculation and management of these variances when the process is used to represent a service, such as *Open Bank Account,* are addressed in Chapters 5 and 8.

Quantity Structure Backflush from Sales and Operation Planning to Cost Center Accounting/Activity-Based Costing

The sales and operation planning (SOP) functionality within SAP is a forecasting and planning tool that integrates the sales plans with the production plans. The SOP consists of two components: (1) logistics functionality and (2) costing functionality. Since the focus of this book is cost related, the logistics functionality of this tool will not be addressed. The SOP functionality supports the creation of different "what-if" scenarios that are used to determine the impact on available capacity and profits. In most organizations, planning is performed separately in each of the corresponding areas. The sales managers plan the forecasted sales quantities. Simultaneously, cost center and process managers prepare their plans for the year; product managers create new cost estimates; and so on. The SOP function integrates these processes from the separate planning philosophy and provides a tool to focus on how these individual plans interrelate. Exhibit 7.14 provides a conceptual overview of the SOP functionality.

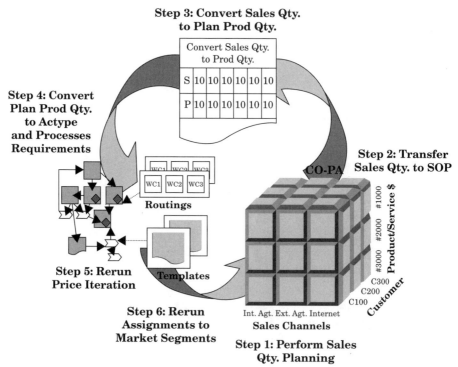

Exhibit 7.14   Sales & Operation Planning Overview

In Step 1, the sales quantities are planned. In Step 2, the sales quantities are transferred from CO-PA to SOP. To simplify this example, in Step 3, the sales quantity plan is accepted as the production quantity plan. Once the planned production quantity is known, these requirements can be transferred to CCA and ABC (Step 4). The routings and templates are used in the backflush to determine what quantities of actypes and processes are required to support the production plan. These quantities will most likely deviate from the cost center and process plans originally generated. In Step 5, the price calculation is rerun to see the impact on the actype and process rates. These rates and new quantities are used for revised standard cost estimates, to rerun allocations into CO-PA, and to determine the final impact on gross and contribution margins (Step 6).

The SOP functionality can support an integrated planning cycle. However, it requires that organizations at least create an integrated plan on paper before supporting it by a system. Most organizations have not been able to move beyond the political intricacies that can make this planning process very difficult. If they can, the PC with AZC module integration is the most comprehensive application of the Activity-Based Budgeting concept.

Process Impact on Excess/Idle Capacity Management

With the ability to backflush and determine the impacts on actype and process quantities, excess/idle capacity is now visible. The lack of visibility of capacity management issues has long been a weakness in nonintegrated solutions. For example, if *Prod/Serv #1000* is eliminated, the quantities of *Receipt FG* and *Final Inspection* process required is reduced. These processes consume resources that are most likely a measure of capacity for a cost center, such as MACHR or LABHR. Therefore, less capacity is required due to a product being eliminated. The rates need to be recalculated to recognize that the portion of fixed costs within the resource unit rate has increased and to increase the portion of fixed costs that other processes will consume. To avoid the fixed cost death spiral, the excess/idle capacity can be attributed to a different level of the P/L rather than fully absorbed by the remaining products.

Process Impact on New Products or Enhancements

Product costing supports the generation of estimated costs for a new product. It allows the user to enter material, labor, processes, and any other costs believed to be necessary for the product creation. Cost impacts of product enhancement changes can be determined by accessing the current product structures and altering them to reflect the enhancements.

IMPLEMENTATION GUIDELINES

The CO module product costing functionality is very robust. Depending on analysis and reporting requirements, implementation can become detail oriented and configuration intensive. Integrating the ABC functionality requires a company to support a holistic conceptual view. Exhibit 7.15 provides several implementation guidelines to consider.

Timing for Process Recognition

The requirement for when the process cost should be recognized drives the determination of the information flow designed. If process costs need to be recognized immediately, the direct activity allocation is required. If another time frame is acceptable or if there is a defining event, then the template or inclusion on the routing may be used.

Routing/Work Center Design Change to Support Processes

Including the process directly on the work center of the routing will require changes to the work center and routing definitions. Depending on the level of information and the number of processes to be included, structural changes to the

Type	Implementation Guidelines
Conceptual Design	When do the process costs need to be recognized?
System Design	What are the impacts of including a process on the work centers?
System Design	How should the linkage of the different templates be designed?
Organization Impact	What are the impacts of process inclusion on inventory valuation?

Exhibit 7.15   ABC Integration with Product Costing Implementation Guidelines

work center/routing, such as the number of work centers on a routing, may be required to support the new requirements. Additionally, adding the process view to the work centers and routings may require new departments in the organization to embrace the ABC philosophy.

Template Linkage Design

Several connecting steps are used to assign the template to the material master for a product. These steps form different combinations of templates and ways for the template determination to be created. If more than one template is required to assign process costs to a material, a hierarchy of templates can be created (i.e., templates including other templates). Therefore, the design of the templates and how they are grouped determines which process costs are attributed to what products. The different potential designs of the template linkages with the material master determines which templates are selected and when.

Process Inclusion in Inventory

Including the process costs in the inventory valuation can become a sensitive subject. Decisions as to which processes to include, when to change the standard, and how or if to reevaluate current inventory need to be addressed. It is also important to weigh the needs for process analysis with inventory requirements since only those processes marked as inventoriable will be included for variance calculations.

SUMMARY

"The great advantage of [integrated ABC] is that current data is available permanently in fine detail. In costing all products, process utilization is directly visible."[2] The integration of Activity-Based Costing with the product costing analysis capabilities within SAP provides several benefits including, but not limited to:

- The ABC process assignment of overhead costs to product costs can provide a more accurate assignment method that supports better decision making for decisions such as product profitability, appropriate product mix, product elimination, and product enhancements.
- Process costs are included in inventory valuation.

- The template functionality supports a more advanced ABC to PC design due to its ability to handle complex cost drivers and support complicated formulas for assignments with little effort. The template also supports the dynamic determination of which process to assign to what products and when during the production life cycle.
- The ABC submodule has real-time access to operational data and driver information without the need to design, build, and support interfaces.

Exhibit 7.16 provides a summary of this chapter and the key points to remember from each of the subsections.

NOTES

1. Operative Linkage of CO-ABC with Product Costing White Paper, SAP AG, p. 4.
2. Ibid., p. 5.

Summary Area	Summary Description
Area-Specific Focus	
Different types of production strategies supported	Example: Make-to-Sales order, Make-to-Stock, Engineer-to-Order, Repetitive, Kanban, Process, Service. Benefit: Process costs included in material costs for any type of production environment.
Different method of product cost planning	Example: quantity-structured and non–quantity-structured. Benefit: Process included in production structures for costing or can be used on-the-fly for product cost determination.
Different cost estimates supported	Example: Standard (Frozen), Modified (Revised), Current/Production Version Specific, Inventory. Benefit: Process included in all forms of cost estimates being used for variance determinations, product pricing, inventory valuation, etc.
Different methods of transfer pricing supported	Example: Legal, Group, and Profit Center valuations. Benefit: Process included in the valuation whether for an external or internal view.
Different variance categories supported	Example: Resource Usage, Input Quantity, Lot Size. Benefit: Process included in production variance calculations for determining areas of improvement.
Information Flows	
Direct Activity Allocation (actual costs only)	Example: *Test Engine* process to the Service order. Benefit: Real-time recognition of the process driver and resulting cost charge at standard process rate.
Template (plan and actual)	Example: *Final Inspection* process to production order. Benefit: Dynamic recognition of the process driver and resulting cost charge. Ability to accommodate complex formulas.
Process on the routing (plan and actual)	Example: *Receipt FG* process to the production order. Benefit: Identification of process impacts on work centers/routings, ability to backflush at standard if desired, ability to use work center formulas, such as determining maintenance costs based on machine time.
Sample Business Decisions	
Which processes impact production or rate for service orders and when?	Supported by the direct activity allocation of a process, the process to routing assignment, and the templates, all using a microstandard of the process. Benefit: Resource and process consumption by each production/service order is made transparent.
What are the impacts of process cost on valuation, inventory, planned product costs, and production costs?	Process inclusion with cost estimates. Benefit: Process costs are included in product pricing, inventory planned, actual and target production costs as well as in the variance calculations.

Exhibit 7.16   Table for Process Integration with Product Costing Summary

What process variances exist and what drives those variances?	Several variance categories include the process in the calculation if it is marked as an inventoriable process. Benefit: Determine why processes are under- or overutilized.
What are the impacts of Sales and Operational planning on planned process outputs?	Provides the ability to backflush the entire quantity structure, from planned sales quantities through production planning, and into cost center and process requirements. Organizational ABB. Benefit: Optimizes resource/process needs throughout the organization. Helps to set capacities correctly.
Where is excess/idle capacity generated if a product/service is eliminated?	By using the backflushing capabilities to accurately determine capacity requirements and needs, areas where excess/idle capacity exist are highlighted. Benefit: Indicates areas where excess/idle capacity will exist.
What are the process cost impacts on future products or enhancements?	Ability to quickly and easily create product cost estimates that include processes as well. Benefit: Can determine if the new product/service or enhancement should be produced.
Implementation Guides	
Timing for process	When do the process costs need to be recognized?
Routing work center design change to support processes	What are the impacts of including the process on the work centers?
Template linkage design	How should the linkage of the template be designed?
Process inclusion in inventory	What are the impacts of the process inclusion on inventory valuation?

Exhibit 7.16   (*continued*)

8

INTEGRATED ACTIVITY-BASED COSTING WITH MARKET SEGMENT ANALYSIS

Chapter 4 provided a brief overview of the profitability analysis capabilities supported by CO. As stated earlier, CO-PA supports two methods of market segment analysis: (1) account based and (2) costing based. Costing-based analysis is used to support a sales and marketing view; account-based analysis focuses on reconciliation with financial accounting. As the focus here is segment analysis, the costing-based, marketing view is the CO-PA method used for all examples within this chapter.

The profitability analysis module provides the organization with multidimensional planning and analysis of profits, enabling managers to view profitability in terms of many analytical views as well as intersections of these dimensional views. Dimensional views may include a customer dimension, a product dimension, and/or many other user-defined dimensions. These views enable managers to analyze market segments and the profit/loss data in a meaningful and relevant perspective. This multidimensional functionality is a powerful tool, which only increases with the accommodation and integration of ABC. Activity-Based Costing is simply a more accurate assignment of product and overhead costs via processes. By integrating ABC data, cost assignments to multidimensional analysis provide a better picture of which market segments are providing the company with the most benefit.

MULTIDIMENSIONAL ANALYSIS CAPABILITIES

By now, the meaning of Activity-Based Costing should be clear. But what exactly does "multidimensional planning and analysis" mean? The following three sections cover a description of this capability, an example of the benefits provided as compared to a two-dimensional view of cost objects, and sample multidimensional reporting functionality of SAP.

Multidimensional Functionality: The Cube

As mentioned in Chapter 2, many stand-alone ABC systems support the common two-dimensional or hierarchical approach of assigning costs to cost objects. Workarounds can be created in the model design to simulate a multidimensional approach, but doing this can be tedious. In the two-dimensional method, process costs are assigned to one cost object reporting dimension, such as product, and then an allocation is performed to move those costs to another dimension or level of the hierarchy, such as product/customer. Multidimensional reporting recognizes that a hierarchical relationship might not reflect reality, because costs may be directly associated with one or more dimensions. Therefore, multidimensional functionality supports the ability to post directly to an intersection of two or more reporting dimensions. Instead of assigning process costs to just the product and then allocating to a product/customer view, the process costs using the multidimensional approach posts directly to the intersection of product/customer, eliminating the need for the allocation.

Exhibit 8.1 illustrates this capability as a multidimensional "cube." Obviously, the potential analytical dimensions far exceed the three dimensions in the

Exhibit 8.1 Multidimensional
Cube Example

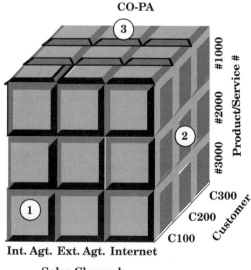

illustration. Most SAP clients actively using this functionality exceed three dimensions; in fact, over 19 dimensions are provided as standard functionality depending on the SAP release implemented. Some standard dimensions include: company code, plant, distribution channel, product, customer, and sales organization. Clients can further expand the dimensional analysis by adding their own user-defined dimensions, such as a strategic business unit for fire and casualty insurance or product/service attributes such as V6 engine or first-class ticket. The possibilities are limited only by imagination and hardware performance. Each additional reporting dimension and the total number of values for that dimension exponentially increases the required size of the database.

The three dimensions of the cube in Exhibit 8.1 are Sales Channel, Customer, and Product. The Sales Channel characteristic for the examples in this chapter represents the three modes of sales methods for this sample organization. The Sales Channel values are *Int. Agt.* for Internal Agents, *Ext. Agt.* for External Agents, and the *Internet.* To further illustrate, assume an organization that maintains its own sales representatives maintains relationships with third-party agencies selling its products/services and provides Internet access for purchases as well. The intersection of the dimensional values defines the market segments. Exhibit 8.2 provides a description of the dimensions labeled in the Exhibit 8.1 example.

A cube is generally used to graphically represent the multidimensional database and reporting capabilities because more than three dimensions are difficult to depict pictorially.

Comparison of Two-dimensional versus Multidimensional Analysis

What is the benefit of being able to post directly to an intersection? The answer is the accuracy provided via a causal association of costs. The phrase "It is better to be approximately correct rather than precisely wrong" is common. In an integrated multidimensional environment, the design rapidly approaches precisely correct.

Segment	Sales Channel	Customer	Product
1	Internal Agent	C100	3000
2	Internet	C200	2000
3	External Agent	C300	1000

Exhibit 8.2   Example Market Segments

When determining how to attribute costs to the segment P/L, clients usually provide a plethora of sayings, ranging from nice to down right rude. Occasionally people act out how an allocation rule is determined by making a gesture of pulling something out of the sky. The consensus is the allocation methodology is a WAG, translated euphemistically, "We make it up." Many companies still take all costs and randomly or use precisely wrong methods to allocate all their costs to the product (e.g., the gardener to all 40,000 product SKUs.) Worse yet are the managers who want to keep moving costs around the organization, for example, moving the historical rent expense when an insurance policy gets transferred from one sales group in New York to another in New Jersey. This logic is inevitably driven by poorly defined performance measures and bonus structures.

Regardless of the logic, or lack thereof, behind the allocation methods, the ability to post directly to an intersection of dimensions removes the need to make further allocations to impute the other dimensions, which can potentially introduce inaccuracy. The following exhibits illustrate the benefits of using multidimensional postings instead of secondary allocations between dimensions. Exhibit 8.3 depicts the constants/assumptions used for the comparison.

The comparison in the exhibit uses two customers purchasing two products/services. There are two customer-related process costs as well. The first is the *Resolve Complaints* process, which is used to represent non–product-related activities, such as billing issues, shipping problems, and so on. The *Handle Inquiries* process is used to represent a product-related activity of answering questions dealing with the different products. Exhibit 8.4 provides the relevant sales information and how the postings are performed within the multidimensional database.

The two key pieces of information in this exhibit are the segment information and the activity/process assignment. Within SAP, each reporting dimension and combination is assigned a segment number (depicted in the exhibit as Segments 1 through 10). Note that Segments 5 and 6 are single-dimension postings

Constants	Name	Cost	Sales Price
P1000	Prod/Serv 1	$ 80.00	$ 200.00
P2000	Prod/Serv 2	$ 100.00	$ 300.00
A1	Resolve Complaints	$ 50.00	
A2	Handle Inquiries	$ 30.00	

Exhibit 8.3 Comparison Constants

Sales Information and Cube Postings							
Segment	Cust. Char.	Prod. Char.	Quantity	Revenues	Costs		Activity
1	C100	P1000	100	$20,000.00	$ 8,000.00		
2	C100	P2000	200	$60,000.00	$20,000.00		
3	C200	P1000	200	$40,000.00	$16,000.00		
4	C200	P2000	100	$30,000.00	$10,000.00		
5	C100		200		$10,000.00		A1
6	C200		200		$10,000.00		A1
7	C100	P1000	50		$ 1,500.00		A2
8	C100	P2000	80		$ 2,400.00		A2
9	C200	P1000	50		$ 1,500.00		A2
10	C200	P2000	120		$ 3,600.00		A2

Exhibit 8.4   Sales Information and Cube Postings

since the *Resolve Complaints* process *A1* is only a customer-related activity compared to the customer/product-related activity of *Handle Inquiries*. For this example, the *Handle Inquiries* process quantities are larger for P2000 since the
P1000 product is a less complex or a more familiar product. The *Handle Inquiries*
process costs are directly posted to the intersection for the customer and product.

In contrast, a two–dimensional-based ABC system posts this cost to either
the product or the customer dimension and requires an additional allocation
method to interpolate these costs to the combined dimensions. Exhibit 8.5 illustrates the sample two-dimensional allocation calculation.

A percentage formula is used to determine the percentage for each of the potential combinations based on sales quantity for this example. This percentage is
then used to allocate the costs from the Customer to the Customer/Product dimensions. Exhibit 8.6 depicts the resulting allocation.

All process costs for the two–dimensional-based approach now reside at the
customer/product level. The two dark grayed numbers are used as examples below. Exhibit 8.7 illustrates the comparison of the resulting P/Ls via both methods.

Note that the two numbers from Exhibit 8.6 add up to the C100 costs for the
P1000 in Exhibit 8.7. Also important to note is that the total number as shown in
the customer P/Ls for both methods have the exact same result. Therefore, the

Two-Dimensional Allocation from Customer to Customer/Product						
Cust. Char.	Formula	%	Prod. Char.	Formula	%	Quantity
C100	P1000/P1000+P2000	0.333	P1000	C100/C100+C200	0.333	100
C100	P1000/P1000+P2000	0.667	P2000	C100/C100+C200	0.667	200
C200	P1000/P1000+P2000	0.667	P1000	C100/C100+C200	0.667	200
C200	P1000/P1000+P2000	0.333	P2000	C100/C100+C200	0.333	100

Exhibit 8.5   Two-Dimensional Customers to Customer/Product Allocation

Exhibit 8.6   Two-Dimensional Allocation Results

Customer	Customer/Product	Costs
C100	C100-P1000 A1 C100/P1000 A2 Prod/Serv 1000	$ 3,333.33 $ 1,300.00 $ 8,000.00
C100	C100-P2000 A1 C100/P2000 A2 Prod/Serv 2000	$ 6,666.67 $ 2,600.00 $ 20,000.00
C200	C200-P1000 A1 C200/P1000 A2 Prod/Serv 1000	$ 6,667.67 $ 3,400.00 $ 16,000.00
C200	C200-P2000 A1 C200/P2000 A2 Prod/Serv 2000	$ 3,333.33 $ 1,700.00 $ 10,000.00

misleading information is at the customer/product level. If the sales representative is trying to analyze which markets to focus on, the same general conclusion would be drawn from both methods. Customer 100 should be focused on more so than Customer 200, and Customer 100 should be given incentives to purchase more of Product/Service 2000. However, the two-dimensional method would lead the sales representative to focus on selling Product/Service 2000 to Customer 200 as well, instead of Product/Service 1000. The conclusion could be that Product/Service 2000 is always the best product to push in the market when, in reality, the cost-to-serve differences between Product/Service 1000 and 2000 suggest otherwise. Additionally, if performance measures are based on certain numbers, then the multidimensional approach can aid in holding accountable managers responsible for making the decisions.

	Multidimensional P/Ls		Two-Dimensional P/Ls	
Customer P/L	**C100**	**C200**	**C100**	**C200**
Revenues	$ 80,000	$ 70,000	$ 80,000	$ 70,000
Prod/Serv. Cost	$ 28,000	$ 26,000	$ 28,000	$ 26,000
Cust. Costs	$ 13,900	$ 15,100	$ 13,900	$ 15,100
Margin 1	**$38,100**	**$28,900**	**$38,100**	**$28,900**
C100 by Prod/Serv.	**P1000**	**P2000**	**P1000**	**P2000**
Revenues	$ 20,000	$ 60,000	$ 20,000	$ 60,000
Prod/Serv. Cost	$ 8,000	$ 20,000	$ 8,000	$ 20,000
Cust. Costs	$ 1,500	$ 2,400	*$ 4,633*	*$ 9,267*
Margin 2	**$10,500**	**$37,600**	**$ 7,367**	**$30,733**
C200 by Prod/Serv.	**P1000**	**P2000**	**P1000**	**P2000**
Revenues	$ 40,000	$ 30,000	$ 40,000	$ 30,000
Prod/Serv. Cost	$ 16,000	$ 10,000	$ 16,000	$ 10,000
Cust. Costs	$ 1,500	$ 3,600	$ 10,067	$ 5,033
Margin 2	**$22,500**	**$16,400**	**$13,933**	**$14,967**

Exhibit 8.7   Profit/Loss Statement Results Comparison[1]

The two-dimensional (matrix) approach produces two inaccuracies.

1. To see process costs for more than one dimension, an allocation has to be made based on some driver. This example used sales volume as the dimensional driver. This driver may not be highly correlated to the true driver of the process, and therefore this allocation can introduce inaccuracy.
2. If process costs are to be allocated to more than one dimension, usually the system using this method forces *all* process cost to be allocated to the intersection. In Exhibit 8.7, taking the customer-only related process costs for *Resolve Complaints* and splitting them to the customer/product level leads to an erroneous analysis.

Saying that the errors are minimal and have almost no relevancy on the profitability numbers is not an argument in favor of allocating between the dimensions. Quite the opposite; it simply shows that there is no reason to waste system resources or time if the allocation results are minimal or irrelevant. Instead of making a wasted allocation that provides no value and only helps to hide information, simply incorporate a multilevel view where responsibility can be managed instead of fully burdening the product with clutter.

The two-dimensional method as demonstrated is approximately accurate and overall has supported analysis results similar to the multidimensional method. However, this is a simplistic example. As volumes increase or other dimensions are added, the margin for error expands. This analytical error may be acceptable if a rough-cut view is desired, but if more sensitive decision making is required based on the segment analysis, an analytical price is paid.

Sample MultiDimensional Reporting with SAP

The example in the previous section demonstrated where the reporting information from the two-dimensional view can be misleading. With the integration of process information and the robust reporting capability provided by CO-PA, users are able to create multilevel margin P/Ls to more accurately reflect the true correlation of costs for the market segments and why those costs occur. Exhibit 8.8 is an example of this type of report.

This multilevel P/L illustrates the different product/service costs broken out by marginal and full costs. Also, the over-underabsorption that is directly related to the product can be clearly viewed. These product costs roll up to the customers, which roll up to their corresponding strategic business units, which roll up to the enterprise view. Only four levels have been provided for the sake of simplicity. However, users can define as many levels as needed to accurately reflect their organization. The multilevel view provides users with the ability to drill down in the report. With a drill-down functionality, impacts of fixed/proportional costs and over-underabsorption can be clearly seen. This view aids in key business decisions, such as which products to market/eliminate, who are the customers providing the most benefit, and what mode of distribution is most cost efficient.

Additionally, slice-and-dice reporting allows all the analytical layers to be peeled away as needed and provides a continual drill-down to the lowest level desired. Ultimately the lowest level of detail, the transactional line item, may be determined. The transactional detail provides the ultimate means for an audit trail and demonstrates the tight integration of the system. Arguments ranging from who made the posting to whether it is accurate can be eliminated because this information is readily available at all times. This ready availability removes the traditional defense of unprovable accuracy from managers of the business segment. In most systems, as in stand-alone ABC systems, the information is not at a transactional level and cannot provide immediate validation of the results.

INFORMATION FLOWS

In order to support ABC information being used for market segment analysis, ABC needs to be completely integrated with CO-PA and its reporting tool. This

Enterprise Operating Result:

	Marginal		Full Cost	
	Standard	Actual	Standard	Actual
Total SBU Contrib. Margins	$881,020	$930,690	$480,970	$306,580
Corporate Overheads			80,500	105,870
Contribution Margin	$881,020	$930,690	$400,470	$200,710
Operating Result	-		-	

Strategic Business Unit 3
Strategic Business Unit 2
Strategic Business Unit 1

	Marginal		Full Cost	
	Standard	Actual	Standard	Actual
Total Sales Channel Margins	$387,300	$389,450	$ 21,885	$28,650
SBU Overloads			62,500	71,000
SBU Contrib. Margin	$387,300	$389,450	-	-
SBU Gross Margin			($40,615)	($42,350)

Customer: #300
Customer: #200
Customer: #100

	Marginal		Full Cost	
	Standard	Actual	Standard	Actual
Total Product Margins	$826,300	$799,950	$97,005	$86,960
Sales Channel Costs				
Resolve Complaints	32,500	31,000	82,500	81,000
Customer Overheads	28,000	28,000	28,000	28,000
Customer Contrib. Margin	$765,800	$740,950	36,330	34,180
Customer O/U Absorption	-	-	-	(8,760)
Customer Gross Margin			($49,825)	($47,460)

Product/Service: #3000
Product/Service: #2000
Product/Service: #1000

	Marginal		Full Cost	
	Standard	Actual	Standard	Actual
Total Product Margins	$291,830	$279,940	$71,700	$68,260
Std. Product Cost	2,500	2,200	8,500	9,000
Production Variances	0	700	-	-
Answer Product Questions	15,000	13,080	19,000	18,075
Product Overheads	-	-	24,250	33,630
Product Contribution Margin	$274,330	$263,960	-	-
Product O/U Absorption	-	-	-	9,040
Product Gross Margin	-	-	$19,950	($1,485)

Exhibit 8.8 Multi-levels, Contribution Report Example

integration is provided by using business processes to allocate/assign product and overhead costs to market segment P/Ls.

Product Costs to Market Segments

Chapter 7 addressed the area of the process costs being integrated with the production cost objects for determining the process impacts on the cost estimates and for actual capturing of production-related process costs. Subsequently, the process costs are then assigned to market segments via the product costing submodule rather than directly from the ABC submodule.

The process costs that are related to any of the production objects are included in the market segments via a cost estimate. A product valuation strategy can be defined within the market segment reporting area that defines which cost estimate will be used and when the product cost will be valuated. The frozen standard cost estimate generally is used, and valuation usually is selected to occur in real time versus at period end. Exhibit 8.9 depicts the flow of process cost through PC to PA.

When the *Sales Qty.* is posted to the database, the standard cost estimate is also posted due to real-time valuation. Therefore, if 100 *Sales Qty.* are posted for an order, each standard cost estimate component is multiplied by 100 and posted. How the lines are displayed is determined by report definition. Each component of the standard cost estimate can be displayed on a separate line in the report. This allows the process components of the standard cost estimate to be clearly visible in the market segment report.

Actual production costs and their variances calculated in the product costing area are assigned to the appropriate market segment when the product cost object is closed and settled during the period or at period-end close. Exhibit 8.10 displays the impact on market segment reporting.

The selected standard cost estimate is used to bring in the planned cost for a product, including the process costs. The variances are settled from the production orders. Standard plus the variances provide actual product costs. If a moving average system is defined within SAP, at period end the transactional postings made during the period using the standard rates to determine costs will be updated with the actual rates and actual costs. The variances are included in the finished goods valuation and thus in cost of goods sold (COGS).

An engineering report can be generated for a product market segment comparing the frozen standard to a current cost estimate. The difference is due to engineering changes. This report highlights the impact of process reengineering on the standard product costs. Also, a break-even report for a product market segment can be created that includes the process view.

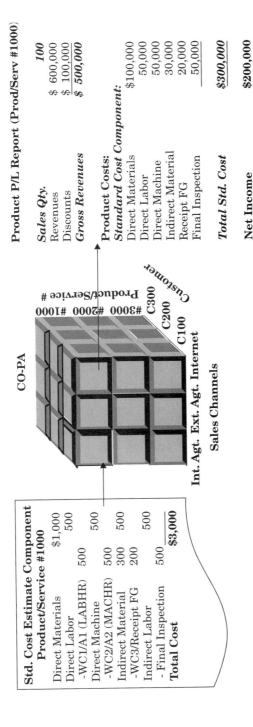

Product P/L Report (Prod/Serv #1000)

Sales Qty.	*100*
Revenues	$ 600,000
Discounts	$ 100,000
Gross Revenues	*$ 500,000*

Product Costs:
Standard Cost Component:

Direct Materials	$100,000
Direct Labor	50,000
Direct Machine	50,000
Indirect Material	30,000
Receipt FG	20,000
Final Inspection	50,000
Total Std. Cost	*$300,000*
Net Income	**$200,000**

Exhibit 8.9 Product Process Cost to Market Segments

Std. Cost Estimate Component
Product/Service #1000

Direct Materials		$1,000
Direct Labor		500
-WC1/A1 (LABHR)	500	
Direct Machine		500
-WC2/A2 (MACHR)	500	
Indirect Material	300	500
-WC3/Receipt FG	200	
Indirect Labor		500
- Final Inspection	500	
Total Cost		**$3,000**

CO-PA

Product/Service #

#1000 #2000 #3000

C100 C200 C300 Customer

Int. Agt. Ext. Agt. Internet

Sales Channels

237

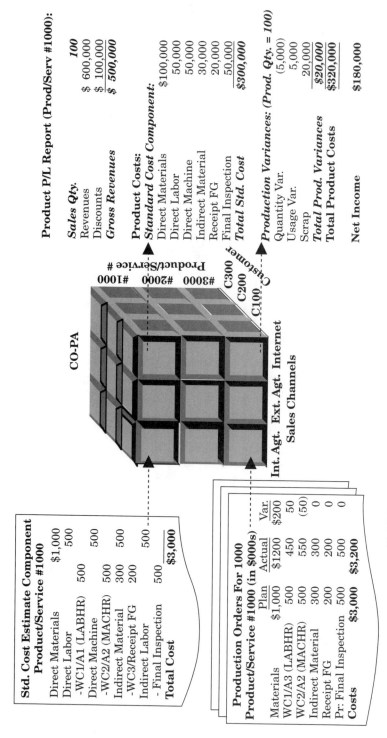

Product P/L Report (Prod/Serv #1000):

Sales Qty. **100**

Revenues	$ 600,000
Discounts	$ 100,000
Gross Revenues	***$ 500,000***

Product Costs:
Standard Cost Component:

Direct Materials	$100,000
Direct Labor	50,000
Direct Machine	50,000
Indirect Material	30,000
Receipt FG	20,000
Final Inspection	50,000
Total Std. Cost	*$300,000*

Production Variances: (Prod. Qty. = 100)

Quantity Var.	(5,000)
Usage Var.	5,000
Scrap	20,000
Total Prod. Variances	*$20,000*
Total Product Costs	*$320,000*

Net Income	$180,000

CO-PA

Product/Service #
#1000 #2000 #3000

Customer
C300 C200 C100

Sales Channels
Int. Agt. Ext. Agt. Internet

Std. Cost Estimate Component
Product/Service #1000

Direct Materials		$1,000
Direct Labor		500
-WC1/A1 (LABHR)	500	
Direct Machine		500
-WC2/A2 (MACHR)	500	
Indirect Material		500
-WC3/Receipt FG	300	
Indirect Labor	200	
- Final Inspection	500	500
Total Cost		**$3,000**

Production Orders For 1000
Product/Service #1000 (in $000s)

	Plan	Actual	Var.
Materials	$1,000	$1200	$200
WC1/A3 (LABHR)	500	450	50
WC2/A2 (MACHR)	500	550	(50)
Indirect Material	300	300	0
Receipt FG	200	200	0
Pr: Final Inspection	500	500	0
Costs	**$3,000**	**$3,200**	

Exhibit 8.10 Production Variances Assigned to Market Segments

Service and Non–Product-Related Costs to Market Segments

The previous section described how product and production process costs are attributed to the market segments. However, service cost and other overhead costs have not been addressed. The business process can be used easily to represent a service. In the banking industry, for example, the services of *Open Bank Account, Perform Wire Transfer, Process Mortgage Loan,* and so on, can be represented as business processes. The appropriate market segments can then consume these business processes. The market segment reporting in CO-PA can generate reports on which processes are occurring at certain locations, or branches within locations, by specific customer groups, such as commercial or personal. Also, all other overheads can be allocated/assigned using business processes as well, such as sales, general, and administrative activities.

Assignment/Allocation Methodologies

Process costs are assigned from the ABC submodule to the market segments in PA in four ways:

1. Business process assessment cycle
2. Direct activity posting
3. Indirect activity posting
4. Template

These methods have different impacts on the information provided, timing of the posting, and the level of accuracy of the allocation.

Business Process Assessment Cycle   The only value-based allocation method between the business process to market segment is a PA assessment cycle. This type of posting is not intended to be real time and is usually a period-end closing activity. When creating the PA assessment cycle, the sending process, receiver characteristics, and tracing method are defined. The methods available are based on a fixed percentage, fixed portion, fixed dollar, and variable portions, which is used with both quantities and dollar amounts. The quantities and values are captured in value fields within CO-PA, which are basically the rows used in reports—for example, transportation costs, sales quantity, revenues, and so on. These value fields can be used to create tracing factors to certain market segments. Exhibit 8.11 depicts an example of marketing processes being allocated to a market segment using a PA assessment cycle.

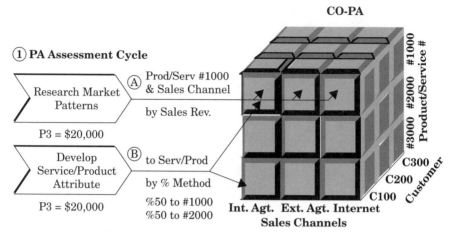

Exhibit 8.11   PA Assessment Cycle Example

In the exhibit, the three reporting characteristics of the multidimensional cube are Sales Channel, Customer, and Product/Service. Two examples of the PA assessment cycle also are provided.

Example 1 The *Research Market Patterns* process will be allocated to Prod/Serv #1000 and each of the Sales Channels (Internal Agents, External Agents, and Internet) based on Sales Revenue. The PA assessment cycle will read the database for the market segments and determine the percentage split necessary to make the allocation. This method is also referred to as peanut-butter spreading the overhead costs.

Example 2 The *Develop Service/Product Attributes* process will be split between the market segment for *Prod/Serv* #1000 and #2000 by a 50%-50% ratio. During period-end closing, the PA assessment cycle will be executed. Exhibit 8.12 illustrates the corresponding results.

The *Research Market Patterns* process (A) has $20,000 of actual costs for Period 3. The cycle calculates the split between the Sales Channel characteristic as 66.67% *Int. Agents,* 11.11% *Ext. Agents,* and 22.22% *Internet* based on the Period 3 Sales Revenue. The Period 3 P/L Report for *Prod/Serv #1000* shows the total amount for the allocation of $20,000. If the Sales Channel characteristic is used for drill-down on the report, the profitability of *Prod/Serv #1000* can be seen by Sales Channel, as depicted on the right-hand side of the exhibit.

The *Develop Product/Service Attribute* process (B) shows only the percentage share for *Product/Service #1000,* that is, $10,000. The PA assessment cycle

Period 3 Market Segment P&L:
Prod/Serv #1000   by Sales Channel View

	Total	Int. Agents	Ext. Agents	Internet
Revenues	$450,000	$300,000	$50,000	$100,000
COGS	$ 90,000	$ 60,000	$10,000	$ 20,000
Process Costs:				
(A) Research Market	$20,000	$ 13,334	$ 2,222	$ 4,444
(B) Develop Attribute	$10,000			
Net Income	**$330,000**	$226,666	$37,778	$ 75,556

Exhibit 8.12   PA Assessment Cycles Results

would find $20,000 of Period 3 costs for the *Develop Product/Service Attribute* process and multiply by the 50% defined in the cycle to determine the $10,000 allocation.

Note that the profits for *Prod/Serv #1000* across the three sales channels do not add up to the $330,000. This is because the lower-level report would not include the second allocation for the *Develop Service/Product Attribute* process that is posted only to the Product/Service and not the Sales Channel reporting dimension.

The CO-PA drill-down, slice-and-dice reporting, makes this market segment reporting tool very robust. Many layers can be added to provide a more detailed view of the organization and its market segments. Taking this example one step higher in the organization, a report could be run for the product group, which contains *Product/Service #1000*. Processes for supporting marketing campaigns for that product group could be allocated to that level. Doing so allows users to develop a clear picture of what is driving the costs of the organization and at which level of management. The product does not take the burden of all the allocated costs; if it did, erroneous product mix and rationalization decisions would be created.

Direct Activity Allocation   A direct assignment of process costs to a market segment is made via the Direct Activity Allocation (DAA). Given that the exact quantity is known, this is a quantity-based method of assigning process costs to a market segment. Exhibit 8.13 illustrates a posting charging the market segments for its direct usage of a business process.

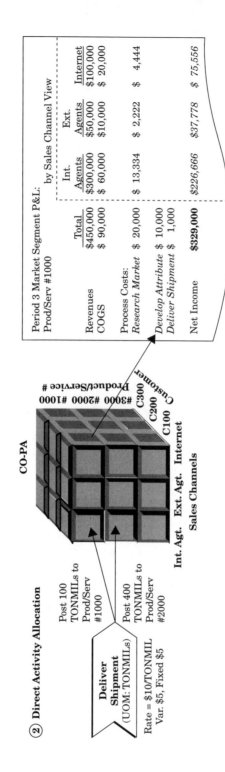

② **Direct Activity Allocation**

CO-PA

Deliver Shipment (UOM: TONMILs)

Rate = $10/TONMIL
Var. $5, Fixed $5

Post 100 TONMILs to Prod/Serv #1000

Post 400 TONMILs to Prod/Serv #2000

Product/Service #
#3000 #2000 #1000

Customer
C300
C200
C100

Int. Agt.   Ext. Agt.   Internet

Sales Channels

Period 3 Market Segment P&L:
Prod/Serv #1000

by Sales Channel View

	Total	Int. Agents	Ext. Agents	Internet
Revenues	$450,000	$300,000	$50,000	$100,000
COGS	$ 90,000	$ 60,000	$10,000	$ 20,000
Process Costs:				
Research Market	$ 20,000	$ 13,334	$ 2,222	$ 4,444
Develop Attribute	$ 10,000			
Deliver Shipment	$ 1,000			
Net Income	**$329,000**	$226,666	$37,778	$ 75,556

Exhibit 8.13   Direct Process Posting to a Market Segment

242

For this example, an interface to a transportation scheduling system brings across the process driver quantity for *TONMILs*. The *Deliver Shipment* process has a rate that contains a variable and a fixed portion. The impacts of this direct process posting to a market segment can be seen on the segment P/L for Prod/Serv #1000. The *Deliver Shipment* process posting to a market segment is a real-time, transaction-based posting. This means that once the transaction is completed, the money is actually moved from the *Deliver Shipment* process to the market segment. Therefore, if the market P/L is run any time within the month, the impact of that process posting can be seen on the report immediately. The transactional posting takes place using the standard rate for the *Deliver Shipment* process that has already been defined. If the actual value is required, at period end, when all actual process rates have been calculated, an adjustment posting for the difference will be made to the transaction posted.

A direct process–to–market segment posting can be used only to post actual process driver quantities. It is used most commonly for the following reasons:

- Quantities by cost object are actually captured.
- It enables users to make an ad hoc charge. These types of charges are random in nature.
- The DAA is used as the receiver of an interface or Excel upload that provides process drivers for market segments from an external system instead of interfacing into the CO-PA database. The determining factors of whether to interface through this transaction or to the CO-PA database are based on many variables, such as systematic requirements, sizing impacts, and when the required system resources are available (period-end processing may consume too many system resources).
- External process drivers also can be interfaced into this transaction or brought through via the logistics information system (LIS) if real-time reporting of those drivers or the resultant movement of costs using these drivers is required. As stated above, if information must be readily available within a period time frame, this charging method may be the best solution.

Indirect Activity Allocations The indirect activity allocation (IAA) is addressed in detail in Chapter 5. The IAA works between the market segments and processes similar to how it works between the cost centers and processes. The difference when using the IAA between processes and market segments is that a value field, whether value or quantity based, imputes the process quantity instead of the process quantity imputing a resource driver quantity. The example in Exhibit 8.14 illustrates an IAA between the market segment and process using the market segment driver *Sales Qty* to impute the plan and actual process outputs.

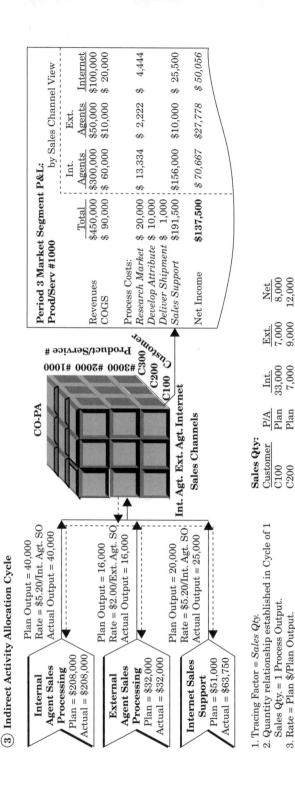

Exhibit 8.14 Process–to–Market Segment Indirect Activity Allocation Cycle

244

The PA assessment cycle contains three segments. The first is used to assign the *Internal Agent Sales Processing* process to the Sales Channel *Int. Agt.* and any other combination of reporting dimensions that the *Sales Qty* was posted to. This would include the product/service #, the customer #, division, perhaps region, and so forth. A quantity relationship is established by defining that for every *Sales Qty,* one *Internal Agent Sales Processing* process is required. Similarly, the second segment is used to assign the *External Agent Sales Processing* process to the *Ext. Agt.* Sales Channel. Finally, the third segment for the *Internet Sales Support* process is to be assigned to the *Internet* Sales Channel. When the cycle is run, taking only Customer *C100* and *Int. Agt.* Sales Channel as the example, the system will read the database for all *Sales Qtys* posted to any segment that includes the dimensions *C100* Customer and *Int. Agt.* Sales Channel. Based on the ratio (quantity relationship) defined, a posting of one *Internal Sales Processing* process for each *Int. Agt. Sales Qty* will be made to Customer *C100*.

The indirect activity allocation cycle between the process and the market segment will inversely calculate what the process consumption should be and make the posting. This is simply an example to show systematic functionality and not necessarily a best-practice method for assigning sales processing costs. It is also not the only way in which this type of process assignment can be made. For example:

- The IAA is used for this example rather than the direct activity posting because the sales and distribution module automatically updates the correct market segment with the Sales Qty information. To use the direct activity posting method would require a person, interface, or Excel upload to make these assignments.

- A template can be used for this assignment just as easily and would be used if it was necessary to have these postings made within a period versus as a period-end closing activities. The template also could be used if there is a need for a more complex *"IF-THEN"* relationship to be defined other than a simple one-to-one ratio. See the following section for a detailed example of the template.

- In this example, there is a process for each type of *Sales Processing* simply because it allows process rates to be compared for analysis. However, one *Sales Processing* process can be used and a template created with "IF-THEN" statements, such as: IF the Sales Channel is *Internet* THEN charge 0.80 times the *Sales Processing* process, or IF the Sales Channel is *Int. Agt.* THEN charge 1.20 times the *Sales Processing* process. This method supports one process, master data record, and rate, but different cost charges due to conditions or complexity.

- Within the IAA, there are other methods for defining the relationship between the process and market segment other than inversely calculated, such as posted quantity or fixed quantity. The fixed quantity method defines a fixed amount of a process driver quantity to be allocated out to the cost objects. The posted quantity can be used to split known process quantities to the cost objects. For example, an organization captures the 2000 pallets for the *Build Pallets* process, but not by pallets by customer. The process driver quantity can be split to the customers based on the assumption that more *Sales Qty* requires more *Build Pallets*. The IAA will then read the *Sales Qty* by customer and determine the split of the 2000 *Build Pallets* process driver quantities to each customer.

Templates Unlike the templates among cost centers, processes, and product/production cost objects, templates used to assign process costs to the market segments have only one environment option, the profitability analysis costing-based (PAC) environment. (See Exhibit 8.15.) The templates used for characteristics are linked via the template determination assignment; for example, the Customer characteristic uses the *CustServ* template *Sales Processing* template.

Exhibit 8.16 illustrates the structure definition of the *CustServ* template based on the PAC environment used to assign the *Handle Inquiries* and *Resolve Complaints* processes to the appropriate customers. The "Type" field is 01 for a business process since the sender objects are business processes. The "Object" field is populated with the actual process code to be assigned with this template, e.g., *Handle Inqs*. The "Name" field and "Un." field are automatically populated from the master data records of the processes, e.g., *Handle Inquiries* and *Ea* for Each, respectively.

Functions are used to determine the planned/actual amounts of the process to be assigned. Standard functions are provided for this PAC environment as well as additional generated ones. The additional functions are based on the actual definitions of the costing-based operating concern being used. The operating concern is the structure definition of the reporting dimensions (characteristics) and, for costing based, the noncalculated rows (value fields). Because the operating concern structures are user defined, they cannot be provided as standard functions. Therefore, users can select the user-defined characteristics and value fields and generate them to be functions that are provided as standard. The function hierarchies and an example of each available in the PAC environment are:

- Costing-based profitability analysis—PSG #Complaints or PSGSales-Channel
- Sender processes—ProcessActualQuantity

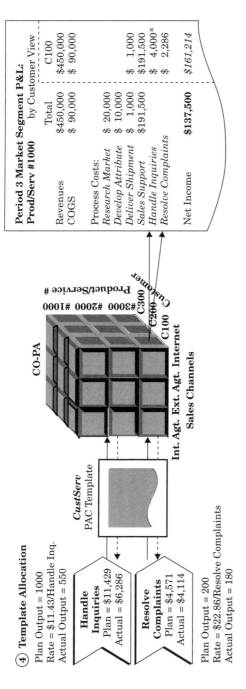

④ Template Allocation

Plan Output = 1000
Rate = $11.43/Handle Inq.
Actual Output = 550

Handle Inquiries
Plan = $11,429
Actual = $6,286

Resolve Complaints
Plan = $4,571
Actual = $4,114

Plan Output = 200
Rate = $22.86/Resolve Complaints
Actual Output = 180

CustServ
PAC Template

CO-PA

Product/Service #
#3000 #2000 #1000
C300
C200
C100
Customer

Int. Agt. Ext. Agt. Internet
Sales Channels

Period 3 Market Segment P&L:
Prod/Serv #1000   by Customer View

	Total	C100
Revenues	$450,000	$450,000
COGS	$ 90,000	$ 90,000
Process Costs:		
Research Market	$ 20,000	
Develop Attribute	$ 10,000	
Deliver Shipment	$ 1,000	$ 1,000
Sales Support	$191,500	$191,500
Handle Inquiries		$ 4,000*
Resolve Complaints		$ 2,286
Net Income	**$137,500**	*$161,214*

Period 3 Driver Qtys.:

Customer	P/A	Inquiries	Complaints
C100	Plan	600	100
C200	Plan	400	100
C100	Act.	370	100
C200	Act.	220	80

1. Report only shows drill-down to C100 Customer.
2. Quantity Relationship Established on Template.
3. Rate = Plan $/Plan Output.
4. Standard Costing system used. Actual Posting = Actual Output * Rate.
5. Target versus Actual Report removes volume variance, showing Variance $0.
6. For simplicity, this example ignores fixed/proportion driver rates and quantities.

*Actual Inquiries adds to be 590; however, each customer is given 20 Inquiries prior to being allocated the additional customer services costs. Therefore, 350 Handle Inquiries process quantities are posted to C100.

Exhibit 8.15   Market Segment Assignment Template

- General data—LISKeyFigure
- Mathematical—Trunc (whole number)

The user-defined characteristics and value fields are included in the costing-based profitability analysis hierarchy—for example, the quantity value field for capturing complaints or the characteristic for sales channel sold through. The function created is generated from adding PSG in front of the user-defined value field or characteristic code. In Exhibit 8.16, the *PSG#Complaints* function is used to populate the plan/actual quantities for the *Resolve Complaints*. The *PSG#Inquiries* is used in a formula, described below, to determine the appropriate quantity to be posted.

The Plan/Actual Activation fields can be selected as Active, Inactive, or Method. In this example, the *Resolve Complaints* process is always active. Therefore, each time the template is run, the quantity in the *#Complaints* value field will be read to determine the actual process driver quantity for the *Resolve Complaints* process and always post the delta quantity from the previous time. A method is used for the *Handle Inquiries* process that defines the process posting to only occur IF PSG#Inquiries>20 THEN ActualProcess Qty = PSG#Inquiries − 20, allowing customers 20 free inquiries before assigning them the process costs indicating extra costs for serving a customer. Note that the PAC template does not have an "Event Activation" field, since the data in the market segments has already occurred and therefore the event (e.g., sale, complaint, inquiry) has been completed.

The template usage to link ABC with market segment reporting and analysis provides two key benefits.

Environment | PAC | Profitability Accounting Costing Based

Template | **CustServ** | Customer Service Template

Type	Name	Object	Un	Plan Quantity	Plan Activation	Actual Quantity	Actual Activation
Business Proc	Handle Inquiries	HandleInqs	Ea	FORMULA	Method	FORMULA	Method
Business Proc	Resolve Complaints	ReslvCmplt	Ea	PSG# Complaints	Active	PSG# Complaints	Active

Exhibit 8.16   Detailed ABC-PA Template Example

1. The template's "IF-THEN" logic is perfect to deal with complexity issues dealing with cost-to-serve assignments. If customer or product complexities are known, they can be incorporated into the quantity structure, instead of creating multitudes of processes for *Resolve Complaints*—Difficult or Easy, or *Handle Inquiries* for Product/Service 1000 versus 2000. This capability reduces master data maintenance and the required resource allocations to the additional processes.

2. The template is a strong planning aid due to the formula capabilities and the complete integration throughout the system. For example, the sales managers have planned to sell 30,000 units of *Product #1000*. However, the shipping managers would prefer to have number of pallets for the product as a key driver for their planning metrics. With the template, a formula can be created that captures the average shipped pallet size of *Product #1000*. When the template runs, it will convert the planned units for the product into the planned number of shipped pallets for *Product #1000*. When executed for actuals, this formula is not necessary. The actual number of pallets will be captured for the shipping managers either in a value field or via a LIS structure.

Exhibits 8.17 and 8.18 provide a summary of the different methods for integrating the ABC information with the market segment. Exhibit 8.17 provides a table comparison of the different methods and uses, and Exhibit 8.18 the pictorial summary to be further addressed in Chapter 9.

Exhibit 8.18 illustrates that the process costs captured in the standard cost estimate are transferred from CO-PC to CO-PA. The other four methods of process costs transfers to market segments are performed via CO-ABC to CO-PA.

SAMPLE KEY BUSINESS DECISIONS

Many key business decisions can be supported by the power of the integration of ABC information with the market segment reporting. A select few are listed in Exhibit 8.19 in order to stress key aspects of the market segment functionality that enhances the integration with Activity-Based Costing/Management.

Real-time Market Segment Reporting

The ability to post process costs directly to a market segment (using a DAA) coupled with a frozen standard process rate provides real-time market segment reporting. Also, templates can be run within a period, providing another method for

Information Flow	Comments	Assignment Basis	Type of Posting	Timing	Usability	Handle Complexity
PA Assessment Cycle	Allocation of processes to market segments based on different basis.	Fixed %, fixed portions, fixed amount, variable tracing based on value field dollars or quantities.	Value based	Period end	Moderate	Limited
Direct Activity Allocation	Direct process charging to the market segments, e.g., customer/ product/region.	Actual quantity only, not valid for plan.	Quantity with value	Real time	Easy	None
Indirect Activity Allocation	Inverse calculation supports imputing quantities and reduces the need to capture actuals for a driver quantity.	Fixed %, fixed portion, fixed quantities, variable tracing based on value field dollars or quantities.	Quantity with value	Period end	Moderate	Limited
Templates	Dynamic determination of the process driver consumed by a market segment.	Simple to complex formulas and "IF-THEN" rules.	Quantity with value	Within period	Advanced	High level easily supported

Exhibit 8.17   Information Flows between ABC and Market Segment Analysis (PA)

assignment of real-time process costs. Both posting/assignment methods, either direct or via the template, can be used to assign the service, if represented by a process, and process costs. Additionally, the valuation strategy for product costs can be configured as either real time or periodic. When selected as real time, the process costs are posted via the standard cost estimate when the product sales occurs. The immediate availability of process information can be used to guide the organization, rather than the normal historical view caused by time lags in most reporting tools that are based on periodic closings.

Both the direct process assignment and the allocation template are quantity-based methods and rely on a defined quantity relationship to build the process

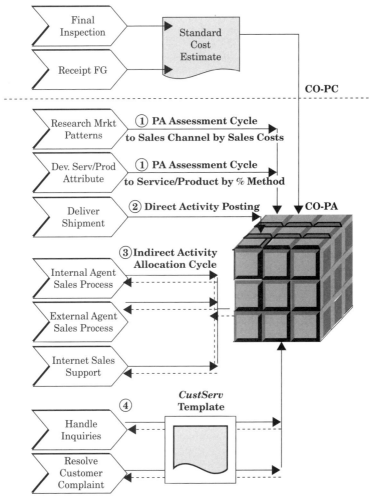

Exhibit 8.18   Process to Market Segment Examples Summary

assignments. The value-based approach is not intended to support a real-time market segment analysis, since it is based on allocations performed during period-end closing. The value-based approach may approximate a real-time view by using a workaround of running the cycles daily. Although this workaround makes an approximation possible, it is not a recommended solution due to the high data volumes generated. Further information on the many ways in which the process costs can be attributed to a market segment is provided above in the "Information Flows" section.

Key Business Decision	Value Based[a]	Quantity Based[a]
What are the processes' cost impacts for real-time profitability or market segment reporting?	--	√
Which process fixed/proportional costs impact margins?	--	√
What is the cost to serve a specific market segment and how can they be reduced?	√	√
Which markets should be targeted or cut?	--	√
If an unprofitable market is cut, what is the contribution to fixed costs that is lost?	--	√
What is the impact of excess/idle capacity on my bottom line?	√	√

[a]— represents not supported. √ represents supported.

Exhibit 8.19   Key Business Decisions Supported by the ABC-PA Integration Sample

True Nature of Process Costs Reflected

Chapter 5 addressed the nature of resource costs reflected onto process costs. With the integration of the process to the market segment, the fixed/proportional components of the processes can be used to support gross and contribution margin reporting. The quantity-based method can readily reflect the true nature of the process costs broken into its fixed and proportional components. Each component can be individually assigned to a separate value field (row) in the market P/L report. The value-based method also can be used to provide a fixed/proportional view of costs. However, it requires some way of deriving a specific dollar or percentage amount to the fixed and variable value fields. Therefore, the value-based method may not provide an accurate reflection of the nature of costs and it does not best support the decision at hand, as indicated in Exhibit 8.19.

Process Costs Assigned Directly to Dimensional Intersections

Recall that accuracy is the benefit of the direct assignment to the dimensional intersections. Once accuracy has been established or an acceptable level of accuracy has been determined and the data are now deemed reliable, process analysis can begin. A process report, or several, can be defined to show all the process costs and the quantities consumed. This information provides the total process impacts on the market segments.

The dimensional comparison used the *Handle Inquiries* process. It was stated that the quantity of this process is higher for Product/Service 2000 due to complexity or potentially new features. The only way to reduce the process costs is to reduce the quantities driving them or to reduce the microstandard of the process. The reports can indicate which processes to focus on first and provide information about whether the issue is localized to one customer, a customer group, or a region. In this example, the focus is on the quantities, not the micro-standard. What drives the quantities can indicate which potential solutions should be investigated. The analysis can highlight the issue as customer related, in which case product pricing can be changed to make sure that these additional costs are covered. The analysis may signify that it is standard across the board and there-fore perhaps product information needs to be reviewed and updated, and so on. This analysis is all predicated on the fact that the appropriate quantities are cap-tured in the corresponding market segment. Given the integrated nature of the SAP system, and its ability to handle complexity issues, there is a higher likeli-hood that these quantities are being tracked elsewhere in the system and at the lowest level therefore available to support this analysis.

The example just given is based on the quantity-based approach. The value-based approach using allocations can also be used to post costs to the dimensional intersections. However, the degree of accuracy and reliability of the data is lower than with the quantity-based method. The value-based approach may be very use-ful for some quick hits and for determining which areas, if any, should be inves-tigated further and possibly changed to a quantity-based allocation to provide the greater accuracy. Since SAP is scalable, it can accommodate either approach or any combinations of approaches toward process reengineering.

Accuracy of Process Assignments

Accuracy goes beyond the ability to reflect the true nature of costs or to assign them directly to an intersection in order to reduce further allocation errors. It en-compasses the ability to accurately address complexity issues via the template. Most ABC systems are designed to aggregate information, losing the granularity, to truly address these issues. If they do try to address the granularity, it is usually by aggregating and then allocating, thereby impacting accuracy or reliability of the data. This approach is usually due to the inability or prohibitive costs to track the quantities at the lowest level. The integrated nature of SAP eliminates some if not all of these issues.

Flexible Multilevel Marginal Profits/Losses

It is a given that before any department is outsourced or a product or a market segment is dropped, an understanding of the fixed costs of the object is required to eliminate erroneous decisions and the "death spiral." When determining whether markets or market segments should be eliminated, flexible multilevel marginal P/Ls are also necessary. These help to identify where the fixed costs reside and the impacts of the eliminations. This analysis requires that the fixed cost and variance liquidations occur at the appropriate level and are not necessarily buried all the way down to the product level. See Exhibit 8.8 for an example.

Managing Inactivity without an "Idle" Process

As stated in Chapter 1, excess/idle capacity conceptually sits on the resources, not the processes. For example, there is no limitation to the # of setups that can be performed for the process *Perform Set-up.* There is a constraint on the available resources, such as *MANHRs,* that can be supplied to perform the process. Systematically within SAP, a process can be defined as anything, which means the process *Run Machine* can be used to replace the resource *MACHR* (machine hour). In this example, there is a constraint on the process output since a limited number of hours are available for which the machine can run. If either the *MANHRS* or *Run Machine* drivers are over- or underconsumed, over-underabsorption on the cost center and/or process occurs. Exhibit 8.20 illustrates an example of the over/underabsorption on both objects and how it is usually moved to the multidimensional cube.

For this example, variance has been generated on the process to demonstrate the capabilities of the SAP system. During planning, the resource drivers have a planned consumption of a one-to-one ratio with the process quantity output. Therefore, the process driver and resource drivers have a planned output of 1,000 each. In the example, in order to induce a variance, the actual resource driver is captured, rather than imputed from the process quantity output, and posted. The *Prod Cost Center #200* worked 100 *MANHRs* more than expected and the *Prod Cost Center #300* worked 100 *MANHRs* less. Rather than creating a process called Excess/Idle capacity, the resource over-underabsorption can be directly assigned to the market segment that has responsibility, such as at the plant level. This example is a standard cost-based example. If a moving average system has been designed within SAP, the over-underabsorption is rolled into the resource and process rates and assignment to the market segments occurs when the process is posted.

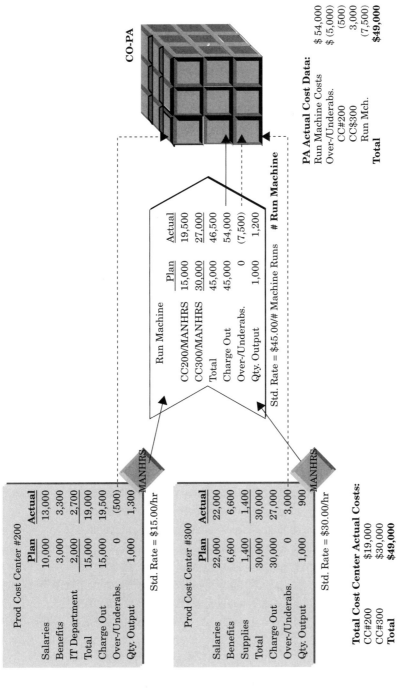

Exhibit 8.20   Capacity Over-Underabsorption to Multidimensional Cube

Prod Cost Center #200

	Plan	**Actual**
Salaries	10,000	13,000
Benefits	3,000	3,300
IT Department	2,000	2,700
Total	15,000	19,000
Charge Out	15,000	19,500
Over-/Underabs.	0	(500)
Qty. Output	1,000	1,300

Std. Rate = $15.00/hr

Prod Cost Center #300

	Plan	**Actual**
Salaries	22,000	22,000
Benefits	6,600	6,600
Supplies	1,400	1,400
Total	30,000	30,000
Charge Out	30,000	27,000
Over-/Underabs.	0	3,000
Qty. Output	1,000	900

Std. Rate = $30.00/hr

Total Cost Center Actual Costs:

CC#200	$19,000
CC#300	$30,000
Total	**$49,000**

Run Machine

	Plan	**Actual**
CC200/MANHRS	15,000	19,500
CC300/MANHRS	30,000	27,000
Total	45,000	46,500
Charge Out	45,000	54,000
Over-/Underabs.	0	(7,500)
Qty. Output	1,000	1,200

Std. Rate = $45.00/# Machine Runs   **# Run Machine**

CO-PA

PA Actual Cost Data:

Run Machine Costs	$ 54,000
Over-/Underabs.	$ (5,000)
CC#200	(500)
CC$300	3,000
Run Mch.	(7,500)
Total	**$49,000**

255

The value of the direct cost center to market segment assignment of over-underabsorption is that the costs of excess/idle capacity can be assigned directly to the appropriate organization level, where it makes more sense, rather than assigning these costs of inefficiencies to the product/customers. Additionally, all costs finally reside in the CO-PA market segments to support complete analysis and reporting.

IMPLEMENTATION GUIDELINES

The design of the market segment reporting is one of the most politically volatile areas of an SAP implementation. Integration of ABC information for analysis and reporting often complicates matters even more. Exhibit 8.21 provides several implementation guidelines to consider during this design process.

Profitability Analysis Costing-Based Template Definition

Templates are created with a defined environment that houses standard equations or fields to be used for formulas. The PAC environment is used for templates between processes and the market segments. Characteristics must to be selected for use with the template, such as product, customer, and distribution channel. These characteristics are used to determine the process template selected to assign overhead costs to the reporting dimensions. For the template example above, configuration defined that the Customer Service template is selected when assigning

Type	Implementation Guidelines
Conceptual Design	Which characteristics should be used to activate the templates and to what level should the templates allocate?
Conceptual Design	What are the sizing impacts of integrating ABC with PA?
System Design	What additional drivers should be used for planning or actuals?
System Design	Will gross and contribution margin reporting be supported?
Organization Impact	What should be the level of reporting?

Exhibit 8.21   Implementation Hints for ABC Integration with Market Segments

process costs to customers. These characteristics also are the only characteristics to which process costs using the template can be allocated. Therefore, the identification of which characteristics will be used to determine the templates and to what level the templates will post is a very important design point.

CO-PA Submodule Sizing

Sizing is always a key issue when it comes to the CO-PA submodule. The addition of the capability to use ABC to allocate process costs only compounds this aspect of PA. When implementing the ABC functionality, new value fields (rows on a report) may need to be added to capture further information and process drivers. Therefore, PA will need to be resized in order to determine the impact of the new value fields and transactional data volumes. In addition, the ABC approach provides a finer level of detail, exponentially increasing data line items that impact the database size and the processing resources needed to perform allocations.

Controlling Module Conceptual Design

When dealing with the CO conceptual design, users must consider the potential impact on which drivers are used in which submodules. The driver usage within the system and from outside the system needs to be reevaluated. With the integration of ABC information into the market segments, the ABC model may need to be expanded or broadened to incorporate drivers already captured with SAP. Also, perhaps allocations already exist in the system that will need to be changed to an ABC approach. These changes might impact the entire CO conceptual design and should not be addressed in an ABC-PA vacuum. Another tip is to determine whether gross and contribution margin market segment reporting is to occur. If so, it is not supported simply via the ABC to market segment design. This view must be incorporated throughout the CO conceptual design, and therefore, it starts with the cost center accounting area.

Shift in Performance Metrics

By using the multilevel reporting capabilities with the already mentioned fixed/proportional and more accurate assignment methodology of ABC, managers can be held responsible for what they truly control. The levels of the market segment reporting should be able to support the different levels of management and management control. When redesigning the reporting requirements, certain performance metrics may need to be changed and/or incorporated. Although performance metrics is a hot topic in the market today, it is still a prickly execution point for implementations.

SUMMARY

Integration of Activity-Based Costing/Management with the market segment analysis capabilities of SAP provides several benefits. These include:

- There is a transactional document link that provides an audit trail and drill-down capability that goes to the actual line-item posting. This tight integration is useful because it helps eliminate the continual battle of managers not believing the information because it is difficult to see where it came from. It also aids with reconciliation activities.
- Using ABC provides a more accurate cost assignment methodology to the market segments.
- The template functionality supports a more advanced process–to–cost object design due to its ability to handle complexity and support complicated formulas for assignments.
- Real-time P/L reporting based on standard process rate supports a more proactive organization rather than historical explanations of events.

Exhibit 8.22 summarizes this chapter and the key points to remember from each subsection.

NOTE

1. The sum of the product margins for a customer (Margin 2) does not necessarily equal the total customer margin (Margin 1). This is due to the step margin used, i.e. not all costs are charged to the product level. In Exhibit 8.7 $20,000 of process costs are charged to the customer margin only for the multidimentional view.

Summary Area	Sumary Description
Area-Specific Focus	*Assignment*
Multi-Dimensional: The ability to assign process costs to a single dimension, such as customer-only process of *Resolve Complaints*. Additionally, the ability to post directly to dimensional intersections, such as for the *Handle Inquiries* process to the Customer/Product intersection.	Example: Assignment to Product1/Customer1. Benefit: Accurate costs portrayal on P/Ls.
Information Flows	
Assessment Cycle: The ability to push down process costs based on a percentage, ratio, or fixed dollar amount. Also used to alleviate over-underabsorptions to other PA levels.	Example: *Research Market Patterns* process cost allocated on the basis of Sales Revenues. Benefit: Ability to allocate costs with less need for accuracy.
Direct Activity Posting: The ability to post processes to a market segment.	Example: *Deliver Shipment* process posted to a customer's P/L. Benefit: Real-time recognition of the process driver and resulting cost charge at standard process rate.
Indirect Activity Allocation: The ability to have the system automatically calculate the required processes needed to support the market segments for plan or actual. No need to capture planned or actual process quantities, as they can be imputed via a relationship with a market segment driver.	Example: *Internet Sales Support* process planned output determined by 1:1 ratio with *Sales Qty.* for Sales Channel *Internet*. Benefit: Reduced driver collection for areas where a strong correlation between drivers can be established.
Template: The ability to have the system automatically calculate the required processes needed to support the market segments for plan or actual. No need to capture planned or actual process quantities, as they can be imputed via a relationship with a market segment driver.	Example: *CustServ* template example and formula for planned shipping pallets using planned sales quantity of products. Benefit: Advanced calculation capabilities that also can handle complexity issues.
Sample Business Decisions	
What are the processes cost impacts for real-time profitability or market segment reporting?	Supported by the direct activity allocation and the templates using a process with a microstandard rate. Benefit: Focuses on being a more proactive organization rather than historical explanations.

Exhibit 8.22 Process Information for Enhanced Segment Analysis Summary

Which process fixed/variable costs impact margins?	Processes consumer resources that have a fixed and variable component. The process costs should therefore not automatically always be considered variable. Benefit: Models true cost behavior and supports break-even reports for services.
What is the cost to serve a specific market segment and how can they be reduced?	Ability to post directly to a single dimension and/or an intersection of dimensions. Not forced to take all customer-specific process costs to the intersection. Benefit: Accuracy.
Which markets should be targeted or cut?	Requires the fixed/variable view and the direct assignment to intersections and most likely the template capabilities to deal with complexity issues. Benefit: Accuracy
If an unprofitable market is cut, what is the contribution to fixed costs that is lost?	Multilevel P/Ls with fixed costs and variance liquidation at the appropriate levels and not buried into the product level. Benefit: More granular information to better support decision making.
What is the impact of excess/idle capacity on my bottom line?	Over-underabsorption for a resource center or process assigned to the appropriate market segment. Benefit: More granular information for decision making dealing with capacity issues.
Implementation Guidelines	
PAC Template Configuration	Which template is called when a characteristic is selected? Which characteristics can receive the template postings?
Sizing Ramifications	What additional drivers will be used to support ABC to market segment analysis? How many additional transactions will be generated?
Conceptual Model Impacts	What are the new drivers, and do they change the CO conceptual design anywhere else? Will gross and contribution margin market segment reporting be supported?
Performance Metric Review	What level of reporting will be designed?

Exhibit 8.22 (*continued*)

9

INTEGRATED ACTIVITY-BASED COSTING

Given that integrated ABC is the core subject of this book, it would make sense for this chapter to be somewhere at the beginning instead of the end of the book. However, all the previous chapters served to establish the building blocks necessary to highlight the key concepts of SAP R/3 integrated ABC and the benefits derived from its utilization. As depicted in Exhibit 9.1, the philosophical groundwork has been laid. The conceptual requirements for the overall view, established. The operational aspects of integrated ABC with the other Controlling module components have been addressed in each chapter, focusing on a specific area of integration. This chapter pulls together the most important points addressed so far in order to provide a complete picture of the integrated ABC capabilities and the impacts of ABC's application throughout an organization.

INTEGRATED ACTIVITY-BASED COSTING CAPABILITIES

Many aspects can be considered the key functionality of the integrated ABC capabilities. These will be highlighted throughout this chapter. However, when focusing on the most beneficial aspects of integrated ABC, several core concepts clearly have predominance. These concepts focus on eliminating systematic issues often encountered when designing ABC models. The largest drawbacks of ABC implementations and the tools used to support these endeavors deal with lack of integration, which compounds the inability to produce accurate and credible information, thereby impacting analysis capabilities. In addition, the tools available to support ABC are not very flexible. Each of these areas is addressed as a separate topic.

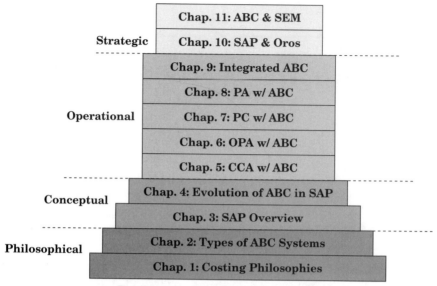

Exhibit 9.1   Chapter Building Blocks

Integration

Integration is the most obvious area to stress, given that ERP systems are designed for this very reason. Implementations of ABC utilizing other ABC support tools are required to interface all information into the application, beginning with the general ledger dollar values to all of the driver quantity information. One of the most common complaints regarding an ABC project is the need to "feed the beast." The ABC model constructed is often very detailed or complicated, and the number of drivers required can be large. This is a twofold problem. First, the ABC model is most likely designed inappropriately to a low level of detail. Second, if the ABC model is justifiable, the amount of drivers needed to support accurate assignments or specific analysis can become extremely large, simply due to the two-step allocation that takes place. The immediate benefit of utilizing ABC within SAP is the elimination of the financial feeds. It is unlikely that SAP CO has been implemented without the FI module. Therefore, the financial information is already directly available for the ABC model. Additionally, many of the driver interfaces are not required. Other SAP modules, such as SD capturing sales quantities or PP tracking production quantities, automatically populate these driver quantities. Capturing necessary driver information is also supported via information systems, which track the number of occurrences for certain transactions, such as the number of purchase orders processed. The degree of integration is impacted by the percentage of usage for the SAP R/3 system. If large sections of the organization or complete functions, such as production or distribution, have not been implemented into SAP, the integration is greatly impacted.

The impact of integration is actually bidirectional. Usually there are interfaces into the ABC support tool. Also, if utilized to truly manage the organization, the results may flow back to other systems. Beyond the inbound connections just mentioned, there are several outbound integration points to other modules. SAP ABC has the ability to post process costs throughout the SAP application. Most notable outbound integration points are those outside of the CO module:

- Capitalizing process costs contained within internal orders or projects
- Updating inventory valuations and cost of goods sold with process costs captured real time for product and production costing
- Recovering process costs that are transferred to sales orders for billing

Accuracy

Tight integration bolsters the accuracy and, most important, the credibility of the information generated from the data produced. Credibility is gained through secure data processing resulting in the inability to manipulate the data or introduce errors. The credibility of the data also is strengthened by the ability to drill-down to actual line items, displaying transaction documents and who created the posting. The integration also increases the accuracy of the information through being real time. Data anomalies can be detected much faster, ensuring the original data information is corrected. Manipulation of the data on the back end becomes unnecessary.

Beyond the actual data collection and processing aspects, accuracy is supported through conceptual design capabilities of the SAP ABC model. The model enables the ability to truly reflect where capacity resides, the nature of the costs on the process, and the cost flows of the organization. As mentioned several times, capacity resides on the resource, not the process. Processes/activities are verbs, not nouns (like an asset), as indicated by the common practice of the process/activity name starting with a verb. Even when capacity is utilized to support only one process, such as MACHR consumed for the *Run Machine* process, this does not negate the fact that there are two separate cost objects involved; a resource object and a process object. The basis of the SAP CO module is designed to support Resource Consumption Accounting (RCA), focusing specifically on the management and control of resources and their capacity. The integration of RCA with ABC provides the most accurate view of capacity within an organization and the application of those capacities to support activities/processes. With the capacity correctly represented by the resource driver, the nature of the process costs is also accurately determined. The process takes on the fixed and proportional nature of those resources consumed. The fixed/proportional components are then further transferred to the consumers of the process. If a true reflection of the cost flows in an organization is replicated in the ABC model, the process is utilized to pass on the accurate costs to the cost objects, by the ability to assign within and outside of the CO module. Specifically, the ability to assign process costs back to a resource center/cost center provides numerous benefits, as discussed in Chapter 5. Not every cost flow in an organization need to be mapped to this level of detail. Both materiality and availability of the data need to be considered. The ability to have a quantity structure representing most of the organization supports imputing drivers based on highly correlated causal relationships for areas where actual data is not captured or materiality is deemed too low. Thus this accurate reflection is much easier to attain and maintain.

Analysis

The increased accuracy in the ability to capture, control, correct, and assign costs throughout the organization aids analysis for process improvement, reengineering, utilization, benchmarking, and outsourcing. Most important is the quantity structure of the cost objects throughout the organization. When a process or a receiver that consumes a process is outsourced, impacts on capacity for the secondary areas also can be seen. The drill-down reporting capability for detecting anomalies is also used for general analysis to determine resources required to support a process, which receivers consume the process costs, and so forth. This drill-down capability is one form of an audit trail for analysis and credibility. Additionally, transparency of the process costs can be designed into the ABC model, utilizing different cost elements, groups, and the primary cost component split. Due to its real-time nature, the ABC model of the SAP system provides information in a timely manner. Many organizations utilizing ABC systems produce information quarterly. The desire to have ABC information every period is one of the main reasons organizations shift to integrated ABC. Although driver data can be captured in real time, often much of the cost data is not available until the end of the period. If the ABC model is based on quantity relationships, standards are utilized during the period to reflect the corresponding cost charges with the actual quantities. The standard method and its resulting information indicates areas where variances are occurring, allowing management to investigate the situation while it is being experienced instead of noting it one or three months later. Therefore, corrective actions can be taken much sooner. The variance calculations of the SAP R/3 system are far more advanced than other ABC tools. These variance calculations are not limited to plan/actual variance, which only indicates poor planning within the organization. The target/actual variance determines what the true variance on the process is or what variance is caused by the process. Additional variances deal with areas such as input price, input quantity usage of the resources, and output variances.

Flexibility

The ability to support integration and accuracy is one thing; supporting flexibility as well is another. Normally integration and accuracy are driven by structure, which directly counters flexibility. However, SAP's integrated ABC provides the necessary technical structure while providing flexibility for supporting the ABC model design. This flexibility is evident in the ability to support multiple methods for driver rate calculations, step-down versus iterative cost flows, intermingling of standard costs or actual costs for differing processes, scalability, and the template allocation. Within SAP, the driver rates are not necessarily just for informational purposes; they can be utilized for actual cost charging. Most ABC applications are based on actual costing with a full-absorption approach. In this case, the process driver rate fluctuates from period to period as utilization fluctuates. This approach assumes that processes are consistent across the year; it does not take into consideration potential seasonality or needs for smoothing. For example, depreciation is normally spread evenly over the year; as activity volumes decrease during certain periods, the process rates rise, punishing the products or services provided in the downturn. When determining rates, SAP can accommodate both a step-down and/or an iterative approach. Many ABC tools do not support iterative relationships beyond simplistic reciprocal flows of values. Therefore, these systems cannot correctly reflects or calculates interrelationship of resource quantities, which greatly impacts the accuracy of the information. Very precise assignments are often made from the process to the receivers. Yet the allocation methodologies to assign the costs to the processes are inaccurate because the interrelationship of resource drivers is ignored or based on unsubstantiated assumptions to begin with.

As previously stated, most ABC models have been designed to be actual costing, full-absorption designs. The biggest benefit of SAP's integrated ABC is the ability to create a standard costing ABC model (i.e., an ABC model utilizing frozen standards), supporting more real-time information and indications of areas of concern due to variances. Additionally, if desired, actual costing can be utilized for some processes. Use of standard costing is common in shared services environments where service agreements have been put in place. In some cases the actual cost of providing the service, represented as a process such as the *Perform Period-End Closing* process, is accepted while for other processes a set price is established. Or different prices are set for given volume levels. This decision is usually driven by the internal organizational agreements or by how variance should be liquidated.

Beyond the flexibility to determine how driver rates are calculated or whether standard costing, actual costing (moving average), or a combination should be utilized, scalability is also supported. A commonly asked question when considering moving from an ABC analytical support tool to SAP's integrated ABC is: Do all costs have to go through the process view? Obviously, within SAP CO, the answer is no. ABC is one costing philosophy supported. Other costs may flow through the costing system in a different manner, such as cost plus, or via an internal order, or directly from the cost center to a market segment. Multiple options are supported since ABC usually is not supported globally throughout an organization. In addition, unless a more accurate costing method is required or there is a need to benchmark the processes, ABC may not be warranted due to materiality.

The final aspect supporting flexibility is the template allocation method. The benefits and capabilities of this method cannot be overstated. Utilizing the template, a dynamic ABC model can be supported, adapting to meet the day-to-day environment to accurately assign process costs throughout the SAP application. The template incorporates four capabilities to enhance flexibility.

1. It can determine which process should be utilized. For example, if a certain aircraft engine code includes the code ATP, then Process 1 is charged versus Process 2. This ability completely eliminates the historical structure of common ABC support tools.

2. It can determine the quantity to be assigned to the receiver objects. The quantity can be as simple as a specific number or can be a complex formula calculation.

3. "IF-THEN" Boolean logic capability takes the quantity calculation one step further and adds conditions to the quantity calculation. Here the flexibility supported by the template helps to determine IF it is for a certain customer THEN the quantity is different than for another customer. Doing this allows complexity to be handled in a statement or rule; the complexity does not need to be designed into either multiple assignment rules or multiple master data records.

4. The template allows for the flexibility to assign process costs when a triggering event has occurred, such as at order creation or during finished good confirmation. This ability supports process costs being recognized in the period the process actually occurs instead of being recognized only at the completion of an event or order. Therefore, process costs can be included in the calculation of work in process, which most ABC applications do not easily support.

Integration, accuracy, analysis, and flexibility are common themes of benefits when considering SAP's integrated ABC. However, these are not the only benefits. The following sections describe other capabilities and benefits. See Exhibit 9.16, provided in the "Summary" section of this chapter, for a combined list of the benefits of SAP's integrated ABC.

INFORMATION FLOWS

Chapters 5 to 8 focused on the information flows between ABC and a particular area of focus. Each chapter addressed different aspects of the allocation methods and the benefits or best uses for each. This section summarizes the key points and benefits of each allocation utilizing the process cost object. Exhibit 9.2 illustrates several of the examples from each of the chapters combined into a CO conceptual design.

Assessments/Distribution Cycles

Exhibit 9.2 provides two assessment cycle examples, labeled 1. First is the allocation of the *Market Research & Development* cost center to the *Research Market Patterns* and *Develop Service/Product Attribute* processes. These costs are then further allocated to the PA market segments using a PA assessment cycle. The assessment and distribution cycles are both value-based allocation methods used to "Push" dollars through the organization. These value-based allocations support common allocation basis of fixed percentages, fixed dollars, ratios, and variable portions. The variable portion option converts quantity measures for actypes, processes, or SKFs into a percentage allocation basis. Assessments and distributions are normally utilized to support a step-down approach to cost allocation. However, they do support the definition of recursive relationships within a cycle. While iterative costs flows between cycles are not automatically supported, they can be accommodated manually. These cycles are generally used to

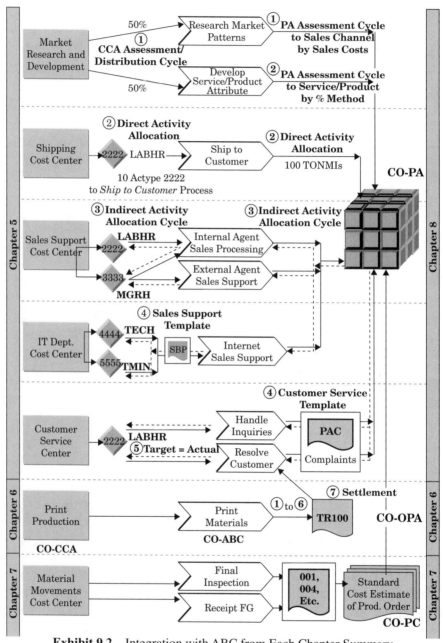

Exhibit 9.2   Integration with ABC from Each Chapter Summary

support full-absorption costing whereby 100% of the sender costs are allocated, yet partial percentages can be utilized to determine the sending amount of expenses. Both types of cycles are periodic allocation methods being executed during the period-end closing procedures and have limited capabilities to handle complexity.

The distribution cycle can be used to allocate dollar values from cost centers or processes to cost centers, processes, work breakdown structures (WBS) on projects, or orders, such as internal orders or even production orders. The distribution cycle debits/credits the same account from the sender to the receiver. Therefore, if several hundred cost elements are being allocated, several hundred line items are generated, posting the debits to the senders and the credits to the receivers. For this reason, the distribution cycle can be system resource intensive, requiring more processing time and database size to house the postings. The cost transfer utilization of the originating primary cost element is usually utilized to support reporting based on a financial accounting basis and not internal cost management. In contrast, the assessment cycle utilizes a secondary cost element for posting the allocation results, for example, 99999 Corporate Allocation. To facilitate a more detailed view of the sending costs breakdown, the allocation structure can be utilized, representing a grouping of costs, for example, 99998 Salary Expenses, 99997 Office Expenses, and 99996 Misc. Assessment cycles also can be used from the process to the market segment cost objects, which is not supported by distribution cycles. Assessment cycles highly correlate to the most common type of assignment methodology supported by stand-alone ABC tools.

Direct Activity Allocations

A direct activity allocation directly charges an actype or process to almost any cost object within SAP, real time. Exhibit 9.2 provides two examples of a DAA, labeled as 2. The actype LABHR of the *Shipping* cost center is directly charged to the *Ship to Customer* process for the time spent preparing and delivering the shipment. The *Ship to Customer* process is then directly charged to the customers based on ton-mileage (TONMI). The DAA is a quantity-based assignment, charging the quantities of a process consumed by another process, cost center, market segment, or any order, such as internal order, maintenance order, or production order. For the process to be directly charged to a cost object, it must have a unit of measure, a secondary cost element, and a rate defined. The most common process unit of measure is "EA" for "Each." The SAP R/3 system comes standard with multiple units of measures and supports user-defined units if a specific one is needed to represent a process. The secondary cost element is utilized in charging for the costs to make the debit/credit postings, relieving the process of the costs, and posting them to the receiving object. The process rate multiplied by the quantity consumed determines the appropriate dollar value for the posting. A standard rate is assumed during the period the quantity is posted, unless a pure actual costing system has been selected. An actual rate can be calculated at period end, and a corresponding adjustment posting is automatically made to relieve the process of any residual expenses.

The DAA is internally utilized throughout the SAP system for making process charges, such as in production confirmation when backflushing is performed if the process is defined on the routing. It exists only in assigning actual period costs and does not apply to plan data. In planning, direct planned consumption of a process or actype quantity is called activity-dependent planning.

Indirect Activity Allocation Cycle

The indirect activity allocation cycle is utilized in some instances like an assessment cycle and in other instances like the direct activity allocation. The "cycle" in the name of this allocation method indicates that it works similarly to the assessment and distribution cycles. The IAA cycle executes periodically and is usually included in the period-end closing procedures. The tracing methods are also similar, such as fixed percentages, variable portions converting actypes, process, SKFs, and value fields into percentages and ratios. The key difference between the IAA and assessment cycle is that quantities are allocated with the corresponding dollar posting based on a standard or actual rate. For this reason, the IAA has fixed quantities as an allocation basis, not fixed dollars. In comparison with the assessment cycle, the IAA provides additional information of quantities. Since the IAA posts the quantities of the process, the secondary cost element of the process will be utilized to make the posting. Therefore, an allocation structure is not an option with the IAA cycle.

If the IAA cycle is defined as inversely calculated, the cycle works like a periodic direct activity allocation for which the quantity is not directly known but can be imputed from another known quantity. Exhibit 9.2 provides one scenario containing two examples of the IAA cycle utilizing the inverse calculated parameter, labeled as 3. The *Sales Support* cost center has two actypes, one for LABHR, representing the sales agents, and the other for MGRH, representing the managers. These resources perform *Internal Sales Agent Processing* and *External Sales Agent Support* processes as well as others not listed. A ratio is established between the actypes and the processes. For example, for each *Internal*

Agent Sales Processing and *External Agent Sales Support* process, 1 minute of the MGHR for review and 6 minutes for managing the partnership, respectively, is required. One *Internal Sales Agent Processing* or *External Sales Agent Support* is required for each individual sale of that type. The only quantity tracked is the actual sales per sales channel. At period end, all sales quantities are known, the actual quantity of each process is also known, and the corresponding consumption of MGHRs is then imputed. The system backflushes through the quantity structure consuming the required resources and processes. The obvious benefit of the inversely calculated IAA is the reduction in capturing actual drivers since a strongly correlated relationship exists that can be used to impute a process and/or actype quantity.

Template Allocation

The inversely calculated IAA is the first assignment method mentioned that back-flushes through a defined quantity relationship. The template allocation also executes by backflushing through a quantity relationship to make a direct process posting to the receiving cost object. The key differences from the IAA are that the template supports within-period postings and conditions to be defined within the correlated relationship. A template can be defined exactly the same as the IAA, yet it supports within-period posting of the quantities. This posting may be desired if users are tracking certain process utilizations by week or supporting market segment P/L reported within the period.

The template can support the same direct relationship between quantities, such as for each sale within the *Int. Agent* sales channel, one *Internal Agent Sales Processing* process is consumed. Or, as continually stressed, templates can support more complex quantity relationships due to conditions or parameters, such as the *Customer Service* PAC template example (Exhibit 9.2). Within the *Customer Service* template, different rules can be defined. For example, the relationship can be established that for every complaint captured as a value field in PA, one *Resolve Customer* process is required. Or the relationship can be established that because *Customer 1* is notoriously a stickler for detail, for every complaint, 1.5 *Resolve Customer* processes should be assigned. Simplistic complexity such as this can also be defined within a cycle by utilizing the weighting capabilities. However, the cycle is still periodic in nature; if the information is needed within the period, the template must be utilized. Although cycles can handle simple weighting for complexity, they cannot support more complex calculations. An example may be drawn from the *Customer Service* template where a rule was established that stated IF more than 20 inquires have occurred, THEN assign one

Handle Inquiries process for each additional inquiry logged. Additionally, within the template, functions can be defined for pulling information residing in other systems to be utilized within calculations or determinations of when a process should be assigned.

The template was specifically designed to address two of the key weaknesses of most ABC models supported by stand-alone tools:

1. In order to support an ABC model at a low level of detail for accuracy, or to provide the information needed for analysis, driver data has to be available. In many cases, for a multitude of reasons or because it is too cost prohibitive, the appropriate driver data is not collected. This issue and/or the inability to appropriately impute the missing driver data lead to limitations (e.g., areas left unaddressed or aggregation of drivers) being designed into the ABC model.

2. Other than needing "to feed the beast," the ABC model also must be built and maintained. Stand-alone ABC systems are usually historical views and updated once every quarter or annually. This information structure is useful for analytics recognizing trends, yet for daily operations and transactional capturing of an ERP system, it is not an appropriate time frame. Within the operational environment, the ABC model needs to expand and become more accurate and timely, thereby increasing the model maintenance requirements. The inability or lack of desire to support this maintenance frequency in stand-alone tools leads to inaccuracy in the ABC model, such as outdated assignment relationships or building assignments at a higher, more stable level, thereby not supporting the most accurate information.

The template functionality addresses both of these weaknesses.

1. SAP integration provides hundreds of potential drivers already being captured within the system, reducing the need to build and maintain collection systems and interfaces and supporting an expanded ABC model. Additionally, the added ability to define complex formulas calculating quantities consumed, increases accuracy and can be utilized to impute driver quantities excluded from the traditional ABC model.

2. Several different aspects of the template address the typical ABC model maintenance issue. The template can be utilized for several cost objects, reducing the need to create repetitive assignments. The template environment's filtering capabilities provide quick access to the most pertinent information for the type of process costs to be assigned. Filtering supports the ability to define more accurate or potentially complex ABC models in

a user-friendly and expedient manner. Accessing hundreds of standard functions for use in these formulas makes the integrated ABC model creation and maintenance intuitive and fast. Utilizing subtemplates minimizes maintenance by allowing grouping of common processes to feed other processes. In addition, strategy rules for dynamic location and determination of templates can be defined. These rules define where and when a template should be used. Doing so supports a dynamic ABC model rather than a static one. The dynamic nature of the SAP ABC model supports the most accurate assignment of process costs to the true usage and consumers, providing very precise cost object information. For example, assignments to customer groups or product groups are automatically updated as master data is added, deleted, or changed in the SAP applications. For stand-alone ABC, a maintenance process must be in place identifying changes to the source system master data. This maintenance process should indicate the need to update the master data and assignments of the model.

Two other examples are provided in Exhibit 9.2, labeled as 4, the structured business process template for the *Sales Support* and a product costing template, built using any of the production environments, such as 001 for Standard Cost Estimates or 004 for Project Systems. In both of these examples, the template functions like a bill of process (also called bill of costs or bill of resources in other ABC applications). Unlike the bill of cost/resource provided in those tools, the template as the bill of process can also dynamically determine which process should be applied, when that process should be applied, and how much of the process quantity is consumed. The calculations for the quantity can consider both fixed (the process is lot-size independent) and variable (the process is lot-size dependent) consumption of a process simultaneously. Other applications supporting ABC limit the calculation of the process or resource driver quantity to be either fixed or variably consumed.

Target = Actual

The target = actual assignment is the third and final quantity-based method that backflushes through a quantity structure. The target = actual assignment works like the indirect activity allocation in that it is executed during period-end closing and has a simplistic quantity-to-quantity relationship. However, for the target = actual, this relationship is not explicitly defined within the cycle, but derived by the system based on planned relationships. Therefore, the sender driver quantities are known in plan yet imputed for actual. In Exhibit 9.2, labeled as 5, the

Customer Service cost center utilizes the target = actual allocation to assign *LABHR* to the *Handle Inquiries* and *Resolve Customer Complaints* processes. The *Customer Service* cost center manager plans how much *LABHR* will be spent on each process—for example, 1000 to *Handle Inquiries* and 400 to *Resolve Customer Complaints* processes. The *Handle Inquiries* and *Resolve Customer Complaints* processes have planned output defined, 1000 and 200, respectively. The implied relationships are for every *Handle Inquiries,* 1 *LABHR* is required (1000/1000), and for every *Resolve Customer Complaints,* 2 *LABHRs* are needed (400/200). This relationship is used to impute, based on the actual process quantities, the consumption of the *LABHRs* to each process.

The benefits of the target = actual method are that it calculates the target input quantities based on the actual output quantity of a receiver. Therefore, an actual driver quantity by sender is not required to be collected. Additionally, the target = actual method considers recursive assignments, which the indirect activity allocation does not consider.

Overhead Calculation

In Exhibit 9.2, the allocation from the *Print Materials* process to the training internal order has listed multiple potential methods, numbers 1 through 6. Number 6 represents the overhead calculation capability, which supports a cost-plus approach for overhead allocations. The overhead calculation method is a periodic value-based allocation that supports percentage or quantity surcharges from a process to an internal order utilizing a costing sheet. The costing sheet defines which cost elements on the process to include, the overhead rate to be charged, and the secondary cost element to utilize for the posting. The overhead calculation method has some conditional capabilities, however limited, such as distinguishing by company code.

Settlements

Settlements can be utilized only to allocate from an order to a receiver. Therefore, it cannot be used to allocate process costs yet it can be used to allocate to a process. Within the CO module, the main "order" of focus is the internal order. The settlement rule is most similar to an assessment cycle utilizing an allocation structure. They both are executed during period end and are value-based allocations posting dollars and not quantities with a dollar valuation. The main difference is that the internal order only supports as an allocation basis percentage,

fixed dollars, or equivalents (ratios). The main benefit of the settlement allocation is its ability to indirectly carry process cost outside of the costing area to
other modules, such as FI or SD, through settling the costs to a balance sheet account or the customer invoice.

The assignment capabilities and the ability to allocate to almost any object
makes the integrated ABC functionality very advanced. Exhibit 9.3 compares assignment methods that utilize a process in some manner.

SAMPLE KEY BUSINESS DECISIONS

Hundreds of different business decisions are supported via ABC information.
Prior chapters have addressed many of the key business decisions for which
ABC information is utilized. Exhibit 9.4 lists sample key business decisions to
be addressed in this section, touching on and encompassing subjects covered
previously.

Identification, Inputs, and Outputs

The ABC model has to be designed to support whatever analysis is to be performed. Therefore, it is critical that the decisions to be answered or monitored
are understood before initiating an ABC project. The biggest problems of the organization need to be determined, so the ABC model can take these issues into
consideration.

1. Is the focus on understanding how the company performs compared to
   others?
2. Is there a need to benchmark within organizational units for outsourcing
   decisions?
3. Is the main objective to streamline processes to eliminate waste and
   shorten lead times?
4. Or is it to understand how capacity is impacted? Key decisions to be answered must be prioritized and then addressed.

These decisions aid in defining the scope of the ABC model. The scope covers the analysis to be supported, costs to be included (product costing, shared
services, cost-to-serve), organizational units, level of complexity for the first
phase, and so on. With the scope defined, the first three questions listed above can
be addressed. These focus on the identification of the processes, their inputs, and
outputs to receiver cost objects.

Allocation Method	Assessment Cycle	Distribution Cycle	Direct Activity Allocation	Indirect Activity Allocation	Template	Target = Actual	Overhead Calculation	Settlement
Comments	Allocations from processes to any receiver using an assessment cost element or the allocation structure.	Allocations from processes to any receiver using the detailed accounts	Direct process charge to any receiver. Exists only in actuals.	Supports imputing quantities, reducing the need to capture actuals for a driver. Also supports quantity splitting.	Dynamic determination of which process, how much, under what conditions, and when in the life cycle.	Target input quantity imputed from actual receiver quantity based on plan relationship. Only exists in actual.	Process costs can be allocated to an order with a percentage or quantity surcharge.	Internal orders settle to processes. Can transfer process costs to other modules.
Assignment Basis	Fixed %, fixed portions, fixed amount, variable tracing based dollars or quantities.	Fixed %, fixed portions, fixed amount, variable tracing based dollars or quantities.	Actual quantities.	Fixed %, fixed portions, fixed quantities, variable tracing based on value field dollars or quantities.	Simple to complex formulas and "IF-THEN" rules (methods).	Imputed based on planned relationships.	Percentage or quantity rate surcharges.	Percentage, fixed dollar amount, equivalents.
Posting Type	Value based	Value based	Quantity based	Quantity based	Quantity based	Quantity based	Value based	Value based
Timing	Period-end closing	Period-end closing	Real time	Period-end closing	Within period	Period-end closing	Period-end closing	Period-end closing
Usability	Moderate	Moderate	Easy	Moderate	Advanced	Easy	Moderate	Moderate
Handle Complexity	Limited	Limited	None	Limited	High level easily supported	None	Limited	Limited

Exhibit 9.3 Allocations/Assignments Methods Supporting ABC in SAP R/3

Sample Key Business Decisions	Value Based	Quantity Based
What processes are performed within the organization?	√	√
What are the process costs?	√	√
What are the impacts of process costs on the receivers?	√	√
How should capacity be deployed for next year?	--	√
Given current volumes and mix, what processes and resources are required and when?	--	√
How can the processes be improved?	√	√
What processes should be outsourced, and what is the impact to direct and secondary capacity?	--	√

ᵃ— represents not supported. √ represents supported.

Exhibit 9.4   Key Business Decision Supported by ABC Sample

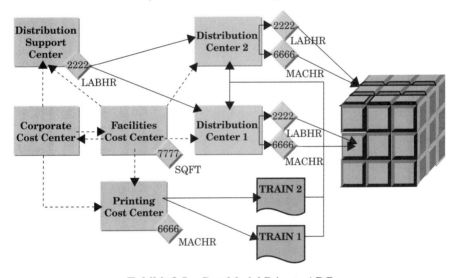

Exhibit 9.5   Cost Model Prior to ABC

Identifying the Processes and Their Inputs (Doing the Right Thing)   Implementing Activity-Based Costing utilizing SAP as the support tool is conducted in a very similar manner to traditional ABC implementations. An activity analysis is performed to define the processes, the inputs to those processes, and the receiving cost objects. Exhibit 9.5 illustrates the organizational structure prior to the activity analysis.

Cost may be accurately or appropriately attributed to the correct cost objects; however, it is difficult to understand how to reduce costs or what the organizational resources are doing. The process object within SAP can be used to represent the lowest-level activity or task, up to the most aggregate view of the process chain. Exhibit 9.6 illustrates the identified individual processes and the aggregate distribution process.

With the processes defined, users gain a better understanding of how resources are converted to cost object expenses to answer the question of how an organization does what it does. Next, the inputs to the process have to be identified. Here the different assignments methodologies and cost objects that can allocate to a process enable a simplistic (value-based) to potentially more complex (supported by a quantity-based, quantity structure) application of inputs to the process. This capability combined with the different rate capabilities and primary cost component split functionality helps to truly define the resource and process driver rates and the costs that generate those rates. The ability to utilize a template as a bill of resources and the internal order to capture event-specific costs for a process aids in accurately depicting the relationships between the processes and all inputs. Doing so is important for supporting improvement endeavors and understanding the impact of process outsourcing decisions. Exhibit 9.7 illustrates the input relationships defined.

Outputs of the Processes   With the inputs accurately identified, an understanding of the consumers of the processes is required. During the activity analysis, the relationships between the processes and the receivers (cost objects) are determined and established. Exhibit 9.8 illustrates several process-to-cost object relationships added to the cost model. One example is the *Enter Document* process consumed by the distribution processes. Another example is the *Schedule Laborers* process consumed by the distribution cost centers.

This exhibit is a small example. The entire model network can become quite large. Augmenting the cost model with the process view adds a level of complexity. However, it also provides information for determining the impacts of process costs on cost centers, event management, job costing, production or service orders, and real-time profitability or market segment reporting. The quality of this information is directly affected by the accuracy of the resource-to-process (input) assignments. A reciprocal cost model, cost center to process to cost center, supports answering questions regarding shared services, such as how much does it cost to provide the services or how does the actual process rate compare to external benchmarks. The process assignment to any order for events, jobs, project, production, or a service aids in the more accurate determination of the costs for that individual order and therefore for the aggregate view of product

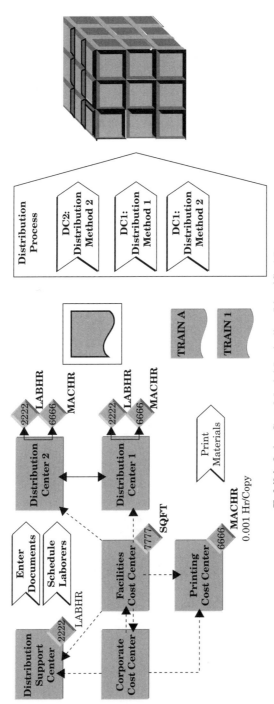

Exhibit 9.6 Cost Model Including Identified Processes

279

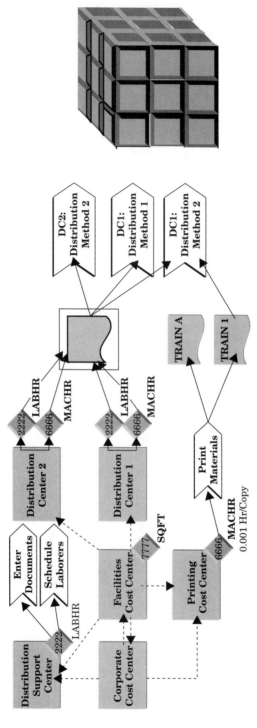

Exhibit 9.7 Inputs to Processes Defined for the Cost Model

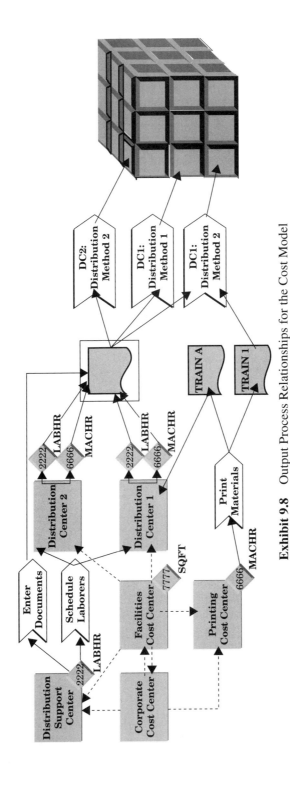

Exhibit 9.8 Output Process Relationships for the Cost Model

costs or service processing, whether for internal or external purposes. Utilizing a process standard rate, cost impacts due to an attribute or to option changes to products or services can be identified or new products/services can be estimated more accurately. The process-to-market segment relationships provide insight into the cost to serve specific markets, identifying which ones to focus on for cost reduction or incentive rewarding projects.

Capacity Management

When defining the assignment methodologies, one must consider whether capacity management is to be supported. If the assignments are designed as value-based allocations, capacity management is not a central focus of the ABC model. Perhaps other concerns are central, such as understanding the processes themselves or allocating expenses in a more accurate manner than traditionally supported. However, to address decisions focusing on questions such as how capacity should be deployed for next year, a quantity structure utilizing quantity-based assignments needs to be designed.

Why focus on capacity management? Anyone who has ever owned or managed a business or organizational unit knows that the name of the game is cash management. Cash management means effectively leveraging the assets of the organization to maximize their usage. The assets of the organization are obvious: cash, people, machines, and materials. To prevent spending more than is required, capacity management is vital for efficiently managing the organization's assets. Capacity management is a key focus for ABC, not because the capacity resides on the process, but because the process is one potential consumer of the capacity and therefore a determining factor for its utilization.

Capacity management begins with planning. In the past, organizations performed planning/budgeting mainly on spreadsheets, estimating a percentage increase in sales volumes or some other key indicator that upper management utilizes as a starting point. The rest of the organization then increases their budgets by a percentage, then management reduces that number. Eventually a bargaining game is played over the numbers. This approach assumes that the business environment has not shifted, the organization has not changed in any way, the same inefficiencies that existed previously remain and have not worsened, and this desired key metric increase has some merit to begin with, other than sounding good to stockholders or being what management wants to have happen. Throughout the year the organization measures actuals against the plan, supposedly receiving key information that indicates ways to change to ensure that the planned figures are realized. In reality, the plan/actual variance simply indicates the inadequacy of the planning process. Managers spend hours manipulating numbers to make them appear as close as possible or at least within a range for which they can contrive plausible excuses for the Plan/Actual variances. With the speed of business ever increasing, this process has become a monthly endeavor, reevaluating and changing the plan/budget based on actual to date. Managers aim to ensure more accuracy simply because the plan is revised or at least manipulated every month. In frustration, some managers throw up their hands, saying: "Perhaps we should scrap this whole budgeting thing and do . . .? "Do what? Current planning/budgeting methods are time consuming and subjective, producing imaginative goals without any true understanding of how meeting those goals impacts on the organization. So what is the solution? Activity-Based Budgeting? The answer is yes, in part.

Chapter 1 addressed Activity-Based Budgeting and the differences when used with Resource Consumption Accounting. Here again we stress that the best solution to the plan/budget cycle quandary encompasses the complete quantity structure, of which ABB is a limited quantity structure. Quantity-structured planning focuses on backflushing output quantities throughout the organization, converting those output quantities to dollars. Activity-Based Budgeting focuses on quantity-structure planning for the activities/processes and the consumption of those processes by the cost objects. Resource consumption accounting focuses on a quantity-structure plan for the resource drivers and the consumption of those drivers by any cost object; a process is one option if used in tandem with ABB. Each philosophy provides valuable information for its particular area. When the two approaches are combined (ABB and RCA), utilizing a quantity-structure, the complete quantity-based network of assignments throughout the cost model is mapped to the true consumers, providing a more accurate reflection of the quantities and therefore capacities consumed. Exhibit 9.9 illustrates this quantity structure. The dark gray and black lines indicate the backflush through the quantity structure. The black lines merely highlight one particular flow as an example.

Defining the quantity structure is basically an industrial engineering exercise to determine the standards between different driver quantities. Once those standards are in place, they are used to backflush starting quantities throughout the costing model network. This example depicts the sales plan being entered for 10,000 of each distribution method. The sales quantities are then backflushed through the quantity structure to determine the impact on all processes and capacities, except for the areas that are not utilizing the quantity structure, such as the *Corporate* cost center. Two assumptions are made:

1. The sales estimates or initial transaction numbers are based on real potential and not overinflated.
2. The standards are generated by analysis, not assumptions.

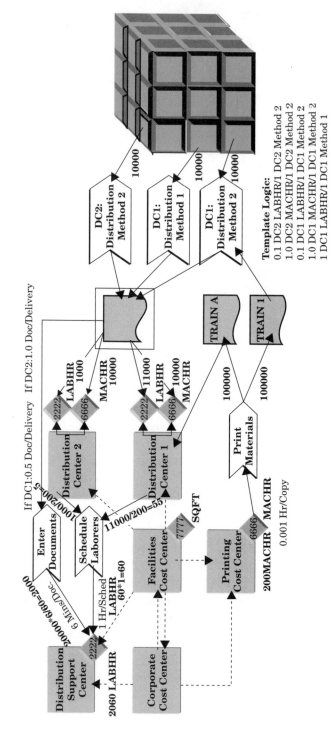

Exhibit 9.9 Quantity-Structured Planning for Capacity Management

Utilizing the initial numbers and the standards as the framework, backflushing shows requirements throughout the model as scheduled, identifying bottlenecks up front, when a purchasing decision can be determined and arranged. Once the quantities have been accepted as the plan, the dollars flow as well. Exhibit 9.10 illustrates a selected section of the model showing the dollars with the quantity structure.

A quantity output of 10,000 for each of the distribution processes is calculated from the sales quantity of 10,000 for each distribution method. This example holds true for either a service or a production company. For instance, the distribution centers (DCs) can represent bank branches. The distribution methods are via teller for method 1 (labor intensive) and via a kiosk for method 2. Or the DCs can represent bottling plants. Then the distribution methods are different sizes of trucks, one requiring mainly manual labor and the other is more automated. Utilizing the standards defined, the *MACHR* and *LABHR* quantities for *Distribution Center 1* and *Distribution Center 2* are determined. The combined *LABHRs* for the *DCs* drive the output of the *Schedule Laborers* process that in turns drives the *LABHR* for the *Distribution Support* cost center. Primary expenses, such as *Salaries* and *Supplies,* are planned for the given output required. The backflush determines the need for 2060 *LABHRs* for the *Distribution Support* cost center. Capacity for that cost center is really 2000 *LABHRs*. Management can make the decision that the difference can be accommodated with the current resources, for example, with overtime.

This example assumes that not all costs within the cost centers are proportional to the amount of output, often an assumption of ABB, which is not realistic. For the *Distribution Support* cost center, most of the labor force is nonsalaried. Therefore, their costs fluctuate directly based on the need for their time, unlike managers who have a fixed salary compared to the output of the cost center. Exhibit 9.11 illustrates the numbers broken into a fixed/proportional view.

With the fixed/proportional expenses throughout the cost model delivering market segment P/L reporting is possible, specifically gross and contribution margins at many levels. An additional level of accuracy is gained by considering fixed and variable quantity consumptions. For example, in addition to the schedule provided per laborer, 20 daily schedules are made each month showing all employees on the schedule. These 20 schedules are fixed regardless of the estimated labor hours required, in order to provide a basis covering minimum requirements and holidays. Exhibit 9.12 illustrates the impact of considering fixed and variable quantity consumptions.

The impact is minimal for this example; however, if production is modeled or the volumes are large, then the impact can be much greater. Note that as the *Distribution Support LABHRs* required increased 40 hours to cover these additional

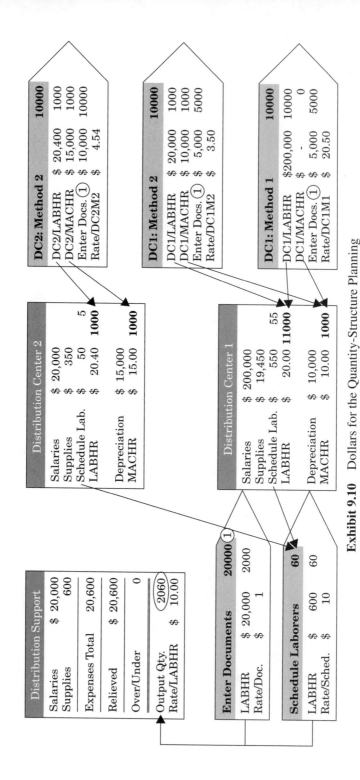

Exhibit 9.10 Dollars for the Quantity-Structure Planning

286

Distribution Support

Account	Fix	Prop.	Total
Salaries	$ 3000	$ 17000	$ 20000
Supplies		600	600
Total	$ 3000	$ 17600	$ 20600
Relieved			$20,600
Over/Under			0
Output Qty			2060
Rate/LABHR	$ 1.46	$ 8.54	$ 10.00

Distribution Center 2

Account	Fix	Prop.	Total	Qty.
Salaries	$ 5,000	$15,000	$20,000	
Supplies		350	350	
Schedule Lab.$	7	$ 43	$ 50	5
LABHR	$ 5.01	$ 15.39	$ 20.40	1000
Depreciation	$15,000	$ -	$15,000	
MACHR	$ 15	$ -	$ 15.00	1000

DC2: Method 2 — 10000

Account	Fix	Prop.	Total	Qty.
DC2/LABHR	$ 5,007	$15,393	$20,400	1000
DC2/MACHR	$15,000		$15,000	1000
Enter Docs.①	$ 1,456	$ 8,544	$10,000	10000
Rate/DC2M2	$ 2.15	$ 2.39	$ 4.54	

DC1: Method 2 — 60

Account	Fix	Prop.	Total	Qty.
DC1/LABHR	$ 916	$19,084	$20,000	1000
DC1/MACHR	$10,000	-	$10,000	1000
Enter Docs.①	$ 728	$ 4,272	$ 5,000	5000
Rate/DC1M2	$ 1.16	$ 2.34	$ 3.50	

DC1: Method 1 — 10000

Account	Fix	Prop.	Total	Qty.
DC1/LABHR	$9,164	$190,836	$200,000	10000
DC1/MACHR	$ -	$ -	$ -	0
Enter Docs.①	$ 728	$ 4,272	$ 5,000	5000
Rate/DC1M1	$ 0.99	$ 19.51	$ 20.50	

Distribution Center 1

Account	Fix	Prop.	Total	Qty.
Salaries	$10,000	$190,000	$200,000	
Supplies		$ 19,450	$ 19,450	
Schedule Lab.$	80	$ 470	$ 550	55
LABHR	$ 0.92	$ 19.08	$ 20.00	11000
Depreciation	$10,000	$ -	$ 10,000	
MACHR	$ 10	$ -	$ 10.00	1000

Enter Documents — 2000①

Account	Fix	Prop.	Total	Qty.
LABHR	$2,913	$17,087	$20,000	2000①
Rate/Doc.	$ 0.15	$ 0.85	$ 1.00	

Schedule Laborers — 60

Account	Fix	Prop.	Total	Qty.
LABHR	$ 87	$ 513	$ 600	60
Rate/Sched.	$ 1.46	$ 8.54	$ 10.00	

Exhibit 9.11   Fixed/Proportional Dollars for the Quantity-Structure Planning

Distribution Support

Account	Fix	Prop.	Total
Salaries	$3,000	$17,330	$20,330	612
Supplies		612	
Total	$3,000	$17,942	$20,942

Relieved $20,942

Over/Under 0

Output Qty. 2100

Rate/LABHR $1.43 $8.54 $9.97

Distribution Center 2　　　　10000

Account	Fix	Prop.	Total	Qty.
Salaries	$5,000	$15,000	$20,000	
Supplies		350	350	
Schedule Lab.	$207	$43	$249	25
LABHR	$5.21	15.39	20.60	1000

Depreciation $15,000 $15,000

MACHR $15 $- $- $15.00 1000

DC2: Method 2　　　　10000

Account	Fix	Prop.	Total	Qty.
DC2/LABHR	$5,207	$15,393	$20,599	1000
DC2/MACHR	$15,000	$-	$15,000	1000
Enter Docs.①	$1,429	$8,544	$9,972	10000
Rate/DC2M2	$2.16	$2.39	$4.56	

Distribution Center 1　　　　

Account	Fix	Prop.	Total	Qty.
Salaries	$10,000	$190,000	$200,000	
Supplies		$19,450	$19,450	
Schedule Lab.	$278	$470	$748	75
LABHR	$0.93	19.08	20.02	11000

Depreciation $10,000 $10,000

MACHR $10 $- $- $10.00 1000

DC1: Method 2　　　　10000

Account	Fix	Prop.	Total	Qty.
DC1/LABHR	$934	$19,084	$20,018	1000
DC1/MACHR	$10,000	$-	$10,000	1000
Enter Docs.①	$714	$4,272	$4,986	5000
Rate/DC1M2	$1.16	$2.34	$3.50	

DC1: Method 1　　　　10000

Account	Fix	Prop.	Total	Qty.
DC1/LABHR	$9,344	$190,836	$200,180	10000
DC1/MACHR	$-	$-	$-	0
Enter Docs.①	$714	$4,272	$4,986	5000
Rate/DC1M1	$1.01	$19.51	$20.52	

Enter Documents　　　　20000

Account	Fix	Prop.	Total	Qty.
LABHR	$2,857	$17,087	$19,945	2000①
Rate/Doc.	$0.14	$0.85	$1.00	

Schedule Laborers　　　　100

Account	Fix	Prop.	Total	Qty.
LABHR	$143	$854	$997	100
Rate/Sched.	$1.43	$8.54	$9.97	

Exhibit 9.12　Fixed/Variable Quantities for the Quantity Structure Planning

Schedule Laborers process quantities, the expense of the planning for the proportional expenses of the *Distribution Support* cost center increased as well.

Efficiency, Improvement, and Outsourcing

With the environment defined and planning performed, whether value based or quantity based, measurement of performance can begin. As actual quantities and dollars flow through the cost model, efficiencies can be determined and indications of areas for improvement can be identified. Once analyzed, if it is determined that the process cannot be further improved and does not adequately perform against benchmarks, then outsourcing becomes a consideration. Each of these management options is addressed in more detail in the following sections.

Efficiency (Do Things Right)   One assumption when defining the cost model, including ABC, is that it is designed with an optimal value chain in mind. Planning then is performed for this environment and actuals are captured to determine how the organization is performing. SAP functionality supports calculations of different variances on the process to identify inefficiencies. For areas where a quantity structure is utilized, actual quantities can be used to determine what the expenses should have been, given the volume output (authorized reporting based on target/actual). Additionally, as the environment changes, the demand for process and resources can be updated continually to ensure a valid control standard at all times.

Improvements   One reason the assumption is made that the cost model for the value chain is already optimized is that during the activity analysis, many process improvements are realized and implemented prior to establishing the final cost model and flows. Once the model is in place, these process improvement endeavors become a continuous focus. The process attribute capability for tagging the process as value-added or non–value-added is useful for reporting in order to indicate areas for investigations. If a value-based cost model is utilized, information is more limited yet can still be designed to provide indicators of where to focus continuous improvement based on increased dollar amounts. Actual rates for processes can be utilized to compare common processes across organizational units. This comparison supports internal benchmarking and indicates sections of the organization that potentially have improved the process in a manner that can be standardized and rolled out to other organizational units. In our example, *Distribution Method 2* has different actual rates between the DCs, mainly due to DC2 having additional requirements for information taking twice as long to produce documentation compared to DC1. Further analysis can be done to determine other causes for differences and to determine if they are anomalies, should permanent trends, be standardized, and so forth.

Outsourcing (Not Doing Things at All)   Efficiency focuses on executing consistently right as defined, such as the tellers in branch 1 performing the same number of transactions in the same targeted amount of time. Improvements are gained by changing the environment, such as removing a step needed to process a transaction or finding new equipment to perform the process faster. Such improvements require the reevaluation of efficiency measures. However, there is the option of not performing the process at all. If the process is not needed and eliminated, this action will result in an improvement. However, if it is needed and it has been determined that the organization cannot perform it efficiently, then outsourcing is an option. Key decisions many organizations face are determining which cost centers, internal services, or processes to outsource. In order to truly understand the ramifications of the outsourcing decision, a quantity structure needs to be in place to highlight areas where excess idle capacity will result, including the support areas. Exhibit 9.13 illustrates this example with the additional printing and training functions.

The decision has been made to automate *DC 1* similar to *DC 2*. As a result, one-half of the customers are expected to shift to using the more automated method. The removal of the manual process impacts all areas except for *DC 2*. Exhibit 9.14 illustrates the results.

It can be seen immediately that the *LABHR* for the *Distribution Support* Center has fallen under the 2000 *LABHR* capacity mark mentioned earlier. An adjustment needs to be made to the schedule for the nonsalaried staff to accommodate the reduction in needed hours. Additionally, the cost of the *Print Materials* process has increased. A decision can be made for potentially outsourcing this process to an outside provider. However, the fixed costs would need to be addressed. The rate of the *Print Materials* process and the rate per *Printing LABHR* resource driver increased because demand decreased while capacity remained the same. A copy machine can be sold or moved to a new cost center that requested a copier.

Many decisions, covering a wide range of areas, can and should utilize ABC information. These decisions usually must also consider other information to make the best overall decision for the organization. Sometimes optimizing the component merely moves the inefficiencies to another area. These key decisions as well as those provided in the last four chapters should be adequate samples of key business decisions to be supported utilizing SAP integrated ABC.

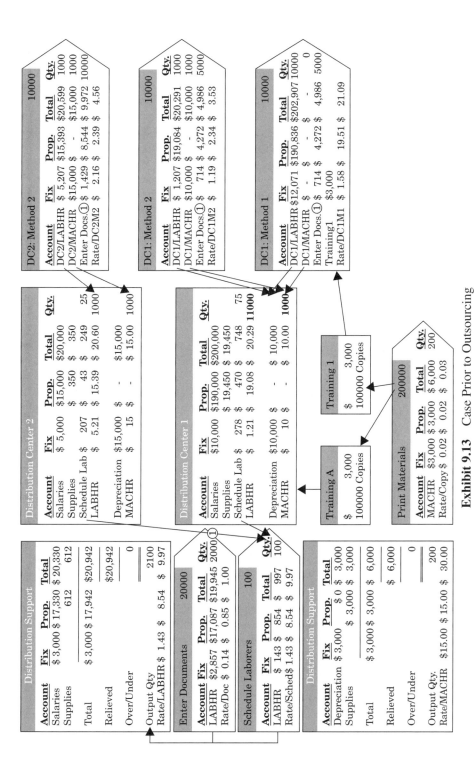

Exhibit 9.13 Case Prior to Outsourcing

291

Distribution Support

Account	Fix	Prop.	Total
Salaries	$3,000	$14,875	$17,875
Supplies		$525	$525
Total	$3,000	$15,400	$18,400
Relieved			$18,400
Over/Under			0
Output Qty			1802.5
Rate/LABHR	$1.66	$8.54	$10.21

Enter Documents — 17500

Account	Fix	Prop.	Total	Qty.
LABHR	$2,913	$14,951	$17,864	1750①
Rate/Doc.	$0.17	$0.85	$1.02	

Schedule Laborers — 52.5

Account	Fix	Prop.	Total	Qty.
LABHR	$87	$449	$536	52.5
Rate/Sched.	$1.66	$8.54	$10.21	

Distribution Support

Account	Fix	Prop.	Total
Depreciation	$3,000	$0	$3,000
Supplies		$1,500	$1,500
Total	$3,000	$1,500	$4,500
Relieved			$0
Over/Under			$4,500
Output Qty:			100
Rate/MACHR	$30.00	$15.00	$45.00

Distribution Center 2

Account	Fix	Prop.	Total	Qty.
Salaries	$5,000	$15,000	$20,000	
Supplies		$350	$350	
Schedule Lab.	$212	$43	$255	25
LABHR	$5.21	$15.39	$20.61	1000
Depreciation	$15,000	$-	$15,000	
MACHR	$15	$-	$15.00	1000

Distribution Center 1 — 15000

Account	Fix	Prop.	Total	Qty.
Salaries	$10,000	$25,909	$35,909	
Supplies		$2,652	$2,652	
Schedule Lab	$217	$64	$281	27.5
Training A.	$4,500		$4,500	
LABHR	$9.81	$19.08	$28.89	15000
Depreciation	$10,000	$-	$10,000	
MACHR	$7	$-	$6.67	1500

Training A

$ 4,500
100000 Copies

Training 1

$ -   0

Print Materials — 100000

Account	Fix	Prop.	Total	Qty.
MACHR	$3,000	$1,500	$4,500	100
Rate/Copy	$0.03	$0.02	$0.05	

DC2: Method 2 — 10000

Account	Fix	Prop.	Total	Qty.
DC2/LABHR	$5,212	$15,393	$20,605	1000
DC2/MACHR	$15,000	$-	$15,000	1000
Enter Docs.①	$1,664	$8,544	$10,208	10000
Rate/DC2M2	$2.19	$2.39	$4.58	

DC1: Method 2 — 15000

Account	Fix	Prop.	Total	Qty.
DC1/LABHR	$14,717	$28,625	$43,342	1500
DC1/MACHR	$10,000	$-	$10,000	1500
Enter Docs.①	$1,248	$6,408	$7,656	7500
Rate/DC1M2	$1.73	$2.34	$4.07	

DC1: Method 1 — 0

Account	Fix	Prop.	Total	Qty.
DC1/LABHR	$-	$-	$-	0
DC1/MACHR	$-	$-	$-	0
Enter Docs.①	$-	$-	$-	0
Training1	$-			
Rate/DC1M1				

Exhibit 9.14 Results of Outsourcing

292

Type	Implementation Guidelines
Organization	How does implementing integrated ABC impact the organization?
Conceptual	What are the main aspects of CO-ABC that can impact the CO conceptual design?
System	What are some crucial areas of concern when implementing ABC in SAP R/3?

Exhibit 9.15   Integrated ABC Implementation Guidelines

IMPLEMENTATION GUIDELINES

Integrated ABC has many benefits as well as many potential areas for issues or concerns. This section provides a broader view than other chapters that covered particular hints or guides for implementation. Exhibit 9.15 lists the areas to be addressed.

Impacts on the Organization

Activity-Based Costing provides more accurate costing information in order to support change management within an organization. Designing and maintaining an ABC model focuses on reflecting what the organization does, who does it, and under what circumstances. Activity-Based Management is about utilizing ABC results for changing the structure and behavior of the organization and its people in order to increase efficiencies and reduce costs. To get the most benefit from this costing philosophy, these efficiencies and savings must be generated at an operational level, not merely for strategic initiatives. Other ERP applications and ABC tools are designed to support analytical or strategic ABC, not operationally integrated ABC. Even bolting an ABC tool onto the main system merely provides an integrated solution; usually it produces ABC data too late to be utilized for operational correction and optimization. To support operationally integrated ABC, the ABC philosophy and the process cost object has to be completely integrated with the day-to-day transaction processing system. Otherwise, the ABC model is merely a historical view, with interfaces from the operational system at an aggregate level. The inclusion of ABC with strategic tools merely supports the same old ABC modeling capabilities in order to show potential impacts on strategies. While this provides very useful information that is needed to make more accurate strategic decisions, it does not garner the savings and optimizations of the operational environment. In this area all other ABC tools fail in comparison to SAP R/3's integrated ABC.

In order to gain these benefits and optimizations, the organization has to change, in most cases severely. These changes may be too large for an organization to absorb all at once. Therefore, an overall conceptual design needs to be established and a migration path mapped out for the organization to follow to gain the costing maturity level desired. To enable this change, performance measurements usually need to be revisited and restructured to support the speed with which the information can be provided and to ensure that the correct decisions are the center of focus. The changes to the performance measurements have to support the new organizational planning and control process. As organizations strive to truly integrate ABC into management decision making, a shift to the quantity-structured approach is necessary. This shift supports Activity-Based Budgeting, which often requires that the organization move from the standard top-down budgeting approach to a quantity-based bottom-up approach. The common practice of slashing the budget by 10% should no longer be pursued since it does not indicate areas where these savings can be collected. The quantity structure used for planning can highlight the areas where efficiencies can be gained. Quantity-based planning removes all fat from the planning process naturally. Any padding of the budget will quickly be apparent through analysis of the plan or once actuals flow through. If the performance measurements are directed toward target/actual comparisons, then managers are rewarded based on control and not on the ability to guess. The only other point to stress here is that implementers of integrated ABC must be prepared to fight. A change enabler, such as a champion in an extremely high position (a C-level: chief financial, executive, or information officer) is definitely needed. Trying to change an organization's costing approach and how people are measured inevitably leads to politics, politics, politics!

Conceptual Design Considerations

Whether starting from scratch or moving away from an ABC modeling tool, several aspects will impact the conceptual decision of the integrated ABC model. Most obvious is the integrated component of the design and the all-encompassing inclusion of costs that normally are not considered in an ABC model, such as capitalization, WIP, inventory valuations, and so on. The most influential aspects are the accuracy, speed, and volume of information. These three variables are dependent on one another, adding a level of complexity when designing an integrated ABC model. First let us consider accuracy. It has already been established that SAP ABC has various functions that increase the accuracy and credibility of the information generated. However, accuracy is greatly impacted by the design of the ABC model. Most organizations design very accurate assignments between the process and receivers, while making assumptions or weak correlations from the resource center to the process or the process to the process. This problem supports providing details that merely give the illusion of precision. If the costs are inaccurate to begin with, splitting them to the cost object in a minute and accurate manner is a meaningless endeavor. Utilizing RCA in tandem with ABC eliminates this issue.

Both the accuracy and speed variables are greatly impacted by designing a quantity-based approach rather than a value-based approach for cost assignment. Assuming the quantity relationships are based on an industrial engineering approach, accuracy will be inherently supported by the highly correlated causal relationships defined. Once the quantity structure is in place, then information can be generated within a period, not periodically or quarterly. In some cases, the decision to have information more readily may outweigh a decision for accuracy or simplicity of the ABC model. Additionally, the focus of the ABC model may shift due to the timing aspect. Many organizations produce large binders of ABC information quarterly for analysis purposes. The ability to receive this information periodically or within a period might overwhelm an organization. Also, the analysis being supported by those binders may have been more focused toward identification of historical trends leading to price changes or discounts to a customer, for example. This type of analysis would not be performed on the short-term basis since week-to-week fluctuations are not sufficient grounds for offering discounts or other incentives for driving customer behavior. Therefore, the integrated ABC model and reporting requirements have to be designed to support both immediate and longer-term analysis requirements. Given that SAP supports allocation methods that can be posted within a period or even daily, the organization might experience the generation of large volumes of data. This system impact can force adjustments to the conceptual design to optimize the information supported and the cost of producing that information.

Areas of Concern When Implementing Activity-Based Costing in SAP R/3

This data volume issue is driven by two dimensions:

1. The integrated ABC model resides on a transactional database rather than receiving an aggregated data interface feed.

2. The design of the interface. If an interface is needed from external systems, where the driver information is posted into SAP can impact volume. The interface can post the driver data as a value field in CO-PA, as a process quantity within CO-ABC, or as SKF in CO-CCA, each resulting in a different impact to the database size. Also, where the necessary data is input can limit which type of allocation method is utilized, thereby impacting the conceptual design. The integrated ABC model should focus on practical allocations weighed against the cost of providing that allocation. Many ABC models go into very low levels of details, driven by the belief that the information is needed. Yet this request for low levels of information is often accompanied by an inability of the user to identify what decision the information supports. Beyond that point, most organizations cling to the idea that every cost absolutely must be allocated to all 300,000 cost objects. In a stand-alone ABC tool where assignments are performed on an aggregate level and quarterly is considered frequent, oftentimes this absurdly low level of detail might be cost justifiable. However, once in a transactional system, there are true costs related to the processing of an allocation. The CPU time and database required to maintain this level of detail might actually cost more than the expenses being allocated. Therefore, a justification exercise definitely has to occur, considering each assignment and whether it is material or addresses a specific business issue. This volume aspect also drives some of the reporting designs, such as pulling from summary tables versus line item tables.

Beyond the pure system impacts of integrated ABC, there are project implementation impacts as well. Previously, when utilizing a stand-alone ABC tool for analysis, a small group within the organization had control and direct access to the model and the information generated. This limited access is also one of the reasons why credibility was questioned. When utilizing SAP to support ABC, access can be granted to any number of users, allowing the ABC philosophy to be reached throughout the organization fairly quickly and providing access to end users never accommodated before. The larger potential user base forces a greater emphasis on training and determining how ABC should be utilized to support decision making. The impact of determining a clear vision of the ABC application for the entire organization is one reason why the prototyping/blueprinting phase of an SAP ABC implementation can take longer than a stand-alone ABC project. Implementation also is affected due to the fact that designing integrated ABC is different from building an ABC model used for analysis. In integrated ABC, the other CO components and modules for addressing the integration throughout the system must be understood. The scope of the SAP implementation drives the size and complexity of the implementation. If SAP is already in place and the project is focusing just on adding ABC functionality, the time frame for implementation can be much shorter.

SUMMARY

SAP's integrated ABC solves many of the issues that arise with traditional ABC, either by a change in philosophy or through system capabilities. This chapter has focused on the weaknesses of traditional ABC and how SAP's integrated ABC can provide solutions. Exhibit 9.16 provides highlights of the key points from this chapter and other chapters.

Category	Traditional ABC	SAP Integrated ABC
Integration	1. Requires inbound interfaces. 2. Limited, if any outbound interfaces.	1. Reduces inbound interfaces. 2. Automatic integration with FI for capitalized process costs, MM for inventory valuations, SD for billing, etc. 3. Integration is impacted by the percentage utilization of the entire SAP R/3 application.
Accuracy (Credibility)	1. Allows data manipulation. 2. Aggregate data feed prevents detail analysis of transaction information. 3. Batch feeds of aggregate data make error detection difficult and delayed when correcting. 4. Varied allocation methods, none as advanced as template allocation. 5. Accurate capacity management is difficult to support and usually handled through an "Idle" activity. 6. Conceptually defined to limit the process cost assignments to flow only to another process or a cost object 7. Has the ability to "create" money. 8. Based on the philosophy of full-absorption costing. 9. ABB focuses primarily on the activity-to-cost object relationship. Consumption of quantities is fixed or variable, not both.	1. Through integration, postings are simultaneous, reducing errors and the opportunity for data manipulation. 2. Drill-down to actual transaction document and who created it. 3. Real-time postings make error detection and correction much faster. 4. Multiple allocation methods to the most advanced template allocation. 5. Tandem ABC and RCA usage supports accurate capacity management. 6. Ability to truly reflect the cost flows of the organization since the process assigns costs to any other cost collector, including a cost center. 7. Debit/credit system cannot create money. 8. Supports full-absorption costing or the more accurate approach of step recovery. 9. ABB is a limited quantity structure, which is completed by a full-quantity structure utilizing RCA. Supports simultaneous consumption of fixed and variable quantities.

Exhibit 9.16   SAP Integrated ABC Summary

Analysis	1. Limited variances capabilities.	1. Extensive variances capabilities.
	2. Static plan/actual reports.	2. Authorized reporting with Target/Actual reports.
	3. Historic view looking backward on what has occurred. Good for historical trends or mid- to long-term decisions, 3 months or more.	3. Forward looking. Real-time nature addresses more timely related questions, such as operational efficiencies, as well as the longer-term decisions.
	4. Limited gross/contribution margin capabilities since the changing nature of costs as they flow through the model are not considered.	4. Extensive gross/contribution margin capabilities by recognition of the changing nature of costs as they flow through the cost model.
	5. Capacity is viewed as residing on an activity/process.	5. Capacity is viewed as residing on the resource, and the process is utilized to convert capacity.
Flexibility (Maintenance)	1. Reconciliation required due to interfaces.	1. Eliminates many reconciliation steps due to integration.
	2. Allocations are mostly value based.	2. Allocations are mostly quantity based.
	3. Usually based on actual driver rates.	3. Multiple driver rate calculation capabilities.
	4. Static ABC model requiring maintenance for master data changes.	4. One data repository for master data changes, no additional updates required.
	5. Static ABC model requiring maintenance for allocation changes.	5. Template supports dynamic model determining which process should be selected for the cost assignment.
	6. Allocations have limited calculation capabilities.	6. Template allocation has advanced calculation capabilities.
	7. Allocations have limited ability to deal with complexity.	7. Template allocation is designed to accommodate complexity.
	8. Cost allocations mostly recognized at final completion of event.	8. Template allocation assigns process costs at trigger points supporting WIP easily.
	9. Based on an actual costing system approach.	9. Supports either a standard and/or actual costing system approach.
	10. Usually a step-down cost flow, or has limited recursive capabilities.	10. Supports a step-down or the more accurate approach of recursive cost flows.

Exhibit 9.16 (*continued*)

Information Flows	
Various Allocation Methods	See Exhibit 9.3 for a complete summary of the allocation methods.

Sample Key Business Decisions	
Identification, Inputs, and Outputs	1. Determine scope. 2. Define activities/processes. 3. Identify inputs to the processes. 4. Determine outputs of the processes. 5. Identify consumers of the processes.
Capacity Management	1. Capacity resides on the resource, not the process. 2. Tandem RCA and ABC is optimal solution. 3. A quantity structure approach should be utilized, of which ABB is a limited quantity structure. 4. Fixed/proportional costs and fixed/variable quantities must be considered.
Efficiency, Improvements, and Outsourcing	1. Measuring for efficiency based on the ideal value chain. 2 Improvements are a continuous process. 3. If the organization cannot meet external efficiency measures, then consider outsourcing.

Implementation Guidelines	
Organizational Impacts	1. Change is absolutely required. 2. Performance measures must be reevaluated. 3. Planning process needs to shift to the quantity structure including ABB. 4. Success relies on a C-level champion. 5. Prepare to fight politics.
Conceptual Design Considerations	1. Inclusion of costs normally outside the scope of ABC models. 2. Accuracy through RCA and ABC utilized together. 3. Speed through real-time capabilities impacts design of system and analysis that can be supported.
Areas of Concern for Implementing ABC in SAP R/3	1. Volume generated due to transaction-level detail versus aggregate data. 2. Where should the interfaced drivers not automatically captured in SAP be populated? 3. Justification exercise for allocations ensuring cost of processing allocations warrants information generated. 4. Additional users have access, which requires a vision of the use of ABC within the organization and increased training requirements. 5. System integration points within the CO module and with the other modules must be understood.

Exhibit 9.16   (*continued*)

_____ PART THREE _____

BEYOND SAP R/3 INTEGRATED
ACTIVITY-BASED COSTING

10

SAP INTEGRATED ACTIVITY-BASED COSTING COMBINED WITH OROS MODELING CAPABILITIES

Earlier chapters addressed the ABC/M capabilities supported by the SAP R/3 business applications. Each of the key integration points between the CO submodules and CO-ABC was covered extensively. All of this information indicates that SAP R/3 provides a very robust costing engine to support a number of costing philosophies, the most important of which is Activity-Based Costing. In addition to the operationally integrated ABC functionality of R/3, SAP can support other analytics via the tandem use of SAP CO with the Oros software package from ABC Technologies.

ABC Technologies, Inc. (ATI), was founded in 1989, at the very beginning of the ABC movement. According to the company's Web page (www.abctech.com), it is the leading provider of Activity-Based Costing software in the world. The Web page states that Oros software supports an integrated solution for "activity-based cost modeling, scorecarding/performance measurement, and planning capabilities enabling organizations to increase profits, seek growth opportunities, reduce costs, and streamline operations." This chapter addresses only the Activity-Based Cost modeling. The Oros software package is a stand-alone ABC system. Therefore, it can be used as an example to represent the type of system addressed in detail in Chapter 2, in the "Distinct Differences" section. This chapter focuses only on the integration of Oros with the SAP R/3 CO module. Chapter 11 addresses the utilization of Oros with the SAP New Dimension Strategic Enterprise Management business application.

In September 1998, SAP AG (SAP) and ATI announced a development partnership to provide a bridging solution between the SAP R/3 ERP and ABC Technologies' Oros software packages. This linkage is supported via the product called the Bridge to SAP (Bridge) provided by ATI. The key aspect about this relationship is that the partnership ensures the continuous support of the Bridge functionality in future releases of both the SAP R/3 and Oros software packages. Other ABC modeling software companies building their own interfaces will not have the advantages gained from this partnership, such as advance knowledge of new functionality being added to SAP, information on upcoming changes to the way Business Application Program Interfaces (BAPIs) are maintained, and a combined vision on the support and use of the two types of products together.

BRIDGE PRODUCT AND FUNCTIONALITY

Many customers are familiar with Oros, SAP CO, or both. However, questions arise when discussing the tandem use of these products and trying to understand what the Bridge actually is and the benefits it provides.

The Bridge is a combined technical venture between SAP AG and ABC Technologies to provide their customers with a seamless interface between the transaction-based operational system and a stand-alone ABC modeling tool. The Bridge is not a stand-alone tool that can function on its own; it must be used in conjunction with both Oros and SAP R/3. The Bridge is provided by ABC Technologies with Oros 4.3 Expansion and higher releases. It enables Oros models to be updated by SAP or to update certain aspects of the SAP CO business application. The Bridge provides a mapping between the Oros and certain SAP CO structures and data. It is basically a user front end on top of a standardized and supported interface for mapping and maintaining synchronization of key data structures and cost assignments between the two systems. The information in this chapter refers to the second release of the Bridge contained within Oros 5.0 Bridge to SAP for R/3 and requiring SAP R/3 Release 4.6C or higher, although many of the functions also are supported for R/3 versions 4.0b, 4.5b, and 4.6a/b. See Exhibit 10.26 at the end of this chapter for a R/3 Bridge Features Matrix by SAP R/3 and Oros Bridge release.

INFORMATION FLOWS

In August 1999, testing of the first Bridge release was completed by Alta Via Consulting, SAP, and ABC Technologies employees. In April 2000 the same group conducted testing on the beta version of the next Bridge release, internally called 4.5 Beta. This testing, combined with actual implementation experience, is used as support for the information provided in the following sections. This section provides only a high-level overview of the information flows supported by the Bridge.

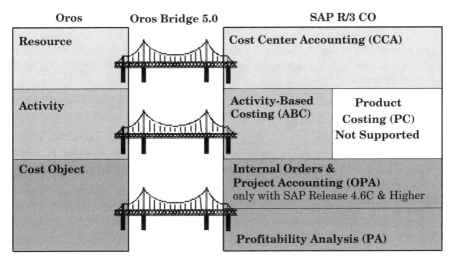

Exhibit 10.1 Bridge Integration Points Overview

The Bridge connects the entire Oros model to portions of the SAP CO module. Access to any information that does not reside within the CO module is not yet supported via the Bridge. Exhibit 10.1 illustrates the key integration points between Oros and the SAP CO application via the Bridge. The areas of connection to the SAP R/3 CO application are the CO-CCA, CO-ABC, CO-OPA, and CO-PA modules. The rest of this section provides details for each of these areas of linkage.

The CO-PC submodule is not linked, due to the tight integration within SAP of the CO-PC module to the production-related modules (i.e., PP—Production Planning; PM—Plant Maintenance; CS-SM—Service Management; PS—Project System; and so on). The integration between costing and how production is accommodated within SAP for varying industries, production strategies, and individual corporate needs creates thousands of variables. Therefore, this integration cannot be supported via a standardized interface such as the Bridge.

Even without this linkage for product costing, the Oros model can be used to build large pieces of the foundation of the SAP CO module, including the processes to be used for product costing and overhead assignments to those processes. Additionally, functionality within SAP can then be added and/or changed to support the product costing needs as well as any additional integration required with other modules used, such as FI (Financials) or SD (Sales and Distribution).

Resource Module to Cost Center Accounting (CCA)

Chapter 5 stressed that the focus of CO-CCA is responsibility accounting, with cost centers representing a departmental view of the organization. The closest relationship within Oros is therefore the Resource module. Exhibit 10.2 depicts the key data structures, assignments, and information shared between CO-CCA and the Oros resource module.[1]

Resource/CO-CCA Master Data　The key master data of both of these modules, Resource and CCA, are the resource/cost centers, the hierarchies, the costs, and the drivers for allocations.

Resource centers/cost centers and hierarchies　Each of the modules, Resource and CCA, contains hierarchies such as resource centers/accounts for Oros and

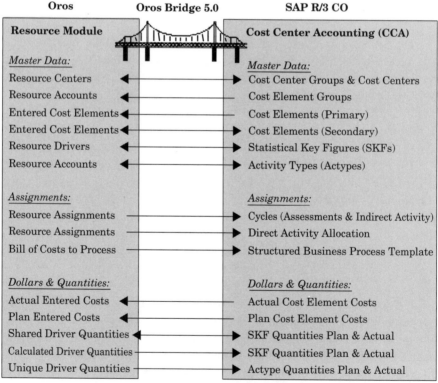

Oros	Oros Bridge 5.0	SAP R/3 CO
Resource Module		**Cost Center Accounting (CCA)**
Master Data:		*Master Data:*
Resource Centers	← →	Cost Center Groups & Cost Centers
Resource Accounts	←	Cost Element Groups
Entered Cost Elements	←	Cost Elements (Primary)
Entered Cost Elements	← →	Cost Elements (Secondary)
Resource Drivers	← →	Statistical Key Figures (SKFs)
Resource Accounts	← →	Activity Types (Actypes)
Assignments:		*Assignments:*
Resource Assignments	→	Cycles (Assessments & Indirect Activity)
Resource Assignments	→	Direct Activity Allocation
Bill of Costs to Process	→	Structured Business Process Template
Dollars & Quantities:		*Dollars & Quantities:*
Actual Entered Costs	←	Actual Cost Element Costs
Plan Entered Costs	←	Plan Cost Element Costs
Shared Driver Quantities	← →	SKF Quantities Plan & Actual
Calculated Driver Quantities	→	SKF Quantities Plan & Actual
Unique Driver Quantities	→	Actype Quantities Plan & Actual

Exhibit 10.2　Cost Center Accounting Integration Resource Module

cost centers for SAP. Within SAP CCA, the standard cost center hierarchy contains all cost centers, often within groups. When downloading from SAP, a cost center group (CCG) must be selected. The selected cost center group can contain the entire standard cost center hierarchy, resulting in the entire SAP organization departmental view, or just a selected cost center group, such as a single strategic business unit, sales unit, distribution center, or plant. The nodes, or cost center groups, on the cost center hierarchy and the cost centers themselves download to become resource centers.

When uploading the Resource module to CCA, the hierarchy of resource centers, except for the resource centers located at the lowest level of each node, is used to generate a corresponding hierarchy of cost center groups, either as an alternative hierarchy or added to the SAP standard cost center hierarchy. The Bridge uses the resource centers on the lowest level of node of the Resource module hierarchy (to which the resource accounts are attached) to generate the corresponding cost centers in CCA. Therefore, the Oros resource center is representative of two different master data elements within SAP, the cost center group and the cost center. Exhibit 10.3 depicts generating cost centers and cost center groups via the Bridge.

The resource centers/cost centers are the senders of and often receivers of costs. Within SAP and Oros, these costs are captured using cost elements. SAP groups cost elements into cost element groups. Oros groups cost elements, in the Resource module, as resource accounts. SAP further differentiates between primary cost elements (G/L accounts) and secondary cost elements (internal cost management accounts used for allocations). The corresponding Oros distinction of cost elements is between entered and assigned (allocated) cost elements.

When downloading cost elements from SAP to Oros, the cost element groups create the resource accounts. The primary *and* secondary cost elements are downloaded as entered cost elements within Oros. On the download, the Oros reference number is populated with the required syntax needed to represent the cost center, cost center group, and cost elements within that group. This syntax assures that the same cost element has a different reference number, which is required by Oros. Within SAP, cost elements within different cost centers utilize the same cost element coding and do not have different numbering. Exhibit 10.4 depicts the cost elements and groups download.

After the download from SAP, an assignment within Oros is utilized to allocate $1,000 of the *Office Costs* within *Purchasing* to the *Salary Costs* within *Receiving*. This assignment illustrates two points. First, only the cost assigned within Oros will show as an assigned cost element. Within SAP, the user-defined cost element number range, for example, 99XXXX, depicts allocated costs using secondary cost elements. The results of allocations made within SAP will appear,

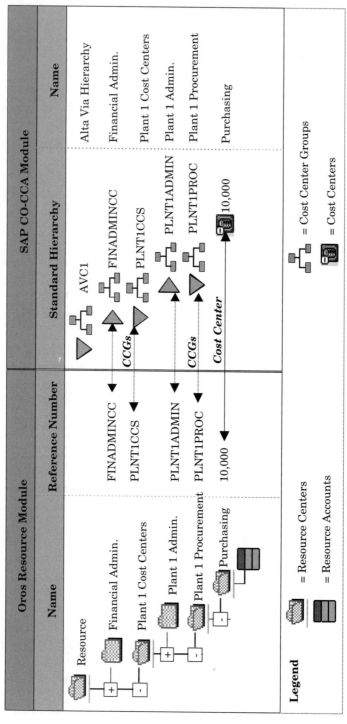

Exhibit 10.3 Resource Centers to Cost Center Groups/Cost Centers Mapping

Oros Resource Module

Name	Reference Number	Costs
Plant 1 Procurement	PLNT1PROC	$22,000
Purchasing	10000	$10,000
Salary Costs	10000.SALARIES	$3,000
Wages	10000.Salaries.430000	$1,000
Benefits	10000.Salaries.431000	$2,000
Office Costs	10000.OFFICE	$7,000
Facilities	10000.OFFICE.990000	$3,000
IT Support	10000.OFFICE.991000	$4,000
Receiving	20000	$13,000
Salary Costs	20000.SALARIES	$13,000
Wages	20000.Salaries.430000	$4,000
Benefits	20000.Salaries.431000	$4,000
Overtime	20000.Salaries.432000	$4,000
Office Costs	10000.OFFICE	$1,000

SAP CO-CCA Module

Reporting Information / Costs

Plant 1 Procurement

10000 Purchasing

		Costs
430000	Wages	$1,000
431000	Benefits	$2,000
	Salary Costs	$3,000
990000	Facilities	$3,000
991000	IT Support	$4,000
	Office Costs	$7,000
	Total Costs	$10,000

20000 Receiving

		Costs
430000	Wages	$4,000
431000	Benefits	$4,000
432000	Overtime	$4,000
	Salary Costs	$12,000
	Total Costs	$12,000

Legend

= Resource Centers = Cost Center Groups

= Resource Accounts = Cost Centers

= Entered Cost Elements

= Assigned Cost Elements

Exhibit 10.4 Resource Accounts/Cost Elements to Cost Element Groups/Cost Elements

on download to Oros, as entered accounts. Second, the actual credit to the *Office Costs* for the $1,000 allocation is not seen in the Oros model, yet is tracked so that the total costs are correct (i.e., the $22,000).

The Bridge cannot upload resource accounts to create SAP cost element groups. However, it can be used to generate secondary cost elements in SAP using attribute tags. Secondary cost elements used for activity types and assessment cost elements are the only type of secondary cost element that the Bridge can create. For example, the Bridge cannot create an internal order settlement account or primary cost elements, since primary cost elements must be created in the SAP FI module prior to being created within CO-CCA.

In order for the costs to be allocated, some drivers or output measures may need to be established. Within Oros, these are called drivers. Within CCA, these are called activity types (actypes) and statistical key figures (SKFs). The actypes can be created in either tool and uploaded or downloaded. When actypes are downloaded from CCA to the Oros Resource module, they are represented as resource accounts, not as drivers, because an actype represents a subpool of costs within a cost center, usually capacity related, that has a specific driver, such as labor hour or machine hour. Therefore, the corresponding Oros object must be able to contain cost elements, hence the resource account. SAP SKFs, such as FTEs, number of employees, and number of purchase orders, download from SAP into Oros, creating a shared driver. Shared drivers used in any Oros assignment that do not already exist within SAP will automatically create an SKF when assignments are uploaded to SAP via the Bridge.

Resource/CO-CCA Assignments   With the master data structures in place and the drivers defined, assignments can be built. Assignments within SAP are not downloadable to Oros. In order to have similar assignments within Oros, they must be manually built or imported using various Oros importing capabilities. Therefore, this section focuses on the ability of the Bridge to upload assignments generating different types of allocation methods within SAP CO. Exhibit 10.5 lists the assignment mappings.

Using the allocation methods listed in the exhibit, the Bridge will create allocations from three areas:

1. Cost centers to cost centers (CCA-CCA [i.e., within Resource module])
2. Cost centers to processes (CCA-ABC [i.e., resource to activity])
3. Cost centers to internal orders (CCA-OPA [i.e., resource to cost object])

When generating the cycles, the Bridge automatically creates the necessary receiver groups within SAP R/3; cost center, process, and internal order groups. The bill of costs assignment capability within Oros is not a direct match with the

Oros Assignment	SAP Allocation Method	SAP Sender Rules	SAP Receiver Rules
Shared Driver	Assessment Cycle	Posted $	Variable portion w/SKF
Evenly Assigned	Assessment Cycle	Posted $	Fixed %
Shared Driver Resource Account = Actype	Indirect Activity Allocation Cycle	Inverse Calculated	Variable portion w/SKF
Evenly Assigned Resource Account = Actype	Indirect Activity Allocation Cycle	Inverse Calculated	Fixed%
Calculated Driver (Quantities only)	Indirect Activity Allocation Cycle	Inverse Calculated	Variable portion w/SKF
No Equivalent Method	Distribution Cycle	Not supported.	
Unique Driver	Direct Activity	Assignments using unique drivers.	
No Equivalent Method	Target = Actual	Not supported.	
Bill of Costs	Template	Structured Business Process templates between cost centers and processes are supported.	
Bill of Costs	Template	Templates to internal orders (007) are not supported.	
No Equivalent Method	Overhead Calculation	Not supported.	
Component Driver	No equivalent method		

SAP supports many more combinations of sender rules and receivers rules within cycles, as addressed in Chapter 5. This is limited to the assignment methods and sender/receiver combinations that the Oros Bridge can create within SAP.

Exhibit 10.5   Resource Module Assignments Uploads to SAP Allocations

SAP template capabilities. The bill of costs cannot support any of the template's flexibility capabilities, such as automatic determination of which process to send, complex formula calculations, and condition parameters for if and when to allocate. However, the bill of costs can be utilized to generate a simplistic template for only the structured business process template. Exhibit 10.6 illustrates the assignments the Bridge supports from resource centers to cost objects when the cost objects represent PA market segments. The Oros Cost Object module also represents the internal orders within CO-OPA. Those assignment Bridge mappings were listed in Exhibit 10.5.

Resource/CO-CCA Dollars and Quantities   Although the allocations defined in SAP CO are not supported for download to Oros, the actual or plan results of

Oros Assignment	SAP Allocation Method	SAP Sender Rules	SAP Receiver Rules
Shared Driver	Assessment Cycle	Posted $	Variable portion w/Value Fields
Evenly Assigned	Assessment Cycle	Posted $	Fixed %
Shared Driver Resource Account = Actype	Indirect Activity Allocation Cycle	Inverse Calculated	Variable portion w/Value Fields
Evenly Assigned Resource Account = Actype	Indirect Activity Allocation Cycle	Inverse Calculated	Fixed%
Unique Driver	Direct Activity	Assignments using Unique Drivers.	
Bill of Costs	Template	PAC Template from Cost Center/Actype to PA Segment is not supported for upload.	

SAP supports many more combinations of sender rules and receivers rules within cycles from CCA or ABC to OPA or CO-PA, as addressed in Chapters 6 and 8, respectively. This is limited to the assignment methods and sender/receiver combinations that the Oros Bridge can create within SAP. Additionally, the Distributions and Target = Actual allocation methods have been removed from this table since SAP does not support these allocation methods between cost centers/ activity types or processes and PA segments.

Exhibit 10.6   Resource to Cost Object (PA Segments) Assignments Upload to SAP

those allocations, as well as other data, can be downloaded. This data is for either dollar values or quantities. Plan cost element dollars can be downloaded from SAP or uploaded from Oros, which allows simulation of plan dollars to occur in Oros and finalized numbers to be uploaded into SAP. The plan can be uploaded/downloaded using different plan versions as well. Since SAP is used for actual capturing, tracking, and controlling, actual cost element values can be transferred only from SAP to Oros. However, actual quantities for actypes can be uploaded from Oros to SAP, since the cost valuation (converting the quantity to dollars using a rate) takes place only in SAP, the operational system. Upload of actual actype quantities is facilitated during the upload of the unique driver assignments. Additionally, actual SKF quantities can be uploaded to SAP, since these are used for information and allocations and have no actual cost valuation or rate.

Activity Module to Activity-Based Costing

The Activity module within Oros corresponds directly to the Activity-Based Costing component of SAP CO. Within these modules, the organizational view is shifted to a process view. Exhibit 10.7 depicts the relationships among the key data structures, assignments, and information shared for CO-ABC and the Oros Activity module.

Activity/CO-ABC Master Data   The original design of the Bridge was based on supporting organizations in their implementing of CO-ABC. Therefore, the activity center hierarchy can be uploaded to generate the business process hierarchy within CO-ABC. With the second Bridge release, functionality was added to support the download of the business process hierarchy and processes in CO-ABC to create the Activity module in Oros. Therefore, activities/processes and groups can be downloaded and uploaded. Exhibit 10.8 illustrates the mapping between the Activity module in Oros and SAP CO-ABC.

The activity centers and accounts are used to represent a higher level of master data than with the Resource module. Instead of the lowest level within a node of the activity hierarchy representing the process, the activity account is used. This difference in approach is due to the philosophical concept that all costs within a process/activity account should be allocated using the same driver. However, the cost center/resource centers usually contain pools of costs within them (the resource account) that have differing resource drivers. Although the activity accounts can generate the business processes, other pieces of information for business processes may then need to be added in SAP—for example, identifying templates associated with the process or populating user-defined master data fields.

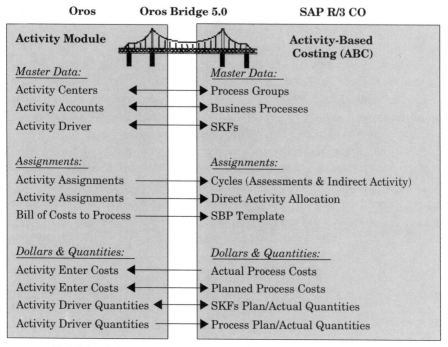

Exhibit 10.7   Activity-Based Costing Linkages Activity Module

Activity/CO-ABC Assignments   Activity assignments within the Activity module or between the Activity and Cost Object module upload from Oros to create either assessments or indirect activity allocation cycles. These cycles move the process expenses within CO-ABC or from CO-ABC to the corresponding cost object within CO-OPA or CO-PA based on fixed percent or variable quantities. Unique driver assignments upload to generate direct activity allocations, either between processes or from a process to internal orders or profitability analysis (PA) segments. When generating the cycles, the Bridge automatically creates the necessary process groups within SAP R/3.

Exhibit 10.9 has the process-to-process (activity-to-activity) and process–to–internal order (activity–to–cost object) allocations that can be generated by the Oros Bridge. SAP process-to–cost center or internal order–to–process assignments cannot be created via the Oros Bridge, since Oros does not support these cost flows. Exhibit 10.10 has the SAP process–to–PA segment allocations that can be generated by the Oros Bridge.

Activity/CO-ABC Dollars and Quantities   With Oros Bridge 5.0, actual and planned SAP process costs can be downloaded to the corresponding activity

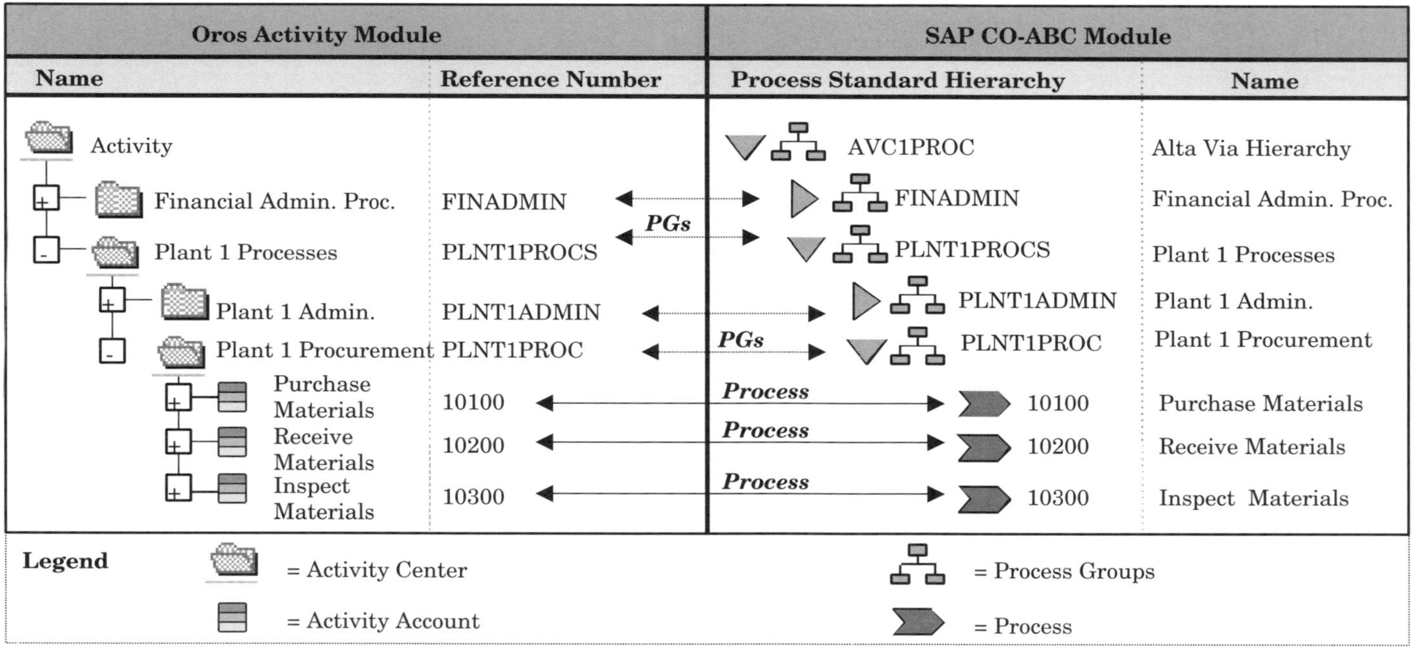

Exhibit 10.8 Activity-Based Costing Linkages Activity Module

Oros Assignment	SAP Allocation Method	SAP Sender Rules	SAP Receiver Rules
Shared Driver	**Assessment Cycle**	Posted $	Variable portion w/SKF
Evenly Assigned	**Assessment Cycle**	Posted $	Fixed %
Shared Driver Activity Account = Process	**Indirect Activity Allocation Cycle**	Inverse Calculated	Variable portion w/SKF
Evenly Assigned Activity Account = Process	**Indirect Activity Allocation Cycle**	Inverse Calculated	Fixed%
No Equivalent Method	**Distribution Cycle**	Not supported.	
Unique Driver	Direct Activity	Assignments using unique drivers.	
No Equivalent Method	Target = Actual ʹ	Not supported.	
Bill of Costs	Template	SBP templates between processes are supported via the Bridge.	
Bill of Costs	Template	Templates between processes and internal orders are not supported.	
Component Driver	No equivalent method		

SAP supports many more combinations of sender rules and receivers rules within cycles. This is limited to the assignment methods and sender/receiver combinations that the Oros Bridge can create within SAP.

Exhibit 10.9   Activity Module Assignments Uploads to SAP Allocations

account in Oros, generating entered cost elements. Exhibit 10.11 depicts the mapping of activity accounts to process with costs downloading.

Both primary and secondary cost elements residing on the process can be downloaded. SAP primary cost elements are assigned to the process either

Oros Assignment	SAP Allocation Method	SAP Sender Rules	SAP Receiver Rules
Shared Driver	Assessment Cycle	Posted $	Variable portion w/Value Fields
Evenly Assigned	Assessment Cycle	Posted $	Fixed %
Shared Driver Activity Account = Process	Indirect Activity Allocation Cycle	Inverse Calculated	Variable portion w/Value Fields
Evenly Assigned Activity Account = Process	Indirect Activity Allocation Cycle	Inverse Calculated	Fixed%
Unique Driver	Direct Activity	Assignments using unique drivers.	
Bill of Costs	Template	PAC template from process to PA segment is not supported via the Bridge.	
Component Driver	No equivalent method		

SAP supports many more combinations of sender rules and receiver rules within cycles from CCA or ABC to OPA or CO-PA, as addressed in Chapters 6 and 8, respectively. This is limited to the assignment methods and sender/receiver combinations that the Oros Bridge can create within SAP. Additionally, the distributions and Target = Actual allocation methods have been removed from this table since SAP does not support these allocation methods between cost centers/activity types or processes and PA segments.

Exhibit 10.10   Activity to Cost Object (PA Segments) Assignments Upload to SAP

through direct postings from the general ledger or through the utilization of distribution cycles for allocations to the process. Note that when cost elements download to the Activity module, the reference number syntax differs from the Resource module. The cost element group name has been left out of the reference number syntax. The "NA" for not applicable is utilized, since the Oros activity does not support a subgrouping of costs below the activity account level (i.e., the cost element group view). SAP supports a cost element group within a process for both information and allocation usage. Reporting functionality utilized with the Oros model can be used to break the cost elements into cost element groups.

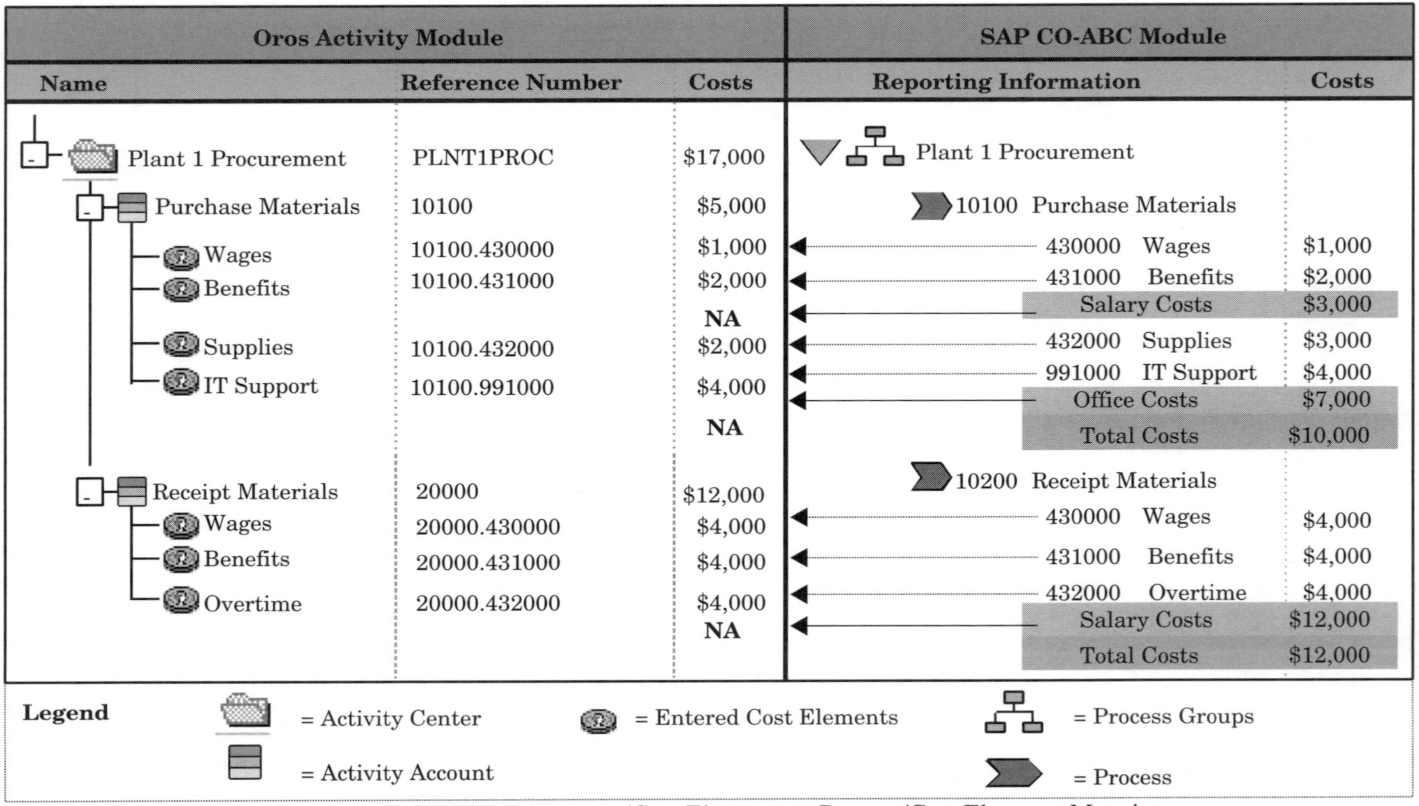

Oros Activity Module

Name	Reference Number	Costs
Plant 1 Procurement	PLNT1PROC	$17,000
Purchase Materials	10100	$5,000
Wages	10100.430000	$1,000
Benefits	10100.431000	$2,000
		NA
Supplies	10100.432000	$2,000
IT Support	10100.991000	$4,000
		NA
Receipt Materials	20000	$12,000
Wages	20000.430000	$4,000
Benefits	20000.431000	$4,000
Overtime	20000.432000	$4,000
		NA

SAP CO-ABC Module

Reporting Information	Costs
Plant 1 Procurement	
10100 Purchase Materials	
430000 Wages	$1,000
431000 Benefits	$2,000
Salary Costs	$3,000
432000 Supplies	$3,000
991000 IT Support	$4,000
Office Costs	$7,000
Total Costs	$10,000
10200 Receipt Materials	
430000 Wages	$4,000
431000 Benefits	$4,000
432000 Overtime	$4,000
Salary Costs	$12,000
Total Costs	$12,000

Legend

= Activity Center

= Activity Account

= Entered Cost Elements

= Process Groups

= Process

Exhibit 10.11 Activity Accounts/Cost Elements to Process/Cost Elements Mapping

318

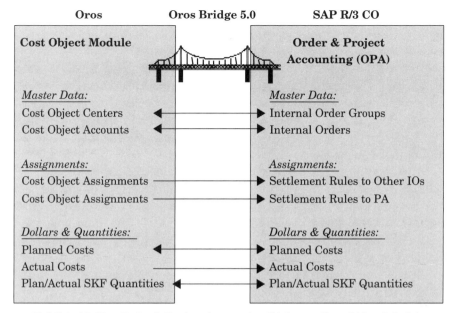

Exhibit 10.12   Order & Project Accounting Linkages Cost Object Module

Planned or actual Oros activity costs can be uploaded to CO-ABC only as planned process costs. As with the Resource module, both planned and actual quantities can be uploaded for either SKFs or for processes.

Cost Object Module to Order and Project Accounting

Recall in Exhibit 10.1, the Oros Cost Object module was mapped to both the SAP OPA and PA modules. Therefore, the cost objects represent different SAP master data elements. The first to be addressed is for the internal orders. The next section covers the Cost Object to CO-PA segment mapping. Exhibit 10.12 illustrates the Cost Object to CO-OPA linkages.

Cost Object/CO-OPA: Internal Order Master Data   Internal orders and internal order groups are the key data structures for the OPA module. The cost object and the cost object hierarchy within Oros represent these key data structures, respectively. The Bridge is capable of uploading and downloading internal orders and groups. Attribute tags and defaults can be defined for the required fields, such as order type, company code, business area, and profit center. Additionally, the optional informational fields can be defined within the default parameters of the

Bridge to be populated on upload. Sample optional fields populated are applicant, applicant telephone, start of work, date work ends, and department.

Cost Object/Internal Order Assignments/Settlements   Internal order settlement rules can be generated for settling to other internal orders, or the more likely scenario of settling internal orders to PA market segments—for example, percentage split to strategic business units for a shared IT hardware upgrade project. The Bridge uses a cost object–to–cost object assignment to create the settlement rule for the internal order.

Cost Objects/Internal Order Dollars and Quantities   As with the other Oros modules, planned primary and secondary costs can be downloaded/uploaded from/to SAP, and different plan versions are supported. Actual primary and secondary costs can only be downloaded from SAP. Exhibit 10.13 illustrates the actual cost download from SAP OPA to a cost object.

The reference number syntax contains the internal order number, making it easier to understand which internal order information was downloaded. Internal orders often have statistical key figures assigned to them. Therefore, actual and plan SKF quantities can be downloaded and uploaded as well.

Cost Object to Profitability Analysis

The Oros Cost Object module also links to the CO-PA module. This linkage focuses on supporting cost-to-serve analysis and assignments from the processes to cost objects (representing customers, products, distribution channels, sales regions, and so on). The integration between Oros and CO-PA is supported for costing-based CO-PA only. Exhibit 10.14 illustrates the linkages between the Oros Cost Object module and SAP CO-PA.

Cost Object/CO-PA: Market Segments Master Data   There are two key data structures within CO-PA: (1) the characteristics (reporting dimensions) and (2) the value fields (reporting values/quantities). When downloading from SAP to the Cost Object module, the characteristic is selected as well as a hierarchy. For example, characteristic *Product* is selected and *Hierarchy 001*. Within the CO-PA, *Hierarchy 001* may contain only the top-selling products, or all products might be included. When the characteristics download, cost object dimensions are created. Not all of the CO-PA characteristics and every value for those characteristics are expected to be downloaded to Oros. The number of CO-PA dimensions (PA market segments) can be extremely numerous (in the millions).

Oros Cost Object Module

Name	Reference Number	Costs
IT Projects	IT Projects	$21,000
Web-based T&E	T&E[400477]	$9,000
Wages	T&E[400477].430000	$1,000
Benefits	T&E[400477].431000	$2,000
		NA
Supplies	T&E[400477].432000	$3,000
Facilities	T&E[400477].996000	$4,000
		NA
Driver Interface	Dr.Int.[400478]	$12,000
Wages	Dr.Int.[400478].430000	$4,000
Benefits	Dr.Int.[400478].431000	$4,000
Overtime	Dr.Int.[400478].432000	$4,000
		NA

SAP CO-OPA Module

Reporting Information	Costs
IT Projects	
400477 Web-based T&E	
430000 Wages	$1,000
431000 Benefits	$2,000
Salary Costs	$3,000
432000 Supplies	$3,000
996000 Facilities	$4,000
Office Costs	$7,000
Total Costs	$10,000
400478 Driver Interface	
430000 Wages	$4,000
431000 Benefits	$4,000
432000 Overtime	$4,000
Salary Costs	$12,000
Total Costs	$12,000

Legend

= Cost Object Center

= Cost Object Account

= Entered Cost Elements

= Internal Order Groups

= Internal Order

Exhibit 10.13 Download of Actual Costs from SAP Internal Orders to Cost Objects

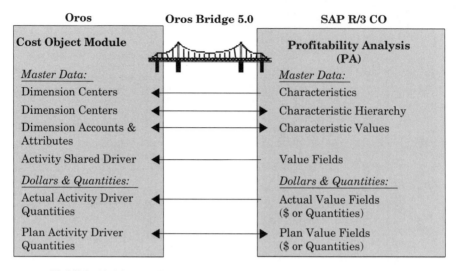

Exhibit 10.14   Profitability Analysis Linkages Cost Object Module

Users should select only the key dimensions required for simulation purposes, such as customer or customer group, product or product group, distribution channel, and region.

Although the Bridge cannot create characteristics within CO-PA, it does support creating the characteristic hierarchy and characteristic values. The attribute hierarchy functionality within Oros can be used to upload as a characteristic hierarchy in CO-PA as well as define the values. Therefore, for the cost objects within Oros, an attribute hierarchy can be created and uploaded, creating a corresponding characteristic hierarchy and values within CO-PA.

Value fields, whether dollar or quantity based, such as revenues, discounts, marketing expenses, sales quantity, and customer complaints, are downloaded as activity shared drivers to be used for activity-to-dimension assignments. The Bridge cannot be used to create value fields.

Cost Object/CO-PA Assignments   The CO-PA segments are usually the final receivers of allocations and do not have additional allocations. However, within CO-PA an allocation method called top-down distribution allows costs within one characteristic to be allocated to a lower level of detail using value fields. For example, process costs are assigned to the distribution channel they support. These costs are then further allocated to all the products sold to each customer within that distribution channel. The top-down distribution allocation is not yet supported via the Bridge. The only cost object–to–cost object assignments that are supported using the Bridge are for internal orders and were addressed in the previous section.

Cost Objects/CO-PA Market Segment Dollars and Quantities   Dollars and quantities within CO-PA are contained within the value fields. As with the other areas, planned dollars and quantities can upload from Oros to SAP. Actual costs or quantities can be downloaded and populate the actual activity driver quantity. Actual driver quantities may be uploaded to post actual value fields that are quantity related.

Oros Synchronization with the SAP Controlling Module

Depending on how the two products are used in tandem, synchronization between the Oros model and the SAP CO conceptual design may need to be performed. The synchronization functionality compares both applications and determines the differences between the master data elements. For example, during synchronization, the Bridge may determine that certain cost centers exist in SAP that do not exist in Oros. Or activities in Oros may exist without a corresponding process within SAP. The synchronization abilities of the Bridge support the ability to add, move, or delete cost centers, processes, and cost objects on the hierarchies. Also, specific field changes on the master records can be synchronized. A few examples are the profit center on a cost center, the description on the activity type or process, or the unit of measure for a SKF.

In summary, the Bridge supports linkages between the most common areas of SAP CO and Oros. The core master data structures are easily uploaded and downloaded. Almost all of the Oros assignments, except for the formulas of calculated drivers and component drivers, are uploadable to generate some form of assignment within SAP. Most planned and actual costs and quantities can be uploaded or downloaded, except actual costs cannot be uploaded from Oros to SAP. These linkages provide the ability to use the two products together in a myriad of ways.

SAMPLE KEY BUSINESS DECISIONS

How these products connect, at least at a high level, is now established. What remains is to determine the key business decisions to support using both of these products. The tandem use of Oros and SAP R/3 CO can support almost any cost-related business decision.

| Which software package provides more ABC functionality? |
| How can these two products be used together and what are the benefits? |
| Which system is used for what type of analysis? |
| Is it necessary to use both software packages? |

Exhibit 10.15   Key Questions About Using Oros and SAP Together Sample

With the relative newness of this development partnership, many questions have arisen regarding how to use the two products together, what benefits can be received, and why should one tool be utilized instead of another. This section addresses these types of questions. The key questions presented in Exhibit 10.15 highlight the abilities and benefits of using these two products in tandem.

Activity-Based Costing Functionality Supported

Neither of these packages is a mere ABC tool. Both support expanded ABC functionality, including Activity-Based Management and Budgeting. The criteria for determining which tool has more ABC functionality will vary from person to person and organization to organization, based on their ABC maturity level, familiarity with the products, needs of the organization, and so on. Chapter 2 addresses most of this comparison. However, regardless of all the potential criteria, the main benefit of ABC functionality is its capability to address any and all permutations of cost assignments as well as its ability to provide the analytical tools needed to perform ABM. When considering only assignment capabilities, SAP ABC has a greater number of different types of assignments, some of which are more advanced, specifically the template allocation functionality. The template allocation combined with the transactional nature of SAP R/3 supports very advanced assignments, with reduced maintenance requirements, providing greater accuracy and more detailed data to produce better management information. As the business environment becomes more complex, and as organizations have a greater need for more sophisticated costing systems, the natural progression will be to shift toward the capabilities of SAP's integrated ABC to be the costing engine. When focusing on the analytical tools needed to support ABM, both tools support differing capabilities. However, Oros, with its speed and flexibility, can support a wider range of analytics and capabilities. For these reasons, the two tools combined provide the best solution to supporting ABM within an organization.

SAP Controlling (CO) Module Functionality Continuum

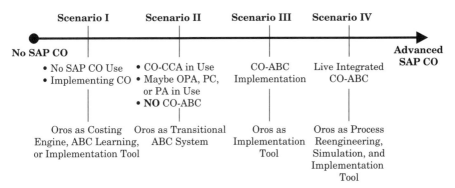

Exhibit 10.16   Four Main Tandem-Use Scenarios

Tandem Usage and Benefits

The answer to how these two ABC systems should be used together is the proverbial consulting answer of "It depends." Each organization's dynamics, culture, politics, SAP knowledge and usage, technical architecture, ABC maturity, systems experience, and resources factor into the equation of how and when to use Oros in tandem with SAP R/3. Exhibit 10.16 illustrates the four main tandem-use scenarios.

Exhibit 10.16 does *not* depict a time line, and it is not necessarily suggested as a phased approach. Organizations just beginning their SAP implementations should consider incorporating all of the CO submodules from the beginning, including CO-ABC, to obtain the most benefits, support internal management from "go live," reduce rework, minimize impacts to inventory valuations, and eliminate unnecessary temporary interfaces. Compared to the additional impact of implementing CO-ABC in the beginning, it is not cost justifiable to delay building CO-ABC to a later phase of the SAP implementation. The steps necessary to build best-practice CO (and not the same old system) are also required for CO-ABC. Therefore, performing them in tandem saves time and money in the long run; that is, to correctly implement CO, an integrated activity analysis is performed to identify the key data structures, allocation methods, analytic needs, and reporting requirements (similar to, yet more encompassing than, the same study typically performed to build an ABC/M model).

Scenario I   This scenario marks the beginning of the CO functionality continuum, where absolutely no CO exists. Oros might be used for ABC learning, as the costing engine, and/or as the implementation tool for the CO module.

In this scenario, the CO module functionality is not in use. This scenario covers companies that have Oros and either have SAP and are not using the SAP CO module or have just purchased SAP. If the organization has SAP and does not utilize the CO module, then Oros is most likely used as the costing engine. However, since CO is not in place, the Bridge cannot be used to download data, so interfaces must be built from SAP to provide required data to Oros. For organizations that have just purchased SAP, Oros can be used to introduce ABC and its capabilities for decision support and as an implementation tool to aid in building pieces of the CO module. There is a common misperception that the Oros Bridge can build the entire CO module. This is absolutely not true. The SAP CO module is much larger than an Activity-Based Costing/Management view, and it requires configuration, which the Oros Bridge cannot generate. Additionally, as mentioned previously, the product costing portions of the model need to be built directly in SAP, due to the integrated links with the logistic modules, and cannot be populated by the Bridge. Although the Oros Bridge cannot build the entire CO module, Oros can be utilized to perform design simulations in order to determine the scope and preliminary design of the CO-CCA, CO-ABC, CO-OPA, CO-PA, and CO-PC modules—that is, the entire CO module. The Bridge will facilitate the transfer of information and structures between the two software packages for much of the key data structures and assignments. Exhibit 10.17 lists the top three benefits of using Oros with SAP CO in Scenario I.

Scenario II   At a minimum, CO-CCA is in use and potentially any of the other submodules, such as product costing (PC) for a manufacturing environment. However, CO-ABC is not used.

Category	Benefits
Organizational Impact	Oros modeling provides a learning experience for the organization to use in order to become familiar with the ABC philosophy, determine areas for application, identify change, management initiatives, etc.
System Design	Implementation tool for creation of key portions of the SAP CO module for cost center hierarchies, cost centers, secondary cost elements, processes, internal orders, CO-PA characteristics, cost center-to-cost center assignments, cost center to process assignments, and process-to-PA segment assignments.
SAP Project Management	A model can be used to represent the CO conceptual design, noting key assumptions and decisions, and for tracking which pieces of the SAP CO model have been built.

Exhibit 10.17   Top Benefits of Oros with Scenario I SAP-CO Functionality

In Scenario I, organizations did not have any CO functionality in place. In this scenario, the basic submodule of CO, cost center accounting (CCA), has been implemented as well as perhaps some of the others. With CCA in place, the Oros Bridge can be used to source data from SAP to Oros. Therefore, the Bridge can replace interfaces from SAP FI to Oros for financial data. Additionally, data from Internal Order and the Profitability submodules can be downloaded, further eliminating potentially existing interfaces. With the key pieces of master data and the data itself downloadable, Oros can be used as the off-line ABC system. Therefore, Scenario II most applies to organizations that:

- Choose to use Oros as their permanent ABC system, not using SAP-ABC, and use the Bridge as the interface
- Intend to implement SAP ABC, using Oros as the interim or transitional ABC system

Exhibit 10.18 lists the top three benefits of using Oros with SAP CO in Scenario II.

Scenario III   This scenario covers the bulk of the current organizations using SAP. In Scenario II, the organization might have just CO-CCA in place. Here all needed pieces of CO are in place (excluding CO-PC for nonmanufacturing environments) except CO-ABC. Therefore, Scenario III is for a CO-ABC implementation.

Many organizations have already implemented most of CO and have been running for several years. If Oros is utilized with this type of organization, then

Category	Benefits
Organizational Impact	Provides ABC results for management decision making even though the SAP ABC implementation is not completed yet. This also begins the learning process of Activity-Based Costing/ Budgeting/Management and prepares the organization for its full use in decision making.
System Design	Reduces the need for most of the interfaces since the Bridge can be used instead. Interfaces from SAP providing data that does not reside in CO would remain in place, unless the data can be linked via LIS into CO.
SAP Project Management	Identifies valuable metrics for determining the scope and time line for subsequent CO submodule implementations, especially CO-ABC. The defined Oros model provides information that enhances the accuracy of the project scoping and estimations.

Exhibit 10.18   Top Benefits of Using Oros with Scenario II SAP-CO Functionality

it is as the off-line side system to support analytical ABC, potentially with interfaces to the SAP R/3 system. In this scenario, Oros can be used to perform rapid
prototyping to determine the scope and preliminary design of CO-ABC and any
other submodules being implemented at the same time, such as CO-PA. The
Bridge can be used to upload the current Oros models, which have been changed
to support the upload, to build the SAP ABC structures and assignments.

Within Scenario III, organizations now have to deal with having potentially
two ABC systems. A determination has to be made defining what each system
should be used for. Another misconception is for organizations to think that SAP
ABC can handle only the summary level of the activities (processes) with the
ABC detail level remaining in Oros. This idea is contrary to the purposes of the
two systems. SAP is the transaction-based tracking and controlling system for
day-to-day operations. Therefore, this transaction level is the lowest level of detail and should be the basis of the detailed activity view. This misconception
comes from a limited knowledge of SAP's ABC calculation capabilities and is
common even among those with relatively deep knowledge of other SAP CO
functionality. How the two products should be positioned when used together is
addressed in the "Implementation Guidelines" section below. Exhibit 10.19 lists
the top three benefits of using Oros with SAP CO in Scenario III.

Scenario IV   All of the required pieces of CO are implemented. If the organization is a service industry, CO-PC may not be implemented.

Category	Benefits
System Design	The already existing Oros models provide valuable information that can be used to shorten the "as-is," "to-be," and gap analysis tasks of the SAP implementation.
System Design	The ability to use the Bridge to upload and download information makes the creation of many of the CO data structures and assignments faster, reducing the time requirements for prototyping and building the final conceptual design of CO.
SAP Project Management	Identifies reporting requirements more efficiently and more quickly. This is important for the determination of the types of reports that will need to be created in SAP R/3 and the amount of time required, and is driven by the determined usage of each system to support certain analytics.

Exhibit 10.19   Top Benefits of Using Oros with Scenario III SAP-CO Functionality

Scenario IV describes the end systems and capabilities that most of the SAP organizations want to have. Within such organizations, SAP supports the integrated ABC model providing monthly process information throughout the organization included in the P/Ls, inventory valuations, cost center consumption reports, and so forth.

In this scenario, the Bridge is used to transfer information from SAP R/3 to Oros to support "what-if" scenarios, simulation activities, and process improvement initiatives. These types of modeling would not occur at the SAP transaction-based operational level due to the integrated requirements. The validity checks within the system provide the benefit of strict audit trails and shared master data repositories. However, these checks do not support simulation activities, since simulations potentially require the construction of "invalid" structures. Therefore, the Bridge provides a way of transferring organizational structures from SAP R/3 to Oros to be used for simulations. Exhibit 10.20 lists the top three benefits for using Oros with SAP CO in Scenario IV.

Once the "what-if" or simulation results indicate that an organizational change should be made, the operational system is changed to reflect the new accepted change (i.e., permanent shifts are incorporated into the SAP operational system).

These four scenarios cover the entire CO functionality continuum, from no CO functionality to a completely integrated SAP ABC model. Within each, examples of how Oros can be utilized were illustrated, varying from being the actual ABC costing engine, to being part of the implementation methodology, to becoming the simulation support tool. These four scenarios and examples are not all-inclusive. Each organization or project has to analyze how the two products should be used together based on needs and requirements.

Analytics Everywhere

A third misconception is that SAP R/3 is not an analytical tool, that only side systems can support analysis. This idea is absolutely not true. SAP houses the transactions and therefore can provide a myriad of analytical information covering key performance metrics; benchmarking; variance analysis; event costing; inventory valuations; outsourcing; "what-if" analysis; responsibility accounting; resource utilization; investment strategies; operational efficiencies; excess/idle capacity; and profitability by products, customer, and regions, among other areas. SAP applications can be used to analyze almost anything currently occurring in the implemented organizational environment. What SAP R/3 cannot easily accommodate is

Category	Benefits
Conceptual Design	Determining impacts of "what-if" analysis. For example, the operational level ABC model is downloaded from SAP to Oros and minor changes are performed for several "what-if" scenarios to review the impacts, such as: "What-if" we ship to customer 1 from DC 3? Here the focus is not necessarily that the model has changed but the information flowing through it is different.
Conceptual Design	Focused modeling for process engineering can take place within Oros and then be incorporated into the SAP R/3 integrated structures. For example: Process improvement impacts for the purchasing department or a manufacturing plant can be modeled, and if it is determined that the changes result in higher efficiencies, then the new design can be incorporated into SAP R/3. In this case, the SAP model is downloaded and Oros is used to model structural changes to determine impacts—for example, eliminate process 2 and 3 and incorporate a new process of 4. Or the Oros model can be used for very specific one-time analysis, e.g., determining which distribution channels drive overhead costs higher. Here the focus is on changing the model to provide improvements or at least indications of areas for improvement.
Conceptual Design	Simulation at a higher or more aggregate level can take place within Oros for strategic envisioning. These simulations of the operational ABC model provide information on the impacts of strategic initiatives, such as shifting from a labor intensive to an automated approach, or other corporate strategies such as an acquisition or divestiture, etc. Here the focus is how large-scale projects or strategic initiatives will impact the operational model. Where core SAP R/3 does not provide these benefits, functionality of the new SAP product, Strategic Enterprise Management (SEM), has been designed specifically to support simulation activities. For ABC/B/M simulations, SEM utilizes Oros with its own version of the Bridge. Chapter 11 addresses this topic.

Exhibit 10.20   Top Benefits of Using Oros with Scenario IV SAP-CO Functionality

optimization of the current environment or simulating what will happen if a certain change is encountered, beyond what is planned for in the upcoming budget cycle. Side systems, such as SAP's Strategic Enterprise Management (SEM) and Advanced Planning and Optimization (APO), are designed specifically to support this type of analysis. The combination of SAP CO and Oros supports the bulk of the analysis organizations desire.

Organizational Impact	Determine the overall view for the use of the two together.
System Design	What are the requirements for using the two together?
Conceptual Design	How does the Oros model need to change to work with SAP?

Exhibit 10.21   Oros Bridge Implementation Guidelines

Moving Forward

A symbiotic relationship exists between these two products, not a mutually exclusive one. Many organizations assume that Oros is no longer needed once SAP's integrated ABC is implemented. Some of these organizations were using Oros as their costing engine, utilizing custom integration to various source data. Once the costing calculations move to SAP, they believe that Oros is no longer needed. Scenario IV provides several reasons why Oros might still be utilized once SAP ABC is implemented. Additionally, the current Oros models that move to SAP probably reflect only a small portion of the organization, such as a plant, or only certain types of costs, such as product costing. The Oros modeling capabilities can be used to model other areas of the organization or types of costs, such as cost to serve and shared services. Once the model is accepted within the organization, the new model pieces can be uploaded into SAP using the Oros Bridge.

IMPLEMENTATION GUIDELINES

Obviously the biggest questions arise around how to use these two products together, since there is a large overlap in capabilities. During an implementation, this aspect must be clearly defined. In addition, the requirements for using the two products together and any changes to the current costing design have to be accommodated. Exhibit 10.21 lists the implementation areas to be addressed in this section.

Product Positioning

Since every instance where these two products will be used in tandem differs based on SAP functionality implemented, model sophistication, organization

As the Costing Engine	SAP usually has more processing power capabilities and database size because it almost always resides on much larger and more powerful hardware than Oros. SAP also provides more advanced allocation/assignments methods, utilizing the template. Given that the transactional data already resides in SAP, there is no need to move the data off-line to perform cost allocations and calculations to then bring the results back to SAP.
One Organizational Model	SAP usually is implemented to support the entire organization, such as multiple companies, countries, divisions, strategic business units, sales offices, etc. This is true even if ABC is not used for the entire organization.
As the Dynamic ABC Environment	SAP can be the one data repository for master data structures throughout the organization. Therefore, the SAP ABC model has access to or can automatically be updated with the new master data values, such as customers, products, vendors, sales areas, distribution channels, etc., depending on the design of the model. If a quantity-based model is built, the ABC model can be designed to dynamically change to replicate the current environment. Therefore, the SAP ABC model can more easily reflect the true organizational structures and appropriate costs flows.
Timely Operational Reporting	SAP provides real-time capturing of actual data, providing more timely management feedback. Reporting can be performed within period, at period end, quarterly, annually, etc. Since the SAP ABC model can be designed to be dynamic, reporting of the ABC information is generally more frequent and accurate. The Oros model needs to be updated to reflect model changes. Many organizations make these changes on a quarterly basis.
Operational to Strategic Analysis Using Current Environment	SAP is used to provide current environment analysis, such as plan/actual/variance, determination of what should the costs have been given the actual volumes (actual/target/variance), operational efficiencies, drill-back to documents that contribute the costs, etc. Additionally, the transactional data can be aggregated to support some strategic analysis from SAP R/3 as well.

Exhibit 10.22   Primary Uses of SAP CO in an SAP/Oros Environment

scope, corporate politics, and so on, each implementation will have to define how the two will be used in the most beneficial manner for the organization. Chapter 2 illustrates the strengths and weakness of both systems. The previous section of this chapter, "Tandem Usage and Benefits", provides several examples of ways the two products can be used together and the benefits to be gained. Exhibits 10.22

For Process Reengineering and New Structures Impact Analysis	Oros can be used to support process engineering and new structures impact analysis. Although SAP can be designed to have a dynamically changing ABC model to reflect the organization, it is still a current view of the organization (i.e., reality). Oros modeling can support analysis of impacts to the current ABC model due to potential master data structures changes.
For "What-If" and Simulation Analysis	SAP is used for tracking of actual data. Simulating actual data for specific analysis is not easily accommodated within SAP R/3 and requires plan versions to be used. Oros is much better suited for developing quick models or making changes to models in order to perform "what-if" and simulations for specific analysis.
As an SAP Implement- ation Tool	Oros can be used as an implementation tool for prototyping and building pieces of SAP-CO. The ABC model is built in Oros, or a current model is changed and then the Bridge is used to upload key pieces to reduce CO build time.
As the SAP CO Visual Cost Assignment View	SAP does not provide a graphical depiction of the cost flows designed within CO. However, the user-friendly Oros front-end provides a method for creating a model used to represent the cost flows designed in SAP, whether they are process related or not. When decisions are considered that may impact the current CO model, this Oros model provides a visual representation of the CO cost flows, helping to highlight potential assignment impacts that then need to be further analyzed.
As a Documentation Tool	In the Oros model created to depict the CO cost flows, documentation for the data structures, assignments, reasoning of key decisions made during the implementation, issues, design changes, etc., can be captured.

Exhibit 10.23   Primary Uses of Oros in an SAP/Oros Environment

and 10.23 list primary ways to use each tool with the other. The focus for SAP CO is on the current environment, its daily fluctuations, and information for control and tracking to make decisions for today or tomorrow. The SAP R/3 focus is mainly execution, not strategic.

The Oros focus is on swift changes of the current environment to determine improvements, implications, advantages, and impacts. This focus requires being detached from the data integrity and validation controls of the SAP R/3 system. The focus instead is on future or potential fluctuations to the environment. Oros is strategic in nature, not execution driven. The other uses of Oros are new applications or approaches for use of the software, specifically designed for the support of SAP implementations.

SAP Release Requirements		4.0B	4.5B	4.6A/B	4.6C
ABC Technologies Requirements	Oros 4.3	SAP Add-on CD hot packages up to 27	SAP add-on CD hot packages	Standard	Not supported
	Oros Bridge Release 5.0	Some new functionality not supported	Some new functionality not supported	Some new functionality not supported	Standard

Exhibit 10.24   System Requirements for a Bridge Implementation

Implementation Requirements

A Bridge implementation has two types of requirement needs: (1) system need and (2) knowledge. The system requirements are listed in Exhibit 10.24.

Knowledge will have to be bought, either through training or consulting, or more likely a combination of both. The following are a few examples of the knowledge needs for a Bridge implementation:

- A technical understanding of how to change the Oros model(s) to upload. Attribute and syntax usage indicates to the Bridge what the Oros objects represent in SAP, where to place the required information, and so forth.
- A solid conceptual understanding of both products, to change current Oros models to upload into the correct places within SAP, building a viable business case. The following section explains why the Oros model would need to change.
- A team member(s) experienced with designing and implementing both software packages; training is not a replacement for experience. For the SAP side, this knowledge needs to include all of the CO submodules as well as experience with other SAP modules for understanding integration impacts, such as PP (production controlling), MM/FI (inventory valuation), links for P/Ls within CO-PA, and impacts of the SD module. For Oros, this knowledge is an understanding of the Oros modeling capabilities as they apply to the Bridge-supported functionality.
- An understanding of the advantages and disadvantages of each tool in order to determine how both should be used within the organization in the future (positioning the use of Oros and SAP ABC within an organization).

A Bridge implementation usually is not confined to merely linking Oros with SAP CO. These endeavors often encompass a multitude of goals, such as further implementation of some SAP CO submodules, a revamping of the current ABC approach in the organization, and adapting to external or internal changes requiring a whole new approach to data collection and information generation. The scope of a Bridge implementation can be as narrow as the actual usage of the two systems together, to as wide as a component in a whole advanced cost management initiative.

Changing a Current Oros Model to Fit SAP

If the current Oros model was not designed from scratch specifically to upload to SAP, then changes need to be made. These changes break out into two categories: (1) technical changes and (2) changes related to model design.

Technical Changes to Current Oros Models   The technical changes consist of attribute tagging and syntax requirements. Attributes are tagged to data structures in order for the necessary required master data fields in SAP to be populated. For example, in order for the activity account in Oros to generate a process in SAP, the activity account needs to have attribute tags assigned that are used to populate the required process fields, such as company code, business area, profit center, and secondary cost element if a default one is not used. Defaults can be selected within the Bridge parameters; however, if different information is to be used for an activity, the tag is used. Additionally, attribute tags are used to determine the secondary cost element to be used for an assignment upload, if the default is not desired, and to indicate that a resource account represents an activity type. Most of these attributes can be populated automatically by the Bridge for a large number of the master data field properties.

   The resource accounts and activity accounts in a current Oros model may already have attribute tags; however, most likely they are not ones required for SAP upload nor would they be in the correct syntax code required. There are syntax requirements for the attribute hierarchy, the attribute values, and the reference numbers in order for the upload from Oros to SAP to work. For example, the reference number for the activity account must be no longer than 12 digits in order for the process to be generated in SAP. This is due to SAP field requirements, such as length of the code. Another reference number syntax example is the syntax for cost elements so that SAP can determine the corresponding cost element. For example, planned costs being uploaded for the resource cost element with reference number *1000.Salaries.400000* indicates to SAP that this is the *400000* cost element contained within the cost element group *Salaries for cost center 1000*. The attribute hierarchy syntax pertains to the naming of the hierarchy node; for example, "SAP R/3 Activity Types" must be used for the activity type attribute hierarchy node. The attribute values themselves also have syntax requirements. For activity types and statistical key figure attribute values, the syntax is Description [Code.Unit], with the code being 6 digits or less and the unit of measure being two digits or less; an example would be # of Employees [FTE.EA].

Model Design Changes to Current Oros Models   The technical changes required to a current Oros model are relatively minor compared to potential changes to the model design. A current Oros model can most likely upload into SAP and function. However, it may not support the business requirements, might need to be expanded to include more advanced allocation methods, or possibly be completely changed due to integration desires. Also, there are some philosophical differences, such as the view of resource pools, which often drive Oros models to be modeled in a different way from how SAP CO-CCA would be designed.

Activity-to-Activity Assignments   Since Oros is developed to support the traditional ABC philosophy, it follows the cost flow of resource to activity to cost object. Assignments are not supported going from the process back to the resource. Therefore, many Oros models have activity-to-activity assignments representing further burdening of the costs prior to the cost object consumption. Since SAP supports any cost flows between objects, some of these assignments would be changed to allocate costs from a process to the true consumer of the process, which may be a cost center. The "Step-down versus Recursive" section of Chapter 5 provides an example of the benefits of this cost flow.

Differing Assignment Capabilities   This section does not necessarily have to do with changes to the Oros model itself but with a change to the costing model being supported by both systems. SAP has more advanced assignment methods—templates—that may be used. When shifting from Oros to SAP ABC, a reevaluation of the ABC model needs to be made to determine which pieces should be shifted to a quantity-based approach to take advantage of the more advanced assignment capabilities. The Oros Bridge allows users to keep the two models, the one in SAP and the one in Oros, in sync from a master data standpoint. However, the two models can quickly become out of sync depending on the desired assignment capabilities. The positioning of the products within the organization will drive how much of a difference can be accepted between the allocation methods in the two models.

Access to New Data   The integrated nature of SAP provides access to drivers automatically tracked in the system. The Oros model may not have these more appropriate drivers, since a method for capturing that driver information did not exist. For example, the "number of sales orders" driver might be replaced by "number of sales orders line items." Also, a calculated driver can be automatically determined for new master data structures instead of having to manually update the value. For example, the "number of pallets shipped" driver can be calculated by dividing the "sales qty" by the "number of units per pallets." The "sales qty" changes by period, but the "number of units per pallet" is a fixed number for a product. When a new material is created in SAP, this information will be populated on the material master and can be automatically included for calculation purposes. Since SAP master data structures provide many informational fields for products, vendors, customers, and sales orders, the driver may need to be changed to accommodate access to the more appropriate data.

Aligning Master Data Structures   The objects within Oros may not necessarily equate to the same corresponding object in SAP; for example, activity accounts are not always a process in SAP. Within Oros, the resource accounts may be designed to be pools of G/L costs. In order to make allocations between support units, activity-to-activity assignments are designed. Since SAP is based on the RCA philosophy, the cost centers are not corresponding pools of G/L accounts but clearly delineated areas of responsibility. Some cost centers are activity type output dependent, in which case these are actually pools of capacity costs. In this sense, some of the Oros master data structures can represent one of two master data structures in SAP. For instance, an activity account may be used in Oros for making maintenance assignments to several maintenance activities. Therefore, some activities in a current Oros model would really be cost centers in SAP. If the Oros model is built from scratch, downloading the CCA module to the Resource module, this misalignment does not occur. Also, some of the activities in current Oros models might be activity types once uploaded to SAP.

Users must define what capabilities and costing model are to be supported. Then the pieces can be evaluated from the current Oros model to determine what changes may need to be made. Once the changes have been identified and the amount of work estimated, a decision can be made on whether to build a new Oros model or make changes to the current Oros model.

SUMMARY

SAP and Oros both provide a great deal of functionality. Their capabilities are based on the different natures inherent in being a stand-alone tool or an integrated tool. The SAP and ABC Technologies partnership guarantees a standardized interface provided via the Bridge that will be consistently updated and maintained in future releases of SAP and Oros. Therefore, the partnership is an integrated solution supporting the functionality of both strategic and operational ABC. Exhibit 10.25 summarizes the main aspects and benefits of using Oros with SAP CO. See Exhibit 10.26 for an R/3 Bridge Features Matrix.

NOTE

1. Additional functionality, which is not included, may be added prior to book release.

Summary Area	Summary Description
Area-Specific Focus	
The Bridge	A user front end to an interface mapping master data structures and assignments between the SAP CO module and Oros.
Information Flows	
Resource Module to Cost Center Accounting	The Oros Resource module most closely maps to the Cost Center Accounting module. SAP masters data structures for cost center groups, cost centers, and cost elements can upload/download. Assignments generally generate assessment or indirect activity allocations in SAP. The structured business process template and direct activity allocations are supported as well. Planned/actual quantities can upload/download. Planned/actual costs can only be downloaded from SAP to Oros. Only planned costs can be uploaded to R/3.
Activity Module to Activity-Based Costing	The Oros Activity Module maps to the Activity-Based Costing module in SAP. Processes can be downloaded/ uploaded. Assignments can be created via the Bridge for assessments, indirect activity allocations, direct activity allocations, and the structured business process. Any template that allocates processes to a receiver other than a process cannot be created using the Bridge. Planned/ actual quantities can upload/download. Planned/actual costs can be downloaded from SAP to Oros. Only planned costs can be uploaded to R/3.
Cost Object Module to Order and Project Accounting (Internal Orders)	One use of the Cost Object module is to represent internal orders. Internal orders and groups can be uploaded/ downloaded. Cost object to cost object assignments can be used to generate internal order settlement rules. Planned/ actual quantities can upload/download. Planned/actual costs can be downloaded from SAP to Oros. Only planned costs can be uploaded to R/3.
Cost Object Module to Order and Project Accounting (Internal Orders)	The Cost Object module is also used to represent the PA market segments. The Bridge works only with costing-based CO-PA. Characteristic values and hierarchies can be created in either tool by upload or download. Value fields can only be downloaded. Planned/actual quantities can upload/download. Planned/actual costs can only be downloaded from SAP to Oros. Only planned costs can be uploaded to R/3.

Exhibit 10.25   Using Oros with SAP CO Summary

Which software package provides more ABC functionality	Many variables can be used to determine the answer to this question. The main strength of ABC is its assignment methodology and analytical capabilities. In this case, SAP CO has more types of allocations and more advanced allocation functionality via the template allocation, although some more advanced component-based assignments are not supported by R/3.
How can these two products be used together, and what are the benefits?	Depending on where the organization is in the controlling functionality continuum, this answer varies. *Scenario I*: With no CO in place, Oros used with SAP provides the benefit of ABC experimentation as a costing engine, an implementation tool, and a representation of the CO conceptual design. *Scenario II*: With CO-CCA in place, but no CO-ABC, Oros used with SAP provides the benefits of ABC results, reduced interface requirements, and identification of CO-ABC project estimating metrics. *Scenario III*: CO-ABC implementation projects using Oros provide the benefits of reducing "as-is" phase, actually constructing master data structures and assignments, reducing build time, and aid in report requirements definitions. *Scenario IV*: With CO-ABC in place, using Oros in conjunction provides the benefits of "what-if" analysis, process reengineering modeling, and strategic simulations.
Which system is used for what type of analysis?	SAP can support analytical information pertaining to capacity management, event costing, operational efficiencies, what the cost should have been, etc. Oros is better suited for analysis for impacts to the current organizational structure or modeling potential future organizational model changes.
Is it necessary to use both software packages?	Scenario IV provides benefits for fully using both packages together. Additionally, Oros could be used to further model organizational areas that are not currently using an ABC approach. Once defined, the new areas can be moved into SAP CO-ABC.

Implementation Guides

Oros & SAP CO Positioning	Determine the overall view for the use of the two together.
Implementation Requirements	What are the requirements for using the two together?
Technical and Model Changes	How does the Oros model need to change to work with SAP?

Exhibit 10.25 (*continued*)

	SAP R/3 Version							
	4.0B		4.5B		4.6A+B		4.6C+	
	Oros Bridge with SAP Version							
Uploading Structure (Master Data) to R/3 CO	4.3	5.0	4.3	5.0	4.3	5.0	4.3	5.0
CO-CCA								
Upload Cost Centers and Cost Center Hierarchy as an Alternative Group								☑
Upload Cost Centers and Hierachy as part of the Standard Hierarchy								☑
Upload Cost Centers and Hierarchy from the Activity Module								☑
Upload Cost Center/Activity Types from the Resource Module	☑	☑	☑	☑	☑	☑	☑	☑
Upload Cost Center/Activity Types from the Activity Module		☑		☑		☑		☑
CO-ABC								
Upload Business Processes	☑	☑	☑	☑	☑	☑	☑	☑
Upload Structured Business Process Templates using Bills of Costs	☑	☑	☑	☑	☑	☑	☑	☑
CO-PA								
Upload Characteristic Hierarchy and Characteristics Values								☑
CO-OPA								
Upload Internal Orders								☑
General								
Upload Secondary Cost Elements (category types 42 and 43 only)	☑	☑	☑	☑	☑	☑	☑	☑

	SAP R/3 Version							
	4.0B		4.5B		4.6A+B		4.6C+	
	Oros Bridge with SAP Version							
Download Master Data (Structure) to ABCPlus	4.3	5.0	4.3	5.0	4.3	5.0	4.3	5.0
CO-CCA								
Download Selected Cost Center Hierarchy to Resource Module	☑	☑	☑	☑	☑	☑	☑	☑
Download Activity Types to Resource Module	☑	☑	☑	☑	☑	☑	☑	☑
Download Cost Centers, Hierarchy, and Activity Types to Activity Module								☑
Download Cost Elements Based on Selected Cost Element Group	☑	☑	☑	☑	☑	☑	☑	☑
CO-ABC								
Download Business Process Hierarchy								☑
Download Company Codes as Attributes	☑	☑	☑	☑	☑	☑	☑	☑
Download Profit Centers as Attributes	☑	☑	☑	☑	☑	☑	☑	☑
Download Business Areas as Attributes	☑	☑	☑	☑	☑	☑	☑	☑
CO-PA								
Download Characteristic Value Profitability Segments	☑	☑	☑	☑	☑	☑	☑	☑
Download Selected CO-PA Characteristics and Hierarchy	☑	☑	☑	☑	☑	☑	☑	☑
Download Selected Value Fields as Drivers	☑	☑	☑	☑	☑	☑	☑	☑
CO-OPA								
Download Internal Orders								☑
General								
Download Secondary Cost Elements (category types 42 and 43 only)	☑	☑	☑	☑	☑	☑	☑	☑
Download Statistical Key Figures as Shared Drivers	☑	☑	☑	☑	☑	☑	☑	☑

	SAP R/3 Version							
	4.0B		4.5B		4.6A+B		4.6C+	
	Oros Bridge with SAP Version							
Assignments (Cycles and Settlement Rules)	4.3	5.0	4.3	5.0	4.3	5.0	4.3	5.0
Upload Resource to Resource Assignments (Cost Center to Cost Center)		☑		☑		☑		☑
Upload Resource to Activity Assignments (Cost Center to Business Process)	☑	☑	☑	☑	☑	☑	☑	☑
Upload Resource to Cost Object Assignments (Cost Center to CO-PA Segments)		☑		☑		☑		☑
Upload Resource to Cost Object Assignments (Cost Center to Internal Orders)		☑		☑		☑		☑
Upload Activity to Activity Assignments (Business Processes to Business Processes)	☑	☑	☑	☑	☑	☑	☑	☑
Upload Activity to Cost Object Assignments (Business Processes to CO-PA Segments)	☑	☑	☑	☑	☑	☑	☑	☑
Upload Activity to Cost Object Assignments (Business Processes to Internal Orders)		☑		☑		☑		☑
Upload Cost Object to Cost Object Assignments (Internal Orders to CO-PA Segments)								☑
Upload Cost Object to Cost Object Assignments (Internal Orders to Internal Orders)								☑
Upload Shared Drivers (used in assignments) as Statistical Key Figures	☑	☑	☑	☑	☑	☑	☑	☑
Upload Unique Drivers (used in assignments)	☑	☑	☑	☑	☑	☑	☑	☑
Upload Results of Calculated Drivers (used in assignments)		☑		☑		☑		☑
Upload % Drivers (used in assignments)	☑	☑	☑	☑	☑	☑	☑	☑
Option to Upload Activity Assignments as Assessments								☑

Exhibit 10.26   R/3 Bridge Features Matrix

Source: Oros® Bridge with SAP® R/3 help documentation provided by ABC Technologies, Inc.

Download Period Data to ABCPlus	SAP R/3 Version							
	4.0B		4.5B		4.6A+B		4.6C+	
	Oros Bridge with SAP Version							
	4.3	5.0	4.3	5.0	4.3	5.0	4.3	5.0
Upload and Download Periodic Data from Plan Version 000 only	☑	☑	☑	☑	☑	☑	☑	☑
Upload and Download Periodic Data from Plan Versions other than 000								☑
Download Actual/Plan Cost Element Costs	☑	☑	☑	☑	☑	☑	☑	☑
Download Actual/Plan Business Process Costs		☑		☑		☑		☑
Download Actual/Plan Internal Order Costs								☑
Download Actual/Plan Statistical Key Figure Quantities	☑	☑	☑	☑	☑	☑	☑	☑
Download Actual/Plan Value Field Quantities from CO-PA	☑	☑	☑	☑	☑	☑	☑	☑
Download Revenue Values	☑	☑	☑	☑	☑	☑	☑	☑
Download Sales Quantities	☑	☑	☑	☑	☑	☑	☑	☑

Upload Period Data to R/3 CO	SAP R/3 Version							
	4.0B		4.5B		4.6A+B		4.6C+	
	Oros Bridge with SAP Version							
	4.3	5.0	4.3	5.0	4.3	5.0	4.3	5.0
Upload Plan Cost Element Costs	☑	☑	☑	☑	☑	☑	☑	☑
Upload Plan Business Process Costs		☑		☑		☑		☑
Upload Plan Internal Order Costs								☑
Upload Actual/Plan Statistical Key Figure Quantities	☑	☑	☑	☑	☑	☑	☑	☑
Upload Plan Value Field Quantities to CO-PA								☑
Upload Control Indicators for Activity Types	☑	☑	☑	☑	☑	☑	☑	☑
Upload Control Indicators for Business Processes	☑	☑	☑	☑	☑	☑	☑	☑

Synchronization of Resource/Activity/Cost Object Group	SAP R/3 Version							
	4.0B		4.5B		4.6A+B		4.6C+	
	Oros Bridge with SAP Version							
	4.3	5.0	4.3	5.0	4.3	5.0	4.3	5.0
Changes in R/3 with Oros as Master								
Delete/Move/Add Cost Centers								☑
Delete/Move/Add Cost Elements								☑
Move/Add Business Processes								☑
Move/Add Characteristic Values								☑
Changes in Oros with R/3 as Master								
Delete/Move/Add Cost Centers								☑
Delete/Move/Add Business Processes								☑
Delete/Move/Add Characteristic Values								☑
Add/Redefine Drivers from SKFs and Value Fields								☑

Exhibit 10.26 (*continued*)

11

ACTIVITY-BASED COSTING/MANAGEMENT WITH STRATEGIC ENTERPRISE MANAGEMENT

The SAP R/3 core business applications focus on business process automation, capturing, and tracking of transactional information throughout the organization. This data can be used to provide valuable information for day-to-day operational execution, monitoring, controlling, and auditing. However, data is often not presented or generated to support initiatives that are less structured in nature. To support these more analytical (nontransactional focused) initiatives, SAP provides the New Dimension products. The New Dimension products focus on the optimization and simulation of several areas; for example, advanced planning and optimization (APO) focuses on logistics, customer relationship management (CRM), and strategic enterprise management (SEM). The SEM functionality and its support of ABC/M capabilities is the focus of this chapter.

STRATEGIC ENTERPRISE MANAGEMENT

The "buzz" in the business world today is the "new economy." In the old economy, organizations determined a strategy and then executed against it. In the new economy, the market environment changes so fast that the strategy is often outdated before the organization even begins to support it. Today's tools enabling strategic management must be flexible enough to quickly adjust strategic scenarios to highlight ways for generating profits first. Strategic enterprise management is now more focused on speed and agility. Organizations require tools to assist them to swiftly answer such questions as:

- What information do we need to determine the strategy and how do we capture it?

- How do we involve the stakeholders in this process in order to assess, meet (preferably exceed), and manage their expectations?
- What are the simulated impacts and planned requirements to support different strategies?
- Once a strategy is defined, how do we get everyone to move toward it, and what, if any, corrective steps should be taken?
- When all is said and done, what are our final results?

The SAP SEM application supports the strategic management process for addressing these specific questions. Strategic initiatives cover a varied arena of concepts, from identifying markets to enter or exit; considering mergers, acquisitions, or divestments; and determining how to maximize the organization as a whole to achieve certain objectives and performance targets. Key components to support these types of decisions and answer the questions listed focus on:

- The ability to gather the required information
- Identification of the individual or organizational stakeholders
- Scenario simulations
- The ability to monitor the performance and consolidate information

The SEM software provides capabilities specifically targeted to aiding with each of these areas. The following is a brief overview of the SEM component modules.

Business Information Collection

Business information collection (BIC) is designed to support answering the questions: What information do we need to determine the strategy and how do we capture it? Business information collection focuses on automating the collection of external information. Strategic business decisions rely on vast amounts of information. This information tends to be more external (outside of the organization) in nature the higher the level of the strategic decision being considered, such as requiring competitor data, analyst estimates on market conditions, or future inflationary impacts. As the strategic decisions narrow to be more operational in nature, the required information tends to be internal in nature, such as operational systems information and planned estimates. Internal data is usually more structured and therefore easier to collect. External data is usually unstructured and sourced through environments such as the Internet. The BIC functionality supports the accessing, collecting, and storing of the external-type data.

Stakeholder Relationship Management

Strategic decisions are evaluated based on the value creation potential for stakeholders. In order to better assess which opportunities should be pursued, the organization needs to have a clear understanding of its stakeholders. Stakeholder relationship management (SRM) addresses this need and further answers the question: How do we involve the stakeholders in this process in order to assess, meet (preferably exceed), and manage their expectations? Stakeholder relationship management provides many tools to aid with identifying, determining the interests and needs of, and communicating with the stakeholders of the organization. These tools cover areas such as the stakeholder map and relevance matrix, questionnaire generator, database, value proposition modeling, communication processor, simulation processor, window, and value report builder. The stakeholder map/relevance matrix aids with the identification of the stakeholders and weighing their attributes, such as power, expectations, and risk. Every organization has many different stakeholders, such as shareholders, regulatory agencies, customers, suppliers, employees, home office, and environmental agencies. Each stakeholder group has different expectations and interests. The stakeholder database is utilized to capture this information as well as data collected from the stakeholder questionnaire. This questionnaire is geared toward determining stakeholders' expectations. The different stakeholders may have conflicting expectations; therefore, stakeholder value proposition modeling is provided to weigh the expectations of stakeholders against one another. Beyond determining the stakeholders' expectations, SRM also focuses on the management of those expectations through communication. The stakeholder communication processor supports automatic updates to be provided to stakeholders via different communication methods, such as mail, e-mail, and faxes. The communication processor can also automate incoming communications. Another method for managing stakeholders' expectations is to provide them with enterprise models that simulate effects of changes to key data, such as inflation rates and currency valuations via the stakeholder simulation processor. Stakeholders can gain access to these models and identified reports via the stakeholder window. The reports can be produced utilizing the stakeholder value report builder, which supplies targeted information to groups of stakeholders based on their interests.

Business Planning and Simulations

Business planning and simulation (BPS) supports the creation of different types of business models and simulations to aid strategic through operational decisions.

Therefore, the BPS component addresses the question: What are the simulated impacts and planned requirements to support different strategies? When supporting planning requirements, BPS enables different types of planning, such as top-down planning versus bottom-up planning, or both, within a centralized or decentralized planning process. The BPS planning capabilities work much like an integrated Excel sheet residing on a data warehouse. They provide the opportunity to have truly integrated planning capabilities that roll up and can be updated at consolidated levels throughout the planning process. These plans can be for one-time analysis to answer specific high-level strategic decisions or a completely integrated fiscal year operational plan at the lowest organization unit in the enterprise.

BPS provides many standard manual planning functions that support steps usually performed during the planning process. Examples are the *Copy* function to copy actuals to plan, *Currency Conversion, Depreciation* calculations, and *Distributions* for spreading information down and across the organization. In addition to the standard functions, easily created user-defined formulas and global parameters are supported. BPS also has linkages with two other tools to aid with modeling and simulation, ABC Technologies' Oros software (Oros), and Powersim Studio Enterprise 2000 (Powersim). Chapter 10 reviewed the capabilities of the Oros ABC modeling tool. Powersim is a software application that supports system dynamic modeling, which addresses nonlinear relationships over a time series. The Powersim capabilities are highlighted through examples located in the "Sample Key Business Decisions" section later in this chapter.

Corporate Performance Monitor

Transparency of information in the marketplace through, for example, the Internet has made it difficult to gain a sustainable advantage through a new or unique strategy. The new strategic approach is available very quickly to everyone, and spin-off versions abound. In the new economy, creating the strategy first no longer provides organizations with a prevailing competitive edge. Shortening the internalization and execution of a strategy is critical to obtaining advantages. Once the strategic initiatives have been defined, the operational environment needs to be aligned to support the execution of that strategy. Doing so requires clear objectives and metrics (key performance indicators) for evaluating the deployment of that strategy. It also requires clear communication of the vision and how that vision should be executed. The corporate performance monitor (CPM) specifically supports these endeavors, answering the questions: Once a strategy is defined, how do we get everyone to move toward it and what, if any, corrective steps should be taken? The

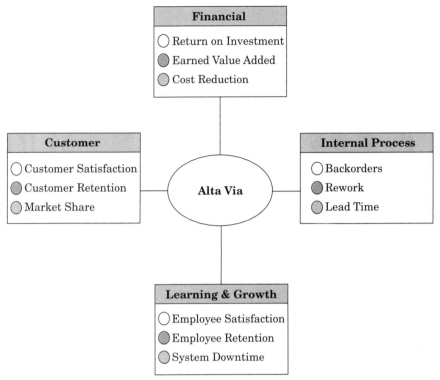

Exhibit 11.1   Balanced Scorecard Sample

CPM submodule provides two main approaches for viewing information, the Balanced Scorecard and the Management Cockpit.[1] The Balanced Scorecard provides a visualization of the requirements of the organization in order to turn strategic objectives into operational deployment. Exhibit 11.1 illustrates an example of a Balanced Scorecard.

As the Balanced Scorecard is rolled out to lower levels of the organization, it becomes even more operationally focused in its content. With a Balanced Scorecard for each operational area, through all levels of management, each group understands the key areas to focus on for supporting the decisions and goals it is trying to attain in order for the organization as a whole to be optimized. Key performance indicators (KPIs) at any management level might be ABC driven; for this Balanced Scorecard example, costs for non–value-added processes are utilized to support the *Financial* indicator of *Cost Reduction*, and KPIs for efficiencies of activities are utilized to support the *Internal Process* indicator for reducing *Lead Time*.

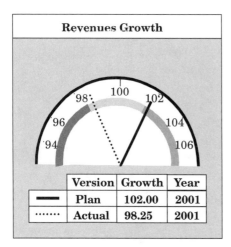

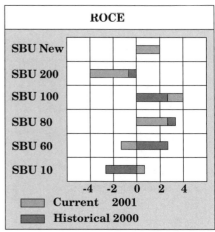

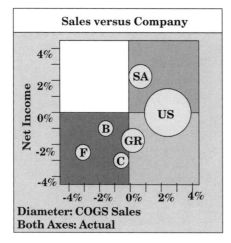

Exhibit 11.2 Management
Cockpit Partial Example

In addition to the visualization provided via the Balanced Scorecard, the Management Cockpit is available as well. The Management Cockpit is software and, if desired, a specially equipped room that displays key decision support information graphically in a visually appealing manner that is easy to interpret. It is utilized to provide upper management with key indicators of how the entire organization is performing. Exhibit 11.2 illustrates a partial example of the Management Cockpit. The screen normally displays six graphics at a time; the room usually has four walls each with six logical displays.

Business Consolidations

Business consolidation (BCS) supports organizations with performing consolidation activities and answering the final question: When all is said and done, what are our final results? Consolidations can be performed to meet external (based on statutory and taxation regulations) or internal management requirements, such as by profit center, business unit, or process. Whether for external or internal consolidations of units or companies, BCS supports eliminations, such as for revenues, investment income, expenses, payables, and receivables. It also supports the necessary currency translations, allocation of balance sheet accounts to other units, manual adjustments, and carrying forward of balances. Business consolidation provides a data and consolidations monitor that visually depicts the progress of the consolidations process. It supports the consolidations of both actual and planned data.

Each individual component of SEM provides a great deal of functionality focused on automating and accelerating a particular area within strategic enterprise management. Activity-Based Costing information can be accessed and utilized throughout each of these components. Business information collection can search and gather unstructured information from the Internet indicating benchmarking metrics for certain processes, methods for process reengineering, or new academic approaches to ABC applications within organizations. Via stakeholder relationship management (SRM), specific stakeholder groups can receive reports including information on the reduction of non–value-added activities. Business planning and simulation supports the application of ABC/M throughout the strategic process in many different ways, such as accessing the SAP R/3 ABC data that resides in BW as a basis for plan scenarios, utilizing the Oros ABC modeling tool, or building a Powersim model to determine the cost of a process within a time series. The corporate performance monitor (CPM) can incorporate any of the ABC data to be visualized in a Balanced Scorecard or in the Management Cockpit. Finally, business consolidations (BCS) can be utilized to perform legal external consolidation and, more important, internal management consolidation utilizing ABC information, especially for shared service entities.

INFORMATION FLOWS

As with all SAP products, the key with SEM is integration. SAP has always supported complete integration within and between its products. Strategic enterprise management follows the same path. It has tight integration between the

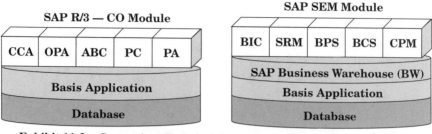

Exhibit 11.3   Comparison Technical Structure Between SAP R/3 and SEM

components of SEM and with the separate SAP R/3 system. Integration with the SAP R/3 system is provided via the link with the business warehouse. Strategic enterprise management functions similar to R/3 in that it is an application requiring a basis layer and a database. SAP R/3 and SEM can utilize many different databases, such as Informix and Oracle. Strategic enterprise management also requires a data warehouse, specifically SAP-BW. Exhibit 11.3 simplistically illustrates a comparison example of the SAP R/3 and SEM technical structure.

The BW is structured similarly to the CO-PA cube (operating concern) but consists of many more potential cubes and supports much more sophisticated reporting capabilities. Each BW cube (info_cube) consists of info_objects, which are either characteristics (reporting dimensions) or key figures (values fields for capturing quantities and dollars to be reported). In order for ABC information to be utilized in strategic decisions supported by SEM, it needs to reside in a BW cube or multiple cubes. There are several ways to populate BW with ABC data, of which the following are addressed:

- Use of the R/3 business applications
- Use of SEM-BPS planning layouts
- Use of the Oros Bridge with BPS
- Use of Powersim with BPS

SEM and SAP CO Business Application Integration

Any system can be utilized to feed the business warehouse with desired ABC data. Once that data resides in BW, it can be used by any of the SEM components. Therefore, almost anything can be the source of ABC information. If the system is non-SAP, then extractors (used to extract (interface) data from the source system) need to be built to bring the information into the BW structures. If SAP R/3 is utilized as the core business application, most likely SAP already provides the extractors to

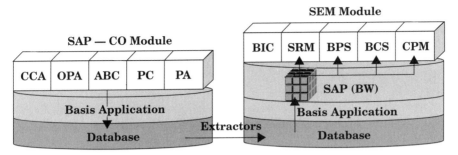

Exhibit 11.4   CO-ABC Data Extracted to BW

access this information. The design and construction of extractors to pull the desired information out of the source systems into any data warehouse, including BW, is the most time-consuming and expensive portion of a data warehousing implementation. The benefit of utilizing SAP R/3 with BW is, of course, integration. Many of these extractors have already been built and shipped as business content in the BW application, which reduces the effort required to populate the BW structures from SAP core applications. Additionally, retractors (putting information back into the source system) are provided that take information from BW back to areas within other SAP applications. These retractors are developed to aid with populating planned data back to the R/3 system, such as planned sales volumes posted to the CO-PA module to be utilized as drivers for the CO-ABC model. Exhibit 11.4 illustrates the extraction of ABC data from the SAP R/3 application.

SAP R/3 CO-ABC master data records and attribute information for a process, planned and actual data, process driver rates, and the results of allocations are all accessible for extraction. With the CO-ABC data available in BW:

- SEM-BPS can utilize process costs or process rates for plans, whether for strategic simulation or for low-level operational planning.
- SEM-BCS can utilize the information in internal management consolidations.
- SEM-CPM can access key ABC metrics to populate the Balance Scorecard and Management Cockpit.
- SEM-SRM can report this ABC information to interested stakeholders.

SEM-BPS Planning Layouts

The main data capture point for ABC plan data into SEM is through BPS planning layouts. The main structure entity of SEM-BPS is the planning area, which defines the BW cube or cubes from which the data is retrieved and to which the data will be posted—for example, the *Operational Planning Area* or the *Finan-*

cial Planning Area. (See Exhibit 11.5.) The planning area defines all of the characteristics, such as sales area, plant, distribution channel, distribution center, customer, region, and customer group, that will be utilized for the plan. The planning area also defines the key figures, such as G/L accounts and driver quantities, that can be planned against these characteristics. The planning area can be defined to suit any organizational need or level. Within the planning area, several planning levels are defined. The planning level is normally utilized to represent a focus for planning, such as production, sales, cost center, or balance sheet. The planning level defines the characteristics required for that type of planning, such as distribution channel, distribution center, product, and customer, for the distribution planning level, ignoring the other characteristics in the planning area. Therefore, the planning level is a more defined slice or view of the cube. A planning level can also be restricted to certain characteristic values as well, such as distribution channel *Direct*, if desired. The lowest level is the planning package, which also represents a further delineation of characteristic choices. The planning package is restricted to (inherits) the value chosen for both the planning area and planning level, for example, distribution channel *Direct*. The planning package also can define characteristic values not yet restricted, such as *Distribution Center 1* only within the distribution channel *Direct*. The planning area therefore defines the cube(s) where the data will reside; the planning level defines a section or grouping of the data within that cube(s); and the planning package is a slice of the data within that grouping. Exhibit 11.5 illustrates the hierarchy of *Operational Plan Area* planning areas, focusing on the *Distribution Planning* planning level, and specifically the manually entered data for the *Distr. Center 1* planning package.

The planning areas, levels, and packages define what is being planned. How planning is performed is defined by the planning function section. BPS provides planning functions, such as *Manual Planning, Activity Based Mgmt., Dynamic Simulation,* and so on, which are associated with the planning levels. Therefore, all planning packages within a planning level can utilize the same functions, layouts, or calculations. When a planning level or planning package is selected, the planning level is shown as the top node of the planning function area, such as *Distribution Planning* being the first line under the planning function section of the exhibit.

The manual planning function supports creating user-defined layouts for manually entering plan data. Manual planning utilizes a wizard (an automated, prompt-based guide) to quickly define the planning layouts in only three steps. Microsoft Excel runs "in place" within SEM-BPS, supporting on-line control and bidirectional data transfer with the BW cube. The planning layouts allow an organization to create a standardized planning form to support the different types

Planning Area

- Operational Plan Area
  - Cost Center Planning
  - Sales Planning
  - Distribution Planning
    - Distr. Center 1
    - Distr. Center 2
- Financial Plan Area
  - Income Statement

Parameters   Distr. Cost Layout

Microsoft Excel - Planning_Layout

File Edit View Insert Format Tools Data Window Help

Times New Roman   12   B I U $ %   100%

B23

	A	B	C
1	Company Code	AVC1	
2	Currency	USD	
3	Distribution Channel	Direct	
4	Distribution Center	1	
5	Fiscal Year	2002	
6	Version	0	

	A	Sales Qty.	# Pallets	# Loads	# UnLoads	# Intra DC Moves	Costs	
7								
8	Product 1000	10000	100	10	10	150	$	850
9	Product 2000	15000	120	12	12	240	$	1,320
10	Product 3000	12000	100	10	10	100	$	600
11	Product 4000	13000	130	13	13	260	$	1,430
12	Product 5000	16000	200	20	20	200	$	1,200
13	Product 6000	20000	200	20	20	200	$	1,200
14								

Planning Function

- Distribution Planning
  - Process Quantities & Costs
  - Manual Planning
- Distr. Cost Layout
  - Activity-Based Mgmt.
  - Dynamic Simulation

Exhibit 11.5   SEM-BPS Planning Areas, Planning Levels, and Planning Packages

of planning, such as cost center, headcount, sales, distribution, fixed assets, and production. These layouts read and write data to the BW cubes at which point the information is available for other planning layouts, the other SEM components, or even other systems. The *Distr. Cost Layout* is utilized to change *Sales Qtys* for the *Distribution Planning* level and is seen in Exhibit 11.5.

In addition to manual planning, standard planning functions are provided to define calculations for the different plans, such as *Copy, Depreciation,* and *Revaluation.* One option within the standard planning functions is for the definition of a formula. For this example, the formula planning function was used to create the *Process Qtys & Costs* calculation. The *Sales Qty.* key figure was planned utilizing the *Sales Planning* level (not shown) and updated via the *Distribution Planning* level. The *Process Qtys & Costs* planning function is then used to calculate the number of resulting *Pallets* and process output quantities for the *Load Truck, Unload Truck,* and *Move IntraDC* processes for the *Distribution Planning* level based on the *Sales Qty.* The cost for each process is utilized within the formula to calculate the distribution costs. The manual planning layout in the exhibit, *Distr. Costs Layout*, can be utilized to make updates or to view the results of the *Process Qtys & Costs* calculations. The formulas are user defined to support any calculations that are required within the organization. Global parameters (variables) can be defined as well, ensuring consistency, such as inflation will be 2.2% for next year, mileage expense will be $0.34/mile, and so on. Additionally, BPS supplies standard planning layout templates already supporting integrated profit and loss, balance sheet, and cash flow statements. The next two sections address the other planning functions listed, *Activity-Based Mgmt.* and *Dynamic Simulation.*

SEM-BPS and Oros Integration

Chapter 10 addressed the integration of SAP R/3 CO-ABC with the Oros modeling tool. The relationship between ABC Technologies Inc., and SAP AG extends to include integration of Oros with SEM-BPS. This linkage between Oros and SEM-BPS is also supported by the ABC Technologies' Bridge product. The Bridge between Oros and SEM-BPS is different from the Bridge to R/3, because there is no overlap in capabilities between Oros and SEM-BPS as there is with Oros and CO-ABC. Therefore, there is no need for a mapping exercise as with Oros and CO-ABC, where structures and assignments need to be aligned between the two systems. BPS does not currently support any ABC modeling capabilities on its own other than to access the data from the CO-ABC module or what can be built within formulas. Therefore, Oros functions as an embedded stand-alone ABC application, with the information and the model itself capable of being accessed and saved through SEM-BPS to a BW info_cube.

This connection supports the direct creation and execution of Oros ABC models within the SEM-BPS application. An Oros model can be utilized to create info_object (characteristics) master data values such as cost centers, cost elements, processes, products, customers, and regions. The Oros Bridge cannot create the info_objects themselves, only master data values and hierarchies. Since SEM is not the operational transaction-based system, actual values can be uploaded from Oros to SEM-BPS to be included in the BW info_cube. Additionally, SEM-BPS can download info_objects to build the Oros model and can populate the model with actual or planned data. Once SEM-BPS builds the master data structures, the Oros assignments can be designed and the model can be calculated. Exhibit 11.6 illustrates an Oros model being accessed by SEM-BPS via the Bridge. The Oros 5.0 Bridge (not shown) facilitates the transfer of information from Oros to SEM-BPS and vice versa. When the Oros model is to be updated, selecting a button on the Bridge will open the Oros application and model as a second screen.

The inclusion of the Oros application within SEM-BPS provides ABC/M analysis capabilities when determining different scenarios. This functionality can be used to determine areas for process improvements and impacts on strategic decisions based on product costs calculated via Oros, or to provide a visualization of the supply chain being analyzed, to list a few examples. The integration with the Oros model supports having many other allocation capabilities for utilization within SEM-BPS. The most recognizable benefits of the Oros and SEM-BPS linkage are central maintenance, global access, and support for ABB within SEM.

SEM-BPS and Powersim Integration

The CO-ABC data is determined at the lowest level of operations and reflects the current environment's information. The Oros ABC model can be at an operational level; more likely, when utilized with SEM, it is at a higher level, focusing more on strategic analysis needs. The Oros model can take into account changes to the current operational environment, such as adding a new sales office or making changes to products. Regardless of the level addressed by the ABC model, strategic, midlevel, or operational, the constants utilized within the Oros and SEM-BPS models are usually fixed. An analysis of the ABC impacts over time is not easily supported within a nonsystem dynamic tool. Linkages between Powersim and SEM-BPS address this need. Powersim is a strategic modeling tool focusing specifically on dynamic modeling, which takes into account time series and causal diagrams. Powersim is a very user-friendly tool to display and understand cause and effects of certain parameters to the entire model over time.

Planning Area

- Operational Plan Area
  - Cost Center Planning
  - Sales Planning
- Distribution Planning
  - Ad-Hoc Package
  - Distr. Center 1
- Financial Plan Area
  - Income Statement

Planning Function

- Distribution Planning
  - Process Qtys. & Costs
  - Manual Planning
  - Activity-Based Mgmt.
- Oros Model 1
  - Dynamic Simulation

Parameters

Resource (Period 1) — **Oros Model 1**

Name	Reference Number	Costs
Distribution Center 1	DC1	
Shipping	10000	$22,000
Salary Costs	10000.SALARIES	$10,000
Wages	10000.Salaries.430000	$3,000
Benefits	10000.Salaries.431000	$1,000
Office Costs	10000.OFFICE	$2,000
Facilities	10000.OFFICE.990000	$7,000
IT Support	10000.OFFICE.991000	$3,000
Receiving	20000	$4,000
Salary Costs	20000.SALARIES	$13,000
Wages	20000.Salaries.430000	$4,000
Benefits	20000.Salaries.431000	$4,000
Overtime	20000.Salaries.432000	$4,000
Office Costs	10000.OFFICE	$1,000

Exhibit 11.6 Oros Model Working with SEM-BPS

Powersim models can be generated to understand trade-off decisions, such as between preventative and emergency maintenance, or to model soft issue impacts, such as customer satisfaction or employee morale.

The linkages between Powersim and SEM-BPS support the ability to utilize ABC information located in a BW info_cube as data within a Powersim model. For example, process rates can be utilized as a constant to determine cost impacts, or process quantities can be utilized in a model analyzing efficiency of a value chain. Additionally, Powersim can be utilized to determine ABC information. A model can be designed to determine the impact to process rates over time that can then be utilized within the Oros model to determine the impacts to product costing. Exhibit 11.7 illustrates a Powersim model with SEM-BPS.

This exhibit contains a portion of a model determining the impact to *Shipping Costs* due to *Shipments* over the next five years. The model is extremely simplistic and does not take into consideration causal feedback loops, the core strength of Powersim, in order to focus just on the inclusion of the ABC information within the model. Within the model, the *Shipping Costs* contains formulas that translate the shipping volume into number of *Unload Truck* and *Load Truck* processes required. The constant of $5 for each process is maintained throughout the five years. The $5 rate can be entered manually or calculated within Oros or SAP R/3 CO-ABC and accessed from BW by Powersim. The results of this model are the determined *Shipping Costs* for the next five years. The process rates maintained at $5/process will require the process managers to increase process efficiency, thereby reducing cost per process each year by the same percentage as inflation. The constants can be changed quickly to see the impact of the change to the overall model.

These methods of integrating ABC data into SEM provide the ability to support ABM decisions at varying levels. The ability to pull SAP R/3 ABC information and to use a BPS planning layout supports the utilization of operational ABC information within SEM. From SAP R/3 the historical and current process costs, process rates, and process quantities can be populated into BW, allowing them to be utilized for determination of future costs and for performance comparisons. The linkage via the Oros Bridge with the Oros modeling capabilities supports process improvement endeavors, different allocation capabilities for planning, and a visualization of the cost flows within the organization. The ability to include any ABC data within Powersim models aids in determining future impacts either to or from process costs, rates, and quantities over a time series. The Powersim capabilities supporting the modeling of soft issues (employee morale) help to highlight impacts for change management, which is often extensive during ABC initiatives. With these integration capabilities, ABC information can be utilized easily to support any type of strategic decision.

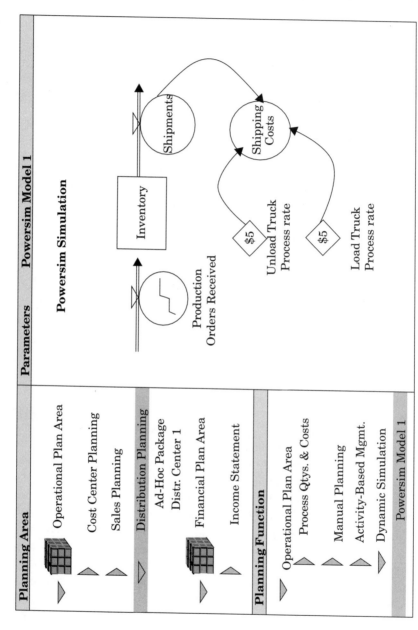

Exhibit 11.7 Powersim Model for SEM-BPS

SAMPLE KEY BUSINESS DECISIONS

Strategic analysis and support covers a wide area of topics focusing on the optimization of the organization's resources at a macro- and microeconomic level, to determination of potential growth markets, or competitor analysis, and so on. The focus of this chapter is on the support of ABC/M via the components of SEM. Each component can be impacted in some way or can impact the ABC/M initiatives within the organization. These ABC/M initiatives can feed information for any level of strategic decisions. These different decision levels consist of:

- High-level strategic analysis such as mergers and acquisitions
- Midlevel tactical analysis such as make/buy decisions
- Operational-level analysis such as the integrated financial plan

High-Level Strategic Analysis

High-level strategic analysis usually focuses on large capital expenditures that will greatly impact the organization as a whole. Sample decisions are mergers, acquisitions, or divestments, launching into a new sales channel or product market, facilities expansions across countries or globally, and a shift in core business concepts such as a low-volume, high-quality provider to the low-cost producer. These types of decisions are considered high level because they are not tightly tied with the operational-level environment, seeking more externally related data, and have a longer time frame, greater than five years. They utilize operational data at a very aggregated level to support the decisions, such as a blended product costs instead of the product cost by plant, or the available capacity by country instead of individual sites. Taking the merger example, several different SEM capabilities aiding this decision process focus on the ease of including the merger company's information, the ability to perform modeling, and the support to simulate softer issues. The corporate or divisional financial information can be added to the SEM-BPS planning layouts using Excel to include the potential merger in the financial information of the current organization. This information can then be consolidated in SEM-BCS and eliminations performed for areas that will be seen as a single entity in the future. Information on key common metrics from the other company can be utilized to visualize through the Balanced Scorecard if the merger will help to meet certain goals and objectives and can highlight potential areas of weakness. An Oros model can be utilized to determine the impacts of a new, shared supply chain to ensure that the economies of scale desired through the merger actually are realized. A Powersim model can be utilized to estimate potential impacts to customer satisfaction or employee morale, to determine if common products cannibalize one another and which ones to rationalize, or to simulate the labor resources available in different locations for the next decade to support back-office procedures. This simulation can aid in the decision of where to consolidate certain support functions due to the merger.

Midlevel Tactical Analysis

Somewhere in between determining which competitor or complement to acquire and planning how many of product 1000 to produce in period three in Santiago, Chile, are midlevel strategic decisions. Midlevel strategic analysis supports strategic decisions focusing on the next two to five years and rely more heavily on operational information. The operational information considered is generally at a grouped level, such as information by plant, product line, or branch office, instead of at a very aggregated level. Even though these decisions consider operational information, the margin of error for the decision is greater than the tolerance level set for operational decisions. This type of decision level focuses on decision support for make-buy decisions, reviewing technology changes, determination of appropriate inventory levels, assessing customer behavior, and identifying workforce needs, for example. Activity-Based Costing information can enable insight into any of these decisions.

The make/buy and workforce needs decisions illustrate the benefits gained from this level of strategic decision utilizing the tools within SEM. When considering whether to make or buy a core product or service, an Oros model can be used to determine the estimated costs to make a product at different plants or provide the service through different locations. This information can be utilized for a Powersim simulation that depicts the impact of other constants over a period of time, such as inflation rates, unemployment rates, and sales volumes. The results of the simulation indicate when future potential shifts should be considered. For example, Product 1000 is most profitable when sourced from the São Paulo, Brazil, plant for years 2000 to 2002, at which time, based on the variables within the simulation, sourcing from the Santiago, Chile, plant becomes more profitable. Adaptation of the same simulation can highlight when a new plant or added capacity is required.

When determining workforce needs, a BPS planning layout can be utilized to perform headcount planning for the next year or several years. This information then can be utilized within an Oros model of the HR and training departments to determine the process costs for hiring, training, and supporting the workforce. A Powersim model can utilize these process rates to determine the costs of cultivating people with particular skills (i.e., a management training program or trade expertise) within the workforce, based on retention rates, employee satisfaction, time to expertise, and training needs. The results of this simulation can help to design future HR policies and procedures to increase retention, estimate training and HR costs, and identify the number of new hires needed to maintain the workforce level required to support future strategic goals.

The results of both of these examples can be utilized to determine key performance indicators to be included at different levels within the Balanced Scorecard for the current year to drive toward the decisions supported by the simulations. Planned expenses can be more readily explained, such as the need to hire more management trainees to support future strategies. Additionally, the simulations highlight hidden assumptions contained within the organizational model that often are not considered or visible when planning for the short term, such as the next fiscal budget.

Operational-Level Analysis

Once the organization has determined the strategy to be executed, the organizational units need to be aligned to support the objectives. The Balanced Scorecard helps to visualize KPIs in order to move the organization toward the same goals. However, these metrics and goals then need to be converted into estimated expenses to determine if the strategy is executable. Therefore, at some level the strategic cost management system—for example, SEM and BW—must overlap with the capabilities supported by the operational cost management system, such as SAP CO. An overlap example is the SEM capabilities for supporting an integrated fiscal year plan at the lowest organization levels, potentially replacing planning performed in the core SAP R/3 system.

Many organizations struggle with the creation of the financial plan from year to year. As an organization grows and becomes more complex and larger in scale with global impacts due to multiple companies, multiple currencies, and multiple strategic units, the yearly fiscal planning activity and the integration or consolidation of such plans can become a nightmare. Some organizations do not plan at the operational level and therefore have trouble manipulating the SAP R/3 business application to support their higher-level organizational requirements. A user-friendly, integrated, flexible planning tool is provided by SEM BPS. Since SEM-BPS does not rely on only SAP information, organizations can use it as their planning tool for all purposes, regardless of whether they use the SAP business applications or not. Therefore, companies that have not completely rolled out SAP or do not have a standard global SAP template can combine all of the information and have one repository for an integrated plan, whether at the strategic or operational level.

The combination of access to data from different systems via BW, the ABC modeling capabilities of Oros, and the dynamic simulation for understanding impacts over time supported by Powersim make the SEM application an extremely powerful tool to support decision-making needs.

IMPLEMENTATION GUIDELINES

Several areas must be considered when constructing a strategic cost management tool incorporating Activity-Based Management capabilities that utilizes SAP products. These areas focus on the identification of the ABC data required and, more important, how that data is captured, stored, and accessed. Also, since SAP products' greatest strengths and benefits are based on integration, this aspect should also be considered. The integration aspect covers two different areas:

1. Integration between the SEM components themselves to support ABM
2. Integration of SEM with the ABC/M functionality of the SAP CO application

Design and Feeding the BW Info_Cubes and Info_Objects

The first area for consideration is the identification of the data needed and the determination of how to capture that data. Detailed analysis must be performed up front to ensure that the info_cubes are designed to support the information needed to make the decisions in the time required. The type of analysis to be performed and the decisions to be supported drive the design of the info_objects, such as the reporting dimensions (characteristics) and the key figures. These represent individual pieces of information that then need to be grouped together to identify the info_cubes. The design of info_cubes is driven by many different parameters, such as reporting, authorization, sizing, data types, and accessing needs. For example, info_cubes can be designed based on data type (plan or actual), data area (sales, production, financials), the main structure focus (key figure or characteristic based), or level of access (upper management, operational level). The info_cube design also considers volume of both the data to be gathered and the number of reporting dimensions. Additionally, the sourcing of the information can drive the design, such as costs or driver data to be extracted from different areas within SAP R/3, such as financials, sales, or purchasing. Other sources are also reviewed, such as systems utilized to support pieces of the organization not yet on SAP, legacy systems not converted, data devices such as hand-helds feeding ABC driver information, Microsoft Access databases with standards or survey results for ABC allocations, or data provided by external agencies, perhaps for process benchmarking metrics. Exhibit 11.8 illustrates the different parameters driving the design of the BW structures.

ABM Integration within SEM Components

Beyond ensuring the structure is in place to capture and control the data needed, the integration points between the SEM components themselves need to be considered. A determination of which cubes are populated with data accessed or generated by multiple components of SEM needs to be made. The goal is to support single sourcing of information to ensure data integrity and eliminate reconciliation. The analysis design phases of the individual components need to have checkpoints to cover integration to ensure that BPS supports the plan of a metric to be

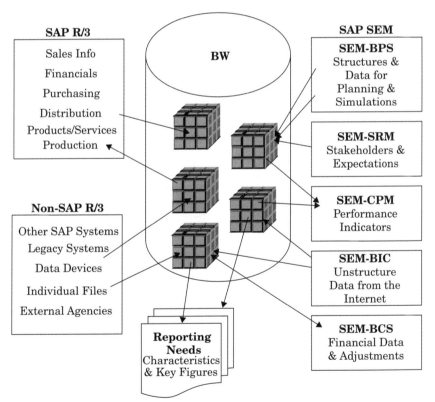

Exhibit 11.8   Design of BW Info_Cubes

utilized within the Balance Scorecard, for example, or that the plan data is structured so that it can be consolidated within BCS for comparisons with actuals.

ABC/M Integration Between SAP SEM & SAP R/3

The requirements of a strategic cost system focus on the speed of decision making, a higher reliance on external data, and a different tolerance level for a margin of error, and so on. However, to ensure that a strategy can be executed, a link to the operational environment has to be maintained at some level. How integrated that link is, and at what level, depends on the utilization of costing functionality within both the operational cost management and the strategic cost management tools. If the costing requirements of the organization are simplistic, the strategic cost management tool will have a large overlap in capabilities. However, as the costing requirements become more intricate and complex, it is unlikely that the strategic cost management system can emulate the same capabilities, for example, integration such as the sales and operation planning or template allocations of SAP R/3. At this point, an overall cost management design must be considered and a decision made as to the types of analysis and reporting to be supported by each tool. In addition, areas of overlap must be considered, focusing on the ability to support each requirement. Exhibit 11.9 illustrates one potential costing design utilizing all of these SAP products.

For this example, SEM BPS is utilized within the organization to support an operational-level integrated financial plan. Potentially, Oros ABC models or Powersim simulations also may be utilized within SEM-BPS. Since, for this example, the plan data is at a very low level within SEM and SAP R/3 has the corresponding actual data, a decision must be made: Will the plan data be retracted back to SAP R/3 to perform plan/actual/variance reporting, or will actual data be extracted to BW to perform the reporting? Beyond the reporting capabilities aspect of this decision, the true driver of this schematic is the ABC functionality requirements. If more advanced ABC functionality is utilized within the organization, such as utilizing template allocations, integrating the ABC information throughout the product costing area, or executing sales and operation planning to determine process and resource requirements, then the SAP R/3 costing engine must be utilized. Therefore, plan data for sales volumes would need to be retracted to SAP R/3 to support backflushing through the quantity structured portions of the ABC model, potentially determining the cost centers plans. Or the cost center plans can be performed within SEM and populated back to CO-CCA, where they are flushed through the ABC model within R/3 and the results of those allocations are transferred to BW for reporting against or to be utilized in other

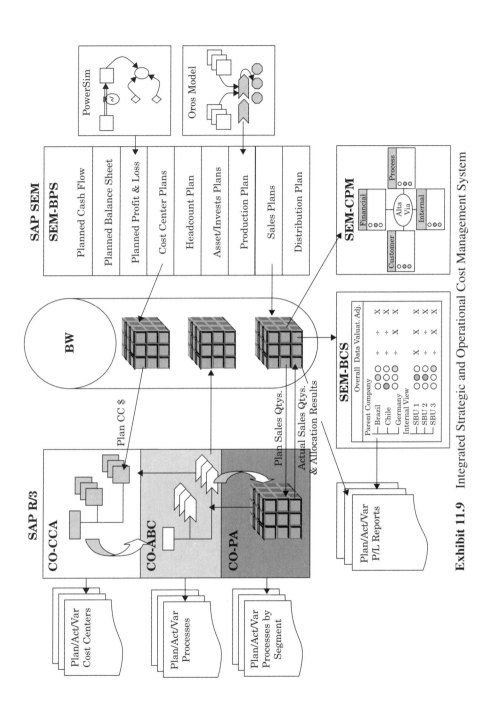

Exhibit 11.9 Integrated Strategic and Operational Cost Management System

BPS plans. Many different variations are possible depending on the ABC requirements and how much of the more advanced ABC functionality is utilized within SAP R/3.

SUMMARY

The SEM module combines and provides tools to support all the key areas of the strategic management process. The core benefits of utilizing SEM are integration, simulation, and usability/flexibility. Strategic enterprise management continues to be built on the SAP strategy of always supporting integration, within a product such as SEM itself, between its own products such as with SAP R/3, and with other applications. The simulation capabilities are supported via the ability to change parameters and have the results ripple through the different scenarios. Simulation is also supported by the Oros modeling capabilities focusing on ABC and Powersim system dynamic models for nonlinear, causal feedback loop simulations across time series. In addition, simulations are supported through having the capability to alter numbers and see the results without necessarily saving the data. This capability is supported via a special memory buffer that allows data to be changed within the SEM-BPS model and simulations to occur without saving to the database. Therefore, simulated changes can be calculated over and over until the best option is identified, at which time the information is then saved to the BW cubes. Usability and flexibility are provided through the ability to create the planning layouts via the Excel layout wizard, standard planning functions and planning structures already made available. Exhibit 11.10 summarizes this chapter.

NOTES

1. Robert S. Kaplan and David P. Norton. *The Balanced Scorecard: Translating Strategy into Action* (Cambridge, MA: Harvard Business Press, 1996). Dr. Patrick M. Georges originally created the Management Cockpit. N.E.T. RESEARCH provides the Management Cockpit room and training. The Management Cockpit is a trademark of SAP AG.

Summary Area	Summary Description
Area-Specific Focus	
SEM-BIC	Business Information Collection is used to capture unstructured information utilized in strategic scenarios.
SEM-SRM	Stakeholder Relationship Management aids with the identification, classification, and management of, as well as communication with, the stakeholders of the organization.
SEM-BPS	Business Planning and Simulation supports planning from a high-level, purely analytical focus to the lowest-level organizational operational plan. BPS includes the Powersim application and linkages with the Oros software via the Bridge, further supporting ABC modeling and system-dynamic simulation capabilities.
SEM-CPM	Corporate Performance Monitor provides visualization and control of how the organization is performing in order to support the identified objectives and goals. The visualization is supported through the Balance Scorecard and the Management Cockpit.
SEM-BCS	Business Consolidations supports the consolidation activities for both external (legal) and internal (management) consolidation for both plan and actuals.
Information Flows	
SEM and SAP CO	Extracts have been provided standard from SAP CO to populate the BW cubes with the required ABC information.
SEM BPS Layouts and Functions	BPS Planning Layouts can be utilized to enter plans, generate plans with functions, and modify both dollar and quantity values for the resources, process, or cost objects, to be utilized for ABM decision support.
SEM and Oros Bridge	The Oros application can be utilized to model the ABC/B aspects and impacts to the organization.
SEM and Powersim	Powersim models can simulate impacts to the organization, or anything, especially those impacts driven by soft issues. These models can utilize or determine ABC information.

Exhibit 11.10   Summary Table for SEM Utilized to Support ABM

Key Decisions	
High-level Strategic	SEM is designed to aid with the decisions focusing on high-level strategic areas such as mergers and acquisitions, changes to core competencies, etc.
Mid-level Tactical	Oros and Powersim models are very robust tools to calculate results to be utilized in midlevel strategic decisions focusing on tactical decisions, such as capacity management and workforce requirements.
Operational	The strategic cost management system must be linked at some point to the operational cost management system. This will introduce an area of overlap in capabilities, such as performing an integrated fiscal year plan.
Implementation Guides	
BW Cube Design	The ability to support the transfer of ABC information is dependent on the design of the BW info_cubes.
ABM within SEM	Conceptual design for the utilization of each of the SEM components must take into consideration the overall desire to support ABM.
SEM and SAP R/3	Full utilization of ABM for strategic to operational decisions support relies on a cohesive costing conceptual model, which should be supported by both applications.

Exhibit 11.10   (*continued*)

GLOSSARY

ABAP: The programming language used in the SAP software products.

ABB: Sce *Activity-Based Budgeting.*

ABC: See *Activity-Based Costing.*

ABM: See *Activity-Based Management.*

Activity: See *business process.*

Activity account: A master data object within the Oros Analytics software application to represent an activity. The activity account is the receiver/sender for assignments.

Activity analysis: The process of identifying the activities performed within an organization, the inputs to the activities, the consumers of the activities, and the metric related to the activities for either benchmarking or allocation tracing.

Activity-Based Costing (ABC): 1. The method of measuring the cost and performance of activities and cost objects. Activity-Based Costing assigns costs to business processes (also called activities) based on their use of resources. The costs incurred by business processes are assigned to cost objects (i.e., products, services, customers, orders, etc.) based on their utilization of these processes. Activity-Based Costing recognizes the causal relationship between cost drivers and business processes. 2. The system component module of the SAP Controlling module that supports integrated ABC using SAP R/3.

Activity-Based Budgeting (ABB): The method of utilizing process output measures and their relationships with the cost of the process as a means for determining the budget expenses of the process.

Activity-Based Management (ABM): A discipline that focuses on the management of activities as a route to continuous improvement. Activity-Based Management draws heavily on ABC for information.

Activity center: A master data object within the Oros Analytics software application to represent a grouping of activities. An activity center can include other activity centers, thereby establishing a hierarchy of centers and activity accounts.

Activity decomposition: See *activity analysis.*

Activity type: Classifies the output of a cost center according to type of cost or service. Activity types enable the performance of internal cost tracing by describing the output of the cost center. Explains the basis of variability of the account. Activity types are tools to trace costs driven by consumption quantities. Examples of activity types include labor hours, machine hours, kilowatt hours, and square feet. For example, production cost center "A" manufactures semifinished parts. The activity types are minutes of drill time and minutes of welding time. These activity types can be quantified and measured. Every semifinished part is drilled for 30 minutes and welded for 5 minutes. A different price can be calculated for each activity type.

Actual activity type rate: The total value of actual costs on an activity type divided by the actual quantity of the activity type results in the actual rate or actual activity type price. This price is used in actual internal cost allocations. See also *standard activity type rate.*

Actype: See *activity type.*

Allocation: The movement of costs from a sending cost structure to a receiving cost structure. Internal cost allocations carry details of where the costs originated. Allocations can be performed in a number of ways:

- Distribution
- Assessment
- Direct activity allocation
- Indirect activity allocation
- Target/actual calculation of activity type
- Template allocation
- Costing sheets
- Settlements

Allocation cost element: A collection of related individual cost elements. Most of the cost allocation techniques in the controlling module use allocation cost elements (secondary cost elements). The assignment of costs to an allocation cost element is retained throughout the allocation chain and can be used for monitoring the flow of values. This grouping decreases the number of elements analyzed and enhances transparency in subsequent evaluations. For example, all salary and wage cost elements could be combined under the allocation cost element personnel costs. Allocation cost elements are different from cost element groups in that cost element groups are used primarily for reporting and analysis purposes.

Allocation structure: A mapping of cost elements into one or more allocation cost element(s) for use with assessment cycles. The allocation structure reduces the creation and maintenance of the assessment cycles.

AP: Accounts Payable.

APO: Advanced Planning and Optimization module.

AR: Accounts Receivables.

Assessment cycle: A simple method of apportioning costs using suitable tracing factors. The tracing factors act as allocation bases. However, assessment does not calculate or post internal prices or activity type quantities to receivers. Assessment does not monitor activity type flows.

Assignment: See *allocation.*

ATI: ABC Technologies, Inc.

Attribute (characteristic): A property that describes an object or process. Object characteristics may include weight, height, and color. Process characteristics may include external value added or degree of complexity.

AUC: Asset under construction.

B2B: Business to business.

Backflushing: The process whereby using, for example, sales quantities to derive a production plan and an overhead cost plan using previously established quantity standards. See also *planning.*

BAPI: Business Application Program Interface.

BCS: Business Consolidation module.

Benchmarking: Identifying a standard capacity measure, process/activity, driver metric, or unit rate to be utilized for comparison purposes against internal or external information to determine efficiency and to indicate areas of improvement.

BIC: Business Information Collection module.

Bill of materials (BOM): A listing of materials (e.g., raw, semifinished, or finished) required to produce a product.

BOM: See *bill of materials.*

BPP: Business Process Planning.

BPS: Business Planning and Simulation module.

Bridge: The ABC Technologies' standardized interface to the SAP Controlling module.

Budget: The end result of the top-down process of allocating a pool of money to cost entities within the functional areas of applications. The budget differs from a plan in that it is not based on standard quantities but entails the downward distribution of dollars.

Business process: Indicates what the corporation does with its resources (e.g., people, machines, etc.) in conducting its business. Business processes create a model of activities flowing across cost centers. They describe the operations of the corporation. One goal of ABC is to allocate costs, generated by activities, to cost objects. Business processes enable the user to perform this type of analysis. The SAP system supports many cost tracing methods to move costs to other processes, cost objects, or business segments. Examples of business processes include creating a customer order, designing a new product, and developing a blueprint for a customized order.

Business segment: See *profitability segment.*

CCA: See *cost center accounting.*

CE: See *cost element.*

Chart of accounts: Organized list of general ledger account master records that are required for one or more company codes. The chart of accounts includes every general ledger account and the account number, name, and control information. The user can define more than one chart of accounts for a given SAP client. However, each company code can have only one chart of accounts.

Client: An independent unit on the highest level of the SAP R/3 system. The client contains the configuration required to adapt the standard SAP R/3 software to support the organization's business requirements.

Client dependent: Configuration of the SAP R/3 software performed within a client that does not impact (make changes to) any other client that resides within the same SAP instance.

Client independent: Configuration of the SAP R/3 software performed within a client that impacts all other clients that reside within the same SAP instance. The configuration change updates database structures that impact the entire instance. ABAP code modifications are also client independent.

Closing: The periodic process whereby closing of primary postings, internal and external batch allocation of costs, and settlements are achieved.

CO: See *controlling module.*

Company code: Independently balanced organizational or accounting unit within a client. Balance sheet and income statements can be produced for each company code. These statements comply with external reporting requirements. Several company codes can be defined for a client to track independent enterprises.

Component: A compartmentalized grouping of code that supports a subfunction of the module. For example, the PC (Product Costing) component of the CO (Controlling) module focuses on controlling the planning/actual transactions utilized to support product costing.

Controlling: The business function that enables problem/opportunity identification, analysis, and decision support. Controlling enables strategic, tactical, and operational decisions. Tasks include planning, monitoring, reporting, advising, and informing.

Controlling module (CO): The SAP R/3 module responsible for supporting the controlling transactions and activities of an organization.

Cost allocation: See *allocation.*

Cost center: A unit (department) within a company distinguished by area of responsibility, location, or accounting method and representing individual company accounting units. Cost elements can be assigned to a cost center. The user can post costs and activities on the cost centers where they originated directly or use internal tracing methods. SAP contains a range of control parameters for cost center planning, analysis, allocation, and reporting.

Cost center accounting (CCA): The component of the Controlling module utilized to support responsibility accounting, departmental planning, capture of actual expenses for cost centers, performing cost center allocations, and reporting from a cost center organizational viewpoint.

Cost center group: A number of cost centers that have similar attributes and are considered as a unit for performance measurement, analysis, or allocation purposes.

Cost center hierarchy: The standard hierarchy defined within the cost center accounting component where all cost centers for the organization are defined. The cost center hierarchy contains every cost center within the client, while the cost center group may contain only some of the cost centers.

Cost component split: Grouping of cost elements to view an aggregation of costs. The cost component split aggregates specific cost elements to provide a higher-level view of costs for the product costs. For example, all material accounts are grouped into the cost component for materials or all labor-related activity type cost elements are grouped into a cost component for direct labor. See also *primary cost component split.*

Cost element: Criteria for classifying all of the costs arising in a company code. Whenever costs are posted, they must be assigned to a primary or secondary cost element. Primary cost elements are maintained as part of the general ledger account master. Secondary cost elements have no counterpart in the financial accounts. They are maintained exclusively in cost accounting.

Cost element group: A combination of several cost elements. Groups can be used for selection, reporting, allocation, or planning.

Cost flow/accumulation: The normal flow of value and quantities as well as their accumulation into different objects throughout the system.

Cost object: 1. Collects costs on the basis of the consumption of processes and resources. Cost objects can be production orders, plant maintenance orders, internal orders, cost centers, processes, or profitability segments. 2. A specific SAP cost object actually called cost object that is utilized as an internal unit of control, decision, and responsibility.

Costing sheet: A method of allocation within the SAP R/3 application utilized to apply a surcharge or percentage overhead increase based on a cost element. For example, a costing sheet is often constructed to apply a percentage increase based on the production material costs in order to account for overhead costs.

CPU: Computer process unit.

CS: Customer Service module.

Cycle: An iterative procedure from senders to receivers in which costs are apportioned. A cycle contains the sending and receiving structures, along with the rules for allocating costs. Each cycle consists of one or more segments. Each segment (executed sequentially, in an order defined by the user) allocates costs.

DAA: See *direct activity allocation.*

DC: Distribution Center

Delta version: If more than one set of data is needed for comparative analyses, each set is stored as a different plan version. For purposes of valuation and balancing with the general ledger, only one version of actuals can be active at any one time. If a new version draws on an existing version, for alternate analysis purposes, it is called a delta version. Delta versions are used in CO-ABC.

Direct activity allocation (DAA): A method of direct charging costs from senders to receivers. This method of allocation requires activity type quantities or process quantities consumed and a price per activity type or process unit. Value allocation from the activity type to the receiver object is done at quantity multiplied by price: $Q \times P$.

Direct allocation: See *direct activity allocation.*

Direct costs: Expenses traced directly to the consuming receiver, such as production labor hours for a product production order.

Distribution: A cost tracing mechanism used to apportion costs. It is useful when it is difficult to clearly define individual activity types in a cost center or if entering all of the activity types present in the cost center is too complicated. Distribution maintains the original cost element detail on the receiver, and sender and receiver are documented in the cost accounting document. Distribution uses fixed percentages, fixed amounts, statistical key figures, or posted amounts to allocate costs.

Driver: A measure indicative of output effort that directly impacts the costs of the consumer.

EC: Enterprise Controlling module.

ECP&E: Easy Cost Planning and Execution functionality in SAP.

Enterprise resource planning: Utilized to describe software applications that provide functionality to support several business functions, such as human resources, financials, supply chain management, and costing, for transactional processing of planning, capturing actual information, internal flow of data, and reporting.

Enterprise wide system (EWS): See *enterprise resource planning.*

ERP: See *enterprise resource planning.*

FI: Financial Accounting module.

FTE: Full time equivalent.

Fixed costs: Costs that do not vary with the volume of output.

Fixed quantities: Quantities that do not vary with the volume of the consumer (receiver) output.

Forecasting: The practice of using year-to-date actuals to predict spending/revenue/profit figures for the remainder of a fiscal year (i.e., trending).

Full absorption costing: A method of costing that assigns all manufacturing costs to the products or services, including those that do not vary with output volumes.

GUI: Graphical User Interface.

General ledger (G/L): Ledger with all organization's financial accounts. The balance sheet and profit-and-loss statements are based in the general ledger.

HR: Human Resources module.

IAA: See *indirect activity allocation.*

IBU: Industry business unit.

IE: Industrial engineering.

IM: Investment Management module.

IT: Information technology.

Imputed costs: Costs that represent operational expenditure or do not correspond to expenditures either in content or in timing. Common imputed costs include depreciation, interest, maintenance reserves, and social costs.

Indirect activity allocation (IAA): The quantity of activity type consumed by the receiver is often unknown. In these cases, it is impossible to use direct activity allocation. Indirect tracing mechanisms allow the user to move costs when this information is not available while still posting quantity times price using an activity type. This method is the indirect activity allocation.

Indirect costs: Costs that are allocated to the receiving consumer because the costs cannot be traced directly; production overhead costs are an example.

Integrated: A single system with the capability to support the entire organization.

Integrated ABC system: One system with the capability to support the Activity-Based Costing philosophy throughout the different functional applications of the organization, such as human resources, financials, sales, production, and distribution.

Interfaced: Two systems that have a communication structure in place allowing information to move from one system to another.

Internal orders: A cost accounting instrument for the detailed planning and controlling of costs. Internal orders monitor objects within the Controlling module (advertising and marketing expenses), overhead orders (which can be linked to cost centers), or productive orders (capital spending or construction orders). An internal order is an event management object.

KPI: Key performance indicator.

LE: Logistic Execution modules.

LIS: Logistics Information System

MM: Materials Management module.

MPS: Master production schedule.

MRP: Materials replenishment planning.

Master data: Data relating to individual objects, which remains unchanged over extended periods of time. Master data contains information that is used in the same manner for similar objects. For example, the master data of a supplier includes name, address, and banking information; the master data of a user in the system includes name, authorizations, mailing address, printer, and so on.

Market segment: See *profitability segment.*

Module: A logical grouping of program code based on functional distinctions within the organization.

Non–value-added process/activity: A process that is perceived as not contributing to customer value or to the organization's needs. The designation "non–value added" reflects a belief that the process can be redesigned, reduced, or eliminated without reducing the quantity, responsiveness, or quality of the output required by the customer or the organization. However, some activities that do not add value for the final customer are necessary to operate the business. External reporting to government agencies is an example.

OM: Overhead Management.

OPA: See *order and project accounting.*

Operational level: The planned and/or actual performance of a lowest-level organizational unit, such as a cost center, for a period. The operating level represents the output and is measured in output quantity, production time, machine hours, expenses, and the like.

Operational ABC: The application of ABC in an operational system used for capturing day to day transactions. Operational ABC is integrated into the structures and cost valuations of the transactional system; parallel ABC is used for analysis purposes only.

Order: A cost collector utilized to capture the costs of a specific event, such as a production order, maintenance order, service order, or sales order. See also *internal order.*

Order and project accounting (OPA): A component of the Controlling module that supports controlling the costs of internal orders and projects.

Outsourcing: Contracting a third party to perform a specific process or an entire department's responsibility, such as the preventative maintenance process or the entire printing cost center. Processes and departments are outsourced when an organization deems them to be outside of a core competency or if cost savings will result.

Overhead costing: Traditional method of costing in product accounting that assigns direct costs to the cost object, then applies indirect costs (overhead) in proportion to the direct costs, expressed as a percentage rate/surcharge.

PA: See *profitability analysis.*

PAC: Profitability Analysis Costing-based template environment.

PC: See *product costing.*

PCA: See *profit center accounting.*

PM: Plant Maintenance module.

PP: Production Planning module.

PS: Project System module.

Periodic cost allocation: An allocation carried out after all primary postings for the period are completed.

Parallel ABC: The CO-ABC application supporting stand-alone ABC module without impacting the Controlling module cost flows.

Planning: The bottom-up process of setting quantity standards in each of the functional areas: cost centers, processes, product costing, and profitability analysis. A plan is based on quantities and standard dollar values throughout. Traditional accounting systems allow the user to allocate and document actual costs. More sophisticated controlling systems require the facility to plan quantities, activities, costs, and revenues in detail. Planning has three goals:

1. To plan the structure of the company's future operations for a particular period. Precise goals and objectives account for internal and market factors.

2. To control business transactions within the planned time period to ensure the plan is met. Interactive planning allows the user to adapt target requirements to any changing factors.

3. To monitor efficiency after the completion of the accounting period by comparing the plan to actual results and analyzing the variances to plan.

Plan version: A collection of year-dependent identifiers and control parameters for planning data. If more than one set of data is needed for comparative analyses, each set is stored as a new plan version. When utilizing SAP R/3, one standard version is created automatically for planned and actual costs. This version is called version 0. In addition to the standard version, users can create any number of alternative planning versions, as analysis needs require.

Planned activity type quantity: The planned cost center activity type quantity required to meet demand, measured in the corresponding physical or technical units of output. The planned activity type quantity reflects resource capacity.

Primary cost element: Costs for input factors and resources procured externally. Includes brought-in parts, raw materials, supplies, and services. These costs are located in the Financial Accounting and the Controlling module.

Primary cost component split: A cost component split defined in order to show a view of the costs that contribute to an activity type or process unit rate. For example, the primary cost component split for the activity type LABHR shows that the $10 unit rate for the activity type LABHR consists of $7 salary-related expenses, $2 of corporate overhead, and $1 of supplies.

Process: See *business process.*

Process group: A number of processes that have similar attributes and are considered as a unit for performance measurement, analysis, or allocation purposes.

Product costing (PC): The component of the Controlling module utilized to support standard product cost creation and the capture of actual production costs.

Profitability analysis (PA): The component of the Controlling module utilized to support multilevel profit-and-loss statements, reporting of market segments, and planning of sales volumes.

Profit center: An organizational unit responsible for within-company financial statement reporting, such as plants or business units.

Profit center accounting (PCA): The component of the Enterprise Controlling module utilized to support profit center accounting from a profit-and-loss view as well as with limited balance sheet reporting. PCA is accessible from within the Controlling module as well.

Profitability segment: A segment composed of a number of reporting dimensions (characteristics). It is a cost and/or revenue object in the profitability analysis component. Examples include: Country "United States," Region "East," Product group "Toys," Consumer group "Wholesale," Industry "Chemicals," Product group "Fertilizers," or any combination of these characteristics.

Proportional costs: Costs that vary with the volume of consumer output.

QM: Quality Management module.

Quantity-based allocation: An allocation that utilizes a driver quantity as the means for determining the cost valuation. Quantity-based allocations require a driver that has a unit rate. Utilization of a quantity metric, such as number of full-time equivalents (FTEs), is not a quantity-based allocation, since a rate is not associated with the FTE and the metric is converted to a percentage basis for allocation. See also *value-based allocation.*

Quantity structure: The linking of individual quantity-based allocations that move costs from the cost center to a process and then to the final cost object. This linking of quantity-based allocations defines causal relationships between the output quantities of the cost object to processes and process output to cost center activity type outputs.

RCA: See *resource consumption accounting.*

Receiver: A cost object that receives costs from a sending cost object. Receivers can be cost centers, activity types, processes, orders, market segments, or cost objects.

Resource: An element acquired by the enterprise and employed/deployed by it to perform certain functions.

Resource account: A master data structure within the Oros Analytics that represents a grouping of cost elements.

Resource assignment: In the Oros Analytics software, the assignment used to assign resource accounts to activity accounts.

Resource center: A master data objected within the Oros Analytics application that represents a grouping of resource accounts. A resource center can include other resource centers, thereby establishing a hierarchy of centers and resource accounts.

Resource consumption accounting (RCA): The method of measuring the cost and the consumption of costs to the cost objects. Resource consumption accounting assigns costs to activity types based on their use of resources. The costs incurred by activity type are assigned to cost objects (i.e., products, services, customers, processes, other cost centers, orders) based on their utilization of these activity types. Resource consumption accounting recognizes the causal relationship between cost centers and activity types with their corresponding consumers.

Resource output: The identified output of the cost center/department which is consumed by other cost objects. Examples are labor hour, machine hour, CPU minutes.

Responsibility accounting: An accounting method that focuses on the costs of an organizational unit, holding accountable the person directly responsible for that unit.

Routing: The master data structure that identifies the work centers and tasks required to convert materials into the final product.

SAP: The company providing the SAP ERP software as well as other software applications.

SBP: Structure Business Process template environment.

SD: Sales Distribution module.

SEM: Strategic Enterprise Management module.

SM: Service Management module.

SOP: Sales and Operation Planning.

SOP Backflushing: See *backflushing*.

SRM: Shareholder Relationship Management module.

Secondary cost elements: Internal costs that are found only in the Controlling module, not in the Financial Accounting module. They result from internal cost allocations and assessments.

Segment: A combination of different reporting dimensions used to represent a subset of the data within the system. An example is information on product a for customer a in Europe.

Sender: A cost object that sends cost to a receiving cost object. A sender can be a cost center, activity type, internal order, process, or cost object.

Settlement: The allocation method utilized to relieve the internal order of costs to a receiving cost object.

Simulation: The practice whereby some or all of the parameters in a total model are changed to evaluate/analyze the implications. Parameters that can be changed are values, quantities, and structures.

SKF: See *statistical key figure.*

Stand-alone ABC system: A system supporting the ABC philosophy that is interfaced to one or more systems utilized to support the organization.

Standard activity type rate: The total value of costs planned on an activity type divided by the planned quantity of the activity type results in the planned rate or standard activity type price. This price is used in planned or actual internal cost allocations. See also *actual activity type rate.*

Standard cost system: A system that uses direct labor and material consumed as the primary means for apportioning overhead (i.e., by means of surcharges). This system was acceptable when total overhead was a small percentage of total cost of sales. As industries have evolved, the proportion of indirect overhead costs has grown tremendously. As a result, traditional cost systems incorrectly calculate the cost of products.

Standard hierarchy: A tree structure for classifying all cost centers or processes from a cost accounting point of view. See *cost center hierarchy* and *standard process hierarchy.*

Standard price/cost: The unit rate defined for an activity type of process.

Standard process hierarchy: The main hierarchy defined within the Activity-Based Costing component where all processes for the organization are defined. This process hierarchy contains every process within the client; the process group might contain only a portion of the processes.

Statistical key figure (SKF): An entity utilized for capturing a metric for internal cost allocation. A common example is using the number of square feet or square meters to allocate the rental cost of a warehouse. Another example is allocating company cafeteria costs based on the number of employees in each department.

Statistical posting: An informational posting made to a second master data object for reporting purposes. For example, a maintenance cost posting the actual costs to the responsible cost center and an informational positive to an internal order merely for tracking the cost over the life of the vehicle.

Statistical ratio: See *statistical key figure.*

Target costs: The calculated results of what the actual costs should have been given the actual volume level. Target costs are generated from the planned costs.

They are divided into fixed and variable components. Costs are adjusted for actual operating volume levels. Target costs are not the same concept as target costing.

Target = actual allocation method: An allocation method that takes a defined planned relationship between any two drivers (activity types or processes) and applies that relationship to determine the actual quantity posting. For example, production utilizes a machine hour activity type. For every machine hour, 1 kilowatt hour of electricity is required. The target = actual relationship will apply 1 kilowatt hour for every machine hour posted to a production order.

Template allocation method: A method that supports the ability to utilize Boolean "IF-THEN" logic to create complex business logic for the allocation of cost elements, activity types, and processes to any cost object.

Tracing: See *allocation*.

Transactional: A system that performs and controls the business transactions and resulting documents.

Unit rate: See *standard activity type rate* and *actual activity type rate*.

Value-added process/activity: A process perceived to contribute to customer value or to satisfy an organizational need. The attribute "value added" reflects a belief that the process cannot be eliminated without reducing the quantity, responsiveness, or quality of output required by a customer or organization.

Value-based allocation: An allocation method that utilizes a percentage, ratio, or metric to assign the costs from one cost object to another, such as from a cost center to a process. A driver quantity rate is not utilized to determine the cost valuation. See also *quantity-based allocation*.

Variable quantity: A quantity that varies with the volume of the consumer output.

Variance: The difference generated when comparing the actual results to the expected results.

Variance liquidation: The practice whereby variance from standard is allocated to an object or the initial absorber of the cost to arrive at an actual cost.

Version: See *plan version*.

WM: Warehouse Management module.

Work center (WC): A master data structure that reflects a work area within a plant. Work centers may be created around common tasks being performed or types of materials being consumed within an area, or based on resource types, such as people related or machine related.

INDEX